How Judges Think

How Judges Think

Richard A. Posner

HARVARD UNIVERSITY PRESS
Cambridge, Massachusetts
London, England
2008

A Caravan book. For more information, visit www.caravanbooks.org

Library of Congress Cataloging-in-Publication Data

Posner, Richard A.
How judges think / Richard A. Posner.
p.   cm.
Includes index.
ISBN-13: 978-0-674-02820-3 (alk. paper)
1. Judicial process. 2. Judicial process—United States. I. Title.

K2300.P67 2008
347'.012—dc22   2007037826

Contents

How Judges Think

Introduction

In my youthful, scornful way, I recognized four kinds of judgments;
first the cogitative, of and by reflection and logomancy; second,
aleatory, of and by the dice; third, intuitive, of and by feeling or
"hunching"; and fourth, asinine, of and by an ass; and in that same
youthful, scornful way I regarded the last three as only variants of each
other, the results of processes all alien to good judges.[1]

Ivan Karamazov said that if God does not exist everything is permitted, and traditional legal thinkers are likely to say that if legalism (legal formalism, orthodox legal reasoning, a "government of laws not men," the "rule of law" as celebrated in the loftiest Law Day rhetoric, and so forth) does not exist everything is permitted to judges—so watch out! Legalism does exist, and so not *everything* is permitted. But its kingdom has shrunk and grayed to the point where today it is largely limited to routine cases, and so a great deal is permitted to judges. Just how much is permitted and how they use their freedom are the principal concerns of this book. These concerns have been made especially timely by the startling (to the naïve) right turn by the Supreme Court in its latest term (ending in June 2007).[2] The turn resulted from the replacement of a moderately conservative Justice (O'Connor) by an extremely conservative one (Alito), and so underscores the question of the personal and political elements in judging and thus of the sense in which the nation is ruled by judges rather than by law. If changing judges changes law, it is not even clear what law is.

1. Joseph C. Hutcheson, Jr., "The Judgment Intuitive: The Function of the 'Hunch' in Judicial Decision," 14 *Cornell Law Quarterly* 274, 275–276 (1929).
2. Linda Greenhouse, "In Steps Big and Small, Supreme Court Moved Right: A 5–4 Dynamic, with Kennedy as Linchpin," *New York Times*, July 1, 2007, § 1, p. 1.

1

I feel a certain awkwardness in talking about judges, especially appellate judges (my main concern), because I am one. Biographies are more reliable than autobiographies, and cats are not consulted on the principles of feline psychology. At the same time, I am struck by how unrealistic are the conceptions of the judge held by most people, including practicing lawyers and eminent law professors, who have never been judges[3]—and even by some judges. This unrealism is due to a variety of things, including the different perspectives of the different branches of the legal profession—including also a certain want of imagination. It is also due to the fact that most judges are cagey, even coy, in discussing what they do. They tend to parrot an official line about the judicial process (how rule-bound it is), and often to believe it, though it does not describe their actual practices.[4] There is also the sense that judging really is a different profession from practicing or teaching law, and if you're not in it you can't understand it. I remember when I was appointed receiving a note from a court of appeals judge in another circuit with whom I was acquainted, welcoming me to "the club." This book parts the curtains a bit.

The difficulty outsiders have in understanding judicial behavior is due partly to the fact that judges deliberate in secret, though it would be more accurate to say that the fact that they do not deliberate (by which I mean deliberate *collectively*) very much is the real secret.[5] Judicial deliberation is overrated. English judges traditionally did not deliberate at all, as that would have violated the ruling principle of "orality," whereby everything that judges did had to be done in public so that their behav-

---

3. A notable example is Harvard law professor Henry Hart's time-and-motion study of Supreme Court Justices: Henry M. Hart, Jr., "The Supreme Court, 1958 Term: Foreword: The Time Chart of the Justices," 73 *Harvard Law Review* 84 (1959), which I discuss in chapter 10.

4. Robert Keeton, a federal district judge and before that a Harvard Law School professor, acknowledged in his treatise on judging that judges make "value-laden" rulings. Robert E. Keeton, *Keeton on Judging in the American Legal System* 15 (1999). But he did not explore the sources of those values. His treatise has no index entry for either "politics" or "ideology."

5. Though a pretty open one. "When I first came on the court [the U.S. Court of Appeals for the District of Columbia Circuit], I imagined that conferences [on cases] would be reflective, refining, analytical, dynamic. Ordinarily they are none of these. We go around the table and each judge, from junior to senior, states his or her bottom line and maybe a brief explanation. Even if the panel is divided, the discussion is exceedingly crisp. The conference changes few minds. Assignments are made, life goes on." Patricia M. Wald, "Some Real-Life Observations about Judging," 26 *Indiana Law Review* 173, 177 (1992). Chief Justice Rehnquist described Supreme Court conferences similarly. See chapter 10.

ior could be monitored;[6] hence those seriatim opinions that baffle the American law student and perhaps the English one as well. In almost all cases a brief discussion among the judges before deciding enables convergence on a single majority opinion in lieu of a separate opinion by each judge.

The confidentiality of the judicial process would not matter greatly to an understanding and evaluation of the legal system if the consequences of judicial behavior could be readily determined. If you can determine the ripeness of a cantaloupe by squeezing or smelling it, you don't have to worry about the produce clerk's mental processes. But the consequences of judicial behavior are often more difficult to determine and evaluate than the consequences even of other professional services, such as medicine. Many of the decisions that constitute the output of a court system cannot be shown to be either "good" or "bad," whether in terms of consequences or of other criteria, so it is natural to ask whether there are grounds for confidence in the design of the institution and in the competence and integrity of the judges who operate it.

The secrecy of judicial deliberations is an example of professional mystification. Professions such as law and medicine provide essential services that are difficult for outsiders to understand and evaluate. Professionals like it that way because it helps them maintain a privileged status. But they know they have to overcome the laity's mistrust, and they do this in part by developing a mystique that exaggerates not only the professional's skills but also his disinterest.[7] Judges have been doing this for thousands of years and have become quite good at it—so good as to have achieved a certain opacity even to their fellow legal professionals, including law professors as well as practicing lawyers. Judges have convinced many people—including themselves—that they use esoteric materials and techniques to build selflessly an edifice of doctrines unmarred by willfulness, politics, or ignorance.

There is nevertheless considerable dissatisfaction with our legal system,[8] as there is with our system of health care. Like health care, law is

---

6. Robert J. Martineau, *Appellate Justice in England and the United States: A Comparative Analysis* 101–103 (1990).

7. Richard A. Posner, *The Problematics of Moral and Legal Theory*, ch. 3 (1999).

8. See, for example, Philip K. Howard, *The Collapse of the Common Good: How America's Lawsuit Culture Undermines Our Freedom* (2001); Walter K. Olson, *The Litigation Explosion: What Happened When America Unleashed the Lawsuit* (1991).

said to be too expensive (it certainly costs more per capita than the legal systems of the nations with which we tend to compare the United States), too intrusive into private and commercial life, too prone to error, too uncertain, and simply too large (the nation has a million lawyers). For these reasons it is contended to be a source of immense indirect costs on top of the expenses to the litigants. The accusations may be true, though assessing their truth is not the project of this book and is especially daunting because it is even harder to estimate the benefits of our legal system than its costs. Legal rights are options that may have value even if never exercised, but how to value such options? And legal duties deter harmful conduct—but how effectively is extremely difficult to determine too.

Supposing the criticisms have merit, the question is whom to blame. If all that judges do is apply rules made by legislatures or the framers of the Constitution (or follow precedents, made by current or former judges, that are promptly changed if they prove maladapted to current conditions), then the responsibility for the mess (if it is a mess) must lie with the legislators or the Constitution's framers, or with the political process more generally. But suppose that most rules laid down by legislative bodies are all right and the problem is willful judges—judges who make up their own rules, or perhaps ignore rules altogether, instead dispensing shortsighted justice on the basis of the "equities" of each case, and as a result create enormous legal uncertainty. The policy implications and hence the path of reform would depend on which explanation was correct (both might be). And what if the basic problem is that the structure of American government, and the American political culture more broadly, *compel* judges to make rather than just apply rules of law? What looks to the critics of the judiciary like willfulness might actually be the good-faith performance of a vital judicial role, and if judges refused to play it, insisting instead, as some legal thinkers urge (the "legalists," of whom more shortly), on limiting themselves to passively applying rules made elsewhere, the legal system might be worse than it is.

The answers are bound up with issues of judicial behavior. To illustrate, everyone will agree that contracts are vital to the operation of markets, and almost everyone will agree that the legal enforcement of contracts is important to the efficacy of contracts. Contract law is administered by judges. (Sometimes they are private judges—arbitrators—

but the effectiveness of arbitration depends on the enforceability of arbitrators' awards.) Being a part of the common law, it is also created by them. The law they create and the way in which they enforce it are deliberate acts, just as business decisions and decisions by legislatures are deliberate acts. Whether judicially made doctrines and decisions are good or bad may depend therefore on the judges' incentives, which may in turn depend on the judges' cognition and psychology, on how persons are selected (including self-selected) to be judges, and on the terms and conditions of judicial employment. Similarly, American antitrust law is far more the creation of judicial decisions than of antitrust legislation: the most important antitrust laws are as skimpy and vague as most provisions of the Bill of Rights. We ought therefore to be interested in how antitrust law has been shaped by the motivations, constraints, and other influences that play on judges. The Supreme Court has actually called the Sherman Act "a common-law statute,"[9] and common law is of course made by judges, not legislators.

The judicial mentality would be of little interest if judges did nothing more than apply clear rules of law created by legislators, administrative agencies, the framers of constitutions, and other extrajudicial sources (including commercial custom) to facts that judges and juries determined without bias or preconceptions. Then judges would be well on the road to being superseded by digitized artificial intelligence programs.[10] But even legal thinkers who believe passionately that judges should be rule appliers and unbiased fact finders and nothing more do not believe that that's how all or even most American judges behave all the time. Our judges have and exercise discretion. Especially if they are appellate judges, even intermediate ones, they are "occasional legislators." To understand their legislative activity, one must understand their motivations, capacities, mode of selection, professional norms, and psychology.

Achieving a sound understanding of judicial behavior is thus of more than merely academic interest; it is a key to legal reform. Yet its academic interest is also considerable because of the unusual incentives and constraints, so unlike those in most jobs, that shape judicial behavior, espe-

9. Leegin Creative Leather Products, Inc. v. PSKS, Inc., 127 S. Ct. 2705, 2720 (2007).
10. I do not know why originalists and other legalists are not AI enthusiasts.

cially in the U.S. federal system, and because the analysis of that behavior may offer insights into the general subject of managing uncertainty.[11] Uncertainty is as salient a feature of our legal system as expense is of our medical system, and decision making under uncertainty is a deservedly important topic in economics, organization theory, and other fields.

Like other writing by judges about judging, this book is heavily influenced by my own judicial experience, consisting of more than a quarter century as a federal court of appeals judge (seven years as chief judge of my court), with occasional forays into the district court to preside at trials, mainly civil jury trials. But the mode of the book is scholarly rather than confessional. In this respect it resembles my book on the regulation of sexuality, a subject otherwise remote from the study of judicial behavior. That book was motivated by my "belated discovery that judges know next to nothing about sex beyond their own personal experience, which is limited," and one of my aims was to "bring to the attention of the legal profession the rich multidisciplinary literature" on the subject.[12] Judges, like other "refined" people in our society, are reticent about talking about sex, but judges are also reticent about talking about judging, especially talking frankly about it, whether to their colleagues or to a larger professional audience. This reticence makes the scholarly study of judicial behavior at once challenging and indispensable.

The book emphasizes positive rather than normative analysis—what judges do, not what they should do—but I do discuss normative issues and propose a few modest reforms, as well as making occasional suggestions for further research. Positive and normative analysis cannot easily be separated when one is dealing with people's deliberate actions, for unless they are evil or cynical people, the best explanation for their actions is unlikely to be that they are deliberately flouting the norms of their society. If it is deeply wrong for a judge to base a decision on the flip of a coin, an aleatory theory of judicial behavior is unlikely to be sound. The grounds of a judge's decisions may be wrong, but they are

---

11. About which I have written at length in relation to catastrophic risk and also to the reform of the U.S. intelligence system. See my books *Catastrophe: Risk and Response* (2004); *Preventing Surprise Attacks: Intelligence Reform in the Wake of 9/11* (2005); *Uncertain Shield: The U.S. Intelligence System in the Throes of Reform* (2006); *Countering Terrorism: Blurred Focus, Halting Steps* (2007).

12. Richard A. Posner, *Sex and Reason* 1, 4 (1992).

unlikely to be outside the ballpark of norms and values prevailing in the society.

The book's primary focus is on federal appellate judges, including Supreme Court Justices (the subject of Part Three, though discussed in the other parts as well). But there is some discussion of trial judges, state court judges, judges in foreign nations similar to the United States,[13] and arbitrators (private judges).

I begin with a discussion of the existing theories (attitudinal, strategic, organizational, economic, psychological, sociological, pragmatic, phenomenological, and legalist) of judicial behavior and of the evidence for and against each. These theories are expounded in a rich literature ignored by most academic lawyers (though this is changing[14]) and by virtually all judges.[15] The theories provide background and support to my own analysis, which draws heavily on labor economics and on the psychology of cognition and emotion. It is the stress I lay on psychology that has led me to entitle the book *How Judges Think* rather than *Judicial Behavior.*

My analysis and the studies on which it builds find that judges are not moral or intellectual giants (alas), prophets, oracles, mouthpieces, or calculating machines. They are all-too-human workers, responding as other workers do to the conditions of the labor market in which they work. American judges, at least, are not formalists, or (the term I prefer, as it carries less baggage) legalists. Legalists decide cases by applying preexisting rules or, in some versions of legalism, by employing allegedly distinctive modes of legal reasoning, such as "legal reasoning by analogy." They do not legislate, do not exercise discretion other than in ministerial matters (such as scheduling), have no truck with policy, and

---

13. That is, nations that have an independent judiciary, as many do not. See, for example, Gretchen Helmke, *Courts under Constraints: Judges, Generals, and Presidents in Argentina* (2005); *Law and Economic Development* (Hans-Bernd Schäfer and Angara V. Raja eds. 2006).

14. See, for example, Gregory C. Sisk and Michael Heise, "Judges and Ideology: Public and Academic Debates about Statistical Measures," 99 *Northwestern University Law Review* 743 (2005).

15. The richness is well illustrated by James L. Gibson, "From Simplicity to Complexity: The Development of Theory in the Study of Judicial Behavior," 5 *Political Behavior* 7 (1983). As the date of his article shows, the literature has been around for many years. That it has not caught on with the legal professoriat may be in part because of its death of implications for the understanding or reform of legal doctrine and in part because it challenges the mystique of an apolitical judiciary, in which lawyers and law professors are heavily invested.

do not look outside conventional legal texts—mainly statutes, constitutional provisions, and precedents (authoritative judicial decisions)—for guidance in deciding new cases. For legalists, the law is an autonomous domain of knowledge and technique.[16] Some legalists are even suspicious of precedent as a source of law, because it is infected by judicial creativity.

But if judges are not legalists, what are they? Might they simply be politicians in robes? Empirical scholars have found that many judicial decisions, by no means limited to the Supreme Court, are strongly influenced by a judge's political preferences or by other extralegal factors, such as the judge's personal characteristics and personal and professional experiences, which may shape his political preferences or operate directly on his response to a case. No responsible student of the judicial system supposes that "politics" (in a sense to be explained) or personal idiosyncrasy drives *most* decisions, except in the Supreme Court, which indeed is largely a political court when it is deciding constitutional cases. Legalism drives most judicial decisions, though generally they are the less important ones for the development of legal doctrine or the impact on society.

But one must be careful about dividing judicial decisions (or judges) into legalist and political, or, what is closely related, asserting a Manichaean dualism between law and politics. The dualism works only when "law" is equated to legalism, and that is too narrow. Justice Scalia was not stepping out of his proper role as a judge when he said in *Richardson v. Marsh* that "the rule that juries are presumed to follow their instructions is a pragmatic one, rooted less in the absolute certitude that the presumption is true than in the belief that it represents a reasonable practical accommodation of the interests of the state and the defendant in the criminal justice process."[17] This is just as proper a judicial state-

---

16. "Legal formalists emphasize the specifically legal virtues of the clarity, determinacy, and coherence of law, and try to sharpen the distinction between legislation and adjudication. Roughly, they can be divided into rule-formalists and concept-formalists. The former place more value on determinacy, emphasizing the importance of clear rules and strict interpretation, while the latter emphasize the importance of system and principled coherence throughout the law." Thomas C. Grey, "Judicial Review and Legal Pragmatism," 38 *Wake Forest Law Review* 473, 478 (2003). Modern American formalists—comprising what one might call the School of Scalia—are mainly rule-formalists. Id. at 479. "The most important thing [for Scalia] is that law should be put in the form of rules wherever possible." Id. at 499.

17. 481 U.S. 200, 211 (1987).

ment as the legalist assertions for which Scalia (he of such pronounce-
ments as that the "rule of law" is the "law of rules"[18]) is more famous.
This is so even though the statement has political implications. Criminal
defendants are at a disadvantage if a judge's or prosecutor's missteps can
be forgiven by the judge's telling the jury to disregard them, for the bell
cannot be unrung; the jurors cannot exclude what they should not have
heard from their consideration of the defendant's guilt.

"Law" in a judicial setting is simply the material, in the broadest
sense, out of which judges fashion their decisions. Because the materials
of legalist decision making fail to generate acceptable answers to all
the legal questions that American judges are required to decide, judges
perforce have occasional—indeed rather frequent—recourse to other
sources of judgment, including their own political opinions or policy
judgments, even their idiosyncrasies. As a result, law is shot through
with politics and with much else besides that does not fit a legalist
model of decision making.

The decision-making freedom that judges have is an *involuntary* freedom. It is the consequence of legalism's inability in many cases to decide
the outcome (or decide it tolerably, a distinction I shall elaborate), and
the related difficulty, often impossibility, of verifying the correctness of
the outcome, whether by its consequences or its logic. That inability,
and that difficulty or impossibility, create an open area in which judges
have decisional discretion—a blank slate on which to inscribe their decisions—rather than being compelled to a particular decision by "the
law." How they fill in the open area is the fundamental question that this
book addresses, though lurking in the background and occasionally
coming to the fore is the question how they *should* fill it in.

Although judges often exercise a political judgment in the open area,
"political" is an equivocal term that must be carefully parsed before it
can be usefully applied to judicial behavior. It could refer to a judge
whose decisions reflect his loyalty to a political party. It could refer to a
judge whose decisions faithfully mirror the platform of a political party,
though as a matter of conviction rather than of party loyalty. It could refer to a judge whose decisions reflect a consistent political ideology,
which might be "liberal" or "conservative" and thus correlated (though

18. Antonin Scalia, "The Rule of Law as a Law of Rules," 56 *University of Chicago Law Review* 1175 (1989).

imperfectly) with the Democratic or Republican Party platform, but which might instead be an ideology embraced by neither major party, such as libertarianism or socialism. The empirical literature that refutes legalism as a complete or even approximate description of actual judicial behavior does not distinguish among these different gradations of "political." "Political" could even describe decisions based on purely technical policy judgments, judgments that involve finding the best means to agreed-upon ends; any issue of governmental policy is in that sense "political." At the opposite extreme, a judge might be "political" in a sense divorced from policy: he might, like a legislator, use charm, guile, vote trading, and flattery to induce other judges to go along with him, though his aim might be to produce legalistic decisions. (He might thus be what is called in a variety of nonpolitical settings "a good politician.") The strategic theory of judicial behavior, discussed in chapter 1, emphasizes political judging in this "means" rather than "ends" sense. Many legislators have no policy preferences of their own, but are merely political brokers for their constituents. Judges, however, unless elected, do not have constituents.

Ringing changes on the "political" might seem to exhaust the possible nonlegalist factors in adjudication. It does not begin to. The possible other factors (call them "personal") include personality traits, or temperament (and thus emotionality at one end of the temperament spectrum and emotional detachment at the other end), which are more or less *innate* personal characteristics. They include personal *background* characteristics, such as race and sex, and also personal and professional *experience*. The political or ideological factors that influence adjudication may themselves be by-products of personal factors rather than products of an informed, disinterested, and coolly analytical study of public issues. Also figuring in judicial decisions are *strategic* considerations, already alluded to, which need not be related to either the political views or the personal characteristics of a judge. A judge might join the majority opinion in a case not because he agreed with it but because he thought that dissenting publicly would magnify the effect of the majority opinion by drawing attention to it. ("Dissent aversion" helps to explain, as we shall see in chapter 1, the puzzling effect of panel composition on appellate decisions.) *Institutional* factors—such as how clear or unclear the law is, salary and workload, and the structure of judicial promotion—also influence judicial behavior.

The political and personal factors create *preconceptions,* often unconscious, that a judge brings to a case. This can explain how judges can think their decisions uninflected by political considerations but neutral observers find otherwise. This explanation saves judges from the accusation of pervasive hypocrisy without denying the force of the empirical literature on political judging.

Judicial preconceptions are best understood, we shall see, with the aid of Bayesian decision theory. Not that this is how judges themselves would describe their thought processes. And "Bayes's theorem" is not the only term I shall be using that is likely to alarm some readers of a book about judges. Nor are "occasional legislators" and "dissent aversion" the only others. Readers will have to brace themselves for "reversal aversion," "ideology drift," "tolerable windows," "utility function," "Sartrean bad faith," "option value," "risk aversion," "zone of reasonableness," "monopsony," "cosmopolitanism," "authoritarian personality," "alienation," "agency costs," "rule pragmatist," and "constrained pragmatist." I do not apologize for these terms or, more generally, for discussing judicial thinking in a vocabulary alien to most judges and lawyers. Judicial behavior cannot be understood in the vocabulary that judges themselves use, sometimes mischievously.

Because behavior is motivated by desire, we must consider what judges want. I think they want the same basic goods that other people want, such as income, power, reputation, respect, self-respect, and leisure. If the typical judicial weighting of the various goods is distinctive, it is because of the incentives and constraints that the office of judge creates, or more broadly the context of judicial action. An important part of that context is legal uncertainty, which creates the open area in which the orthodox (the legalist) methods of analysis yield unsatisfactory and sometimes no conclusions, thereby allowing or even dictating that emotion, personality, policy intuitions, ideology, politics, background, and experience will determine a judge's decision.

Among the institutional factors that influence judicial behavior in the open area is the structure of the judicial career, which affects selection and self-selection into the judiciary and the incentives and constraints that click in once a person is inducted into that career. I compare different types of judicial career and different types of judiciary and also examine proposals for modifying the career structure, such as by raising judicial salaries steeply or limiting the length of judicial terms in office.

My analysis of the career structure of federal appellate judges (including Supreme Court Justices) confirms the absence of significant external constraints on their judicial behavior (such as salary, promotion, or removal) and thus the scope of the judges' freedom from efforts by their "principals" (whoever exactly they are—a matter of some uncertainty) to control these their agents.

But I must not ignore the possibility that this freedom is tightly restricted by a range of *internal* constraints, including what I call "judicial method." This consists of analytical tools for managing uncertainty and producing what legalists regard as objective decisions. We shall see that the legalist tools—including those most hallowed ones of reasoning by analogy and strictly interpreting statutes and constitutions—come up short: the first is empty and the second has, despite appearances, a large discretionary element.

I must also not ignore academic criticism of judges as a potential constraint on judicial behavior, since the absence of strong constraints opens a space for the normally weak ones to exert significant influence. But academic criticisms of judges tend to fall on deaf ears these days because of changes in the legal academy that have driven judges and law professors so far apart intellectually that the faculties of the elite law schools are becoming alienated from the judiciary. My complaint is not, as one might think, that academics are too critical of judges; in many respects they are insufficiently critical. My complaint is that the current academic critique of the judiciary is unrealistic about judges, unhelpful to them, and indeed rather uninterested in them unless they happen to be Supreme Court Justices.

The emphasis that I place on the American judge's extensive (though not complete) freedom from internal and external constraints is not intended to suggest that judicial behavior is random, willful, or political in a partisan sense. Most judges, like most serious artists, are trying to do a "good job," with what is "good" being defined by the standards for the "art" in question. The judicial art prominently includes the legalist factors, and so those factors figure prominently in judicial decisions—and rightly so. But innovative judges challenge the accepted standards of their art, just as innovative artists challenge the accepted standards of *their* arts. As there are no fixed, incontestable criteria of artistic excellence, so there are no fixed, incontestable criteria of judicial excellence.

And in law as in art, the innovators have the greater influence on the evolution of their field.

So what exactly are judges doing when they are judging in the open area? If they are not merely applying preexisting rules in a logical or otherwise mechanical fashion, might they not be implementing a consistent judicial philosophy? But no; we shall see that judicial philosophies (such as "formalism," "originalism," "textualism," "representation reinforcement," "civic republicanism," or, the newest contenders, "active liberty" and "judicial cosmopolitanism") are either rationalizations of decisions based on other grounds or rhetorical weapons. None is a politically neutral lodestar guiding judges' decisions.

What term, then, best describes what most American judges do? Readers of my previous writings on judicial behavior will expect me to say that it is "legal pragmatism," to divide judges into legalists and pragmatists, and then, by classifying legalism as a pragmatic strategy, to turn all our judges into pragmatists. That would be too facile. But pragmatism *is* an important component of American judicial behavior and figures importantly in this book. It is widely misunderstood to be an "anything goes" approach to judging, like extreme versions of legal realism. It is not. The pragmatic judge is a *constrained* pragmatist. He is boxed in, as other judges are, by norms that require of judges impartiality, awareness of the importance of the law's being predictable enough to guide the behavior of those subject to it (including judges!), and a due regard for the integrity of the written word in contracts and statutes. The box is not so small that it precludes his being a political judge, at least in a nonpartisan sense. But he need not be one unless "political" is given the broadest of its possible meanings that I reviewed earlier, in which the "political" is anything that has the slightest whiff of concern for policy. A pragmatic judge assesses the consequences of judicial decisions for their bearing on sound public policy as he conceives it. But it need not be policy chosen by him on political grounds as normally understood.

A judge can be political without being pragmatic; an ideologue is not a pragmatist. Most judges who oppose abortion rights do so because of religious belief rather than because of a pragmatic assessment of such rights. (Many who support such rights are ideologically driven as well.) They may offer pragmatic objections to abortion in an effort to enlist the support of judges who are not religious or whose religious beliefs do not include a rejection of abortion. But that is window dressing. A pro-lifer, judicial or otherwise, to whom you point out that one of the benefits of abortion rights is that they reduce future crime rates, because unwanted children are more likely to grow up to be criminals than wanted ones,[19] will look at you with horror rather than commend you for having made an interesting pragmatic point that he will add to the balance of good and bad consequences of abortion rights to help guide his decision.

The issue of what influences play on judicial behavior is most acutely raised with respect to the U.S. Supreme Court. The Justices operate with even fewer constraints than the lesser federal judges, except for the political constraint imposed by public opinion. That constraint is greater for the Justices because their decisions have more visibility and a greater impact on society (that is the main reason for the greater visibility). So it is in the Supreme Court, especially when it is deciding constitutional cases, that we expect, and find, the most strenuous and least successful efforts to demonstrate that judges are, or can be, legalists. For that is where the stakes usually are highest, not only because of the nature of the issues that constitutional law deals with but also because of the difficulty of changing constitutional law other than by the Court's overruling previous decisions. It is also where the decisional guidance provided by the orthodox legal materials is weakest. So it is there that we find innumerable competing proposals of comprehensive theories to limit judicial discretion, several of which I examine in Part Three. The most desperate of them is the quest for global judicial consensus, a kind of secular natural law. Judicial cosmopolitanism (not to be confused with the influential philosophical doctrine of cosmopolitanism) is manifested in the Supreme Court's increasing propensity to cite foreign judicial decisions as authorities in American constitutional cases. In doing this the Court overlooks profound differences in judicial structures and outlook between the United States and foreign countries.

Were the entire argument of the book that American judges (in contrast to most foreign judges) have a great deal of discretion—that they do not just apply rules made by the legislative and executive branches of government, by earlier generations of judges, or by judges of higher courts—many readers would respond, "So what else is new?" But most

---

19. John J. Donohue III and Steven D. Levitt, "The Impact of Legalized Abortion on Crime," 116 *Quarterly Journal of Economics* 379 (2001).

of the book is about what judges do when they are not just applying rules. It is an effort to develop a positive decision-theoretic account of judicial behavior in what I am calling the open area—the area in which a judge is a legislator. I argue that the reasons for the legislative character of much American judging lie so deep in our political and legal systems and our culture that no feasible reforms could alter it, and furthermore that the character of our legal system is not such a terrible thing. The falsest of false dawns is the belief that our system can be placed on the path to reform by a judicial commitment to legalism—to conceiving the judicial role as exhausted in applying rules laid down by statutes and constitutions or in using analytic methods that enable judges to confine their attention to orthodox legal materials and have no truck with policy.

I hope that these arguments persuade, or at least that the book contributes to a more exact and comprehensive understanding of how judges behave, why they behave as they do, what the likely consequences of such behavior are, and what intellectual tools are best suited to analyzing such questions.

I

The Basic Model

Nine Theories of Judicial Behavior

There are many positive (that is, descriptive as distinct from normative) theories of judicial behavior.[1] Their primary focus is, as one would expect, on explaining judges' decisions. The theories are the attitudinal, the strategic, the sociological, the psychological, the economic, the organizational, the pragmatic, the phenomenological, and, of course, what I am calling the legalist theory. All the theories have merit and feed into the theory of decision making that I develop in this book. But all are overstated or incomplete. And missing from the welter of theories—the gap this book endeavors to fill, though in part simply by restating and refining the existing theories—is a cogent, unified, realistic, and appropriately eclectic account of how judges actually arrive at their decisions in nonroutine cases: in short, a positive decision theory of judging.

I begin with the attitudinal theory,[2] which claims that judges' deci-

---

1. For reviews of the literature, see Lawrence Baum, *Judges and Their Audiences: A Perspective on Judicial Behavior,* ch. 1 (2006); Barry Friedman, "The Politics of Judicial Review," 84 *Texas Law Review* 257 (2005). For an anthology suggestive of the diversity of the literature, see *Supreme Court Decision-Making: New Institutionalist Approaches* (Cornell W. Clayton and Howard Gillman eds. 1999).

2. See, for example, Jeffrey A. Segal and Harold J. Spaeth, *The Supreme Court and the Attitudinal Model Revisited* (2002); Robert A. Carp and Ronald Stidham, *Judicial Process in America* 294 (2001) (tab. 10–1); William N. Eskridge, Jr., and Lauren E. Baer, "The Supreme Court's Deference Continuum: An Empirical Analysis (from *Chevron* to *Hamdan*)" (Yale Law School, May 11, 2007); Andrew D. Martin, Kevin M. Quinn, and Lee Epstein, "The Median Justice on the United States Supreme Court," 83 *North Carolina Law Review* 1275 (2005); Micheal W. Giles, Virginia A. Hettinger, and Todd Peppers, "Picking Federal Judges: A Note on Policy and Partisan Selection Agendas," 54 *Political Research Quarterly* 623 (2001); Tracey E. George, "Developing a Positive Theory of Decision Making on U.S. Courts of Appeals," 58 *Ohio State Law*

sions are best explained by the political preferences that they bring to their cases. Most of the studies that try to test the theory infer judges' political preferences from the political party of the President who appointed them, while recognizing that it is a crude proxy. The emphasis is on federal judges, in particular Supreme Court Justices. State judges are of course not appointed by the President, and sometimes the method of their appointment—for example, by nonpartisan election—makes it difficult to classify them politically.[3]

Justices and judges appointed by Democratic Presidents are predicted to vote disproportionately for "liberal" outcomes, such as outcomes favoring employees, consumers, small businessmen, criminal defendants (other than white-collar defendants), labor unions, and environmental, tort, civil rights, and civil liberties plaintiffs. Judges and Justices appointed by Republican Presidents are predicted to vote disproportionately for the opposite outcomes.

Other evidence of a judge's political leanings is sometimes used in lieu of the party of the appointing President, such as preconfirmation editorials discussing the politics or ideology of a judicial nominee.[4] A neglected possibility is a fourfold classification in which the intermediate categories would consist of judges appointed when the President and the Senate majority were of different parties ("divided government"). However, Nancy Scherer finds no difference in the decisions of federal district judges appointed by "divided" versus "united" government,[5] and I find only a small difference (as shown in Table 1[6]) in the case of federal court of appeals judges appointed by Republican Presidents. But when

Journal 1635, 1678 (1998). For criticism, see Frank B. Cross, "Political Science and the New Legal Realism: A Case of Unfortunate Interdisciplinary Ignorance," 92 *Northwestern Law Review* 251 (1997); Barry Friedman, "Taking Law Seriously," 4 *Perspectives on Politics* 261 (2006).

3. Paul Brace, Laura Langer, and Melinda Gann Hall, "Measuring the Preferences of State Supreme Court Judges," 62 *Journal of Politics* 387 (2000); Carp and Stidham, note 2 above, at 296–297.

4. Jeffrey A. Segal and Albert D. Cover, "Ideological Values and the Votes of U.S. Supreme Court Justices," 83 *American Political Science Review* 557 (1989); Segal et al., "Ideological Values and the Votes of U.S. Supreme Court Justices Revisited," 57 *Journal of Politics* 812 (1995). See also Martin, Quinn, and Epstein, note 2 above, at 1285–1300.

5. Nancy Scherer, "Who Drives the Ideological Makeup of the Lower Federal Courts in a Divided Government?" 35 *Law and Society Review* 191 (2001).

6. Some of the classifications used in the data set from which the statistics in Tables 1 and 2 are drawn are erroneous, such as classifying all votes for plaintiffs in intellectual property cases as "liberal." I have corrected such errors; for the details of the corrections and a fuller analysis of the data, see William M. Landes and Richard A. Posner, "Judicial Behavior: A Statistical Analysis" (University of Chicago Law School, Oct. 2007).

Table 1   Judicial Votes in Courts of Appeals as Function of United versus Divided Presidency and Senate, 1925–2002 (in percent)

Vote	Republican President		Democratic President	
	Republican Senate	Democratic Senate	Democratic Senate	Republican Senate
Conservative	55.8	55.9	49.6	55.3
Liberal	37.1	35.9	43.5	37.9
Mixed	7.1	8.2	6.8	6.8

Sources: Appeals Court Attribute Data, www.as.uky.edu/polisci/ulmerproject/auburndata.htm (visited July 17, 2007); *U.S. Court of Appeals Database,* www.as.uky.edu/polisci/ulmerproject/ appctdata.htm, www.wmich.edu/~nsf-coa/ (visited July 17, 2007). Votes were weighted to reflect the different caseloads in the different circuits. "Mixed" refers to multi-issue cases in which the judge voted the liberal side of one or more issues and the conservative side of the other issue or issues.

Table 2   Judicial Votes in Courts of Appeals as Function of United versus Divided Presidency and Senate, Judges Serving Currently (in percent)

Vote	Republican President		Democratic President	
	Republican Senate	Democratic Senate	Democratic Senate	Republican Senate
Conservative	66.9	63.2	49.7	57.0
Liberal	25.6	27.0	39.5	35.6
Mixed	7.5	9.8	10.9	7.5

Sources: Appeals Court Attribute Data, www.as.uky.edu/polisci/ulmerproject/auburndata.htm (visited July 17, 2007); *U.S. Court of Appeals Database,* www.as.uky.edu/polisci/ulmerproject/ appctdata.htm, www.wmich.edu/~nsf-coa/ (visited July 17, 2007). Votes were weighted to reflect the different caseloads in the different circuits. "Mixed" refers to multi-issue cases in which the judge voted the liberal side of one or more issues and the conservative side of the other issue or issues.

the President is a Democrat, it makes a significant difference whether the Senate is Democratic or Republican, probably because the Republican Party is more disciplined than the Democratic Party and therefore better able to organize opposition to a nominee.

Table 2 is similar to Table 1 except limited to currently serving judges. Notice that the effects of divided government on judicial voting are more pronounced than in Table 1, consistent with the strong Republican push beginning with Reagan to tilt the ideological balance of the courts rightward. Notice also that federal judicial decisions as a whole tilt toward

Table 3   Ideology of Currently Serving Justices and the Appointing President

Justice's Ideology	President's Ideology		
	Conservative Republican	Moderate Republican	Democratic
Conservative	4	1	0
Liberal	0	2	2

Table 4   Conservative and Liberal Supreme Court Justices as Function of United versus Divided Presidency and Senate, Justices Serving Currently

Justice	Republican President		Democratic President	
	Republican Senate	Democratic Senate	Democratic Senate	Republican Senate
Conservative	3	2	0	0
Liberal	0	2	2	0

the conservative end of the spectrum and that the tilt is more pronounced among currently serving judges.

Presidents differ in their ideological intensity, and taking account of that difference can improve the accuracy of the attitudinal model. Seven of the nine current Supreme Court Justices were appointed by Republican Presidents, but it is more illuminating to note that four conservative Justices were appointed by conservative Republicans (Scalia and Kennedy by Reagan, and Roberts and Alito by the second Bush), two liberal Justices by a Democratic President (Ginsburg and Breyer, appointed by Clinton), and one liberal and two conservative Justices appointed by moderate Republicans (Stevens by Ford, Souter and Thomas by the first Bush). See Table 3.

There is also a divided-government effect in Supreme Court appointments, as shown in Table 4.

Whatever the method of determining a judge's political inclinations, and whatever the level of the judiciary (Supreme Court, federal courts of appeals—on which there is now an extensive literature[7]—or federal dis-

7. Christina L. Boyd, Lee Epstein, and Andrew D. Martin, "Untangling the Causal Effects of Sex on Judging" (Northwestern University School of Law and Washington University School of Law and Department of Political Science, July 28, 2007); Cass R. Sunstein et al., *Are Judges Po-*

trict courts[8]), the assumed inclinations are invariably found to explain much of the variance in judges' votes on politically charged issues. The hotter the issue (such as abortion, which nowadays is much hotter than, say, criminal sentencing), the greater the explanatory power of the political variable. The attitudinal theory is further supported by the unquestionable importance of politics in the appointment and confirmation of federal judges;[9] by the intensity of congressional battles, almost always politically polarized, over the confirmation of federal judges and particularly Supreme Court Justices; and by the experiences of lawyers and judges. Every lawyer knows that the accident of which judges of a court of appeals are randomly drawn to constitute the panel that will hear his case may determine the outcome if the case is controversial. Every judge is aware of having liberal and conservative colleagues whose reactions to politically charged cases can be predicted with a fair degree of accuracy even if the judge who affixes these labels to his colleagues would not like to be labeled politically himself.

Further evidence is the tendency of both Supreme Court Justices and court of appeals judges to time their retirement in such a way as to maximize the likelihood that a successor will be appointed by a President of

litical? An Empirical Analysis of the Federal Judiciary (2006); Thomas J. Miles and Cass R. Sunstein, "Do Judges Make Regulatory Policy? An Empirical Investigation of *Chevron*," 73 *University of Chicago Law Review* 823 (2006); Ward Farnsworth, "The Role of Law in Close Cases: Some Evidence from the Federal Courts of Appeals," 86 *Boston University Law Review* 1083 (2006); Jeffrey A. Segal, Harold J. Spaeth, and Sara C. Benesh, *The Supreme Court in the American Legal System* 236–242 (2005); Daniel R. Pinello, *Gay Rights and American Law* (2003); Frank B. Cross, "Decision Making in the U.S. Circuit Courts of Appeals," 91 *California Law Review* 1457, 1504–1509 (2003); David E. Klein, *Making Law in the United States Court of Appeals* (2002); Emerson H. Tiller and Frank B. Cross, "A Modest Proposal for Improving American Justice," 99 *Columbia Law Review* 215, 218–226 (1999); George, note 2 above; Richard L. Revesz, "Environmental Regulation, Ideology, and the D.C. Circuit," 83 *Virginia Law Review* 1717 (1997); Sheldon Goldman, "Voting Behavior on the United States Courts of Appeals Revisited," 69 *American Political Science Review* 491 (1975). For an interesting case study of how the political preferences of court of appeals judges affect decisions, see Paul J. Wahlbeck, "The Development of a Legal Rule: The Federal Common Law of Public Nuisance," 32 *Law and Society Review* 613 (1998).

8. C. K. Rowland and Robert A. Carp, *Politics and Judgment in Federal District Courts* (1996); Gregory C. Sisk, Michael Heise, and Andrew P. Morriss, "Charting the Influences on the Judicial Mind: An Empirical Study of Judicial Reasoning," 73 *New York University Law Review* 1377 (1998); Ahmed E. Taha, "Judges' Political Orientations and the Selection of Disputes for Litigation" (Wake Forest University School of Law, Jan. 2007), http://ssrn.com/abstract= 963468 (visited Sept. 2, 2007).

9. On which see, for example, Lee Epstein and Jeffrey A. Segal, *Advice and Consent: The Politics of Judicial Appointments* (2005); John R. Lott, Jr., "The Judicial Confirmation Process: The Difficulty with Being Smart," 2 *Journal of Empirical Legal Studies* 407 (2005).

the same party as the one who appointed the retiring Justice.[10] Still another bit of evidence is what might be called "ideology drift"—the tendency of judges to depart from the political stance (liberal or conservative) of the party of the President who appointed them the longer they serve.[11] A judge closely aligned with the ideology of the party of the President who appointed him may fall out of that alignment as new, unforeseen issues arise. A judge who was conservative when the burning issues of the day were economic may turn out to be liberal when the burning issues become ones of national security or social policy such as abortion or homosexual rights.

There is more: the outcome of Supreme Court cases can be predicted more accurately by means of a handful of variables, none of which involves legal doctrine, than by a team of constitutional law experts.[12] While there is a high correlation between how a given federal appellate judge (court of appeals judge as well as Supreme Court Justice) votes for the government in nonunanimous (hence "close") constitutional criminal cases and in nonunanimous statutory criminal cases, there is a low correlation between the votes of different judges for and against the government in criminal cases.[13] Some judges have a progovernment lean-

10. Ross M. Stolzenberg and James Lindgren, "Politicized Departure from the United States Supreme Court" (University of Chicago and Northwestern University, Mar. 18, 2007); James F. Spriggs and Paul J. Wahlbeck, "Calling It Quits: Strategic Retirement on the Federal Courts of Appeals, 1893–1991," 48 *Political Research Quarterly* 573 (1995); Deborah J. Barrow and Gary Zuk, "An Institutional Analysis of Turnover in the Lower Federal Courts, 1900–1987," 52 *Journal of Politics* 457, 467–468 (1990). Another straw in the wind is the surprising finding in a recent study that Supreme Court law clerks' self-described political identity (Democratic or Republican) influences the political valence of their Justices' votes. Todd C. Peppers and Christopher Zorn, "Law Clerk Influence on Supreme Court Decision Making" (Roanoke College, Department of Public Affairs, and University of South Carolina, Department of Political Science, June 14, 2007).

11. See Andrew D. Martin and Kevin M. Quinn, "Assessing Preference Change on the US Supreme Court," 23 *Journal of Law, Economics and Organization* 365 (2007); Susan Haire, "Beyond the Gold Watch: Evaluating the Decision Making of Senior Judges on the U.S. Courts of Appeals" (University of Georgia, Department of Political Science, 2006).

12. Andrew D. Martin et al., "Competing Approaches to Predicting Supreme Court Decision Making," 2 *Perspectives on Politics* 761 (2004); Theodore W. Ruger et al., "The Supreme Court Forecasting Project: Legal and Political Science Approaches to Predicting Supreme Court Decisionmaking," 104 *Columbia Law Review* 1150 (2004). The variables are "(1) circuit of origin; (2) issue area of the case; (3) type of petitioner (e.g., the United States, an employer, etc.); (4) type of respondent; (5) ideological direction (liberal or conservative) of the lower court ruling; and (6) whether the petitioner argued that a law or practice is unconstitutional." Id. at 1163.

13. Ward Farnsworth, "Signatures of Ideology: The Case of the Supreme Court's Criminal Docket," 104 *Michigan Law Review* 67 (2005); Farnsworth, note 7 above.

ing, others a prodefendant leaning, and these leanings appear to be what drives their votes in close cases whether the case arises under the Constitution or under a statute—though from a legalist standpoint the text of the enactment being applied ought to drive the outcome, and there are huge textual differences between the Constitution and statutes. Apolitical judges would not be expected to vote the same way in both types of case.

All this is not to say that *all* judicial votes are best explained as politically motivated,[14] let alone that people become judges in order to nudge policy closer to their political goals. We shall see in subsequent chapters that to explain the political cast of judicial decisions does not require assuming that judges have conscious political goals. No attitudinal study so finds, and data limitations cannot explain the shortfalls. Even at the level of the U.S. Supreme Court many cases do not involve significant political stakes, but that cannot be the entire explanation either. Think of Oliver Wendell Holmes. The publication of his correspondence after his death revealed that he was a rock-ribbed Republican, yet he voted repeatedly to uphold liberal social legislation (such as the maximum-hours law at issue in the *Lochner* case, in which he famously dissented) that he considered socialist nonsense. He may of course have been an exception among Supreme Court Justices in this as in so many other respects. He may have few successors in point of political detachment in today's more politicized legal culture.

We get a sense of the attitudinal model's predictive limitations in Tables 5 and 6, in which judicial votes that lack any political valence are coded as "other," and the liberal, conservative, mixed, and other votes are correlated with the party of the President who appointed the judge who cast the vote. Notice that apart from the substantial percentage of votes that were either mixed or other, a large percentage of conservative votes were cast by putatively liberal judges (judges appointed by Democratic Presidents) and a large percentage of liberal votes were cast by putatively conservative judges. Notice, as in the earlier tables, the apparent trend toward the increased politicization of court of appeals voting re-

14. See, for example, Cross, note 7 above; Cross, note 2 above, at 285–311; Sunstein et al., note 7 above; Daniel R. Pinello, "Linking Party to Judicial Ideology in American Courts: A Meta-Analysis," 20 *Justice System Journal* 219 (1999); C. Neal Tate and Roger Handberg, "Time Binding and Theory Building in Personal Attribute Models of Supreme Court Voting Behavior, 1916–88," 35 *American Journal of Political Science* 460 (1991); Sheldon Goldman, "Voting Behavior on the United States Courts of Appeals Revisited," 69 *American Political Science Review* 491 (1975).

Table 5 Judicial Votes in Courts of Appeals as Function of Party of Appointing President, 1925–2002 (in percent)

Vote	Republican President	Democratic President
Conservative	42.2	37.6
Liberal	28.1	33.3
Mixed	5.9	5.1
Other	23.9	23.9

Sources: Appeals Court Attribute Data, www.as.uky.edu/polisci/ulmerproject/auburndata.htm (visited July 17, 2007); *U.S. Court of Appeals Database,* www.as.uky.edu/polisci/ulmerproject/appctdata.htm, www.wmich.edu/~nsf-coa/ (visited July 17, 2007). Votes were weighted to reflect the different caseloads in the different circuits. "Mixed" refers to multi-issue cases in which the judge voted the liberal side of one or more issues and the conservative side of the other issue or issues.

Table 6 Judicial Votes in Courts of Appeals as Function of Party of Appointing President, Judges Serving Currently (in percent)

Vote	Republican President	Democratic President
Conservative	51.2	42.5
Liberal	22.9	33.1
Mixed	7.3	7.6
Other	18.7	16.9

Sources: Appeals Court Attribute Data, www.as.uky.edu/polisci/ulmerproject/auburndata.htm (visited July 17, 2007); *U.S. Court of Appeals Database,* www.as.uky.edu/polisci/ulmerproject/appctdata.htm, www.wmich.edu/~nsf-coa/ (visited July 17, 2007). Votes were weighted to reflect the different caseloads in the different circuits. "Mixed" refers to multi-issue cases in which the judge voted the liberal side of one or more issues and the conservative side of the other issue or issues.

sulting from judicial appointments by Republican Presidents. But notice, too, that the differences between the two types of judge, exhibited in the first two rows of the tables, though significant, are only partial. And a comparison just of means obscures the fact that the distributions overlap; some judges appointed by Republican Presidents are less conservative than some appointed by Democratic Presidents. This does not refute the attitudinal model, but it does highlight the fact that the party of the appointing President is an imperfect proxy for a judge's judicial ideology. One reason is that ideological issues important to judges need not have salience in political campaigns; capital punishment is a current example. Another reason is that judges pride themselves on being politically independent rather than party animals.

An explanation for the attitudinal model's predictive limitations that would hold even if all decisions involved significant political stakes is that a case may pose a conflict between two political values, both of which are important to a judge, as when, for example, a civil rights suit (liberal) is brought challenging affirmative action (a conservative bête noire). One might think that in such a case the political considerations would cancel and the decision could be attributed to conventional legal reasoning. But no; the political considerations are unlikely to weigh equally in the judge's mind, and if they do not, the heavier may determine his decision. A notable example is *Buchanan v. Warley.*[15] Decided at a time when the Supreme Court was strongly disinclined to invalidate racially discriminatory laws, it nevertheless invalidated a southern ordinance that forbade blacks to live on any block in which whites were in the majority, and vice versa. The ordinance had blocked the plaintiff, a white, from selling property to a black. The Court distinguished mere "social rights"—the right of blacks to associate with whites (and likewise of whites *not* to associate with blacks, a "right" that the whites who remained in the neighborhood were denied), which the Court had refused to recognize in *Plessy v. Ferguson*—from "those fundamental rights in property" that the Fourteenth Amendment was intended to secure to blacks on equal terms with whites.[16] The distinction is not found in the equal protection clause. Michael Klarman argues persuasively that the Court simply thought government interference with property rights a worse affront to personal liberty than segregation of schools and other public facilities, especially since the person complaining that his property rights were being infringed was the white seller.[17] The upshot was that the Court issued a liberal decision, rejecting racial segregation in private housing.

The attitudinalists' traditional preoccupation with politically charged cases decided by the Supreme Court creates an exaggerated impression of the permeation of American judging by politics.[18] Most cases decided

15. 245 U.S. 60 (1917).

16. Id. at 79.

17. Michael J. Klarman, *Unfinished Business: Racial Equality in American Law* 83–84 (2007).

18. Brian Leiter, *Naturalizing Jurisprudence: Essays on American Legal Realism and Naturalism in Legal Philosophy* 187, 188 n. 22, 192 (2007).

by American courts are neither politically charged nor decided in the Supreme Court. And to use the political party of the appointing President as a proxy for a Justice's political inclinations misleadingly implies that *partisan* politics pervades Supreme Court decision making. A President invariably appoints most judges (usually more than 90 percent) from among members of his own political party, but once appointed they are more likely to want to be good judges than to want to toe anyone's political line. You do not find judges saying, even to themselves, "How would Bill Clinton [or George Bush, etc.], who appointed me, decide this case?" Nevertheless, in the frequent cases in which a political judgment is required to "close the deal" because legalist analysis of the case leads nowhere, the judge is likely to lean toward the position that the political party to which he belongs (or belonged) would support, for it is usually not an accident that he belongs to that party rather than another. But "lean toward" is different from "identify with." Supreme Court Justices are political, but politically independent. Most of them, indeed, are outside (either more liberal or more conservative) the range bounded by the political preferences of the President and the Senate that confirmed them.[19]

Any amount of political judging challenges orthodox conceptions of the judicial process, however, and the attitudinalists have shown that there is plenty at all levels of the American judiciary (though more, the higher the level). Yet their findings, while heresy to the legal establishment, have the paradoxical effect of blunting criticisms of the courts as acting undemocratically when they invalidate legislative and executive acts. As explained by Mark Graber,

> Judicial review is established and maintained by elected officials. Adjudication is one of many means politicians and political movements employ when seeking to make their constitutional visions the law of the land. Elected officials provide vital political foundations for judicial power by creating constitutional courts, vesting those courts with jurisdiction over constitutional questions, staffing those courts with judges prone to exercising judicial power, assisting or initiating litigation aimed at having those courts declare laws unconstitutional, and passing legislation that encourages justices to make public policy in the guise of statutory or constitutional interpretation. Judicial review

19. Michael Bailey and Kelly H. Chang, "Comparing Presidents, Senators, and Justices: Interinstitutional Preference Estimation," 17 *Journal of Law, Economics and Organization* 477, 508 (2001).

does not serve to thwart or legitimate popular majorities; rather that practice alters the balance of power between the numerous political movements that struggle for power in a pluralist democracy.[20]

The judge who orients his judicial philosophy to the ideology of the President who appointed him (or the electorate that elected him) might be thought the democratic judge, who amplifies rather than undermines the people's choice. Those who regard the Presidency as the most perfect embodiment of the democratic principle should applaud such judges.

The strategic theory of judicial behavior (also called the positive political theory of law), to which I now turn, hypothesizes that judges do not always vote as they would if they did not have to worry about the reactions to their votes of other judges (whether their colleagues or the judges of a higher or a lower court), legislators, and the public.[21] Some of the strategic theorists are economists or political scientists who model politics as a struggle among interest groups and use game theory to sharpen the analysis. Others study historic struggles between the judiciary and other branches of government.[22] At its core the theory is just common sense: whatever a judge wants to accomplish will depend to a considerable degree on other people in the chain of command, broadly understood. At its periphery, however, the theory becomes fanciful, as when the votes of Supreme Court Justices on issues of statutory interpretation are predicted to depend on whether the same political party controls Congress that controlled it when the statute was passed. The

20. Mark A. Graber, "Constructing Judicial Review," 8 *Annual Review of Political Science* 425, 427–428 (2005).

21. See, for example, Daniel B. Rodriguez and Mathew D. McCubbins, "The Judiciary and the Role of Law: A Positive Political Theory Perspective" (forthcoming in *Handbook on Political Economy*); Symposium, "Positive Political Theory and the Law," 15 *Journal of Contemporary Legal Issues* 1 (2006); Stephen J. Choi and G. Mitu Gulati, "Trading Votes for Reasoning: Covering in Judicial Opinions" (New York University School of Law and Duke University School of Law, Sept. 2007); Thomas H. Hammond, Chris W. Bonneau, and Reginald S. Sheenan, *Strategic Behavior and Policy Choice on the U.S. Supreme Court* (2005); Lee Epstein and Jack Knight, *The Choices Justices Make* (1998); Andrew F. Daughety and Jennifer F. Reinganum, "Speaking Up: A Model of Judicial Dissent and Discretionary Review," 14 *Supreme Court Economic Review* 1 (2006); Forest Maltzman, James F. Spriggs II, and Paul J. Wahlbeck, *Crafting Law on the Supreme Court: The Collegial Game* (2000); McNollgast [Matthew D. McCubbins, Roger G. Noll, and Barry R. Weingast], "Politics and the Courts: A Positive Theory of Judicial Doctrine and the Rule of Law," 68 *Southern California Law Review* 1631 (1995); William N. Eskridge, Jr., "Overriding Supreme Court Statutory Interpretation Cases," 101 *Yale Law Journal* 331 (1991).

22. Charles Gardner Geyh, *When Courts and Congress Collide: The Struggle for Control of America's Judicial System* (2006).

idea is that the Justices will feel freer to depart from the original meaning of the statute if the party that controlled Congress when the statute was passed is no longer in power.[23]

The strategic theory is compatible with the attitudinal,[24] as it is a theory of means and the attitudinal theory one of ends. The judge who wants the decisions of his court to conform to his political preferences will be likely to choose a voting strategy that promotes that goal, although he *could* care just about expressing his political views and not about their adoption. Brandeis was a judge of the second type, Holmes of the first, with an occasional aberration—such as *Buck v. Bell*,[25] the "three generations of imbeciles are enough" case. Holmes's mistaken belief in the importance for the nation's future of the eugenics law that he was voting to uphold is palpable.

But the strategic theory is compatible with any other goal-oriented theory of judicial motivation as well. Even a legalist judge might adopt a voting strategy designed to maximize the likelihood that his views will be adopted, as distinct from a strategy of always voting in conformity with those views, come what may. That is a possible, though highly controversial, interpretation of *Bush v. Gore*. The five conservative Justices voted for the liberal outcome (the vindication of constitutional voting rights) and the four liberal Justices voted for the conservative outcome. Both camps must have been aware that it would make a difference, should there be a vacancy on the Court, whether the President was a Republican or a Democrat. A more innocent example is a judge who forgoes a public dissent in a case because he fears it would lend prominence to the views of the majority or that if he dissented too often his colleagues would be annoyed and retaliate (perhaps unconsciously) by paying less heed to his views in other cases. Few judges are completely insensible to strategic considerations (though Justice Scalia, our most

23. See, for example, Lee Epstein, Jack Knight, and Andrew A. Martin, "The Supreme Court as a *Strategic* National Policymaker," 50 *Emory Law Journal* 583 (2001); John A. Ferejohn and Barry R. Weingast, "A Positive Theory of Statutory Interpretation," 12 *International Review of Law and Economics* 263 (1992); Robert A. Dahl, "Decision-Making in a Democracy: The Supreme Court as a National Policy-Maker," 6 *Journal of Public Law* 279 (1957).

24. See George, note 2 above, at 1665–1696; Max M. Schanzenbach and Emerson H. Tiller, "Strategic Judging under the U.S. Sentencing Guidelines: Positive Political Theory and Evidence," 23 *Journal of Law, Economics and Organization* 24 (2007).

25. 274 U.S. 200 (1927).

prominent legalist judge, comes close). In effect they trade off principle against effectiveness.

What I shall call the sociological theory of judicial behavior, because of its focus on small-group dynamics and hence on appellate judging, is an application or extension of the strategic theory, combined with the attitudinal theory. Drawing on both social psychology and rational choice theory, it hypothesizes that panel composition (federal courts of appeals normally sit in three-judge panels, randomly selected from the members of the full court, of which there might be as many as 28, and even more when senior judges are included) influences outcomes. Specifically, a panel having a Republican or Democratic majority is likely to decide differently from one that is all Republican or all Democratic (bearing in mind the special sense in which a judge is usually classified in studies of the political element in judicial behavior as "Republican" or "Democratic"—on the basis of the party of the President who appointed him).[26] And similarly a panel in a sex discrimination case in which all the judges are male is likely to decide the case differently than a panel that contains a female judge.[27]

Several explanations for why panel composition should have this curious effect—why, that is, a majority would ever yield to the wishes of the minority—have been hypothesized. One is that the odd man out acts as a whistleblower, threatening to expose in a dissenting opinion the majority's position as unprincipled. A less contentious hypothesis is that he may simply bring to the panel's deliberations insights that the other judges, with their different political orientation, have overlooked. Either way his presence is an antidote to the tendency of collective deliberations of the like-minded to drive them to extreme conclusions, as the literature on group polarization finds.[28]

26. See, for example, Sunstein et al., note 7 above; Thomas J. Miles and Cass R. Sunstein, "The Real World of Arbitrariness Review" (forthcoming in *University of Chicago Law Review*); Joshua B. Fischman, "Decision-Making under a Norm of Consensus: A Structural Analysis of Three-Judge Panels" (Tufts University, Department of Economics, May 2, 2007); Sean Farhang and Gregory Wawro, "Institutional Dynamics on the U.S. Court of Appeals: Minority Representation under Panel Decision Making," 20 *Journal of Law, Economics and Organization* 299 (2004); Frank B. Cross and Emerson H. Tiller, "Judicial Partisanship and Obedience to Legal Doctrine: Whistleblowing on the Federal Courts of Appeals," 107 *Yale Law Journal* 2155, 2175–2176 (1998).

27. Boyd, Epstein, and Martin, note 7 above.

28. See Alice H. Eagly and Shelly Chaiken, *The Psychology of Attitudes* 655–659 (1993); references in Sunstein et al., note 7 above, at 75–77 nn. 26–30. The focus of the panel-composition

But a bigger factor than either of these may be differences among panel members in intensity of preference for a particular outcome,[29] coupled with the phenomenon of "dissent aversion." Suppose that for reasons of or correlated with ideology, or because of personal background or experiences, emotion, or any other factor likely to stir up a disagreement difficult to resolve by reasoned argument, one member of the panel feels strongly that the case should be decided one way, while the other two judges, though inclined to vote the other way, do not feel strongly. One of those two may decide to go along with the third, the dissentient judge (especially if the case is unlikely to have much significance as a precedent), either treating intensity as compelling evidence of a correct belief or to avoid conflict, perhaps in the conscious or unconscious hope of reciprocal consideration in some future case in which *he* has a strong feeling and the other judges do not. Once one judge swings over to the view of the dissentient judge, the remaining judge is likely to do so as well, for similar reasons or because of dissent aversion.

Most judges do not like to dissent (Supreme Court Justices are an exception, for reasons I explain later in the chapter). Not only is it a bother and frays collegiality,[30] and usually has no effect on the law, but it also tends to magnify the significance of the majority opinion. Judges also do not like dissents from their decisions, which is *why* dissents fray collegiality. Judges do not like to be criticized, to bother having to revise a draft opinion in order to parry any solid punches thrown by the dissent, or, worst of all, to lose the third judge to the dissenter.

---

literature on three-judge panels makes sense, incidentally, because the larger the panel (for example, the nine-judge panel in the U.S. Supreme Court), the less bargaining power a dissentient judge has.

29. As proxied by the ideological "distance" between the dissenting judge and his majority colleagues with respect to the particular case. The greater the distance, the more likely a dissent. Virginia A. Hettinger, Stefanie A. Lindquist, and Wendy L. Martinek, "Separate Opinion Writing on the United States Courts of Appeals," 31 *American Politics Research* 215 (2003).

30. See, for example, Collins J. Seitz, "Collegiality and the Court of Appeals: What Is Important to the Court as an Institution Is the Quality of the Working Relationship among Its Members," 75 *Judicature* 26, 27 (1991). For evidence, see Stefanie A. Lindquist, "Bureaucratization and Balkanization: The Origins and Effects of Decision-Making Norms in the Federal Appellate Courts," 41 *University of Richmond Law Review* 659, 695–696 and tab. 5 (2007). She finds that dissent is more frequent in federal courts of appeals the more judges the court has. This is what one expects if there is dissent aversion, because the larger the court, the less frequently any two of its judges will sit together, and so the less each will be motivated to invest in collegiality.

Dissent aversion reflects the simultaneous difficulty and importance of collegiality. Appellate judging is a cooperative enterprise. It does not work well when the judges' relations with one another become tinged with animosity—and that is always a danger because of the way in which the members of the cooperative enterprise are selected. Judges neither choose their colleagues and successors, as members of law firms and academic faculties do, nor are chosen (and retained or replaced) by a stable, uniform management layer above them. With the Presidency alternating between the parties, judges of the same federal court are invariably appointees of antagonistic principals. What is more, because there are no uniform criteria for the selection of judges, the judges of the same court tend to be diverse in background and ability, which is a source of tension as well as of an enriching variety of experiences and insights. Maintaining collegiality under such conditions requires continuous efforts at minimizing sources of irritation—such as dissents.

The panel-composition effect that has received the most attention is the ideological—the liberal moderating the conservative majority, the conservative moderating the liberal majority. Ideological disagreement is unlike a disagreement over the best means to an agreed end because ideological disputants rarely argue from shared premises. A liberal on a panel with two conservatives is unlikely to produce facts or arguments to change the ideology of his colleagues, or vice versa. But if he feels more strongly about how the case should be decided than the other judges do, this implies that he would derive greater benefits than they from a decision of the case his way and in turn that he would be willing to incur greater costs to get his way, as by writing a dissent. His threat to dissent is thus a credible threat to impose costs on his colleagues (the costs arising from their dissent aversion) if they refuse to yield to his preference. If those costs exceed the benefits to his colleagues of deciding the case their preferred way because they do not feel strongly about the outcome, they will give way.

Were there no dissent aversion, the panel-composition effect would probably be slight. It is true that the deliberations of the like-minded can produce group polarization, resulting in a more extreme opinion than the average opinion of the group's members before they began to deliberate; for whoever in the group holds the extreme opinion will be pushing on an open door when he tries to persuade the others to accept it. This could well happen in a court of like-minded judges. But it would be unlikely to happen when, in a diverse court, some panels happened to be composed of like-minded judges, as they would be from time to time. Remember that judges do not engage in much collective deliberation over a case (in fact less than most juries do). Whether or not a member of the court known to disagree with two judges is on a panel with them, they know that if it is a contentious case other members of the court would vote differently. The presence of one of those other members on the panel would probably therefore not add much information to what the two judges already know about the diversity of views within the full court concerning the issues in the case. Those other judges are likely to be a real presence at the panel's deliberations, though not as vivid, as influential, a presence as the panel's members.

Jury holdouts are a parallel phenomenon to the panel-composition effect under dissent aversion. A juror who feels very strongly about what the verdict in the case should be will be willing to incur costs by protracting the jury's deliberations. By thus imposing costs on the majority as well, he may induce the majority to yield to him, compromise with him, or report to the judge that the jury is hung. The requirement (not always imposed in civil cases any longer) that a jury verdict be unanimous strengthens the holdout's hand relative to that of the dissentient judge on a three-judge panel. This is important because there are strong pressures to conform to prevailing views in most social settings,[31] including that of jury deliberations; the pressures are weaker in the judge setting because of the long and honorable tradition of dissent. But while requiring unanimity strengthens the hand of the holdout juror, the fact that the jury majority can at low cost walk away from the case by declaring the jury hung weakens it. And if the jury does hang, there will be a new trial, in which the party favored by the current holdout is quite likely to lose. The majority of the new jury probably will favor the other party, just as the majority of this jury did, and there is unlikely to be a holdout next time because holdouts are rare.

What I have been calling the sociological theory of judicial behavior, incorporating as it does strategic calculation, emotion (intensity of preference for one outcome or another will often reflect or create an emo-

---

31. On these "uniformity pressures," see, for example, Rod Bond, "Group Size and Conformity," 8 *Group Processes and Intergroup Relations* 331 (2005); Lee Ross and Richard E. Nisbett, *The Person and the Situation: Perspectives on Social Psychology* 27–46 (1991); Bibb Latané, "The Psychology of Social Impact," 36 *American Psychologist* 343 (1981).

tional commitment), and group polarization, straddles the economic and the psychological theories of judicial behavior—theories that overlap, though to see this requires a careful definition of "economic" and "psychological." A narrowly economic theory of human behavior that models it as the product of hyperrational choice and a narrowly psychological theory that models it as the product solely of nonrational drives and cognitive illusions do not overlap, but they also do not do justice to either the economic or the psychological perspective on human behavior. Rationality in economics means elementary consistency and instrumental rationality (fitting means to ends), and so can accommodate a good deal of emotional behavior and cognitive limitedness, while psychology embraces the study of cognition in the large, including the cognition of normal people, the cognitive shortcuts that substitute for formal reasoning, and the social influences at work in group polarization and dissent aversion.

A promising psychological approach focuses on strategies for coping with uncertainty, a fundamental characteristic of the U.S. legal system. This approach highlights the importance and the sources of preconceptions in shaping responses to uncertainty,[32] is supported by studies of judges, and plays a starring role in the theory of judicial behavior developed in this book. The radical uncertainty that besets judges in many of the most interesting and important cases makes conventional decision theory largely inapplicable to judicial decision making and necessitates eclectic theorizing.

The economic theory of judicial behavior treats the judge as a rational, self-interested utility maximizer.[33] He has a "utility function,"

32. See, for example, Rowland and Carp, note 8 above, ch. 7.
33. See, for example, Richard A. Posner, "What Do Judges and Justices Maximize? (The Same Thing Everybody Else Does)," 3 *Supreme Court Economic Review* 1 (1993); Posner, *Overcoming Law*, ch. 3 (1995); Richard S. Higgins and Paul H. Rubin, "Judicial Discretion," 9 *Journal of Legal Studies* 129 (1980); Thomas J. Miceli and Metin M. Cosgel, "Reputation and Judicial Decision-Making," 23 *Journal of Economic Behavior and Organization* 31 (1994); Christopher R. Drahozal, "Judicial Incentives and the Appeals Process," 51 *SMU Law Review* 469 (1998); Andrew F. Daughety and Jennifer E. Reinganum, "Stampede to Judgment: Persuasive Influence and Herding Behavior by Courts," 1 *American Law and Economics Review* 158, 165–167 (1999); Susan B. Haire, Stefanie A. Lindquist, and Donald R. Songer, "Appellate Court Supervision in the Federal Judiciary: A Hierarchical Perspective," 37 *Law and Society Review* 143 (2003); Gordon Foxall, "What Judges Maximize: Toward an Economic Psychology of the Judicial Utility Function," 25 *Liverpool Law Review* 177 (2005); Gilat Levy, "Careerist Judges and the Appeals Process," 36 *RAND Journal of Economics* 275 (2005); Gillian K. Hadfield, "The Quality

as economists term the complex of objectives that guide rational action. The "arguments" (elements) of the judicial utility function include money income, leisure, power, prestige, reputation, self-respect, the intrinsic pleasure (challenge, stimulation) of the work, and the other satisfactions that people seek in a job. The arguments of the utility function can be manipulated by the employer to alter the behavior of the jobholder, and also to affect who seeks or is willing to take the job. Much of the strategic and even the sociological theory of judging can be subsumed under the economic theory.

Leisure preference in the judicial utility function may help explain the emphasis that judges place on "judicial economy," and hence their fondness for doctrines such as harmless error, waiver, and forfeiture; the pressure that some judges exert on litigants to settle cases before trial; and excessive delegation of judicial tasks to law clerks and other staff. Income preference is illustrated by evidence that if judicial incomes are made to depend on the volume of litigation, as was once the case in Britain, judges will lean in favor of expansive rights for plaintiffs—but not too expansive, as that might cause litigation to dry up by motivating potential defendants to steer a wide berth around any activity that might give rise to a suit.[34] Judges' responses to retirement options are also consistent with the standard assumptions about rational self-interested behavior.[35] Another empirical test of the economic model finds that "all else equal, [district] judges with stronger preferences for publishing opinions, those with lighter workloads, or those who are able to write

---

of Law: Judicial Incentives, Legal Human Capital and the Evolution of Law" (USC Center in Law, Economics and Organization Research Paper No. C07–3, Feb. 21, 2007), and references therein. For a first-rate contribution by a legal philosopher not associated with the "law and economics" movement, see Frederick Schauer, "Incentives, Reputation, and the Inglorious Determinants of Judicial Behavior," 68 *University of Cincinnati Law Review* 615 (2000).

34. Daniel Klerman, "Jurisdictional Competition and the Evolution of the Common Law" (forthcoming in *University of Chicago Law Review*). See also Drahozal, note 33 above, at 472 n. 16; Todd J. Zywicki, "The Rise and Fall of Efficiency in the Common Law: A Supply-Side Analysis," 97 *Northwestern University Law Review* 1551 (2003).

35. David R. Stras, "The Incentives Approach to Judicial Retirement," 90 *Minnesota Law Review* 1417 (2006); Albert Yoon, "Pensions, Politics, and Judicial Tenure: An Empirical Study of Federal Judges, 1869–2002," 8 *American Law and Economics Review* 143 (2006); Christopher J. W. Zorn and Steven R. Van Winkle, "A Competing Risks Model of Supreme Court Vacancies, 1789–1992," 22 *Political Behavior* 145, 155 (2000); Barrow and Zuk, note 10 above. See also Stolzenberg and Lindgren, note 10 above, at 14.

publishable decisions more efficiently [are] more likely to publish their decisions."[36]

The economic theory of judicial behavior has to surmount two difficulties. One is neglect of psychological factors—of cognitive limitations and emotional forces that shape behavior along with rational calculation. But cognitive limitations can be modeled as costs of processing information, and we saw in discussing dissent aversion how emotion (there viewed as the precondition for making credible threats) can be an efficient instrument of utility maximization. In chapter 4 we shall see how the costs of processing information are often so great as to make intuition—a telescoped form of thinking—a more rational method of arriving at a judicial decision than logical, step-by-step reasoning.

The other difficulty that the economic theory faces is that of identifying the incentives and constraints that shape the vocational behavior of workers whose work is so structured as to eliminate the common incentives and constraints of the workplace. Federal judges cannot be removed from office, short of gross misconduct, and cannot be docked pay, exiled to undesirable judicial venues, or paid bonuses. Their powers vis-à-vis each other (for example, to preside, to make opinion assignments, to be promoted to chief judge) are determined by seniority[37] rather than by appointment. And their opportunities for promotion to a higher court, which in the case of federal court of appeals judges means to the Supreme Court of the United States, are too limited to make concern with being promoted play a major role in the thinking of most of them (or of any Supreme Court Justice, unless he thinks himself a candidate to become Chief Justice). Furthermore, judges are forbidden to sit in cases in which they might have a personal stake, such as a case in which a relative is a party or a lawyer for a party, or in which one of the parties is a corporation in which the judge owns stock.

So it is as if the designers of the federal judiciary had set out to remove every possible stick and carrot to which judges might respond; perhaps

36. Ahmed E. Taha, "Publish or Paris? Evidence of How Judges Allocate Their Time," 6 *American Law and Economics Review* 1, 25 (2004).

37. The Chief Justice of the United States is separately appointed. But the chief judge of a federal court of appeals is simply whoever is the most senior judge of the court, in regular service (that is, not a "senior" judge in the sense of a judge who has taken senior status and is therefore entitled to work part-time), who is not yet 65 years old when the position becomes vacant.

they did. And with self-interest in the usual sense out of the picture, economic analysis of judicial behavior might seem blocked at the threshold. But self-interest is not really out of the picture; it is rather that a judge's votes cannot be explained by reference to *standard* self-interest variables, such as price; there are other self-interest variables. In addition, economic analysis of judicial behavior can draw on Friedrich Hayek's biggest legacy to economics—recognition that limitations of knowledge present an economic problem even when the persons whose behavior is being analyzed are assumed not to be self-interested. Hayek's criticism of central planning was based on the difficulty of aggregating information by means other than the price system rather than on the motivations of the central planners.

The interplay of self-interest and of limitations of knowledge is illustrated in the judicial arena by attempts to evaluate judicial performance. Objective evaluations might generate searing criticisms that would shame judges into behaving themselves because shame, like guilt, is a cost. (Criticism can induce guilt as well as shame, of course.) But the information necessary for such evaluations is difficult, maybe impossible, to obtain.[38] This is due partly to the ability of an appellate judge to hide behind his law clerks, to whom he can delegate much of his job, including the writing of judicial opinions. (Trial judges cannot hide as well, because they have to preside over trials in open court.) A further obstacle is that the criteria of a good judge are contested. And even when they are agreed upon, their application to a difficult case is likely to be fraught with subjectivity. We shall see in chapter 11 that even that most celebrated of modern decisions, *Brown v. Board of Education,* can confidently be adjudged "correct" only by virtue of widespread acquiescence in its result (the test of time). While a scientific theory can be supported or undermined by observing whether its adoption results in the consequences that the theory predicts, the consequences of a judicial doctrine or decision often cannot be determined. There is not even agreement that the test of a judicial decision or doctrine should be the goodness or badness of its consequences. Some legal thinkers believe that law oriented toward consequences is illegitimate.

With the criteria for evaluating judicial action unsettled, evaluations

38. See generally Symposium, "Empirical Measures of Judicial Performance," 32 *Florida State University Law Review* 1001 (2005), and further discussion of the issue in chapters 5 and 6 of this book.

of judicial performance are likely to be contaminated by the evaluator's politics. This enables judges to take the easy path of dismissing academic criticism of their work as being the product of politics (plus envy and ignorance of judicial working conditions) and to dismiss journalistic criticism as likewise the product of politics and ignorance. These dismissals are self-serving and sometimes unjust, but they blunt the influence of criticism on judicial performance. In addition, most judges are largely unaware of media criticism of their work and particularly of academic criticism.

The economic theory of judicial behavior overlaps not only the strategic, sociological, and psychological theories but also the organizational and the pragmatic. The former builds on the insight that an agent and his principal, such as a judge and the government that employs him, have divergent interests and that the principal will try to create an organizational structure that will minimize this divergence and the agent will resist.[39] From this standpoint the highly prized institution of the "independent" judiciary presents a paradox, for what sense can it make for an agent to be independent of his principal? Yet some nonjudicial agents, ranging from commissioned salesmen to physicians, are authorized by their principals (their patients, in the latter example) to operate with considerable independence, and this can be consistent with the basic economics of principal-agent relations.

An example of how the judicial process is structured to motivate the judge-agents is the doctrine of precedent. Although precedents can be distinguished and even overruled, they have some authority, which means that there is a cost to circumventing or eliminating a precedent. Since any published decision of an appellate court is a precedent, the doctrine raises the cost of judicial error and so can be expected to make judges more careful in deciding a case and explaining the decision in an opinion that will create an appropriate precedent. Consistent adherence to precedent by appellate judges also makes it more likely that lower

---

39. See Haire, Lindquist, and Songer, note 33 above; Donald R. Songer, Jeffrey A. Segal, and Charles M. Cameron, "The Hierarchy of Justice: Testing a Principal-Agent Model of Supreme Court–Circuit Court Interactions," 38 *American Journal of Political Science* 673 (1994); and chapter 5 of this book, which focuses on the organizational theory of judicial behavior. Jonathan Matthew Cohen, *Inside Appellate Courts: The Impact of Court Organization on Judicial Decision Making in the United States Courts of Appeals* (2002), analyzes how the court system solves problems of communication, coordination, and control within and between courts.

courts will be the faithful agents of those judges, because they will be receiving clearer directives.[40]

"Pragmatism," in the sense in which the word is used in the pragmatic theory of judicial behavior, will require careful definition. But for now it is enough to note that the word refers to basing judgments (legal or otherwise) on consequences, rather than on deduction from premises in the manner of a syllogism. Pragmatism bears a family resemblance to utilitarianism and, in a commercial society like ours, to welfare economics, but without a commitment to the specific ways in which those philosophies evaluate consequences. In law, pragmatism refers to basing a judicial decision on the effects the decision is likely to have, rather than on the language of a statute or of a case, or more generally on a preexisting rule. So it is the opposite of legalism—or so it seems; the reality is somewhat different, as we shall see in subsequent chapters.

The phenomenological theory of judicial behavior[41] is a bridge from the pragmatic theory to the legalist theory, with which I shall end the chapter. Whereas psychology studies primarily the unconscious processes of the human mind, phenomenology studies first-person consciousness—experience as it presents itself to the conscious mind. So we might ask what it *feels* like to make a judicial decision.[42] The question interests some judges (not all, by any means), and some of these self-conscious judges, most famously Cardozo in *The Nature of the Judicial Process*, have published their impressions. I discuss that literature in chapter 9. Most judicial self-descriptions turn out to be of pragmatic judges, though the word rarely appears. This does not mean that most judges are pragmatists. The judges who internalize the "official" line, which is legalism, take for granted what they do, so they feel no urgent need to explain and defend it. And of course it is perilous to infer behav-

40. Ethan Bueno de Mesquita and Matthew Stephenson, "Informative Precedent and Intrajudicial Communication," 96 *American Political Science Review* 755 (2002).

41. See Edward Rubin and Malcolm Feeley, "Creating Legal Doctrine," 69 *Southern California Law Review* 1989 (1996); Duncan Kennedy, "Strategizing Strategic Behavior in Legal Interpretation," 1996 *Utah Law Review* 785 (1996); Kennedy, "Freedom and Constraint in Adjudication: A Critical Phenomenology," 36 *Journal of Legal Education* 518 (1986). Cf. Edward L. Rubin, "Putting Rational Actors in Their Place: Economics and Phenomenology," 51 *Vanderbilt Law Review* 1705 (1998). I discuss Kennedy's article "Freedom and Constraint in Adjudication" in chapter 8.

42. For a lucid introduction to the phenomenology of judgment (not necessarily a legal judgment—the author's principal example is the Judgment of Paris in Greek mythology), see Wayne M. Martin, *Theories of Judgment: Psychology, Logic, Phenomenology*, ch. 5 (2006).

ior from protestation. But the self-declared pragmatists are a little more credible than the self-declared legalists. They are swimming against the tide, asserting the less respectable position and thereby courting controversy. They at least are demonstrating the courage of their convictions.

This brings me last to the legalist theory of judging. Battered though it has been by legal realists and pragmatists, "crits" (that is, members of the Critical Legal Studies movement), political scientists, economic analysts of law, and other skeptics, it remains the judiciary's "official" theory of judicial behavior. It is proclaimed most emphatically by Justices of the Supreme Court, since the Court is in fact a political court, especially in regard to constitutional law, and therefore especially in need of protective coloration.

Legalism, considered as a positive theory of judicial behavior (it is more commonly a normative theory), hypothesizes that judicial decisions are determined by "the law," conceived of as a body of preexisting rules found stated in canonical legal materials, such as constitutional and statutory texts and previous decisions of the same or a higher court, or derivable from those materials by logical operations.[43] The treatment decisions of physicians are determined (most of them anyway) by the physicians' understanding of the structure of the physical world, and the aspiration of the legalist is that a judicial decision be determined by a body of rules constituting "the law" rather than by factors that are personal to judges, in the sense of varying among them, such as ideology, personality, and personal background. The ideal legalist decision is the product of a syllogism in which a rule of law supplies the major premise, the facts of the case supply the minor one, and the decision is the conclusion. The rule might have to be extracted from a statute or a constitutional provision, but the legalist model comes complete with a set of rules of interpretation (the "canons of construction"), so that interpretation too becomes a rule-bound activity, purging judicial discretion.

The legalist slogan is "the rule of law."[44] But this, as we shall see in chapter 3, is an ambiguous term. Better (though still somewhat ambiguous, as we shall also see there) is a "government of laws not men." Objectivity, as distinguished from neutrality or impartiality, implies ob-

---

43. Frederick Schauer, "Formalism," 97 *Yale Law Journal* 509 (1988).

44. As in Brian Z. Tamanaha, *Law as a Means to an End: Threat to the Rule of Law* 227–231 (2006); Tamanaha, "How an Instrumental View of Law Corrodes the Rule of Law," 56 *DePaul Law Review* 469 (2007).

server independence. If you ask someone what is 2 + 2, you will get the same answer whether he is a Democrat or a Republican, a theosophist, a libertarian, a Holocaust denier, or a cannibal. And if legal questions are similarly susceptible to being answered by methods of exact inquiry, then it does not matter how different the "men" who administer the laws are, and it is really the "laws" that govern.[45]

Legalism treats law as an autonomous discipline, a "limited domain."[46] Since the rules are given and have only to be applied, requiring only (besides fact-finding) reading legal materials and performing logical operations, the legalist judge is uninterested professionally in the social sciences, philosophy, or any other possible sources of guidance for making policy judgments, because he is not engaged, or at least he thinks he is not engaged, in making such judgments. It thus counts against legalism as a description of the behavior of American judges that the greater availability to them (for example, on the World Wide Web) of extralegal materials that a pragmatist might think relevant to a judicial decision has led to more frequent mention of those materials in judicial opinions.[47] It also counts against the descriptive adequacy of legalism that judges are expected to have "good judgment," to be wise, experienced, mature; none are qualities requisite in a logician.

The legalist theory makes a bookend with the pragmatist theory, but even more dramatically with the attitudinal theory. Judges like to justify their decisions as dictated by "the law," so must not attitudinalists be contending that the judges are lying or deluded? Actually no, unless they believe that judicial decisions are *never* influenced by "the law." Even in politically charged areas such as abortion, gay marriage, affirmative action, labor law, national security, election law, church and state, and voting rights, legalism can be expected to influence at least some judges some of the time. But neither would a legalist deny that judicial decisions are often influenced by the judges' politics, though he

45. This model of judicial objectivity is explicit in Friedrich A. Hayek, *The Constitution of Liberty* 153–154 (1960). See also *Federalist No. 78* (1788) (Hamilton), in *The Federalist Papers* 226, 233 (Roy P. Fairfield ed., 2d ed. 1966), where we read that it is "indispensable that [the judges] should be bound down by strict rules and precedents, which serve to define and point out their duty *in every particular case* that comes before them" (emphasis added).

46. Frederick Schauer, "The Limited Domain of the Law," 90 *Virginia Law Review* 1909, 1914–1918, 1945 (2004).

47. Frederick Schauer and Virginia J. Wise, "Legal Positivism as Legal Information," 82 *Cornell Law Review* 1080, 1080–1082, 1093–1109 (1997).

would deplore the fact. At the level of positive analysis, therefore, there is ample room for a middle ground between legalism and attitudinalism, as in the following summary of the results of an empirical study of judges' adherence to precedent:

> Precedent appears to have a moderately constraining effect on judicial freedom. The associations of ideology and outcome in the cases provide measured support for the realist hypotheses, but the study of cases of first impression refute the most extreme claims of realism. Judicial decisionmaking is influenced by precedent, but also by ideology and other factors. The growth of precedent in an area does not appear to restrict judicial discretion; if anything, the development of the law may increase such discretion.[48]

The middle ground is not the idea that adjudication is part "law" and part "ideology." When the authors of a study of political voting by federal appellate judges, finding areas of law in which the judges' presumed political leanings do *not* seem to influence their votes, conclude that "perhaps [in those areas] the law is effectively controlling,"[49] they are defining "law" too narrowly. Law is suffused with ideology. The true middle ground, as long ago explained by Roscoe Pound, is a tripartite conception of law as legal doctrines (rules and standards), techniques for deriving and applying doctrines (techniques such as *stare decisis*—decision according to precedent—which often means distinguishing or overruling a precedent), and social and ethical (in a word, policy) views.[50]

To which should be added the exercise, in certain circumstances, of pure discretion. When a judge schedules the start of a trial for 9:00 A.M. rather than 9:30 A.M., he is not guided by law in any meaningful sense. He is making a discretionary determination. Yet it is not "lawless." I am therefore led to embrace an adjectival rather than a substantive understanding of "law" in relation to judicial behavior. The analogy is to the

48. Stefanie A. Lindquist and Frank B. Cross, "Empirically Testing Dworkin's Chain Novel Theory: Studying the Path of Precedent," 80 *New York University Law Review* 1156, 1205–1206 (2005). For a particularly compelling articulation of the middle ground between the legalist and attitudinal models, see Klein, note 7 above, ch. 2.

49. Sunstein et al., note 7 above, at 62.

50. Roscoe Pound, "The Theory of Judicial Decision," 36 *Harvard Law Review* 940, 945–46 (1923). See also Leon R. Yankwich, "The Art of Being a Judge," 105 *University of Pennsylvania Law Review* 374, 378 (1957).

proper understanding of "luck." "Luck" is a noun but does not denote a property. To be lucky is to be the beneficiary of a random event, or more commonly of a series of such events (a "run"), rather than to possess something—"luck"—that alters the odds in one's favor. In the expression "he made his own luck," the word "luck" actually denotes its opposite; it denotes a reduction in randomness. Similarly, when we say that a judge's decisions are in conformity with "the law," we do not mean that we can put his decisions next to something called "law" and see whether they are the same. We mean that the determinants of the decisions were things that it is lawful for judges to take into account consciously or unconsciously. A judge is not acting lawlessly unless there is no authorized method by which he could deny some claim that a litigant was urging on him, yet he denied it nevertheless.

But the fact that judges follow precedent regularly even though not invariably does not support the legalist theory as strongly as one might expect. The original precedent in a line of precedents could not have been based on precedent. At the origin of the line must be something else. It might well be a policy judgment or, what often will amount to the same thing, the interpretation of a vague statute or vague constitutional provision—and the policy judgment or the policy-laden interpretation might well be determined by ideology.[51] To describe a case as "easy" because it is "governed" by some precedent[52] is to ignore the possibility that the precedent (or its ultimate ancestor) was the nonlegalist decision of a difficult, perhaps an indeterminate, case and that the decision to adhere to that precedent is an explicit or implicit policy judgment balancing the costs and benefits of adherence, since judges can overrule the prior cases of their court and thus wipe precedents off the books. That is what makes some legalists suspicious of the doctrine of precedent.

When a judge is following a precedent not of his own court but of the court to which his decisions can be appealed, he is not making a political judgment; he is in effect yielding to superior force. Even when a precedent is not binding (for it may not be a precedent of the higher court), it may be so deeply woven into the fabric of the law that its overruling would be unthinkable. (Holmes gave the example of the doctrine of consideration in contract law.) Most cases are not even appealed, because the outcome of the appeal is a forgone conclusion, usually because the

51. For evidence, see Lindquist and Cross, note 48 above, at 1184 (tab. 1).
52. Cross, note 2 above, at 286–287.

case really is "controlled" by precedent or clear statutory language. For the same reason, many potential cases are never even filed. So legalism has considerable sway, and the lower the level at which a legal dispute is resolved, the greater that sway. The higher the level, however, and so the weaker the tug of legalism, the greater the impact of decisions on legal rights and duties. The higher levels of the judiciary, culminating in the Supreme Court, are where a great deal of law is made, to be administered (albeit with imperfect fidelity) in mostly legalist fashion by the lower courts.

Often "following" precedent really means making a policy-based choice among competing precedents or a policy-influenced interpretation of a precedent's scope. Because judges are reluctant to overrule decisions—their preference is for "distinguishing" them to death rather than explicitly overruling them, in order to preserve the appearance of the law's continuity and stability—the landscape of case law is littered with inconsistent precedents among which current judges can pick and choose, resurrecting if need be a precedent that had died but had not been given a decent burial. (This may explain why ideology plays a greater role in judicial decision making the more precedents there are in an area of law.[53]) The problem is particularly serious in the Supreme Court. As a result of the Court's long history and sharp ideological swings, there is a large stock of precedents that not having been formally overruled are available for opportunistic rehabilitation. For only when a court is dealing with a precedent of the court that has appellate jurisdiction over it is the legalist methodology actually *enforced,* and when it is not enforced it often is ignored or overridden. But not always. The risk of reversal by the Supreme Court is so slight these days that courts of appeals (and state supreme courts as well) could get away with a good deal more ignoring of Supreme Court precedent than they do. Lower-court judges follow Supreme Court precedent less out of fear of reversal if they do not than because (in my terms) adhering to precedents created by a higher court is one of the rules of the judicial "game" that judges internalize.[54]

Frank Cross argues that the fact that there is a high affirmance rate of

53. Lindquist and Cross, note 48 above, at 1187–1200.

54. Frank Cross, "Appellate Court Adherence to Precedent," 2 *Journal of Empirical Legal Studies* 369 (2005). To the same effect, see David E. Klein and Robert J. Hume, "Fear of Reversal as an Explanation of Lower Court Compliance," 37 *Law and Society Review* 579 (2003); James L. Gibson, "Judges' Role Orientations, Attitudes, and Decisions: An Interactive Model," 72 *American Political Science Review* 911 (1978).

federal district court decisions by the courts of appeals, and that the rate is higher when the standard of appellate review is more deferential, shows that appellate judges are bowing to the commands of "the law."[55] All it really shows is that most cases are routine (and would not be litigated at all if lawyers were better at predicting judicial outcomes), rather than residing in that uncomfortable open region in which judges are at large. The routine case is dispatched with least fuss by legalist methods. It is in such a case that the virtues of such methods shine; feeling no need to go beyond those methods to decide the case satisfactorily, the judge can plume himself on his self-abnegation without surrendering discretion where it counts. It is also easier to write a convincing opinion affirming a decision after ruling that the lower court's decision was entitled to deferential review, as it is easier to show that a decision is not clearly wrong than to show that it is right.

Cross finds that personal characteristics (including personal background characteristics, such as race and gender), as well as ideology, influence judicial decisions,[56] but that such characteristics, especially personal experience, such as a judge's having been a prosecutor before he became a judge, have much less influence than his ideology as proxied by the political identity of the President who appointed him. This follows, Cross argues, from Presidents' being focused on ideology.[57] If most female lawyers are liberal, a conservative President will still pick women to be judges. But he will be picking them from the minority of women who are conservative, and this will tend to wash out the effect of gender on a judge's decisions. The strategy is consistent with female judges' being on average more liberal than male judges, either in areas of law that may not be important to the appointing authorities[58] or because it is easier for a liberal President to find qualified female judicial candidates who share his ideology than it is for a conservative President to do so.

The fact that ideology is correlated with personal characteristics suggests the possibility, examined in chapter 4, that such characteristics, along with psychological traits, influence the formation of a judge's ideology and thus, at one remove, the judge's decisions in the open area.

---

55. Frank B. Cross, *Decision Making in the U.S. Courts of Appeals* 48–53 (2007).
56. Id., ch. 3.
57. Id. at 92–93.
58. Such as sex discrimination, which is strongly opposed by both political parties, and in which a significant effect of gender on decisions is found; see Boyd, Epstein, and Martin, note 7 above.

Attitudinalists and legalists disagree about the extent of political judging rather than about its existence. One source of that disagreement is that attitudinalists, who mostly are political scientists rather than lawyers, are positive theorists, while most legalists are lawyers, who—inveterately normative as most lawyers are—very much want, and are predisposed by their training and by the mores and understandings of the profession to expect, judges to conform to the legalist conception. Legalists' normative project would be undermined if most judges, and not just an errant minority, turned out to be guided by politics or other factors that do not enter into legalists' conception of "the law." In contrast, since the subject of political science is politics, political scientists expect judging to be imbued with politics—and even want it to be, as demonstrating the power of political science to illuminate behavior.

But what if attitudinalists and legalists alike are wrong about what the law is? What if law in the judicial setting is deeply, intrinsically political, in the sense of responsive to judges' political preferences, but also deeply, intrinsically legalist, in the sense of heavily influenced by conventionally "legal" materials and techniques of decision making? Then strict legalists might be off base both as positive and as normative theorists, while political scientists' positive theory might be off base because they exaggerated the degree to which judicial decisions are motivated by politics. I think both things are true, that legalists have too narrow a sense of what law (or doing law) is and that attitudinalists exaggerate the influence of politics, not only partisan politics but also ideological politics, on judicial behavior, at least below the level of the U.S. Supreme Court. I am not criticizing the attitudinalists' empirical work, but merely trying to characterize accurately what they have found.

Legalists acknowledge that their methods cannot close the deal every time.[59] That is an understatement. Legalist methods fail in many cases that reach appellate courts, and those are precisely the cases that most influence the further development of the law.[60] There are too many vague statutes and even vaguer constitutional provisions, statutory gaps and inconsistencies, professedly discretionary domains, obsolete and conflicting precedents, and factual aporias.

Some of the resulting uncertainties could be dispelled by the adoption of legalist meta-rules, such as that a statute should not be invalidated

59. Notably in Tamanaha's book and article cited in note 44 above.
60. This is the essential insight of legal realism. Brian Leiter, *Naturalizing Jurisprudence: Essays on American Legal Realism and Naturalism in Legal Philosophy* 20 and n. 25 (2007).

unless its unconstitutionality is clear beyond a reasonable doubt, that statutory exceptions are to be construed narrowly, that judges in interpreting statutory or constitutional provisions must never search beneath the surface meaning for the purpose of the provision, or that precedents can be overruled only by legislation. But these rules, though advocated by some legalists, cannot be derived by logical or quasi-logical means from agreed-upon premises; they are not themselves fruits or exemplars of legalistic reasoning. For example, nowhere does the Constitution say that constitutional interpretation must be strict. That rule must be posited; it cannot be deduced. The meta-rules represent policy choices, and policy choices so unsatisfactory that as a result there are no consistent legalists (recall my quotation from Justice Scalia in the introduction[61]) in the judiciary, as distinct from the academy, where reality does not constrain imagination. Nor, once having created a comprehensive system of meta-rules, could judges turn over a new leaf, as it were, and decide all cases in strict conformity with the rules. The rapidly changing social, economic, and political environment would soon knock the rules out of alignment with the circumstances in which they were being applied. New rounds of policy-flavored rule changes would be unavoidable.

Legalists could meet pragmatists halfway, as by accepting the legitimacy of purposive interpretation of rules (see chapter 7). Such interpretation is policy oriented, but the policy need not be that of the interpreter; it may really be the policy that animates the statute—the policy the legislators wanted the statute to promote. So judicial discretion, though not eliminated, would be trimmed. Most legalists are already moderate in the sense of being willing to allow common law judges (and almost all American judges have a common law as well as a statutory and constitutional jurisdiction) to overrule and distinguish precedents and create new common law rules and standards. Legalists in regard to the interpretation of statutes and constitutions, originalists recognize a legitimate role for discretion when judges are wearing their common law hats. They are even willing to recognize a category of "common law statutes," such as the Sherman Act, as I noted in the introduction. These are statutes that judges treat with the same freedom as they treat common law precedents, as when the Court said, again of the Sherman Act, that the Act "cannot mean what it says."[62] The Supreme Court's conservative

61. I give further examples in chapter 9.
62. National Society of Professional Engineers v. United States, 435 U.S. 679, 687 (1978).

legalists joined Justice Kennedy's opinion denominating the Sherman Act a common law statute, without a murmur.

Moderate legalists are matched by moderate pragmatists—pragmatists who believe that the institutional consequences of judicial decisions argue for a judicial approach heavily seasoned with respect for the language of contracts, statutes, and precedents. The two moderate judicial schools may come close enough to enable most cases in the open area to be disposed of with minimum disagreement.[63] But a space will be left in which a legalist methodology might produce substantive policies that would make many pragmatist judges gag. Responsible pragmatists will be guided in interpreting a statute by what they think a legislature of thoughtful nonpartisan representatives of the people would have done had the decision been up to them (unless it is apparent that the legislature did not do this—that the governing statutory provision was the product of an unprincipled compromise). Legalists shudder at the thought, but are not themselves immune to the tug of their political ideology. Far from it, if only because legalism so often fails to yield a determinate result.

Yet the existence of a solid legalist core in judicial decision making even at the highest levels must not be overlooked. Thomas Hansford and James Spriggs point out that while "the [Supreme Court] justices interpret precedent with a keen eye toward moving existing policy closer to their preferred policies,"[64] they also accord considerable weight even to precedents that do not conform to their ideology if the precedents have achieved what the authors call "precedent vitality" by virtue of having been favorably cited in many cases over a substantial period of time.[65] Yet we shall see in chapter 10 that in a recent case a plurality of the Justices reinterpreted *Brown v. Board of Education*, one of the Supreme Court's most hallowed precedents, to make it stand for a conservative principle (affirmative action is unconstitutional) remote from the decision's original liberal meaning.

The percentage of the Court's decisions that are unanimous might seem to place an upper bound on legalism in the Court. Over the past

---

63. "It is, I think, the fact that most originalists are faint-hearted and most nonoriginalists are moderate . . . which accounts for the fact that the sharp divergence between the two philosophies does not produce an equivalently sharp divergence in judicial opinions." Antonin Scalia, "Originalism: The Lesser Evil," 57 *University of Cincinnati Law Review* 849, 862 (1989).

64. Thomas G. Hansford and James F. Spriggs II, *The Politics of Precedent on the U.S. Supreme Court* 126 (2006).

decade an average of 36 percent of decisions in which the Court issued an opinion have been unanimous. Interestingly, as shown in Table 7, this is an increase over the two preceding decades. Does that mean the Court is becoming more legalist? Perhaps so. But an alternative hypothesis is that it is becoming more uniform. Today, unlike in 1975, all the Justices are former federal court of appeals judges. This is the culmination of a trend. In 1950 only one of the Justices was a former federal court of appeals judge (Sherman Minton). Since 1975 only one Justice has been appointed who was not a federal court of appeals judge—Justice O'Connor, and she was a state appellate judge. That all the current Justices are former judges with no political experience confirms the limitations of legalism at the Supreme Court level. For despite their lack of political experience and their having been inducted into the culture of judging, with its legalist traditions, before being appointed to the Court, the Justices are unable to attain the degree of consensus that should be attainable by judges engaged in an essentially logical enterprise, since logical proofs are observer independent.

The percentages in Table 7 are at most only outer limits, because legalism and uniformity are different sources of judicial consensus. A case may present a pure issue of policy that legalist techniques cannot begin to resolve. But if the judges happen to have similar views, which might be based on similar professional experiences, they may reach unanimity as easily as they would in a case that could be formulated as a syllogism. Even as outer limits, however, the percentages are misleading. They ignore the petitions for certiorari that the Justices turn down because they are not minded to disturb a precedent for which they would not have voted in the first place, and the petitions that are never filed because the Court would be sure to deny them on the basis of established precedent or clear constitutional or statutory language.

Table 7 Average Percentage of Unanimous Opinions in the Supreme Court, 1975–2005 (in percent)

1975–1985	21.8
1985–1995	27.5
1995–2005	36.0
1975–2005	28.4

Source: Statistics published annually in the November issue of the *Harvard Law Review.*

Because of dissent aversion, unanimity cannot be used to estimate consensus in the decisions of the lower courts (obviously not in the trial courts, where the judge sits by himself). The dissent rate is much lower than the amount of disagreement. But dissent aversion is very weak in the Supreme Court. The cases the Court hears tend to arouse strong emotions. And the Justices have a lighter workload than lower-court judges, are more in the public eye and therefore more concerned with projecting a coherent judicial philosophy, and are more likely to influence the law even when dissenting, because of the instability of Supreme Court precedent as a consequence of the greater stakes in the cases that the Court decides and the absence of review by a higher court. With their heavier but less momentous caseloads, the courts of appeals are more wedded to precedent than the Supreme Court is, and as a result a dissent in the court of appeals has less influence on the law; the benefits therefore are usually outweighed by the costs, discussed earlier, of dissenting. This may explain the surprising finding that, after adjustment for other factors (an essential qualification), Supreme Court Justices appointed from the courts of appeals are more liberal than other Supreme Court Justices.[66] The former have been socialized by their lower-court judicial experience to be respectful of precedent, and the most controversial Supreme Court precedents are those created in the liberal Warren Court era.

The place of legalism in the work of the Supreme Court is illustrated by *Whitman v. American Trucking Associations*,[67] a unanimous decision though with multiple concurring opinions. Congress had directed the Environmental Protection Agency to prescribe national air quality standards "the attainment and maintenance of which . . . are requisite to protect the public health" with "an adequate margin of safety."[68] The Court held that this directive did not permit the agency to consider the cost of complying with a standard. The agency can consider only whether the standard is necessary to protect the public health with an adequate margin of safety. The "adequate margin" qualification implies that doubts

65. Id. at 25, 126. See also Ronald Kahn, "Institutional Norms and Supreme Court Decision-Making: The Rehnquist Court on Privacy and Religion," in *Supreme Court Decision-Making: New Institutionalist Approaches* 175 (Cornell W. Clayton and Howard Gillman eds. 1999).

66. Landes and Posner, note 6 above.

67. 531 U.S. 457 (2001).

68. 42 U.S.C. § 7409(b)(1).

are to be resolved in favor of finding that a possible standard is indeed "requisite," an approach inconsistent with basing a decision on a comparison of costs and benefits. The majority opinion was by Justice Scalia, who is hardly an ardent environmentalist; had he been a member of Congress when the Clean Air Act was passed, he doubtless would have voted to allow the EPA to consider costs. As explained in Justice Breyer's concurrence, the argument against allowing such consideration is that it lessens polluters' incentive to press for technological innovations that would lower the cost of reducing pollution. Denial of a cost defense is thus "technology-forcing,"[69] which is a shibboleth of environmentalists.

The statutory language provided no handle for recognizing a cost defense. Nor did the legislative history, reviewed at length in Breyer's opinion. Other provisions of the Clean Air Act require the EPA to consider compliance cost. It is unlikely that had Congress intended this to be the case with regard to national air quality standards as well, it would not have said so; it could not have overlooked the issue, a plank in the environmentalists' platform and a salient concern of industry. Also, loopholes in the Act allow the cost of complying with the standards to be brought in by the back door, which minimizes the risk that the EPA will impose on the industry compliance costs absurdly disproportionate to the environmental benefits. This is significant because Justice Scalia acknowledges an "absurdity exception" to the literal interpretation of statutes—incidentally a sign that legalists flinch from embracing the full implications of their position.

Scalia would have been hard-pressed to write a persuasive opinion in support of the opposite outcome. Congress had left little interpretive leeway. Such an opinion would have invited not only intense professional criticism but possible congressional retaliation, since environmentalism is politically popular and Congress does not like the courts to treat its statutes as first drafts that a judge is free to rewrite to promote his personal policy agenda. So here is an example in which a legalist approach (more precisely, an approximation to such an approach, as the Court's analysis was not strictly an exercise in logical deduction) is implied not only by a judicial commitment to legalism but also by the strategic theory of judicial behavior. Such decisions are common even in the Supreme Court, though more so in nonconstitutional cases.

69. 531 U.S. at 492 (concurring opinion).

Common but not typical. Consider *Bell Atlantic Corp. v. Twombly.*[70] Rule 8(a)(2) of the Federal Rules of Civil Procedure requires of a complaint or other pleading only that it contain "a short and plain statement of the claim showing that the pleader is entitled to relief." This is what is called "notice pleading." It supplanted the requirement (which prevailed before the civil rules were promulgated in 1938) that the complaint plead facts that would show that the plaintiff was entitled to the legal relief his suit was seeking. *Bell Atlantic* holds that a complaint charging that an agreement between firms not to compete, in violation of antitrust law, must contain "enough factual matter (taken as true) to suggest that an agreement was made . . . An allegation of parallel conduct and a bare assertion of conspiracy will not suffice."[71] The Court rejected the rule stated in a much-cited earlier decision, *Conley v. Gibson,* "that a complaint should not be dismissed for failure to state a claim unless it appears beyond doubt that the plaintiff can prove no set of facts in support of his claim which would entitle him to relief."[72] The majority in *Bell Atlantic* was concerned that *Conley's* heretofore canonical formula might force a defendant in an antitrust case to conduct expensive pretrial discovery in order to demonstrate the groundlessness of a plaintiff's case.[73] The dissent pointed out correctly that district judges have ample authority to prevent abusive discovery. But the majority said that the rules granting judges that authority "have been, and are doomed to be, hollow."[74]

I am not concerned with which faction had the better case. All that interests me is that nothing in the repertoire of legalism could have decided it, especially in favor of the position in the majority opinion (which nonetheless the four most conservative Justices, all votaries of "textualism-originalism," the currently most influential school of legalism, joined without a peep). Rule 8(a)(2) does not say what the "short and plain statement" is supposed to contain; it does not mention facts. Precedent, as illustrated by the *Conley* case, supported the dissent. But the majority had a good argument, though not a legalist argument, that "notice" (in the term "notice pleading") should be interpreted to require

70. 127 S. Ct. 1955 (2007).
71. Id. at 1965–1966.
72. 355 U.S. 41, 45–46 (1957).
73. 127 S. Ct. at 1967.
74. Id. at 1967 n. 6.

the pleading of *some* facts in an antitrust conspiracy case, as otherwise the defendant may have very little sense of what the plaintiff's claim is. The lower courts had already made the point with reference to charges of conspiracy generally, owing to the vagueness of such charges.[75] The effect of minimal pleading on discovery, and whether it might be out-weighed by the difficulty of pleading details of a conspiracy without pretrial discovery (which follows rather than precedes the filing of the complaint), were issues of antitrust policy and case management policy rather than of the meaning of legal texts. Right or wrong, the decision in *Bell Atlantic* was pragmatic rather than legalist.

Or consider once again *Leegin Creative Leather Products, Inc. v. PSKS, Inc.,*[76] which overruled the almost century-old precedent of *Dr. Miles Medical Co. v. John D. Park & Sons Co.*[77] The earlier case had held that agreements by which a manufacturer places a floor under his distributors' resale price are a per se violation of the Sherman Act, on the ground that they have the same effect as if the retailers had gotten together and decided to fix a minimum price at which to sell the good. That was wrong as a matter of economics, because a manufacturer has no interest in allowing his distributors to cartelize distribution, thus restricting his access to his customers. If the manufacturer places a floor under his re-tailers' prices, it is because the floor serves his interest in competing more effectively against other manufacturers, as by encouraging the re-tailers to provide presale services to customers for the manufacturer's good.[78] So *Dr. Miles* was rightly overruled. But the overruling, and its rightness, owed nothing to legalist thinking. A venerable precedent was overruled because it was bad economics. *Leegin* is a triumph of prag-matism.

Leegin notwithstanding, it would be a mistake to think that precedent has no constraining effect on Supreme Court decision making, even in

75. For example, in Loubser v. Thacker, 440 F.3d 439, 442–443 (7th Cir. 2006), the court remarked that "although conspiracy is not something that Rule 9(b) of the Federal Rules of Civil Procedure requires be proved with particularity, and so a plain and short statement will do, it differs from other claims in having a degree of vagueness that makes a bare claim of 'con-spiracy' wholly uninformative to the defendant. Federal pleading entitles a defendant to notice of the plaintiff's claim so that he can prepare responsive pleadings. That is why courts require the plaintiff to allege the parties, the general purpose, and the approximate date of the conspir-acy" (citations omitted).

76. 127 S. Ct. 2705 (2007).

77. 220 U.S. 373 (1911).

78. Richard A. Posner, *Antitrust Law* 171–189 (2d ed. 2001).

Table 8   Replacement of Supreme Court Justices, 1969–2006

Replaced	Appointed by Republican or Democratic President	Replaced By	Appointed by Republican or Democratic President	Year
Warren	R	Burger	R	1969
Fortas	D	Blackmun	R	1970
Black	D	Powell	R	1972
Harlan	R	Rehnquist	R	1972
Douglas	D	Stevens	R	1975
Stewart	R	O'Connor	R	1981
Burger	R	Scalia	R	1986
Powell	R	Kennedy	R	1988
Brennan	R	Souter	R	1990
Marshall	D	Thomas	R	1991
White	D	Ginsburg	D	1993
Blackmun	R	Breyer	D	1994
Rehnquist	R	Roberts	R	2005
O'Connor	R	Alito	R	2006

constitutional law. Consider Table 8, which lists Supreme Court appointments, and the Justices they replaced, since Nixon began the dismantling of the Warren Court, and notes the party of the appointing President.

The fact that 5 of the 14 replaced Justices and only 2 of the Justices who replaced them were appointed by Democratic Presidents is less important than that, with the exception of Ginsburg's replacement of White, every one of the replacements was more conservative than the Justice he or she replaced, though in some cases, notably Powell's replacement by Kennedy, the difference was slight. Throughout the entire 37-year period the Court has been moving rightward from the Warren Court, and, as expected, its decisions have been more conservative than they would have been had all the replacements been as liberal as the average member of the Warren Court. Yet most of the landmark Warren Court decisions, in areas such as criminal procedure, legislative apportionment, freedom of speech and religion, racial discrimination, prisoner rights, substantive due process, and constitutional rights, and the Warrenesque decisions of the Burger Court, such as *Roe v. Wade,* have remained largely or entirely intact, even though most would have been decided differently by the present Court had they been given to it to decide. The expansion of rights brought about by the Warren Court, and to a more limited extent by the Burger Court, has ceased; retrenchment is in the air. But there is no indication of a wholesale rejection of precedents that most of the current Justices may wish had never been created. So even this most political of courts, in its most political domain, that of constitutional law, is, to a degree, legalistic.

2

The Judge as Labor-Market Participant

Nine overlapping, incomplete, but insightful theories of judicial behavior make for an unwieldy analytic apparatus. They can be integrated by conceiving of the judge as a worker, and thus a participant in a labor market—a rather unusual labor market, to be sure, but a labor market nevertheless.

A market is two-sided—buyers and sellers. A labor market consists on the buying side of a set of employers who want to hire workers for a particular type of job and on the selling side of a set of workers who prefer that type of job to the alternatives open to them. In the federal court system, the President, with the approval of the Senate, hires persons to resolve the class of disputes that Article III of the Constitution places within the judicial power of the United States, mainly cases arising under federal law and cases between citizens of different states even if they do not arise under federal law. The appointing authorities have dual goals that are in tension. First, they want to appoint "good" judges, in the sense of judges who will enforce the legal norms found in the Constitution and federal statutes impartially, free from political interference by the appointing authorities. Not only is an independent judiciary a considerable social and economic good[1] (though not always indispens-

1. A major theme in Kenneth W. Dam, *The Law-Growth Nexus: The Rule of Law and Economic Development* (2006). See also Daniel M. Klerman, "Legal Infrastructure, Judicial Independence, and Economic Development," 19 *Pacific McGeorge Global Business and Development Law Journal* 427 (2007); Klerman and Paul G. Mahoney, "The Value of Judicial Independence: Evidence from Eighteenth Century England," 7 *American Law and Economics Review* 1 (2005); Rafael La Porta et al., "Judicial Checks and Balances," 112 *Journal of Political Economy* 443

able to rapid economic growth—witness China[2]), but it is recognized as such by the dominant groups in our society. And it is not merely a diffuse social and economic value, which might not be perceived clearly by the general public; it benefits the nonjudicial branches of government, and thus the politicians, by providing stability to political settlements.[3] Judicial independence is therefore most likely to be valued when political competition is intense, as it is in the United States, because "by establishing an independent court, politicians currently in office make it more difficult for successors to alter the policies passed today."[4] Like Ulysses tied to the mast, independent judges do not hear (or at least hear more faintly) the siren song of the current political incumbents calling on them to unmake the constitutional and legislative deals of previous generations of politicians.[5]

But second, the appointing authorities want the judges to tilt in favor of the political goals of the Administration (or of the Senate majority, when it is not in the control of the President's party and refuses easy confirmation of his nominees). The political actors know, consistent with the attitudinal theory of judicial behavior, that federal judges have a large measure of discretion. This implies latitude to decide many cases in favor of the policies advocated by either of the political parties without being regarded as usurpative. Once appointed, however, a federal judge, being well insulated from both carrots and sticks, has no incentive to decide cases in such a way as to advance anyone's political goals besides his own—if he has such goals. He does not have to flaunt his political leanings even if they coincide with those of his appointers, be-

---

(2004); Lars P. Feld and Stefan Voigt, "Economic Growth and Judicial Independence: Cross-Country Evidence Using a New Set of Indicators," 19 *European Journal of Political Economy* 497 (2003).

2. Dam, note 1 above, ch. 11. As Dam points out, however, only in poor countries may an independent judiciary not be indispensable to economic growth.

3. William M. Landes and Richard A. Posner, "The Independent Judiciary in an Interest-Group Perspective," 18 *Journal of Law and Economics* 875 (1975); Gary M. Anderson, William F. Shughart II, and Robert D. Tollison, "On the Incentives of Judges to Enforce Legislative Wealth Transfers," 32 *Journal of Law and Economics* 215 (1989).

4. F. Andrew Hanssen, "Is There a Politically Optimal Level of Judicial Independence?" 94 *American Economic Review* 712, 726 (2004). See also J. Mark Ramseyer, "The Puzzling (In)Dependence of Courts: A Comparative Approach," 23 *Journal of Legal Studies* 721 (1994).

5. "Although politicians in countries that keep courts off limits lower their ability to earn political points while in office, they limit their losses while out of office." J. Mark Ramseyer and Eric B. Rasmusen, *Measuring Judicial Independence: The Political Economy of Judging in Japan* 171 (2003).

cause once he is appointed, the President who nominated him and the Senators who confirmed him can do nothing to help or hurt his career. The exception is judges who are avid for promotion (and these, I shall argue, are relatively few), but their best way of signaling fealty is by their decisions; talk is cheap.

Promotion seekers to one side, the best the appointing authorities can do to advance their political goals is to appoint judges who share those goals yet, because they can be expected to confine their political judging to cases in the open area (and perhaps their judging will be "political" in only the broadest sense), are not so political that they will be incompetent judges. This appointment policy preserves the independence of the judiciary but does not eliminate, and in fact confirms, the existence of a political component in judging.

So we know what the buying side of the labor market is looking for and we must now consider what the would-be sellers of judicial labor— the judicial candidates themselves, especially those who succeed in becoming judges—are looking for. They want to be paid a salary for serving as a judge of course. But money is not the principal motivator, as they could command a higher salary in a law practice or even in teaching law. (The judicial wage is held down by monopsony, as explained in chapter 6.) One of the nonpecuniary compensations of a judgeship, for those whose next most attractive alternative would be private practice, is not having clients to kowtow to. Another—the obverse of that unattractive feature of private practice—is being kowtowed to by the lawyers who appear before the judge. Deference is a significant nonpecuniary reward of a judgeship.

Power is one of the sources of the deference that judges receive, though legalists wish it otherwise—for they think that judges should be either transmitters of decisions made elsewhere in the political system or solvers of puzzles. The public executioner has no power because he has no discretion. But power is not the only source of the deference that judges receive; for they, and the legal profession generally, have had some success in "selling" judges to the general public as the very incarnation of the rule of law. So judges are respected. Power is also an independent source of job satisfaction. Many people enjoy exercising power over other people—man is a hierarchical species, like other primates.

Most people who seek or accept a judgeship derive more utility from leisure and public recognition, relative to income, and are more risk averse, than the average practicing lawyer. For despite much self-serving complaining about heavy judicial workloads (judges have been complaining since judicial workloads were much lighter, giving the current complaints a crying-wolf quality), judges having a taste for leisure can indulge their taste more easily than they could as practicing lawyers. A federal judge cannot, as a practical matter, be fired, short of engaging in conduct gross enough to provoke impeachment by the House of Representatives and conviction by the Senate; his salary cannot be reduced (although it can be eroded by inflation—see chapter 6); and the retirement benefits are outstanding. A federal judge is entitled to retire at full pay at age 65 with only 15 years of service. If he prefers, he can take "senior status" rather than retire, and continue working indefinitely full-time or part-time, at his option, still at full pay.

There are only about 800 Article III judges (district judges, circuit judges, and Supreme Court Justices, as distinct from lesser federal judicial officers, such as magistrate judges, bankruptcy judges, and countless administrative law judges)—about 1,200 if senior judges are included—out of a total of about a million lawyers in the United States. Because of their small number, and because they are engaged in conducting highly visible public business, Article III judges tend to be more prominent than even very successful practicing lawyers. Many of them achieve a celebrity status—albeit a very minor one, usually limited to the legal community and often just to the local legal community, except of course in the case of Supreme Court Justices—denied to their practitioner peers.

Since no one is forced to become a judge and the job is not to everyone's liking, there is self-selection—itself reflecting the play of incentives and constraints on behavior—into the judiciary. And so it is plausible that judges actually do have the tastes that I have just listed, and in addition that they have a taste for being a *good* judge. This is an intrinsic satisfaction but it is validated and reinforced by a judge's reputation in the judicial and the broader legal community, and sometimes in other communities as well, such as the academic and political communities, and in the media. Most candidates for a federal judgeship have good enough job alternatives that they would not seek or accept a judgeship unless they thought it an important job, one to be taken seriously and performed conscientiously. Although politics almost always plays a role, and often a decisive one, in a judicial appointment, the elaborate screening of candidates by the FBI, the White House, interest groups, and the Senate Judiciary Committee tends to filter out irresponsible candidates. It might be different if the judicial salary were much higher, however, an issue that I discuss in chapter 6.

To regard oneself and be regarded by others, especially one's peers, as a good judge requires conformity to the accepted norms of judging. One cannot be regarded as a good judge if one takes bribes, decides cases by flipping a coin, falls asleep in the courtroom, ignores legal doctrine, cannot make up one's mind, bases decisions on the personal attractiveness or unattractiveness of the litigants or their lawyers, or decides cases on the basis of "politics" (depending on how that slippery word is defined). Virtually all judges would be distressed to be regarded as politicians in robes, because if they thought of themselves in that light they could not regard themselves as being good judges, and this would deny them a major satisfaction of a judgeship and might well drive them into practice, teaching, or some other nonjudicial vocation.

The hypothesis that judges are motivated by a desire to be good workers is supported by the superficially puzzling existence of a judicial work ethic. The judicial utility function is missing many of the arguments of other workers' utility functions, but one that remains, as we know, is leisure. In the age of the law clerk (federal district judges are entitled to two law clerks, court of appeals judges to three, and Supreme Court Justices to four, and these numbers can sometimes be exceeded through bureaucratic maneuvers[6]), the opportunities for a leisured judicial life, especially at the appellate level, are abundant. Yet most federal judges work pretty hard, often well past the age at which they could retire at full pay—so if they continue to work, they are working for nothing.[7] Many work very hard indeed—too hard, in a few instances; think of

6. For example, federal court of appeals judges are allotted five "slots," which they can use for any combination of law clerks and secretaries. Most of the judges used to have three law clerks and two secretaries, but with the automation of most secretarial work an increasing number of judges have four law clerks and one secretary. In addition, the courts of appeals now employ staff law clerks (sometimes called staff attorneys), who are not assigned to particular judges but are available to help them. Many judges also have interns and externs. And an increasing number of judges (mainly but not only district judges) have career law clerks, who sometimes function as assistant judges. In short, the federal courts are generously staffed.

7. This is consistent with rational behavior and even with leisure preference. As David R. Stras, "The Incentives Approach to Judicial Retirement," 90 *Minnesota Law Review* 1417 (2006), finds, most judges take senior status shortly after eligibility, so they continue judging but have more leisure—yet could have still more leisure by retiring, and without sacrificing pay.

Harry Blackmun. What are they working hard *for*? Some work for celebrity, but most, below the level of the Supreme Court, are content to labor in obscurity. They are laboring to be good judges. Why else would they be working hard? They derive other satisfactions from being a judge, as I have said, such as wielding power, but the enjoyment of them does not require working hard.

There is a parallel between the utility function of judges and that of serious artists, another unusual category of labor-market participants. Serious artists want a good income and some leisure, but they are not income or leisure maximizers. The intrinsic satisfaction of their work (which may be felt by them as compulsion or obsession) is a major argument in their utility function. But bound up with that in most cases is a desire to be able to regard themselves and be regarded by others as good artists. Most judges similarly derive considerable intrinsic satisfaction from their work and want to be able to regard themselves and be regarded by others[8] as good judges. (The nonpecuniary rewards of judging are, as we shall see in chapter 6, a neglected factor in the movement to raise federal judicial salaries.) A difference between the judge and the artist, however, is that the judge exercises power, and with power comes responsibility; conscience should be a stronger motivator of the judge than of the artist. Another difference is that appellate judging is a collaborative enterprise. But we must not exaggerate this difference, for much artistic creation is collaborative too—think of drama, architecture, operas, musicals, films, the ateliers of the great Renaissance painters, and the jointly authored plays of Shakespeare's time.

Artists combine craftsmanship with creativity. But so do judges, displaying craftsmanship in the legalist phase of decision making and creativity in the legislative phase (the phase in which judges exercise discretion to make law, as distinct from passively applying preexisting law), and in both phases working through a legal problem or series of legal problems and wrapping the solutions in a rhetorical package pleasing to their colleagues as their primary audience but also, they hope, to a broader audience as well.

"The mixture of disciplined structure and imaginative freedom, the reworking of traditions into a new idea, the ruthless elimination of dull,

---

8. The importance to judges of the opinion in which they are held by others is emphasized in Lawrence Baum, *Judges and Their Audiences: A Perspective on Judicial Behavior*, ch. 1 (2006).

incongruous or surplus materials, and the creation of a dramatic narrative . . . —not to mention patience, stamina, and attentiveness"—is said to be what gardening and novel writing have in common,[9] but it can serve as a description of judicial opinion writing as well. Novelists and judges further resemble each other in being to a great extent intuitive reasoners, in the sense (discussed at length in chapter 4) that much of their creative thinking is unconscious. A novelist writes a passage one way rather than another because it *feels* right; he may be unable to explain *why* it feels right. A judge often has a strong sense of which way a case should be decided, but when he tries to explain the decision in a judicial opinion the explanation will often turn out to be a rationalization of a result reached on inarticulable grounds, though sometimes the effort to explain will operate to refine and perhaps reverse the intuition that drove his vote.

Norms govern the various art genres, just as norms govern judicial decisions—and in both cases the norms are contestable. Manet could not paint as well, in the conventional sense, as his teacher, Couture; but in the fullness of time Manet became regarded as much the greater painter. Holmes, Brandeis, Cardozo, and Hand are examples of judges who succeeded by their example in altering the norms of opinion writing.

The comparison of judge and artist is more apt with respect to intermediate appellate judges than with respect to district judges (whose principal product is not the written opinion) or Supreme Court Justices. Justices have great power, though it is diluted by the fact that they hear and decide cases in a panel of nine. Intermediate appellate judges have some power, clearly over the litigants in the cases they decide but also over the development of the law (and thus over society at large). And their power is growing as the ratio of Supreme Court to court of appeals decisions falls,[10] although it remains far less than the Justices' power. The federal courts of appeals publish more than 100 times the number of opinions as the Supreme Court, but even if the average court of appeals opinion were one-hundredth as consequential as the average Supreme Court opinion (the percentage is surely lower), the average judge of those courts would have much less power than a Supreme Court Justice because the power of the courts of appeals is divided up among

9. Hermione Lee, *Edith Wharton* 563 (2007).
10. See chapter 10. Cf. Benjamin Kaplan, "Do Intermediate Appellate Courts Have a Lawmaking Function?" 70 *Massachusetts Law Review* 10 (1985).

many more judges; there are more than 20 times as many court of appeals judges as there are Supreme Court Justices. Very few such judges besides Learned Hand have had the impact on the law that the average Justice has had, even though the average quality of Supreme Court Justices is only moderately greater than that of court of appeals judges; it is held down by the highly politicized character of the Supreme Court appointment process. Some federal court of appeals judges, such as Learned Hand and Henry Friendly, have been far abler than the average Supreme Court Justice (let alone the lower-quality Justices), but have been far less powerful, at least when weighted by years of judicial service. (Some Supreme Court Justices have served only briefly.) To those federal appellate judges can be added such state supreme court judges as Roger Traynor, Benjamin Kaplan, and Hans Linde, and of course Benjamin Cardozo and Lemuel Shaw—and Holmes when he was Chief Justice of the Supreme Judicial Court of Massachusetts.

What the intermediate appellate judges have, if they are good, is *influence* over the development of law, just as good writers influence the development of literature. The two professions further resemble each other in the rhetorical cast of their written product (so different from that of a scientific article) and even in the presence of a political dimension, for there is that in literature too. We do not think of imaginative literature as political, but some of it is (though that is not all it is). Think of the politically inflected poetry of such great poets as Eliot and Yeats, and before them of Dante, Shakespeare, Milton, Pope, and Shelley, among countless others, and of novelists ranging from Swift and Dickens to Hemingway and Orwell.

Rapid norm shifts are possible in both art and judging, because the products of these activities cannot be evaluated objectively. There are no crucial experiments, decisive observations, verifiable predictions, or rigorously logical processes for adjudging either a literary work or a judicial opinion great—nothing but the test of time. That is a clue to why recognition that judges are strongly motivated to be good judges does not undermine the attitudinal theory as long as the theorist avoids too narrow a view of the "political" (confining it to the activities and expressed beliefs of politicians and parties) and too crabbed a concept of "the law" as leaving out everything that legalists exclude from the concept. Because the norms of judging are unsettled, two judges can be equally celebrated even though the major decisions of one are better explained by ideology and those of the other by traditional legal craft norms.

I do not mean to romanticize judging by comparing it to creative writing. The judge's assured income is a major difference between him and the creative writer, and offers him a leisure-labor trade-off unavailable to most creative writers. Less able judges (and there is great variance in judges' ability because judicial appointments often are based on political criteria rather than on merit) can be expected to substitute leisure for work because they can delegate much of their work to law clerks but would face high costs of obtaining distinction by working harder. Abler judges face lower costs in the mental effort exerted and leisure forgone of obtaining distinction by hard work and so they can be expected to work harder. The result is a tendency for two tiers of judges to emerge— leaders and followers. Of course, there are journeyman artists as well as journeyman judges, but they work as hard as the masters, which is less true of their judicial counterparts.

A critical difference between the novelist and the judge might appear to be that the former is an independent contractor, rather than an employee of his publisher, while the judge is an employee. But by virtue of judicial independence, the judge (especially a federal judge) is more like an independent contractor than an employee. Not completely, of course; he is salaried; his decisions can be reversed; in extreme cases he can be removed from office. But he has much greater autonomy than an ordinary employee—or even an ordinary independent contractor.

A second critical difference might appear to be that the novelist does not violate the norms of his art by having a political slant or otherwise rejecting the slogan "art for art's sake," but that a judge is supposed to be completely disinterested. How could a judge think himself a good judge if he thought his decisions seasoned with politics or personality? One answer is that he might be sophisticated enough to realize that this just is the nature of American judging. But a more interesting answer is that the nonlegalist influences on a judge are likely to operate subliminally.

The second answer can be explored with the aid of Bayesian decision theory. A judge in a nonjury proceeding who has to decide whether to believe a witness's testimony will often have formed before the witness begins to testify an estimate of the likelihood that the testimony will be truthful. The estimate might be based on previous experience with witnesses in similar cases (perhaps experience that the judge acquired as a practicing lawyer), on a general sense of the honesty of the class of persons to which the witness belongs, or even on the witness's manner of striding to the witness box and swearing to tell the truth and the posture he assumes in the stand. This pre-inquiry estimate is what is called a "prior probability," or just a "prior." The judge might well be unconscious of his having such a prior, and he would be most unlikely to express it in quantitative terms. But it would be there, and it would affect his "posterior probability"—that is, the probability that he would assign to the witness's having testified truthfully after the witness had testified and been cross-examined and after any evidence bearing on his truthfulness had been presented. Each bit of information the judge received that bore on that truthfulness would be likely to alter his prior probability, but not erase it; the prior probability would affect the posterior probability, as in $\Omega(H|x) = p(x|H)/p(x|{\sim}H) \times \Omega(H)$, the simplest version of Bayes's theorem.

Ω is odds; the left-hand side of the equation is the posterior odds that some hypothesis, H, is true; the last term on the right-hand side of the equation, $\Omega(H)$, is the prior odds; x is the new information obtained in the course of the inquiry; p is probability, and $p(x|H)/p(x|{\sim}H)$, the first term on the right-hand side of the equation, is the ratio of the probability that x would have been observed if H was true to the probability that x would have been observed even if H was false $({\sim}H)$. (So if those two probabilities were the same, the new information would not alter the odds; it would be a case of multiplication by 1.) Suppose the hypothesis is that the witness—let us say the plaintiff in a sex discrimination suit—is testifying truthfully, and that before she begins to testify the judge sets (almost certainly unconsciously) the odds that she will be telling the truth at 1 to 3, which is equivalent to a probability of 25 percent (1 out of [1 + 3]). She testifies, producing new information, x. Suppose the probability that x would be observed if she was telling the truth is .6, while the probability that it would be observed if she was not telling the truth is .3, so that the ratio of the two probabilities is 2. When this "likelihood ratio" is multiplied by the prior odds of 1 to 3, the result is posterior odds of 2 to 3 (1:3 × 2 = 2:3), which is equivalent to a 40 percent probability (2 out of 5) that the witness is telling the truth.

This is a *subjective* probability, personal to the particular judge. Another judge might have had different prior odds, resulting in different posterior odds even if both judges would assess the same information (x) the same way. They might of course assess it differently, for the same reason that their priors were different—because they had different "cognitive structure[s] of organized prior knowledge,"[11] based on such things as temperament, personal background characteristics (such as race or sex), life experiences, and ideology; and ideology might in turn be shaped by temperament and other factors discussed in chapter 4.

Suppose the second judge would have set the prior odds at 2 to 1 rather than 1 to 3. Then the posterior odds would be 4 to 1—that is, the judge would think there was an 80 percent probability that the witness was telling the truth. With the judge being the trier of fact (remember that I am speaking of nonjury proceedings) and thus the decider of witnesses' credibility, the difference in subjective probabilities between the two judges might well spell the difference between the plaintiff's winning and losing her case.

Bayesian theory is a way of systematizing the elementary point that preconceptions play a role in rational thought. It is not only impossible as a psychological matter to purge ourselves of them, but it would be irrational to do so, since preconceptions impound information, though it is not always accurate. "Preconception" has a pejorative connotation, which is why I prefer to speak of Bayesian priors. They differ across persons because different persons have different information and also process it differently to form their beliefs.

I used the example of a sex discrimination suit because it is the kind of suit in which judges' priors are likely to differ along political lines or along racial, religious, or gender lines that are correlated with (and often influence) political leanings, or because of different personal or professional experiences or differences in personality. And these attributes might converge to form a general cast of mind that would in turn generate the specific preconceptions that a judge brings to a case. Our perceptions are produced by the interaction between sensory impressions—the impact of the external world on the organs of sense—and a classificatory apparatus in the brain. In Kant's epistemology sensory impressions are made intelligible by being subjected to mind-generated categories such as causation and time. In Friedrich Hayek's epistemology an individual's classificatory apparatus is the product of idiosyncratic factors of

11. C. K. Rowland and Robert A. Carp, *Politics and Judgment in Federal District Courts* 165 (1996).

personality and culture rather than just of basic hardwired features of the brain. (Presumably, as Kant in effect argued, the capacity to perceive two events as cause and effect is hardwired.) The apparatus not only differs among individuals but can be altered by experience, which obviously varies from individual to individual. In other words, people see (literally and figuratively) things differently, and the way in which they see things changes in response to changes in the environment.[12] That is true of judges. As Cardozo said, "We may try to see things as objectively as we please. None the less, we can never see them with any eyes except our own."[13] I assumed that judges' priors are unconscious in order to illustrate how, acting in perfectly good faith, with no sense that they are being influenced by their political leanings, judges may nevertheless behave in conformity with the expectations of the attitudinal theorists. Bayesian theory reconciles judges' behavior (how they vote in cases) with their conscious thinking.

An example of the operation of the theory in judicial decision making is that judges are more likely to convict a criminal defendant than juries are.[14] Through long experience with the criminal justice system, judges learn that prosecutors rarely file cases unless the evidence against the defendant is overwhelming. Prosecutors' resources are very limited relative to the incidence of crime, and so they concentrate on cases in which guilt is clear (as such cases are easier to win without a heavy investment of prosecutorial resources), which are plentiful.

Preconceptions matter even when the only thing the judge is doing is finding facts. That was my example of Bayesian decision making[15] and it is consistent with the evidence cited in chapter 1 that district judges as well as appellate judges engage in political judging. The latitude that a trial judge has in making factual determinations is sometimes referred to as "fact discretion," but that is a misleading term. It makes it seem as

12. See Richard A. Posner, "Cognitive Theory as the Ground of Political Theory in Plato, Popper, Dewey, and Hayek," in *Cognition and Economics* 253, 263–264 (Elisabeth Krecké, Carine Krecké, and Roger G. Koppl eds. 2007).

13. Benjamin N. Cardozo, *The Nature of the Judicial Process* 13 (1921). See also Andrew J. Wistrich, Chris Guthrie, and Jeffrey J. Rachlinski, "Can Judges Ignore Inadmissible Information? The Difficulty of Deliberately Disregarding," 153 *University of Pennsylvania Law Review* 1251 (2005).

14. Theodore Eisenberg et al., "Judge-Jury Agreement in Criminal Cases: A Partial Replication of Kalven and Zeisel's *The American Jury*," 2 *Journal of Empirical Legal Studies* 171 (2005).

15. The scholarly literature on judicial fact-finding as a Bayesian process is extensive. See Richard A. Posner, *Frontiers of Legal Theory*, ch. 11 (2001), and references cited there.

if the judge has a free choice whether to believe or disbelieve a witness, as he would if he were deciding whether to start a trial at 9:00 A.M. or 10:00 A.M., or even whether to accept or reject a legal proposition asserted by a court in another jurisdiction and hence not binding on him. One would like to think that belief in whether a witness is telling the truth is driven by whether he *is* telling the truth. It isn't always. But when it isn't, this is because of the difficulty of distinguishing between truth and falsity rather than because the judge has an option to believe or disbelieve as he wishes. You cannot will belief.

Five phenomena that could be regarded as instances of bias in the finding of facts in a trial setting can be distinguished.

1. *Conscious falsification.* This is rare in our system. If, as I believe, judges try to be good judges, they will not deliberately falsify the facts because that would be a serious violation of anyone's idea of what a good judge does. What is true, however, is that at the appellate level judges have a tendency to report the facts in their opinion in such a way as to make them fit the legal conclusion smoothly or shape the precedent that the decision will create. The scope of a precedent is inferred by reading the court's analysis in light of the facts recited in its opinion. A judge may decide to omit from his opinion a fact that he considers irrelevant even though a layperson might think it important to a complete picture of the factual situation out of which the case arose, because the judge does not want the court in a subsequent case to distinguish his case on the basis of that fact.

2. *Priors shaped by experience, temperament, ideology, or other personal, nonlegalist factors.* These are ubiquitous and uneliminable. No one can ignore all his priors in making a decision. That would mean trying to think in a vacuum. If an arresting officer says one thing and the person he arrested says the opposite, the judge's decision as to which one to believe is likely to be influenced by the judge's background. Was he a prosecutor before he became a judge? A defense lawyer? What experiences has he or members of his family or friends had with police or prosecutors, or for that matter with criminals? Not that these experiences, which may be unrepresentative, are always reliable. But if they are the best data that the judge has to go on, maybe because the other indicators of the witness's credibility are hopelessly inconclusive, it is rational and probably inevitable that he should rely on them as a tiebreaker.

3. *Cognitive illusions.* Although there are various institutional mecha-

nisms for minimizing the effect of cognitive illusions (such as hindsight bias) on fact-finding by judges (as by jurors), they are far from completely effective.[16]

4. *Priors shaped by irrelevant reactions,* such as dislike of a lawyer or disapproval of a party's religion or lifestyle—reactions that have no proper place in judicial decision making. This kind of thing is not too common in our system, for the same reason that deliberate falsification of facts is uncommon. An important rule of the judicial "game"—the game you have to play if you want to be considered a good judge—is judging "without respect to persons," as the judicial oath has it. Reasonably self-disciplined people can set such reactions to one side when making a decision. But that is not true with respect to one's rational preconceptions—nor would we want it to be true.

Because it usually is impossible to compare the findings made by a judge or jury with the "true" facts bearing on the parties' dispute, it usually is impossible to determine which judges' priors are more accurate. So the appointing authorities tend to appoint judges whose priors resemble their own.

5. *Twisting the facts to minimize the likelihood of being reversed.* Appellate review of findings of fact is supposed to be and generally is deferential, while review of abstract propositions of law is plenary. That is, no deference is given to the trial judge's rulings on "pure" issues of law, as distinct not only from findings of fact but also from the application of legal doctrine to facts, as when the issue is whether the defendant was negligent. Since judges do not like to be reversed, both for career reasons (in the case of judges who aspire to promotion to the court of appeals) and for power reasons (reversal nullifies their decision), also for reasons of amour propre, trial judges are sometimes tempted to bend the facts so that they fit snugly into an uncontroversial legal category. For the reasons mentioned above, judges are unlikely to do this consciously, but it is undoubtedly an unconscious tendency.

"Reversal aversion" creates a conflict for judges between role expectations and personal feelings. Suppose the best reading of the precedents is that a decision for the plaintiff will be affirmed, but a careful "nose count" suggests that the current appellate judges, who are known to

16. Chris Guthrie, Jeffrey J. Rachlinski, and Andrew J. Wistrich, "Inside the Judicial Mind," 86 *Cornell Law Review* 777 (2001). See generally *Heuristics and the Law* (G. Gigerenzer and C. Engel eds. 2006).

have different views from the judges who created the precedents, will reverse a decision for the plaintiff. Reversal aversion will push the judge toward deciding for the defendant. But role expectation will push him the other way. He is supposed to decide cases in accordance with "the law," and the law, as the word is usually understood, does not change when new judges are appointed, but only when their votes in a case change it.

This point illustrates the complexity of the judicial utility function. The judge wants to be a good judge and thus decide cases in accordance with the law. He also does not want to be reversed. The balance is pretty even in the case just described. On the one hand the nose-counting judge is not offending deeply against the law, but on the other hand reversal aversion is rarely a very powerful motivator since a reversal usually imposes only a small cost on the judge who is reversed.

An important task of trial judges is sentencing criminal defendants. Anyone who doubts the pervasiveness of judicial discretion, and hence the limitations of legalism as a description of what judges do, should think back to the extraordinary variance in federal sentences that prevailed before the promulgation of the federal sentencing guidelines and that is beginning to creep back into the sentencing process as a result of the Supreme Court's demotion, in the *Booker* decision that I discuss in chapter 10, of the guidelines from mandatory to advisory status. Before the guidelines, the determinants of how severely to punish a convicted defendant within the usually broad limits fixed by Congress had almost nothing to do with legal analysis; they depended, rather, on the judge's attitudes toward such large, contested, broadly ideological issues as personal versus social responsibility for misconduct, the morality of retribution, the feasibility of rehabilitation, and the deterrent effects of criminal punishment. No common law of federal sentencing had evolved to guide judges in deciding on a sentence within the statutory range. That decision had been left to the unchanneled discretion of the individual district judge.

Yet the concern that motivated the creation of the guidelines was the variance in sentences under the system of discretionary sentencing (given the differences in priors across judges) rather than a sense that the system was "lawless" because it conferred so much discretion on judges. Even legalists are quite willing to see a class of rulings denominated "discretionary," though logically such thinkers should consider discretionary rulings, and hence pre-guidelines criminal sentencing, lawless. Legalists have accepted what by their standards are lawless pockets in the law—some huge, such as pre-guidelines sentencing—because they would rather shrink the domain of the law than to subject fuzzy areas of the law to loose standards. In doing this, they unintentionally expand the influence of judges' preconceptions on judicial decisions by expanding the scope of judicial discretion.

What weight should we give to the fact that many, maybe most, judges would if asked deny that they bring preconceptions to their cases?[17] Very little. That denial would reflect in some instances a lack of self-awareness and in others the rhetorical pull, or more bluntly the propaganda value, of the legalist model of judging. Judges want to deny the role of subjectivity in judicial decision making lest they undermine their claim to be a deservedly independent branch of government in which reason rules, obviating a need for political or other external constraints on the exercise of discretion. They want to convince people that they wear blinders that keep them from straying off the beaten path; that they are society's dray horses. They also want to duck blame for unpopular decisions ("the law made me do it"). So they say—you will find this in almost every case involving the interpretation of a statute—that in interpreting statutes judges "start with the words of the statute" and usually end there, thus avoiding the treacherous shoals of purpose and policy, for in interpreting they are merely manipulating words (verbal symbols), like mathematicians. Actually they start with the name of the statute, or some general sense of what it is about, perhaps recollected from previous cases; or with the often tendentiously cropped excerpts from the statute quoted to them by the lawyers; or with the spin that the lawyers place on the statute's words. There is always a context to reading, and it is given in advance of the encounter with the words themselves and shapes the reader's interpretation.

That judges are Bayesians[18] is not the only reason their decisions in nonroutine cases often conform to the attitudinal model even when the

17. For a notable exception, see Henry J. Friendly, "Reactions of a Lawyer-Newly-Become-Judge," in Friendly, *Benchmarks* 1, 14–21 (1967), though his term for preconceptions was "convictions," by which he meant conscious rather than unconscious leanings.

18. In a loose sense. I am not suggesting that they actually apply Bayes's theorem (which most of them have never heard of) or that they typically have the information that would be required to apply it.

judges are wholeheartedly committed to the judicial norm of apolitical adjudication. Another reason is the motivations of the people who hire judges, the President and the members of the Senate. (For remember that like any labor market, the judicial labor market is two-sided.) They want, I said earlier, a judge who will be competent but also will decide cases in the open area in conformity with the President's and the Senators' political preferences. So, apart from the play of unconscious influences, we cannot expect federal judges to be complete political eunuchs, their decisions never influenced by politics because they have no politics. Such political neuters are unlikely to be appointed.

But I remind the reader that partisan politics is not the only politics; and politics shades into ideology, which in turn shades into common sense, moral insight, notions of sound policy, and other common and ineradicable elements of judicial decision making. Politics in these extended senses is the core of the attitudinal model, sensibly construed; the party of the President who appointed the judge is merely a crude proxy for ideology. Nor can the independent interests of the Senators who must confirm the President's nominees be neglected, even when the Senators belong to the same party as the President; for they have a tendency to place patronage above ideology as a judicial qualification.[19]

But even with the model thus qualified, judicial decisions cannot be expected to conform to it perfectly, and in many cases not even closely. Political inclinations, even in the loosest sense of "political," are not the only things that determine a judge's priors. A judge's personal background characteristics, such as race and sex, and his personal and professional experiences are among the nonpolitical, nonlegalist factors that have been found to influence his decisions.[20] A judge might, for example, tend to decide for the government in close cases regardless of what policy the government (local, state, or federal) is trying to enforce in the case before him. Maybe he had worked for the Justice Department

19. See Micheal W. Giles, Virginia A. Hettinger, and Todd Peppers, "Picking Federal Judges: A Note on Policy and Partisan Selection Agendas," 54 *Political Research Quarterly* 623 (2001); Donald R. Songer, Reginald S. Sheehan, and Susan B. Haire, *Continuity and Change on the United States Courts of Appeals* 137 (2000).

20. Besides references in chapter 1, see James J. Brudney, Sara Schiavoni, and Deborah J. Merritt, "Judicial Hostility toward Labor Unions? Applying the Social Background Model to a Celebrated Concern," 60 *Ohio State Law Journal* 1675 (1999); Gregory C. Sisk, Michael Heise, and Andrew P. Morriss, "Charting the Influences on the Judicial Mind: An Empirical Study of Judicial Reasoning," 73 *New York University Law Review* 1377, 1451–1465, 1470–1480 (1998).

in his youth, had been impressed by the competence and disinterest of the department's staff, and had taken away from the experience a warm glow that continues to influence his thinking, all unconsciously. But this example illustrates the difficulty of disentangling the factors that influence judges. For the judge's progovernment leaning may have been what made him go to work for the Justice Department in the first place, rather than being the consequence of that work.

To take another example, judges whose background is law teaching rather than private practice tend to be harder on the lawyers who appear before them because such judges have less insight into the constraints on a lawyer's performance that are imposed by time, money, and client pressures than do judges who come out of private practice. The less forgiving attitude of the ex-academic may affect the strictness with which he enforces deadlines and other procedural rules as well as his attitude toward sanctioning lawyers for mistakes.

Appellate judges promoted from the trial court may be more likely than other appellate judges to vote to affirm a trial judge. They are more sensitive to the advantages that the trial judge has over the appellate court in gaining a deep understanding of a case—especially a case that is actually tried, for then the trial judge will have spent much more time on it than the appellate judges who review his ruling. In addition, having become accustomed to resolving cases without too much concern for creating a bad precedent (the decisions of trial courts are not precedents—that is, they are not authority for deciding a similar case the same way in the future), a former trial judge promoted to the court of appeals may be more likely to focus more on the "equities" of the individual case—the aspects of the case that tug at the heartstrings—and less on its precedential significance than would his colleagues who had never been trial judges.

Personal characteristics not only differ from political leanings but also can work at cross-purposes with, and sometimes overcome, them. Hence the conservative woman who votes for the plaintiff in a sex discrimination suit, the conservative black Republican who favors aggressive enforcement of the Voting Rights Act, and the liberal former prosecutor who sides with the government in criminal cases.

Another reason suggested by Bayesian theory for not expecting judicial behavior to conform perfectly to the attitudinal model even in the open area of judging is that judges differ with respect to the strength of their priors. Judges we call "detached" operate with weaker priors than other judges, whether because of intellectual insecurity and a resulting lack of conviction, a skeptical outlook, or a cool temperament. Learned Hand was a skeptic with a "hot" temper; Holmes a "cool," some think a rather glacial, skeptic—someone who gazed at his fellow human beings through the wrong end of the telescope and saw an anthill. Skepticism might seem paradoxical: how can one be confident about not being confident; equivalently, how can a skeptic fail to be skeptical about skepticism? But the paradox is a challenge only to philosophical skepticism.[21] One can be skeptical about particular claims without being skeptical in general—without doubting, for example, that there is an external world.

That personal background and previous experiences (often correlated—a woman is more likely to have had the experience of being discriminated against on the basis of sex than a man) have an effect on judicial decisions that is independent of politics even in the broadest sense[22] underscores the breadth of judicial discretion arising from the limited guidance that rules or norms of judging provide. Personal background and experience are unreliable grounds for many of the determinations that judges have to make. That a judge is a woman and has had experiences typical of women is a very small part of the information required to decide a sex discrimination case involving a different woman in different circumstances. So the fact that gender, like other personal factors, has been found to play a significant role (even after correction for correlated factors such as ideology) in judicial decisions suggests that often judges lack good information about the merits of a case they have to decide and so are forced to grasp at straws. This injects a disquieting amount of randomness into the judicial process. But the difference between male and female responses to discrimination cases need not reflect prejudice; few judges would *consciously* allow their judgment to be affected by whether they are of the same sex, race, or religion of a litigant or lawyer—that would be a gross violation of the rules of the judicial game. The difference in response is the unavoidable consequence of hav-

21. On which see M. F. Burnyeat, "Can the Skeptic Live His Skepticism?" in *The Skeptical Tradition* 117 (Myles Burnyeat ed. 1983); David Hume, *An Enquiry concerning Human Understanding*, § 12 (1748).

22. As shown in Christina L. Boyd, Lee Epstein, and Andrew D. Martin, "Untangling the Causal Effects of Sex on Judging" (Northwestern University School of Law and Washington University School of Law and Department of Political Science, July 28, 2007), who carefully correct for ideological differences yet still find an independent effect of gender. See also David R. Songer, Sue Davis, and Susan Haire, "A Reappraisal of Diversification in the Federal Courts: Gender Effects in the Courts of Appeals," 56 *Journal of Politics* 425 (1994).

ing to rely on personal experiences to decide a case where there is nothing better to go on.

The point that underlies these examples is that the weaker the incentives and constraints that influence a worker's performance, the wider the range of influences on that performance, especially in the presence of uncertainty, which indeed is one of the things that makes those incentives and constraints bear only weakly on judicial decision making. Yet the existence of a wide range of influences on job performance is not inconsistent with a person's being a good, a loyal, worker. Often in private firms as well as in public institutions some employees will have a great deal of leeway in performing their jobs—and everyone is at the mercy, to some degree, of his preconceptions. But employees of a commercial firm have less discretion than judges. Their performance is easier to evaluate because there is less uncertainty about its quality. For their employer has a financial bottom line and has only to determine (not that that is always easy) the employee's contribution to it. A firm also has tools that have been withheld from the judges' employer for shaping its workers' behavior, even if they belong to a union (as few workers do these days, however).

A corollary is that we can expect greater variance in skills, effort, and other dimensions of performance among judges than among executives of firms. Even if the screening of judicial aspirants were not influenced by politics, and even though the screened judicial candidate is bound to have a longer work history than a young new hire in a commercial firm, the federal judge's freedom from the usual external constraints, coupled with the difficulty of objectively evaluating judicial performance, results in greater variance in the performance of judges than in most private-sector employment.

There is another difference between judges and other workers. Most organizations follow the practice of "management by exception." Routine matters are handled by the workers at the bottom of the organization, but when a nonroutine matter arises the first-line worker refers it to his immediate supervisor, who may in turn, if it exceeds his ability to resolve it, refer it to *his* supervisor, and so on up. In this way the employer economizes on the cost of skilled labor. The judiciary is hierarchical too, but judges at all levels handle both routine and nonroutine matters. The routine cases are those that can be decided by legalist techniques. When cases can be so decided, judges are committed to using those techniques and usually do so. Oddly, perhaps, nothing in their training equips them to deal with the nonroutine cases. The reason may be a desire by the judicial establishment to maintain the pretense that judges just do legalist analysis, that they are entirely rule-bound. But the result is to leave them not only at large but at sea when confronted with a case that cannot be decided by such analysis.

It might seem that leisure preference would lead judges to decide as many cases as possible (or more!) by legalist techniques. Not only are those the techniques the judge knows best and is most comfortable with; but by excluding from the decision-making process a range of often recalcitrant material (such as legislative history, public policy, and the consequences of his decision), legalism demands less of the judge in the way of research. The other side of this coin, however, is that a judgment based on nonlegalist factors may require no research at all—may require no more than knowing who the parties are and which side of the case conforms to the judge's untheorized concept of what is "just" or "fair."

This point suggests that judicial performance in the open area might be improved by training judges in economics. In areas such as antitrust, contract law, public utility and common carrier regulation, corporate, pension, and financial law, intellectual property, procedure and remedies, large swatches of environmental law, and smaller swatches of tort, criminal, and family law, the courts have adopted an economic approach to the resolution of those issues that are not governed by a rule sufficiently hard-edged to be applicable to the facts of a case without need to consider the social consequences of the decision. Questions such as how much unauthorized copying of copyrighted material should be permitted under the "fair use" doctrine; whether a manufacturer should be allowed to forbid his distributors to cut the resale price of his goods below a level specified by him (the issue in the *Leegin* case discussed in chapter 1); when "loyalty rebates" (end-of-year rebates to consumers who buy multiple lines of a seller's products) should be considered anticompetitive; or whether an injured worker can recover damages even though his injury was caused by an "open and obvious" hazard cannot be answered by legalist techniques and should not be answered by untutored intuition. But they perhaps can be answered with a fair degree of objectivity by judges armed with basic economic skills and insights. Objectivity is one of the main aims of legalists. It can sometimes be achieved by methods other than those of legalism.

3

The Judge as Occasional Legislator

Judges' motivations would be uninteresting were judges legalists in the extreme sense endorsed by John Roberts at his hearing for confirmation as Chief Justice. He said that a judge, even if he is a Justice of the Supreme Court, is merely an umpire calling balls and strikes.[1] Roberts was updating for a sports-crazed era Alexander Hamilton's description of a judge as the government official who, unlike an official of the executive or legislative branch of government, exercises judgment but not will,[2] and Blackstone's description of judges as the oracles of the law,[3] implying (if taken literally) an even greater passivity than Hamilton's and Roberts's definitions.

In offering the umpireal analogy, Roberts was trying to navigate the treacherous shoals of a Senate confirmation hearing. And having had a very successful career as an advocate—the batter, not the umpire—it was natural for him to exalt the former's role. (When he became Chief Justice, his perspective quickly changed.) Neither he nor any other knowledgeable person actually believed or believes that the rules that judges in our system apply, particularly appellate judges and most particularly the Justices of the U.S. Supreme Court, are given to them the way the rules of baseball are given to umpires. We must imagine that umpires, in addition to calling balls and strikes, made the rules of baseball and changed

1. Hearing on the Nomination of John Roberts to Be Chief Justice of the Supreme Court before the Senate Judiciary Committee, 109th Cong., 1st Sess. 56 (Sept. 12, 2005).

2. *Federalist No. 78* (1788), in *The Federalist Papers* 226, 227 (Roy P. Fairfield ed., 2d ed. 1966).

3. William Blackstone, *Commentaries on the Laws of England,* vol. 1, p. 69 (1765).

them at will. Suppose some umpires thought that pitchers were too powerful and so they decided that instead of three strikes and the batter is out it is six strikes and he's out, but other umpires were very protective of pitchers and thought there were too many hits and therefore decreed that a batter would be allowed only one strike.

There is a less obvious mistake in Roberts's baseball analogy. Until recently, different umpires defined the strike zone differently, so that pitchers had to adjust their tactics to the particular umpire. The analogy is to the way in which different judges interpret the Constitution differently. The interpretive freedom of umpires was deemed intolerable, and beginning with the 2002 season Major League Baseball installed cameras (the Umpire Information System) to photograph all pitches so that it could be determined objectively whether umpires were calling balls and strikes according to a uniform standard. When the system detects a significant error rate on the part of an umpire, he is disciplined.[4]

If the judiciary had a similar system for evaluating judicial decisions, Roberts's analogy would be spot-on. But of course it does not. As is usually true of "reasoning by analogy," what is interesting about the comparison between umpires and judges is not the similarities but the differences.

Roberts knows that when legalist methods of judicial decision making fall short, judges draw on beliefs and intuitions that may have a political hue, though usually it is not a partisan one[5] and a judge may be unaware that his decision is influenced by his political leanings. He will draw on these intuitions and beliefs in the legalistically indeterminate cases because the judicial imperative is to decide cases, with reasonable dispatch, as best one can. The judge cannot throw up his hands, or stew indefinitely, just because he is confronted with a case in which the orthodox materials of judicial decision making, honestly deployed, will not produce an acceptable result. They may not produce *any* result, as in a case in which two canons of statutory construction are applicable and they point to different results.

"To decide" and "to conclude" are interestingly different modes of res-

4. David Gassko, "The Outside Corner," *Hardball Times,* Feb. 1, 2007, www.hardballtimes .com/main/article/the-outside-corner/ (visited June 27, 2007); Tom Verducci, "Man vs. Machine," *SI (Sports Illustrated).com,* June 4, 2004, http://sportsillustrated.cnn.com/si_online/ news/2003/06/03/sc/ (visited June 27, 2007).

5. Bush v. Gore, 531 U.S. 98 (2000), may be an exception.

olution. It would be odd to speak of a "duty to conclude" or "to reach a conclusion." A decision is an action; a conclusion is a rumination; and in the distinction we can begin to sense the tension explored in chapter 8 between the judiciary and the academy.

There are only a few exceptions to the imperative duty of judges to decide. The "political questions" doctrine is one.[6] The nonreviewability of some administrative rulings where the reviewing court has no law to apply is another.[7] And of course there are cases that are outside a court's jurisdiction, so that, in effect, the only decision the court can make is a decision *not* to decide. But a case cannot be left undecided just because it is a toss-up from a legalist standpoint. A convicted defendant cannot be left unsentenced.

A judge's political preferences do not break the tie every time. Sometimes they are tempered by other concerns—not only case-specific ones but also such institutional concerns of a sort especially prized by legalists as the feasibility of a particular judicial intervention given the limited knowledge and powers of courts, or the effect on the law's stability and a court's standing of too cavalier a view of precedent and statutory text. The weaker the judge's political preference for a particular outcome in a case, the stronger will be the tug of legalist considerations the other way.[8] In this example, as in most routine cases, where legalist analysis promotes the valuable social good of legal predictability, legalism can be understood as a special case of legal pragmatism. It is even possible to imagine legal systems in which a thoroughgoing rather than an intermittent legalism might be the best pragmatic strategy.[9] But even in our system it will sometimes be difficult to distinguish a pragmatist judge from a legalist one. Suppose the pragmatist sees enormous value in rules compared to standards. He will push for rules, and to the extent successful the push will increase the scope for legalism. From the outside he may look just like a legalist judge who thinks law is only law when it involves the application of clear rules. The analogy is to "rule utilitarians," who believe that utility can often be more effectively promoted by means

---

6. See Luther v. Borden, 48 U.S. (7 How.) 1, 46–47 (1849).

7. Citizens to Preserve Overton Park v. Volpe, 401 U.S. 402, 410 (1971). See also 5 U.S.C. § 701(a)(2).

8. For evidence, see H. W. Perry, Jr., *Deciding to Decide: Agenda Setting in the United States Supreme Court* 273–275 (1991).

9. Richard A. Posner, *Frontiers of Legal Theory* 219–220 (2001).

of rules that do not require a comparison of utilities than by trying to evaluate the effect on utility of every act.[10]

Against Roberts's umpireal analogy, therefore, I set the story of the three umpires asked to explain the epistemology of balls and strikes. The first umpire explains that he calls them as they are, the second that he calls them as he sees them, and the third that there are no balls or strikes until he calls them. The first umpire is the legalist. The second umpire is the pragmatic trial judge (as *he* sees them). The third is the appellate judge deciding cases in the open area. His activity is creation rather than discovery.

Roberts may have made a tactical error. His confirmation did not turn on convincing Senators that a Supreme Court Justice is like a baseball umpire. In the spring of 2007, less than two years after his confirmation, he demonstrated by his judicial votes and opinions that he aspires to remake significant areas of constitutional law. The tension between what he said at his confirmation hearing and what he is doing as a Justice is a blow to Roberts's reputation for candor and a further debasement of the already debased currency of the testimony of nominees at judicial confirmation hearings.

Appellate judges are *occasional legislators.*[11] In their legislative capacity they labor under constraints that do not bind the official legislators— rules of standing, for example, and limitations on whom judges may consult and more generally on what methods of inquiry they may employ. An important function of the esoteric (to nonlawyers) distinction between the holding of a case and its dicta (roughly, statements inessential to the outcome)—with only the former having precedential effect— is to limit judges' legislative power by preventing them from promulgating, in the form of judicial opinions, treatises that would have the force of law.[12] But judges also enjoy leeways that official legislators do not. Transaction costs are low (for there are many fewer judges on a panel,

---

10. The analogy ("rule pragmatism") is explored further in chapter 9 of this book.

11. Not a new idea, but it still grates. "The principle of the Swiss Civil Code that where the law is silent or unclear the judge must decide the case as if he were a legislator, still sounds strange to us, even after a century of demonstration, from Bentham through Holmes to Professor Pound and Cardozo and Lord Wright, that this is what in fact happens daily in our courts." Julius Stone, *The Province and Function of Law: Law as Logic, Justice, and Social Control; A Study in Jurisprudence* 500 (2d ed. 1950).

12. Eric Rasmusen, "Judicial Legitimacy as a Repeated Game, 10 *Journal of Law, Economics and Organization* 63, 75 (1994).

even in a supreme court, than there are members of a legislative body at the federal or state level) and constituent pressures usually nonexistent. When deciding constitutional cases Supreme Court Justices are like legislators in a system in which there is no judicial power to invalidate statutes and legislators once elected cannot be removed. And some of the constraints on judges actually are liberating: the fact that they cannot sit in cases in which they have a financial or personal stake enlarges their decisional freedom, just as not being answerable to an electorate does.

Judges may have as many degrees of legislative freedom, albeit only in the subset of legalistically indeterminate cases, as formal legislators do, though unlike them judges cannot as a practical matter tell the government what to do—the lesson of regulatory decrees, for example those requiring school busing, now largely abandoned because judges have learned from painful experience that they do not have control of enough of the levers of power to be able to administer government programs effectively. Judges can tell the other branches of government only what *not* to do. Still, the legislative power that judges do have, though negative, is considerable, especially when the other branches are stopped in their tracks by the Supreme Court in the name of the Constitution, which is so difficult to amend.

The desire of legislators for reelection, combined with the pressures that interest groups exert on electoral politics and legislative activity, goes some distance toward explaining their votes. But federal judges do not have to worry about election, reelection, fund-raising, interest groups, and the like. As a result, the springs of their behavior are mysterious, and we must go beyond the suggestions in the preceding chapters to unravel the mystery.

Judges' legislative power is usually thought to reach its zenith in common law fields. Since common law is explicitly judge created, one might think it would be bound to be even more "lawless" than constitutional adjudication. In fact it is more stable, more objective, more lawlike, and less like "real" legislation than constitutional law is. It deals with subjects on which there is usually a high degree of consensus in both society at large and the judiciary, enabling judges of diverse backgrounds and political commitments to reason from common premises to conclusions that command broad support within the judiciary and the larger political community. That persons of diverse backgrounds, values, and so forth can be brought to agree on a matter is the practical meaning of "objective."

Also there is a kind of competitive process at work in the common law to discipline the exercise of judicial discretion. The same issues arise under the common law of each of the states, and often there are divergent resolutions at first. But gradually consensus emerges as uncommitted judges compare the different resolutions on offer. And in the background is the threat of legislative override to check judicial power to make and remake common law. The Supreme Court, moreover, decides so few cases relative to the lower courts (see chapter 10) that in an effort to control those courts it tends to lay down flat rules (such as the *Miranda* warning, *Roe v. Wade's* trimester rule, or the rule that due process requires a probable-cause hearing within 48 hours of arrest), like a legislature. It does not proceed tentatively from case to case, gradually narrowing broad standards by distinguishing earlier cases, as common law courts do.

We must not confuse "common law" with "case law." Ours is a case law system that includes but is not exhausted in common law. Not only constitutional law (obviously), but also to a considerable extent statutory law, is shaped by judicial decisions, with occasional intervention from the "real" legislators. The open-ended character of common law reasoning (see the quotation from Brian Simpson in the next paragraph) is equally characteristic of American case law that is not common law. But the regularizing features of the common law that I have mentioned are missing from the other areas of case law, constitutional law being only the most conspicuous example. Think not only of antitrust law but also of intellectual property law, pension law, labor law, corporation law, and numerous other fields that have been shaped to a great extent by case law. One is led to wonder how the legalist can regard case law, though it is the bulk of American law, as law at all. How can he defend the overruling of a precedent except in the rare case in which the precedent can be shown to have been based on a logical error? If the precedent just does not conform to modern conditions, its overruling is a legislative act.

Even with its stabilizing features, the common law should make a legalist uncomfortable. As Frederick Schauer explains, "The common law does not view the wrong answer as the inevitable price of invariably crude generalizations. Rather, it treats all generalizations as contingent and perfectible."[13] That does not sound like a "law of rules." Furthermore, as Brian Simpson explains,

> at no period in common law history has there existed a crisply defined form of legal opinion, or a closed canon of justificatory material, or a convention that effectively depersonalizes the court's opinion, as is the case, for example, in France . . . It is of course commonplace to contrast law with policy, or legal rules or precedents with principles, and so forth, *but common law reasoning has never been controlled by conventions that insist on these distinctions,* or require the presentation of justificatory rhetoric in terms of them.[14]

It might seem that judges would legislate only after they had tried and failed to decide a case by reference to the orthodox materials of legislative text and precedent. Some judges do proceed in that way. But others reverse the sequence. They start by making the legislative judgment, that is, by asking themselves what outcome—not just who wins and who loses, but what rule or standard or principle enunciated in their judicial opinion—would have the best consequences. Only then do they consider whether that outcome is blocked by the orthodox materials of legal decision making, or, more precisely, whether the benefits of that outcome are offset by the costs that it would impose in impairing legalist values such as legal stability. An equally pragmatic judge might start the other way around, by asking himself whether the issue in the case was ruled by statutory language, precedent, or some other orthodox source of law that it would be a mistake to disregard. The lawyers in the case would have hurled at him general statements, drawn from cases and statutes, that covered the case as a matter of semantics. But he would want to determine whether the authors of those statements had been referring to the kind of issue confronting him in this case. If not, he would have to make a legislative judgment.

Most judges blend the two inquiries, the legalist and the legislative,[15] rather than addressing them in sequence. Their response to a case is

---

13. Frederick Schauer, *Playing by the Rules: A Philosophical Examination of Rule-Based Decision-Making in Law and in Life* 178 (1991).

14. A. W. B. Simpson, "Legal Reasoning Anatomized: On Steiner's *Moral Argument and Social Vision in the Courts,*" 13 *Law and Social Inquiry* 637, 638 (1988) (emphasis added).

15. A notable example is Holmes. See Thomas C. Grey, "Holmes on the Logic of the Law," in *The Path of the Law and Its Influence* 133 (Steven J. Burton ed. 2000).

generated by legal doctrine, institutional constraints, policy preferences, strategic considerations, and the equities of the case, all mixed together and all mediated by temperament, experience, ambition, and other personal factors. A judge does not reach a point in a difficult case at which he says, "The law has run out and now I must do some legislating." He knows that he has to decide and that whatever he does decide will (within the broadest of limits) be law; for the judge as occasional legislator is still a judge.

The phenomenology of judgment provides useful insights into judicial motivation and thinking. Wayne Martin points out that in making a judgment (it does not have to be a legal judgment) one is conscious of both freedom and constraint.[16] Freedom because to make a judgment is to make a choice, constraint because judgment is a matter of deliberation (not necessarily collective—a trial judge must deliberate), of weighing alternatives; flipping a coin is an escape from judgment. The consciousness of constrained freedom is the same whether one is making an algorithmic judgment or a nonalgorithmic one.[17] The sense of constraint will be stronger in the former case, hence stronger when a judge is deciding a case that lends itself to a legalist analysis than when he is making a legislative judgment. But it will be present in the latter case as well.

That the judge is unconscious of a sharp break between his legalistic and his legislative activity on the bench produces leakage between his consideration of routine and of nonroutine cases. Accustomed to making nonlegalist judgments in the latter, the judge is likely to allow nonlegalist considerations to seep into his consideration of the former. This is especially likely because the case that can be decided by pure logic and the case that can be decided only by making a legislative judgment represent the ends of a continuum and are rarely encountered in the actual work of a court. Often, to decide a case the judges first derive a rule by free rather than literal interpretation of a statute and then apply the rule mechanically to the facts to determine the outcome: a legislative judgment precedes a legalist judgment. And the reverse happens too: the rule

---

16. Wayne M. Martin, *Theories of Judgment: Psychology, Logic, Phenomenology*, ch. 5 (2006).

17. "Most human reasoning is not algorithmic. That is, it does not (overtly at least) proceed in accordance with rules of logic and/or mathematics and/or probability, or any other rules that could be incorporated into a computer program." David Hodgson, "Partly Free: The Responsibility for Our Actions beyond the Physical Processes of Our Brains," *Times Literary Supplement*, July 6, 2007, p. 15.

may be extracted by a literal interpretation of a statute, or of a precedent laid down by a higher court, yet its application may require a legislative judgment (perhaps the creation of an exception to the rule) if the rule, though it is the only one that could apply to the facts of the case, does not quite fit them.

The combination of legalist and legislative elements in many cases further blunts the judge's sense that he wears two hats—that sometimes he is a "real" judge and sometimes really a legislator—and so helps show why few judges think of themselves as occasional or any other kind of legislators. Think of the skier who is taught the rules of skiing—such as that in turning you should shift your weight to your uphill ski, unweight the downhill ski, and make the skis parallel—but who when he starts down the ski slope sets his mind not on following the rules (which if he does he will do by force of habit) but on getting to the bottom in one piece. The busy judge wants to decide the case sensibly and with reasonable dispatch. He does not have the time, the inclination, or the habit of introspection that would make him wonder about the nature of the judgments that he was making en route to his decision, although if he thought about it he might realize that he had not been following the orthodox methodology of judicial decision making at every step.

The amount of legislating that a judge does depends on the breadth of his "zone of reasonableness"—the area within which he has discretion to decide a case either way without disgracing himself. The zone varies from judiciary to judiciary and from judge to judge. Among institutional factors that influence the breadth of the zone is the judge's rank in the judicial hierarchy. The higher it is, the greater his discretionary authority is likely, though not certain, to be. The reason for my hedging is that a judge's authority is diluted by the presence of other judges (if any). A federal district judge sits by himself, a federal court of appeals judge normally with two other judges, and a Supreme Court Justice with eight others. The higher the court, the greater its power, but also the more its power is shared among the judges who decide each case, which limits the individual judge's power.

A judge's zone of reasonableness is likely to widen with experience, as he becomes more knowledgeable and more realistic about the judicial process. But I conjecture that it has a U-shaped relation to intellectual ability. Both the most able and the least able appellate judges are likely to stretch the zone—the most able because they will be quick to see, behind the general statement of a rule, the rule's purpose and context, which limit the extent to which the general statement should control a new case; the least able because of difficulty in understanding the orthodox materials and a resulting susceptibility to emotional appeals by counsel, or, what is closely related, difficulty in grasping the abstract virtues of the systemic considerations that limit idiosyncratic judging, such as the value of the law's being predictable.

The breadth of the zone varies with the field of law. It is narrower in fields of ideological consensus, which at present is the approximate situation in, for example, contract law. In such fields judges share common premises of decision, such as belief in freedom of contract and in the importance of the written contract as a protection against the vagaries of a jury's determination of contractual liability. Shared premises enable judges to reason together to an agreed result. The value of predictability in contract law, hence in judicial convergence on the rules and principles of that law, is obvious. Most contract rules are default rules—that is, rules the parties can contract around. They have to know what the rules are so that they can draft accordingly. Most judges in this most commercial of societies agree on all this. In fields, again illustrated by contract law, in which economic analysis is an accepted tool of judicial decision making, judicial discretion is curtailed by an analytic method distinct from the methods of legalism but not necessarily any less effective in generating outcomes felt as objective, as dictated by methodology rather than left to free choice.

The zone of reasonableness is widest in those constitutional cases in which the judges' emotions are engaged, because the constitutional text provides so little guidance and because emotion can override the systemic factors that induce judges to curb their own exercise of discretion. Rather than thinking that judges can be bludgeoned into agreeing to adopt one of the constitutional theories to channel their discretion, the body politic should bow to the inevitable and, if it is troubled by the exercise of a freewheeling legislative discretion by Supreme Court Justices, insist on greater diversity in appointments in order to make the Court more representative, so that its occasional legislating will tend to track the preferences of the official legislators.

But now to say that appellate judges in many cases are legislators, or even to identify those cases, tells us nothing about their legislative preferences, the policies they enact. Nor is it enough to say, as I did in the preceding chapter, that judges are motivated by a desire to be thought, not least by themselves, "good" judges. That leaves the matter too vague. For what is a "good" judge exactly, especially when he is legislating?

The key to answering this question is that the extrinsic satisfactions of a judgeship—money, power, deference, celebrity—are so meager (except, insofar as extrinsic satisfactions other than money are concerned, in the case of Supreme Court Justices) as to make the intrinsic satisfactions ordinarily crucial in the decision to become and remain a judge. All the more so now that the confirmation process is so protracted and potentially unpleasant and the financial opportunity costs of a judgeship are so great.

One intrinsic satisfaction of judging is the utility that some people derive from public service. But that would be insufficient by itself to attract enough highly competent lawyers to staff the courts; zeal for public service just is not that great in the United States. You have to expect to *enjoy* judging (the activity, not just the post) to agree to become a judge, and to enjoy judging you have to enjoy a process, a protocol, that includes (for an appellate judge) reading briefs and listening to oral arguments (many judges greatly enjoy the give-and-take with the lawyers), negotiating with other judges, formulating rules and standards, recognizing the political and institutional limitations and opportunities of adjudication, enjoying the human comedy revealed by cases, and writing (though today more commonly supervising the writing of, and editing) judicial opinions. And the opinions have to conform to certain rhetorical principles, primarily involving the selection and narration of facts, the handling (sometimes manhandling) of orthodox legal materials, and the unobtrusive weaving into them of policy concerns while perhaps giving the reader an occasional glimpse of the judge's personality.

A defining element of the judicial protocol is what Aristotle called "corrective justice." That means judging the case rather than the parties,[18] an aspiration that is given symbolic expression in statues of Justice as a blindfolded goddess—blindfolded because she is not seeing the individual characteristics of the parties and their lawyers: their party affili-

---

18. That is *all* it means in Aristotle. Richard A. Posner, *Law, Pragmatism, and Democracy* 284–286 (2003). Efforts to give corrective justice a substantive meaning, as in suggesting that it requires or is exemplified by the award of damages to tort victims, are recent and in my view unsuccessful. I return to this issue in chapter 7.

ation, standing in the community, family, personal attractiveness, record of achievement, social class, ethnicity, and so forth. In the judicial oath corrective justice is called deciding "without respect to persons."

Corrective justice is also one meaning of the term "rule of law." Another meaning of that multifaceted term is "a government of laws not men"—that is, that law is the ruler of the nation rather than officials being the rulers. The term "rule of law" is also used to designate a political system in which all public officials are, just like private persons, fully subject to legal process rather than being above it. So the United States is an entire nation under law.

When "rule of law" is used in either of the two senses of "a government of laws not men," the word "law" has to be bulked up a bit; it has to achieve some level of generality, predictability, and publicity, as otherwise it would collapse into raw political power.[19] If judges are not constrained at all, there is no rule of law but only rule by judges. But this is an unsatisfactory dichotomy. We actually want judges to "rule," though only to a degree. Judicial independence empowers judges—licenses and indeed encourages the exercise of judicial discretion—and by doing so weakens the constraints of the formal law on judges and thus undermines the rule of law.[20] Because judicial independence is a great social value, the rule of law cannot be the only guiding light of a judicial system, unless we fuzz it up, as legalists do when they use the term in a vague, encompassing, aspirational Law Day sense to denote an idealized legal justice.

"Corrective justice" is more meaningful than "rule of law" if used just to denote abstracting from the personal characteristics of the litigants and seeing them instead as representatives of interests that have acknowledged significance for the allocation of rights and duties—the careless victim, the reckless driver, the unauthorized copier of copyrighted work, and so forth. In Roberts's metaphor, the judge, like the umpire, does not have preferences between contenders. Where the metaphor misleads is in denying that judges have and implement preferences between rules, or between litigants viewed as representative parties (the prosecutor, not Mr. X; the criminal defendant, not Mr. Y), as

19. See Joseph Raz, "The Rule of Law and Its Virtue," in Raz, *The Authority of Law: Essays on Law and Morality* 210 (1979).

20. Lydia Brashear Tiede, "Judicial Independence: Often Cited, Rarely Understood," 15 *Journal of Contemporary Legal Issues* 129, 159–160 (2006).

umpires cannot do, at least since the advent of the Umpire Information System.

Yet even corrective justice in this "without respect to persons" sense cannot be regarded as an unqualified good, or at least is not so regarded in our legal culture. In criminal sentencing—all the more now that the federal sentencing guidelines have been (as we shall see in chapter 10) demoted to advisory status—considerations that would be deemed improper in a civil case, such as the defendant's honorable war record, are admissible to influence the length of the defendant's sentence. Such considerations also play a role in civil jury cases. These are further illustrations of the inadequacy of conventional conceptions of how the judicial system operates.

A residual confusion in the term "corrective justice" is the implication that there is a legal duty to provide a remedy for wrongs. A modern view held by some scholars,[21] it is not what Aristotle, the originator and still the authoritative expositor of the phrase, said or implied. Corrective justice is the doctrine that the function of the adjudicative process is to correct wrongs rather than to play favorites among the litigants.

A lawyer who does not like the protocol that I have described, or is believed by the Senate not to like it, is unlikely to become a federal judge. Weeding out candidates unwilling to play by the rules is thus one function of the confirmation process. But there is a second function that is of growing importance because, as we glimpsed in the contrast between Tables 1 and 2 in chapter 1, political factors play a bigger role in federal judicial appointments today than they did a generation ago. The rise of the Federalist Society, which has groomed many a conservative lawyer for the bench, is one indicator of the trend, and another is the decreasing percentage of federal judges who are appointed from the ranks of private practitioners (see chapter 6).

The causes are various. One is that the two major political parties have become more national and as a result more focused on ideology and less on patronage.[22] For example, since the Reagan Administration

21. See, for example, Jules L. Coleman, *The Practice of Principle: In Defence of a Pragmatic Approach to Legal Theory*, pt. 1 (2001); Richard A. Epstein, "Nuisance Law: Corrective Justice and Its Utilitarian Constraints," 8 *Journal of Legal Studies* 49 (1979); also references in Gregory Mitchell and Philip E. Tetlock, "An Empirical Inquiry into the Relation of Corrective Justice to Distributive Justice," 3 *Journal of Empirical Legal Studies* 421 (2006).

22. Herbert M. Kritzer, "Law Is the Mere Continuation of Politics by Different Means: American Judicial Selection in the Twenty-First Century," 56 *DePaul Law Review* 423, 425–428 (2007).

the role of patronage has taken second place to ideology in court of appeals appointments. Another factor has been the Supreme Court's insistence on injecting itself into highly emotional controversies, such as those over abortion, homosexuality, the regulation of campaign financing and the electoral process generally, and capital punishment, and doing so provocatively, with aggressive rhetoric, intemperate dissents, and, lately, promiscuous citation of foreign decisions (see chapter 12).

In this environment the confirmation process operates to lop off the ideological extremes in the pool of judicial aspirants. A politicized confirmation process has the paradoxical effect of trimming the political dimension of judging by excluding the aspirants who would be most prone to politicize the judicial process. But the effect is limited. At any moment a court is composed of judges appointed at different times and therefore often in different political circumstances. The mainstream changes over time and this tends to expand the ideological distance between the most extreme judges on a court; each may have been well within the mainstream when appointed yet may be outside the current mainstream.

What I am calling a "protocol" could equally be called a "game." You do not play chess unless you are prepared to play by the rules. The rules of the game of which I am speaking with reference to the judicial process are not legal rules; I am not echoing Roberts. They are rules of articulation, awareness of boundaries and role, process values, a professional culture. Wholehearted compliance with the rules cannot be guaranteed, given judges' freedom from the kind of external constraints that operate on other game players. If you do not play chess by the rules, you are not doing anything. If you do not play judging by the rules, but instead act the politician in robes, you are doing something, and it may be something you value more than you do the game of judging as it is supposed to be played. The distinction is blurred by the fact that the judicial game has a legislative component. Having to make an occasional legislative determination is as we know a correlate of one of the judging game's most important rules—the duty to decide. But the rule that requires occasional legislating jostles uneasily with the other rules, which seek to distinguish the judicial role from the legislative on the basis of a distinctive judicial protocol. As a result, many judges hesitate to acknowledge, even to themselves, as one of the rules of their game a duty to legislate, albeit only occasionally.

The judge's legislative decisions are likely to be determined by two sorts of preference. One is systemic, the other case or issue specific, though not personal or (narrowly) political. The systemic preference is the judge's desire to follow his overall judicial approach, his bent—more grandly, his judicial philosophy (originalism, liberal activism, states' rights, natural law, strict construction, judicial self-restraint, fundamental rights, and so on, it seems, ad infinitum)—if he has one. Not all judges do, but some judges who do not want to be called willful or "result oriented" pride themselves on being guided by a judicial philosophy that overrides their reactions to the equities of the individual case. (In the cliché "Hard cases make bad law," "hard" does not mean difficult; it means tugs at the heartstrings.) Those overall approaches are so malleable, as we shall see in subsequent chapters, that they are little better than rationalizations of decisions reached on other, unacknowledged grounds, such as sympathy for the class to which a litigant belongs, which might consist of people who have lost their jobs, or of drug addicts, prosecutors, accident victims, fraud victims, small businessmen, big businessmen, immigrants, police officers, physicians, members of the executive branch, American Indians, or farmers. These are systemic preferences because they relate to entire classes of litigant. Often they are the product of some general political (not legal) philosophy or outlook—usually a variant of "liberalism" or "conservatism." But a judge is likely also to be influenced by the particulars of the individual case—he may be confronted by a litigant who straddles two litigant classes, one of which the judge looks upon with favor, the other not; examples are the physician who cheats on his taxes and the white supervisor who discriminates against her black underlings. Or the litigant may have characteristics that challenge the judge's stereotypical view of the class to which the litigant belongs.

These are the types of preference that shape a judge's legislative decisions; it remains to consider the forces that influence the formation of a particular judge's preferences.

4

The Mind of the Legislating Judge

We have narrowed our inquiry into judicial mentation to cases in which the judge's vote, in cases fairly described as legislative, is determined not by some declared judicial philosophy and not by the orthodox materials of legal decision making either but by—what? By "politics," that slippery word? Jeremy Waldron slips on that banana peel when he says that

> as a citizen, a judge is Republican or Democrat, liberal or conservative, security-minded or liberty-minded, a Bush supporter or an opponent. We work on the assumption that it is wrong for a judge to decide cases simply on the basis of his or her political views. It happens of course, but we want to prevent it. The principles I have been talking about are supposed to be ways of disciplining oneself in this regard. One figures out a way of interpreting the Constitution precisely so that one's decision in a particular case is not simply at the mercy of one's political instincts. And the trouble with repudiating all such principles as "legalistic," the problem with allowing justices to pursue whatever compromises and strategies seem sensible, is that it seems to undermine this discipline.[1]

To be a "Republican or Democrat," a "Bush supporter or an opponent," is to be a political partisan. But to be "liberal or conservative, security-minded or liberty-minded," is to be political in a quite different sense—in fact in two quite different senses, because a judge might be liberal or conservative in national security cases but not in other cases. Waldron

1. Jeremy Waldron, "Temperamental Justice," *New York Review of Books*, May 10, 2007, pp. 15, 17.

does not mark these distinctions (I also wonder about the intended force of "simply" in the second sentence of the quoted passage and of "seems" in the last), but they are important. Our principal political parties are coalitions; they lack coherent ideologies. A judge may lean more toward the set of policies associated with the Democratic Party or more toward those associated with the Republican Party, but because neither party is ideologically uniform, party affiliation has only limited value in predicting judicial decisions even in the open area, where judges are legislators. A judge might have a view about the relative weight that should be accorded security and liberty in those national security cases to which the orthodox legal materials do not speak clearly, and he might think his view relevant to deciding such cases. That would not make him a political partisan even if he could not defend his weightings of the competing considerations by reference to an impartial study of the subject that he or others had made. Nor would he be a partisan if, rather than or besides having "retail" political views—views on particular issues—he had a "wholesale" view, a general political orientation, or in short an "ideology"—a body of more or less coherent bedrock beliefs about social, economic, and political questions, a worldview that shaped his answers to those questions when they arose in cases in the open area.

Ideology is not the only recourse of judges in the open area. But it is a major one, as the attitudinal literature suggests, and so let us consider the sources of judges' ideologies—a fascinating and understudied question. Moral and religious values are among those sources and are in turn the products of upbringing, education, salient life experiences, occupational experiences, and personal characteristics that may determine what experiences a person seeks. Personal characteristics include race, sex, ethnicity, and other innate identifiers of a person, but also temperament, which shapes not only values but also dispositions such as timidity and boldness that influence a person's response to situations.

The role of schooling both formal and informal in the formation of a judge's outlook was emphasized years ago by Yale law professor Jan Deutsch under the rubric of political socialization. He was speaking of the Justices of the Supreme Court but his observations apply to other judges as well.

> The Court, unlike Congress, is not a social system; the task of a Justice is far more an individual than a group endeavor; and the influence of

other Justices and of the institution on a new member of the Court is correspondingly limited. To a far greater extent than is true in the case of a Congressman, therefore, the search for factors that effectively impose restraints on the discretion of the individual Justice must be carried beyond the realm of his work experience to that of his schooling, both formal and informal. Such an investigation, a branch of the study of political 'socialization,' might profitably begin with an examination of the impact of their professional training on given Justices. For example, to what extent can a particular Justice's perception of the range of discretion he can legitimately exercise be ascribed to a professional training that was primarily 'policy-oriented'?

As the decisions of the Court increasingly lose the appearance of 'logic' that has historically constituted the basis for their public acceptability, studies of the institutional differences between Congress and the Court and of the extent to which the Justices have internalized the constraints on their power implicit in those institutional differences could thus gradually serve to replace appearance with reality, could in time make possible the discarding of those symbols in terms of which the Court's authority has historically been accepted by the public.[2]

Experience, like training, can inculcate values that influence judicial behavior. A judge's professional experiences before he became a judge may have convinced him that labor unions are bad for most workers, for consumers, and for the economy as a whole, or alternatively that a significant fraction of corporate executives are greedy, mendacious, and shortsighted. Such interpreted experiences could congeal into (though could also be formed by) a general antiunion or antibusiness ideology that would influence the judge's vote in close cases involving unions accused of unfair labor practices or corporate executives accused of fraud. And we recall that personal characteristics and professional experience may be entwined—the former may determine the choice of career.

It is no surprise that empirical studies do better at predicting the votes of Supreme Court Justices by including, besides a Justice's presumed political affiliation, such additional explanatory variables as the prestige of his college, his prosecutorial experience or lack thereof, and his prior judicial experience if any.[3] We learn that in the period 1916 to 1988 a Jus-

2. Jan G. Deutsch, "Neutrality, Legitimacy, and the Supreme Court: Some Intersections between Law and Political Science," 20 Stanford Law Review 169, 260–261 (1968).

3. See C. Neal Tate and Roger Handberg, "Time Binding and Theory Building in Personal Attribute Models of Supreme Court Voting Behavior, 1916–88," 35 American Journal of Political

tice was more likely to favor civil rights plaintiffs if he was from the North, if he was from an urban area, if his father had not been a government official, or if he had never worked as a prosecutor; and he was more likely to vote the liberal side of economic issues if he was from an urban area, had long judicial experience,[4] or had never worked as a prosecutor.[5] Race, religion, and gender have also been found, as we know, to be significant predictors of judges' votes in cases that raise issues relating to those characteristics.[6] These correlations identify differences in judicial behavior that come from differences in the background knowledge that judges bring to their judging, but also, in the case of northern, religious, and urban backgrounds, in the values they are likely to have absorbed from their social environment.

The correlations omit psychological variables. Yet psychological factors, including emotions that influence religious belief and give salience to particular experiences, play a large role in ideological formation, at least in societies such as ours in which freedom and mobility expose people to a range of ideological positions. Emotion exerts a huge influence on how people translate their experiences into beliefs,[7] and so on the weights (critical to the balancing tests so widely used in American

Science 460 (1991); Tate, "Personal Attribute Models of the Voting Behavior of U.S. Supreme Court Justices: Liberalism in Civil Liberties and Economics Decisions, 1946–1978," 75 *American Political Science Review* 355 (1981); S. Sidney Ulmer, "Dissent Behavior and the Social Background of Supreme Court Justices," 32 *Journal of Politics* 580 (1970); Ulmer, "Social Background as an Indicator of the Votes of Supreme Court Justices in Criminal Cases: 1947–1956 Terms," 17 *American Journal of Political Science* 622 (1973); Ulmer, "Are Social Background Models Time-Bound?" 80 *American Political Science Review* 957 (1986).

4. Notice that the four liberal Justices on the Supreme Court (Stevens, Souter, Ginsburg, and Breyer) have in the aggregate significantly more judicial experience than the four conservative Justices (Roberts, Scalia, Thomas, and Alito). The relation still holds, though it is weakened, if the remaining Justice, the moderate conservative Kennedy, is grouped with the conservatives.

5. Tate and Handberg, note 3 above, at 473–475.

6. See, besides references in chapter 1, David S. Abrams, Marianne Bertrand, and Sendhil Mullainathan, "Do Judges Vary in Their Treatment of Race?" (University of Chicago, 2007); Darrell Steffensmeier and Chestler L. Britt, "Judges' Race and Judicial Decision Making: Do Black Judges Sentence Differently?" 82 *Social Science Quarterly* 749 (2001); Orley Ashenfelter, Theodore Eisenberg, and Stewart J. Schwab, "Politics and the Judiciary: The Influence of Judicial Background on Case Outcomes," 24 *Journal of Legal Studies* 257 (1995); Gerald S. Gryski, Eleanor C. Main, and William J. Dixon, "Models of State High Court Decision Making in Sex Discrimination Cases," 48 *Journal of Politics* 143 (1986).

7. For illuminating discussions of the relation among emotion, belief formation, and decision making, see Alain Berthoz, *Emotion and Reason: The Cognitive Neuroscience of Decision Making*, ch. 2 (2006); Mary Douglas and Aaron B. Wildavsky, *Risk and Culture: An Essay on the Selection of Technical and Environmental Dangers* (1982).

law) that judges assign to the probable consequences of deciding a case one way or the other.

The role of emotions is related to the fact that belief systems that are called ideologies—"clusters or configurations of attitudes and beliefs that are interdependent or organized around a dominant societal theme such as liberalism or conservatism"[8]—are

> extremely 'hypothesis-driven' rather than 'data driven.' The ideolog is apt to find evidence even in the most commonplace events for the predicted workings of his enemies . . . Belief systems which are less than totally ideologized, while they may not use the same single core account for everything, nevertheless often have the 'top-down' character of imposing abstract and possibly gratuitous interpretations on the ambiguous data presented by the world of events.[9]

For it is implausible that people are libertarians, or socialists, or originalists because libertarianism, or socialism, or originalism is "correct." They can't all be, and probably none is, except in severely qualified form. These isms, like religious beliefs, are indeed hypothesis-driven rather than fact-driven. Nothing is more common than for different people of equal competence in reasoning to form different beliefs from the same information. Think of how sophisticated people reacted to student riots protesting the Vietnam War in the late 1960s and early 1970s: some with horror, fearing social disintegration; others with exhilaration, hoping for transformative social change. They were seeing the same thing but interpreting it in opposite ways. Alternatively they were reacting differently to the same information because of different intuitions, a kind of buried knowledge. Moral psychology is intuitionist and diverse, rather than rationalistic. It includes—besides such traditional liberal values as care for others' suffering and the duty to reciprocate benefits received—group loyalty, respect for authority, and defense of purity or sanctity.[10] This diversity helps to explain the moral intensity with which many people, including many judges, embrace liberal or conservative ideolo-

8. Alice H. Eagly and Shelly Chaiken, *The Psychology of Attitudes* 145 (1993).

9. Robert P. Abelson, "Concepts for Representing Mundane Reality in Plans," in *Representation and Understanding: Studies in Cognitive Science* 273, 274 (Daniel G. Bobrow and Allan Collins eds. 1975).

10. See Jonathan Haidt and Jesse Graham, "When Morality Opposes Justice: Conservatives Have Moral Intuitions That Liberals May Not Recognize," 20 *Social Justice Research* 98 (2007); Haidt, "The New Synthesis in Moral Psychology," 316 *Science* 998 (2007); Haidt, "The Emotional Dog and Its Rational Tail: A Social Intuitionist Approach to Moral Judgment," 108 *Psychological Review* 814 (2001).

gies. I will take up intuition as a factor in judicial decision making shortly, along with its cousins common sense and good judgment. Another cousin, preconception, was discussed in chapter 2. Ideology is preconception writ large—a lens that colors a judge's initial reaction to a case.

Among the intuitions that shape ideology and make ideological differences impossible to bridge by reasoned argument are metaphysical presuppositions, such as free will versus determinism, natural equality versus natural inequality, man as ensouled versus man as big-brained monkey, and original sin versus the original goodness of Rousseau's "noble savage." These presuppositions influence a person's evaluation of severe punishments, welfare programs, high taxes, national security, and paternalistic government. For such an evaluation is likely to depend on whether one thinks a crime a willed evil or an accident of the genes or of upbringing, whether one thinks poverty a deserved state of irresponsible people or a failure of society, whether one thinks altruism a trustworthy motivator of public officials or a false pretense. Metaphysical disputes cannot be resolved to the satisfaction of the disputants, and this is a clue to the existence of unbridgeable disagreements at the core of American law.

Intuition, emotion, and preconception are all forms of telescoped or tacit thinking, as contrasted with explicit, logical, step-by-step reasoning,[11] and all are influenced not only by such obvious factors as upbringing, education, the beliefs of peers, and reigning social beliefs but also by personality. More than half a century ago, influential books by Theodor Adorno (and colleagues—the Berkeley study, as it is known) and by Gordon Allport distinguished between the authoritarian and the nonauthoritarian personality,[12] spawning an extensive literature in social

---

11. On the myriad ways in which actual human thinking departs from the ideal of rigorous, conscious, algorithmic reasoning, see Philip N. Johnson-Laird, *How We Reason* (2006); Miriam Solomon, "Social Cognition," in *Philosophy of Psychology and Cognitive Science* 413 (Paul Thagard ed. 2007). And this includes judicial thinking. See Chris Guthrie, Jeffrey J. Rachlinski, and Andrew J. Wistrich, "Inside the Judicial Mind," 86 *Cornell Law Review* 777 (2001); Jeffrey J. Rachlinski, Chris Guthrie, and Andrew J. Wistrich, "Inside the Bankruptcy Judge's Mind," 86 *Boston University Law Review* 1227 (2006).

12. Theodor W. Adorno et al., *The Authoritarian Personality* (1950); Gordon W. Allport, *The Nature of Prejudice* (1954). For a comprehensive recent analysis of the relationship between personality and ideology, see John T. Jost et al., "Political Conservatism as Motivated Social Cognition," 129 *Psychological Bulletin* 359 (2003).

psychology.[13] Adorno and Allport were curious whether racial prejudice had psychological causes. They concluded that it did—that it was a product of psychological maladjustment. Even earlier, Jerome Frank, an American lawyer of legal realist persuasion and later a federal appellate judge, had in his 1930 book *Law and the Modern Mind* attributed legal formalism to arrested psychological development. Adorno, Allport, and Frank were as one in believing that rigid, dichotomous, "inside the box" thinking—the sort associated with hierarchical attitudes toward political and other forms of authority—was rooted in infantile troubles with one's parents. An authoritarian personality formed in childhood predisposed a person either to irrational prejudices (Adorno and Allport) or to an unwillingness to interpret law flexibly so that it would keep pace with changing social conditions and understandings (Frank). So legalists had authoritarian personalities.

After decades of further research, the belief that an authoritarian personality is a product of maladjustment has dwindled,[14] though one still encounters claims that such a personality is formed when parents are overprotective and excessively controlling and as a result prevent a child from developing mechanisms for coping with frightening situations.[15] The child becomes fearful, and later in life intolerant of challenges to accepted modes of thought or structures of authority.

People do vary in their attitudes toward authority, even though the variance is not well correlated with differences in mental health or an infant's relations with his parents. Social psychologists believe that the variance reflects differences in beliefs, which in turn reflect different learning—from parents, teachers, peers, personal experiences, and the larger society.[16] But this "social learning" approach is not fully convinc-

13. See, for example, *On the Nature of Prejudice: Fifty Years after Allport* (John F. Dovidio, Peter Glick, and Laurie A. Rudman eds. 2005); *Strength and Weakness: The Authoritarian Personality Today* (William F. Stone, Gerda Lederer, and Richard Christie eds. 1993); *The Psychological Basis of Ideology* (Hans J. Eysenck and Glenn D. Wilson eds. 1978); Stanley Feldman and Karen Stenner, "Perceived Threat and Authoritarianism," 18 *Political Psychology* 741 (1997).

14. John Duckitt, "Personality and Prejudice," in *On the Nature of Prejudice,* note 13, at 395, 401–402; Robert A. Altemeyer, *Right-Wing Authoritarianism* 112–115 (1981).

15. Detlef Oesterreich, "Flight into Security: A New Approach and Measure of the Authoritarian Personality," 26 *Political Psychology* 275, 282–286 (2005). See also Christel Hopf, "Authoritarians and Their Families: Qualitative Studies on the Origins of Authoritarian Dispositions," in *Strength and Weakness,* note 13 above, ch. 6.

16. Robert A. Altemeyer, *The Authoritarian Specter* 76–92 and ch. 6 (1996). See also Hans J. Eysenck, *The Psychology of Politics,* chs. 8 and 9 (1998 [1954]). And on the fundamental

ing either. People exposed to similar information and arguments often react differently. How else to explain diversity of religious beliefs within the same community? It would not be surprising if personality, rather than just different learned beliefs, influences where along the liberal-conservative spectrum a judge will be found, especially since genetic factors appear to be important in predisposing a person to develop an authoritarian personality.[17]

What I shall continue to call the authoritarian personality, but without pejorative intent and without attributing it to a psychological deformity, has been found to cause a person to react particularly strongly to threats that seem aimed at society at large—to its dominant beliefs and values, such as marriage and patriotism—as distinguished from merely personal threats. Such a person seeks security through association with a group and its beliefs,[18] sensing that individual resistance would be ineffectual against a society-wide threat. More generally, the authoritarian personality is repelled by disorder, prizes hierarchy and hence fears loss of control, and dislikes ambiguity and ambiguous relationships, such as families that depart from the conventional nuclear-family model.

We can begin to sense the political valence of the authoritarian personality. A study by John Jost and his colleagues lists the core elements of conservative ideology as resistance to change and acceptance of inequality, and the peripheral elements as "desire for order and stability,

point—the unconscious influences of the entire "social surround" in determining attitudes and beliefs—see John A. Bargh and Erin L. Williams, "The Automaticity of Social Life," 15 *Current Directions in Psychological Science* 1 (2006); R. W. Connell, "Political Socialization in the American Family: The Evidence Re-examined," 36 *Public Opinion Quarterly* 323 (1972). And note the parallel to the passage I quoted earlier from Jan Deutsch, discussing the "political socialization" of judges.

17. Kathryn McCourt et al., "Authoritarianism Revisited: Familial Influences Examined in Twins Reared Apart and Together," 27 *Personality and Individual Differences* 985, 1008 (1999); Amy C. Abrahamson, Laura A. Baker, and Avshalom Caspi, "Rebellious Teens? Genetic and Environmental Influences on the Social Attitudes of Adolescents," 83 *Journal of Personality and Social Psychology* 1392 (2002). These findings were anticipated by Private Willis in Act II of *Iolanthe:*

> I often think it's comical . . .
> How Nature always does contrive . . .
> That every boy and every gal
> That's born into the world alive
> Is either a little Liberal
> Or else a little Conservative!

18. Feldman and Stenner, note 13 above.

preference for gradual rather than revolutionary change (if any), adherence to preexisting social norms, idealization of authority figures, punishment of deviants, and endorsement of social and economic inequality."[19] The study finds the following personality traits to be positively correlated with conservatism so understood: dogmatism, intolerance of ambiguity, not being open to experience, fear of death, fear of threat in general, and need for order, structure, and closure.[20] Those are hallmarks of the authoritarian personality.

Suppose a judge was at an impressionable stage in his development during the disorders of the Vietnam War era. If he has an authoritarian personality, the disorders appalled him and probably drove him into the Republican camp. That would not commit him to all the planks of today's Republican platform, but he is likely to be a conservative judge. If on the contrary he is a natural rebel—hates authority whether intellectual or political, and thus is a skeptic in the everyday sense of the word, reveling in contingency and ambiguity—then he is probably a liberal judge.

I am depicting extremes exaggerated to the point of caricature, as well as ignoring the liberal bias of the literature on authoritarian personality, the authoritarianism of communists and other extreme left-wingers,[21]

19. Jost et al., note 12 above, at 342–343. In the parallel formulation by Christopher Weber and Christopher M. Federico, "Interpersonal Attachment and Patterns of Ideological Belief," 28 *Political Psychology* 389 (2007), "right-wing authoritarianism . . . is defined by a constellation of three social attitudes: conventionalism, submission to authority, and aggression against outgroups, which covary to form a highly unitary attitudinal dimension." The authors identify another political psychology that they call "social dominance orientation": "We thus hypothesized that individuals with an anxious attachment style would perceive the world as dangerous and threatening and would in turn endorse the social and cultural aspects of conservatism—in the form of RWA [right-wing authoritarianism]—in order to reduce threat. In contrast, attachment avoidance is marked by interpersonal distrust and by the desire to control others. We thus hypothesized that individuals with an avoidant attachment style would tend to see the world as an uncaring, competitive jungle in which people maximize personal utility and would in turn endorse the economic aspects of conservatism—in the form of SDO [social dominance orientation]—in order to exert control." Id. at 405. An axis related to both RWA and SDO is the "tough-minded"–"tender-minded" axis, on which see Eysenck, note 16 above, at 147.

20. Jost et al., note 12 above, at 366.

21. Jeff Greenberg and Eva Jonas, "Psychological Motivations and Political Orientation—The Left, the Right, and the Rigid: Comment on Jost et al. (2003)," 129 *Psychological Bulletin* 376 (2003); Eysenck, note 16 above; Milton Rokeach, *The Open and Closed Mind: Investigations into the Nature of Belief Systems* (1960). Greenberg and Jonas argue that the relevant polarity is not liberal-conservative but ideological rigidity versus ideological flexibility. Jost et al. respond that although indeed there is left authoritarianism, in the American political culture (with

and the other ideological axes—besides "liberal" and "conservative" in their usual modern meaning—along which judges might fall. Libertarian free marketers are unlikely to be authoritarian; zealots for political correctness, animal liberationists, and ecoterrorists and other radical Greens are quite likely to be so.

I know no actual judge who "presents" as authoritarian. Authoritarianism appears to be a normally distributed (that is, bell-shaped) personality characteristic; each of us has more or less of it. Some liberals have more of it than some conservatives. Liberals have prejudices, like conservatives—just different prejudices. Liberals too want to take sides, want to belong, to be part of an in-group—this is very important to people[22]—that defines itself in part by opposition to a dangerous other. They too at times succumb to the anxious and rigid thinking patterns that they ascribe to conservatives.

Yet, important as these qualifications are, I think that there is a correlation between personality and politics, that most American judges can probably be located along the spectrum that runs from authoritarian/conservative on the right to nonauthoritarian/liberal on the left, and that a judge's location should have some value in predicting his votes in legalistically indeterminate cases that present issues relating to authority, the family, religion, equality, human nature, and other matters in which belief tends to be entangled with strong emotions.[23]

But emphasis must fall on *some* predictive value. An authoritarian judge's ideological convictions might be overridden by concern for institutional values, such as the desirability of crisp rules, which ought to be attractive to a person who has an authoritarian personality. Or he might have weak ideological convictions but a high degree of skepticism concerning the efficacy of the orthodox tools of legal reasoning; this might make him a pragmatic judge difficult to classify politically. His ideology might be incoherent; it might be in conflict with strong personal emotions, rooted in background or experiences, that would sometimes dom-

communism and other left radicalism deader than a doornail) there is a strong positive correlation between conservatism and authoritarian personality traits, and that although conservatives do frequently support change, it is generally change back to some previous status quo. John T. Jost et al., "Exceptions That Prove the Rule—Using a Theory of Motivated Social Cognition to Account for Ideological Incongruities and Political Anomalies: Reply to Greenberg and Jonas," 129 *Psychological Bulletin* 383 (2003).

22. Solomon E. Asch, *Social Psychology* 605–606 (1952).

23. See Johnson-Laird, note 11 above, at 334–335.

inate his ideological commitments. He might have no ideology. There are judges who do not have an authoritarian personality yet have many of the beliefs that authoritarians are expected to have. Holmes (he of "three generations of imbeciles are enough" and many other "tough-minded" dicta that made his not infrequent liberal judicial and personal views all the more striking) is a notable example.

The authoritarian/conservative judge in particular confronts a dilemma that may moderate his ideologically driven legislative enthusiasms. To the extent that his temperament and (closely related to or determined by it) his political ideology predispose him to value order, a desire to promote the conventional rules of the judicial game may vie with his desire to conform the law to his ideology. The judge who wants people to genuflect to the authority of "the law" may feel himself drawn to accepting, indeed to celebrating, the authority of text and precedent even when they block otherwise ideologically appealing results. Intolerance of ambiguity makes a particularly plausible match with preferring rules over standards and strict over loose construction. In chapter 10 we shall see Justice Scalia's fondness for rules overcoming his conservative hostility to the burning of the American flag.

But the kind of dilemma illustrated by the flag-burning cases is usually solved by a judge's elevating constitutional text to the supreme principle of order, corresponding to the Bible or the Koran, with all these sacred texts sharing the fortunate property, to the ideologically ambitious, of profound ambiguity. This ambiguity is due in part to their antiquity, as a result of which they often fit modern conditions poorly, requiring aggressive "interpretation" represented as obedience.

This politically conservative response ("originalism" or "textualism-originalism")—which under different conditions could be a liberal response but is more congenial to conservatives because of its evocation of an era more culturally conservative than today—illustrates a more general tendency of judges to reach backward for the grounds of their decisions. By doing so they can if challenged claim to be employing a different methodology from that of the legislator, who is forward-looking, a methodology that involves deriving conclusions from premises by logical operations as distinct from basing action on a comparison of the social or political consequences of different possible outcomes. But the backward orientation actually enlarges a judge's legislative scope, and not only by concealing that he is legislating. A judge or Justice who is out of step with current precedents reaches back to some earlier body of case law (or constitutional text) that he can describe as the bedrock, the authentic Ur text that should guide decision. And the older the bedrock, the greater the scope for manipulation of meaning in the name of historical reconstruction or intellectual archeology. You cannot, for example, just by staring at the language of the due process clauses of the Fifth and Fourteenth Amendments, determine whether they authorize judges to create abortion rights. You can adopt an interpretive rule that constitutional rights cannot be created by implication but must be stated expressly in the Constitution—more precisely, that specific constitutional rights, such as the right to an abortion, cannot be derived from constitutional rights expressed in general terms, such as the right not to be deprived of liberty without due process of law. But the choice of that interpretive rule is not something that can be derived by reasoning from agreed-upon premises.

The originalist's pretense that it can be makes originalism an example of bad faith in Sartre's sense—bad faith as the denial of freedom to choose, and so the shirking of personal responsibility. Similar examples abound at the liberal end of the ideological spectrum. An example is Justice Breyer's claim in his book *Active Liberty*[24] that liberal judges, too, are interpreters, not creators. The articulation of judicial philosophies by judges is prone to hypocrisy because of the strategic attractiveness of a rhetoric of judicial certitude that declares an opposing view not merely opposed or even mistaken, but "lawless." Jeremy Waldron, who is not an American lawyer, has been taken in by that rhetoric. He believes that good judges really do discipline themselves by submitting to "principles" that rule out politically motivated decisions; and he instances Scalia without considering the possible political motivations of the Justice's adoption of those principles.

Sartrean bad faith need not be conscious. Judges are not villains, and even a villain, according to advice given actors who play villains, is not a villain in his own eyes. The authoritarian judge may have a compelling sense that the only legitimate judicial decision is one generated by legalist analysis. He considers his decisions legitimate, concludes they must therefore be legalist, and constructs a legalist rationale that convinces him that his decision was not the product of a political ideology. His

24. I discuss the book in chapter 11.

legalist leanings will bite in his effort to control future cases by what he says in his opinion. Rather than decide the case on a narrow ground he will be inclined to declare a rule that will confer a broad precedential scope on the decision so that the next case, at least, can be decided deductively. The effort may fail, however, because the scope of a precedent is determined by decisions in subsequent cases that may bring to light considerations that cause the judges in those cases to narrow the rule declared in the earlier case.

Judge Michael McConnell argues that originalism "is not an ideological position, but one that safeguards the distinction between law and politics. Textualist and originalist judges, *at least in principle*, will *on occasion* vote to uphold laws they deeply disagree with, or to strike down laws they would favor, because the basis for constitutional judging (*text, history, tradition, and settled precedents*) is independent of their own preferences."[25] The phrases that I have italicized give the game away. Interpreting an antique text, discerning tradition, and deciding which precedents should be deemed "settled" (why was *Plessy v. Ferguson* not a "settled" precedent?) and what exactly the "settled" precedents mean are tasks so fraught with uncertainty that the judge's preferences as to outcome will not only shape his theory but also determine its application to specific cases. The moderate legalist will admit the propriety of seeking interpretive guidance in a statute's purpose, but textualists-originalists are not purposivists; consider Justice Scalia's campaign against resorting to legislative history to help determine statutory meaning.

Often when impartial analysis does not yield a definite answer to an urgent question, emotion takes over and the role of the conscious intellect is reduced to that of rationalization. A poem by Rudyard Kipling says derisively of people who despise soldiers and police that they make "mock o' uniforms that guard you while you sleep."[26] You are likely to have a strong reaction pro or con to this sentiment and how Kipling expressed it, but you will not be able to defend your view with arguments that would convince someone who has the opposite reaction. If you are intellectually sophisticated you may recognize that your conviction, however strong, cannot be shown to be "right," but at most reasonable.

25. Michael W. McConnell, "Book Review [of Breyer's book]," 119 *Harvard Law Review* 2387, 2415 (2006) (emphasis added).

26. Rudyard Kipling, "Tommy," in Kipling, *Barrack-Room Ballads: And Other Verses* 6, 7 (1892).

Yet that recognition will not weaken the strength of your conviction or its influence on your behavior. A judge is likely to set some emotional reactions to one side, such as a personal liking for a litigant or his lawyer, because they are forbidden moves in the judicial game, because sophisticated people are aware of the perils of basing judgments on likeability, and because decisions so motivated will not advance one's political goals—a litigant's likeability is not correlated with the politics of his case. The emotional reactions triggered by seeing the parties as representatives of groups and therefore focused on their actions rather than on who they are may be just as intense. But acting on those reactions is consistent with deciding cases without respect to persons. Indignation at a wrong is consistent with corrective justice; sympathy for a litigant is not.

The character of an emotional reaction, at once gripping and inarticulable, does not make emotion always an illegitimate or even a bad ground for a judicial decision. The judge has to decide the case even if unable, because he is facing irreducible uncertainty, to reach a decision by algorithmic means. Emotion can be a form of thought, though compressed and inarticulate. It is triggered by, and more often than not produces rational responses to, information.[27] A child runs in front of your car and you swerve without conscious thought. That is more rational than pausing to weigh the pros and cons of running the child down.

The epistemic significance of emotion depends on which emotion is engaged. Some emotions, such as anger, disgust, and happiness, increase a person's certitude. Others, such as uncertainty, hope, surprise, fear, and worry, have the opposite effect. A person who feels certain about an issue will be disinclined to engage in systematic analysis, especially of a taxing sort (in other words, he will substitute emotion for analysis), while when he is uncertain he will have the opposite inclination.[28] This

27. I stress the difference between emotion as a useful cognitive shortcut and emotion as a nonrational influence on belief or behavior ("emotionalism"), citing an extensive literature, in my book *Frontiers of Legal Theory,* ch. 7 (2001). See also Johnson-Laird, note 11 above, ch. 6.

28. Norbert Schwarz, "Feelings as Information: Moods Influence Judgments and Processing Strategies," in *Heuristics and Biases: The Psychology of Intuitive Judgment* 534, 539 (Thomas Gilovich, Dale Griffin, and Daniel Kahneman eds. 2002); Larissa Z. Tiedens and Susan Linton, "Judgment under Emotional Certainty and Uncertainty: The Effects of Specific Emotions on Information Processing," 81 *Journal of Personality and Social Psychology* 973, 985 (2001) ("certainty-associated emotions result in more heuristic processing than do uncertainty-associated emotions, which promote systematic processing").

point underscores the importance of our adversary system, which forces a judge to give a hearing to someone who will challenge the judge's intuition. It also suggests the suite of emotions that one should look for in a judge.

Intuition plays a major role in judicial as in most decision making. The faculty of intuition that enables a judge, a businessman, or an army commander to make a quick judgment without a conscious weighting and comparison of the pros and cons of the possible courses of action[29] is best understood as a capability for reaching down into a subconscious repository of knowledge acquired from one's education and particularly one's experiences[30] (as in "practice to the point of automaticity"[31]). Intuition in this sense is related to "judgment,"[32] as in the proposition that experienced people tend to have "good judgment" because their experiences, though largely forgotten, remain accessible sources of knowledge for coping with challenges that despite being new are not novel, because they resemble previous challenges. Most judges in the American system are highly experienced; most are middle-aged or older, have been judges for a long time, and before becoming judges were engaged in a related activity such as private practice or law teaching. Their experiences nourish their intuitions. Unconscious preconceptions, which play so large a role in the judicial process and are the key to reconciling the attitudinal literature with what judges think they are doing, are products of intuition. This implies incidentally that the more experienced a judge is, the less his decision in a new case will be influenced by the evidence and arguments in that case—which infuriates lawyers.

The choice, which is usually unconscious, between intuitive and conscious problem solving involves a trade-off between the *amount* of available knowledge, including long-buried knowledge that nonetheless

29. There are other meanings of "intuition"—see Lisa M. Osbeck, "Conceptual Problems in the Development of a Psychological Notion of 'Intuition,'" 29 *Journal for the Theory of Social Behavior* 229 (1999)—but they are not germane to my concerns.

30. See, for example, Robin M. Hogarth, *Educating Intuition* (2001); Roger Frantz, "Herbert Simon: Artificial Intelligence as a Framework for Understanding Intuition," 24 *Journal of Economic Psychology* 265, 273–275 (2003).

31. S. Farnham-Diggory, "Paradigms of Knowledge and Instruction," 64 *Review of Educational Research* 463, 468 (1994).

32. Margaret E. Brooks and Scott Highhouse, "Can Good Judgment Be Measured?" in *Situational Judgment Tests: Theory, Measurement and Application* 39 (Jeff A. Weekley and Robert Ployhard eds. 2006).

can be recovered as intuition,[33] and the *precision* with which whatever knowledge one has can be applied to solving the problem. Because the unconscious mind has greater capacity than the conscious mind,[34] the knowledge accessible to intuition is likely to be vast. The alternative to drawing on that knowledge by means of intuition is to apply explicit, step-by-step reasoning to one's smaller stock of conscious knowledge. That is often the inferior choice even when time is not pressing, though it is in many judicial settings. When a decision depends on several factors, you may do better by using your intuition than by trying to evaluate consciously each factor separately and combining the evaluations to form an ultimate conclusion.[35] The costs of consciously processing the information may be so high that intuition will enable a more accurate as well as a speedier decision than analytical reasoning would.[36] This often is true in the open area in law because what makes it open may be the number of factors that are relevant to making a decision. But intuition is important in the disposition of routine cases as well. Judges gain experience in deciding on legalist grounds the cases that can be decided on those grounds, and that experience enables them to decide more rapidly than a novice could, thereby economizing on information-processing costs.

Thus, the more experienced the judge, the more confidence he is apt to repose in his intuitive reactions[37] and the less likely he is to be at-

33. See, for example, "The Logic of Tacit Inference," in Michael Polanyi, *Knowing and Being: Essays* 138 (Marjorie Grene ed. 1969); Richard N. Langlois and Müfit M. Sabooglu, "Knowledge and Meliorism in the Evolutionary Theory of F. A. Hayek," in *Evolutionary Economics: Program and Scope* 231 (Kurt Dopfer ed. 2001).

34. Ap Dijksterhuis et al., "On Making the Right Choice: The Deliberation-without-Attention Effect," 311 *Science* 1005 (2006).

35. Brooks and Highhouse, note 32 above, at 43; Timothy D. Wilson and Jonathan W. Schooler, "Thinking Too Much: Introspection Can Reduce the Quality of Preferences and Decisions," 60 *Journal of Personality and Social Psychology* 181 (1991); Pawel Lewicki, Maria Czyzewska, and Hunter Hoffman, "Unconscious Acquisition of Complex Procedural Knowledge," 13 *Journal of Experimental Psychology: Learning, Memory and Cognition* 523 (1987).

36. See, for example, Lewicki, Czyzewska, and Hoffman, note 35 above; Adrianus Dingeman de Groot and Fernand Gobet, *Perception and Memory in Chess: Studies in the Heuristics of the Professional Eye* 4 (1996); Arthur S. Reber, *Implicit Learning and Tacit Knowledge: An Essay on the Cognitive Unconscious* (1993); Baljinder Sahdra and Paul Thagard, "Procedural Knowledge in Molecular Biology," 16 *Philosophical Psychology* 477 (2003); Ido Erev, Gary Bornstein, and Thomas S. Wallsten, "The Negative Effect of Probability Assessments on Decision Quality," 55 *Organizational Behavior and Human Decision Processes* 78, 92 (1993).

37. See Michael R. P. Dougherty, Scott D. Gronlund, and Charles F. Gettys, "Memory as a

tracted to a systematic decision-making methodology, perhaps involving Bayes's theorem or other complex algorithms, decision trees, artificial intelligence, debiasing techniques, and so forth. Not only would decision making by means of a rigorous methodology be more difficult and time-consuming than intuitive decision making, but its advantages would be obscure because the preconditions for using such a methodology would so often be absent. It is not only that judges do not quantify relevant probabilities, as Bayes's theorem requires; it is that many judicial decisions are made under conditions of uncertainty, precluding quantification of the relevant variables. Thus the very term "decision under uncertainty" is misleading, because the methods that decision theorists use generally require assigning probabilities. When that cannot be done we have "uncertainty" in the sense in which statisticians distinguish "uncertainty" from "risk," and then the use of algorithmic methods of decision making becomes impossible, or desperately difficult.[38] I use Bayes's theorem to dramatize the importance of preconceptions in judicial decision making, not to offer judges the key to making objectively correct decisions.

Even though judges' decision-making methods are often and inevitably opaque because they involve telescoped rather than step-by-step thinking, it might be possible to declare the methods good or bad if it could be determined how often they misfire. Particular decisions, findings, and so forth can sometimes be adjudged right or wrong with a fair degree of confidence. But computing an overall judicial error rate, correlating judicial errors with particular methods of judicial decision making, and determining whether the error rate is "too high" (compared to what?) and would be lower if algorithmic decision making (with all its limitations) were substituted for intuitive decision making are impossible in the present state of our knowledge. Unsound methods of making

---

Fundamental Heuristic for Decision Making," in *Emerging Perspectives on Judgment and Decision Research* 125, 144–149 (Sandra L. Schneider and James Shanteau eds. 2003).

38. See, for example, Richard A. Posner, *Catastrophe: Risk and Response,* ch. 3 (2004); Martin L. Weitzman, "Structural Uncertainty and the Value of Statistical Life in the Economics of Catastrophic Climate Change" (Harvard University, Department of Economics, Oct. 31, 2007). A good way to think about the distinction is in terms of insurance. To be able to compute an insurance premium, an insurance company has to be able to make a quantitative estimate of the risk that the loss to be insured against will occur. When the risk is unknown, insurance against it is a form of gambling because the premium that would compensate an insurer for bearing the risk cannot be computed.

decisions will be abandoned if they are known to lead to bad decisions. But if the goodness or badness of a decision cannot be determined, there will be no pressure to change the existing methods.[39]

So judicial intuitionism is here to stay for the foreseeable future, and for the further reason that it is compelled by the institutional structure of adjudication. Judges cast a great many votes in the course of a year and do not have time to engage in elaborate analytical procedures before each vote is cast, or afterward for that matter. Typically, appellate judges read the briefs in advance of oral argument; discuss the case with their law clerks, also in advance; listen to the argument; and afterward, usually right afterward, discuss the case briefly with their colleagues and take a vote that is tentative but usually turns out to be final. At every stage the judge's reasoning process is primarily intuitive. Given the constraints of time, it could not be otherwise; for intuition is a great economizer on conscious attention.[40]

The role of the unconscious in judicial decision making is obscured by the convention that requires a judge to explain his decision in an opinion. The judicial opinion can best be understood as an attempt to explain how the decision, even if (as is most likely) arrived at on the basis of intuition, could have been arrived at on the basis of logical, step-by-step reasoning.[41] That is a check on the errors to which intuitive reasoning is prone because of its compressed, inarticulate character; hence the value of a judge's having a suite of emotions that does not cut him off from considering challenges to his intuitive take on a case. Beware the happy or the angry judge!

It is an imperfect check, however, because the vote on how the case shall be decided precedes the opinion; and though it might be otherwise, most judges do not treat a vote, though nominally tentative, as a hypothesis to be tested by the further research conducted at the opinion-writing stage. That research is mainly a search for supporting arguments and evi-

39. J. Frank Yates, Elizabeth S. Veinott, and Andrea L. Patalano, "Hard Decisions, Bad Decisions: On Decision Quality and Decision Aiding," in *Emerging Perspectives on Judgment and Decision Research* 13 (Sandra L. Schneider and James Shanteau eds. 2003).

40. Hogarth, note 30 above, at 138. My discussion is focused on appellate judges, but trial judges of course are under comparable—indeed greater—time pressure to make rulings and findings and decide their cases.

41. Another way to put this is that intuition belongs to the logic of discovery rather than to that of justification. See Kenneth S. Bowers et al., "Intuition in the Context of Discovery," 22 *Cognitive Psychology* 72 (1990).

dence. Justificatory rather than exploratory, it is distorted by confirmation bias—the well-documented tendency, once one has made up one's mind, to search harder for evidence that confirms rather than contradicts one's initial judgment.[42] But since it is a public document, it can be scrutinized for conformity to the norms of the judicial process, and in particular for the degree to which it gives legalism its due.

That is something, but it is not everything, because the law is not exhausted in legalism. The published opinion often conceals the true reasons for a judicial decision by leaving them buried in the judicial unconscious. Had the intuitive judgment that underlies the decision been different, perhaps an equally plausible opinion in support of it could have been written. If so, the reasoning in the opinion is not the real cause of the decision, but a rationalization. This is not to denigrate the social value of published opinions but merely to indicate their limitations. They not only aid in catching the errors that are inevitable in intuitive reasoning about complex issues; they not only flag, if only by omission, any gap between the outcome and the capacity of a legalist analysis to generate it; they also facilitate the consistent decision of future cases. The first decision in a line of cases may be the product of inarticulable emotion or hunch. But once it is given articulate form, that form will take on a life of its own—a valuable life that may include binding the author and the other judges of his court (along with lower-court judges) and thus imparting needed stability to law through the doctrine of precedent, though a death grip if judges ignore changed circumstances that make a decision no longer a sound guide. Opinions create, extend, and fine-tune rules; they are supplements to constitutional and other legislative rules.

The opinion provides a rare opportunity, moreover, for judges to make creative use of decision theory, one element of which is recognition of option value. An option is a method of postponing a decision; to buy an option on the purchase of a house that must be exercised within 30 days is to delay by that length of time having to decide whether to buy the house. To write a narrow opinion because one is uncertain about the implications of one's decision is to acquire an option to decide in some future case how broadly or narrowly to interpret the decision.

42. See, for example, Ziva Kunda, "The Case for Motivated Reasoning," 108 *Psychological Bulletin* 480 (1990); Frank B. Cross and Stefanie A. Lindquist, "The Scientific Study of Judicial Activism," 91 *Minnesota Law Review* 1752, 1767–1768 (2007).

The role of intuition in judicial decision making was one of the scandals of legal realism, as in the article by Judge Joseph Hutcheson from which I quoted in the introduction. One interpretation of legal realism is that it is the recognition of the "thinness of the law's propositional content—the inability of the linguistic meanings within the law to tell judges what to do in future cases."[43] In other words, the realists saw through the exaggerated pretensions of legalism. Another interpretation is that judges in a case law system such as ours have a repertoire of interpretive methods that enables them to skirt in many cases the apparent dictates of legal doctrine, including clear statements in statutes and precedents.[44] Judges do not ignore legal doctrine, but they are not straitjacketed by it.

Two things fatally undermined legal realism in the eyes of the professional legal community and later killed off critical legal studies, legal realism's radical grandchild. The first was that the realists exaggerated the open area, sometimes implying that all cases are indeterminate. The second was that the noisier realists imputed willfulness, whether in the form of politics or prejudice or sheer orneriness, to judges. This was not only resented but implausible, because willful judging is such a clear-cut violation of the rules of the judicial game. It is more plausible that judges, like other people who have to make decisions under uncertainty, act in good faith but rely heavily on intuition, and also on emotion both as shaping intuition and as an independent influence on decision making. As a result, judges are not fully conscious of the beliefs that determine their judicial votes. But Jerome Frank's suggestion that judges needed psychotherapy to discipline their intuitions was hardly welcomed by judges and their backers in the professional legal community, even though it implicitly acquitted the judges of conscious bad faith.

Law is a methodologically conservative profession, and "bad boy" rhetoric such as Frank's advocacy of psychotherapy for judges or Fred

43. Michael Steven Green, "Legal Realism as Theory of Law," 46 *William and Mary Law Review* 1915, 1978 (2005).

44. Brian Leiter, *Naturalizing Jurisprudence: Essays on American Legal Realism and Naturalism in Legal Philosophy,* ch. 1 (2007). For a sense of the variety of legal realism, see the anthology *American Legal Realism* (William W. Fisher III, Morton J. Horwitz, and Thomas A. Reed eds. 1993). For an interesting recent attempt to cast legal realism in a constructive, as distinct from the more common oppositional, role, see Hanoch Dagan, "The Realist Conception of Law," 57 *University of Toronto Law Journal* 607 (2007).

Rodell's proposal that the practice of law be made a crime and courts be replaced with administrative agencies including a "Killing Commission to apply its laws about what are now called murder and manslaughter,"[45] like the antics of the "crits," ensured that these scholars would not receive a fair hearing. That the only avowed legal realist to become a Supreme Court Justice—William O. Douglas—flouted perfectly sensible norms of judging[46] also helped to give realism a bad name.

A subtler rhetorical mistake of legal realism was Hutcheson's equating intuition to "hunch." A hunch sounds like a guess, a shot in the dark, and there is that element in judging. But "hunch" is a misleading as well as a belittling description of interpretation and appellate review. Both are areas where intuition reigns, but not in the form of guesswork. Interpretation is an innate, universal, and quintessentially intuitive human faculty. It is field-specific, in the sense that one's being good at interpreting, say, faces or pictures or modern poetry does not guarantee success at interpreting contracts or statutes. It is not a rule-bound activity, and the reason a judge is likely to be a better interpreter of a statute than of a poem, and a literary critic a better interpreter of a poem than of a statute, is that experience creates a repository of buried knowledge on which intuition can draw when one is faced with a new interpretandum. The "canons" of statutory interpretation belong to the ex post rationalizing function of the judicial opinion.

Appellate review is likewise intuitive, though judges pretend otherwise. Opinions recite a variety of standards of review—plenary, clearly erroneous, substantial evidence, some evidence, a modicum of evidence, reasonableness, arbitrary and capricious, abuse of discretion, *Chevron*,

---

45. Fred Rodell, *Woe unto You, Lawyers!* 176, 182 (1939). The book was reissued in 1957 with a new preface, in which Rodell said that he stood by everything he had said in it.

46. Here is a sampling of criticisms of Douglas—none by conservatives. "His [Douglas's] opinions were not models; they appear to be hastily written; and they are easy to ignore." L. A. Powe, Jr., "Justice Douglas after Fifty Years: The First Amendment, McCarthyism and Rights," 6 *Constitutional Commentary* 267, 269 (1989). The carelessness of Douglas's opinions was rooted in his "indifference to the texture of legal analysis, which arises from an exclusively political conception of the judicial role." Yosal Rogat, "Mr. Justice Pangloss," *New York Review of Books,* Oct. 22, 1964, p. 5. "Douglas was the foremost anti-judge of his time." G. Edward White, "The Anti-Judge: William O. Douglas and the Ambiguities of Individuality," 74 *Virginia Law Review* 17, 80 (1988). Douglas "refus[ed] to judge in tax cases." Bernard Wolfman, Jonathan L. F. Silver, and Marjorie A. Silver, "The Behavior of Justice Douglas in Federal Tax Cases," 122 *University of Pennsylvania Law Review* 235, 330 (1973).

Skidmore, and so forth—but the gradations of deference that these distinctions mark are finer than judges want, can discern, or need.[47] The only distinction the judicial intellect actually makes is between deferential and nondeferential review. Deferential review implies that the opposite ruling by the lower court probably would also have been upheld, and thus is inappropriate for reviewing a ruling on a question of law (for example, whether contributory or comparative negligence should be the standard for determining the effect of a victim's negligence on a negligent injurer's tort liability), as that would make the law vary according to which trial judge one happened to be before. But other rulings, such as deciding whether the plaintiff in a particular case was negligent, can vary among judges without unsettling the law. So those rulings are not reversed unless the appellate court is pretty confident that they are wrong, and that confidence—and hence how searching appellate review will be—will vary with the court's assessment of its own competence relative to that of the lower court or agency that made the ruling.[48] If, as in the case of a scheduling decision, there really is no standard for evaluating the correctness of a ruling, or if the ruling resolved a highly technical issue that is the bread and butter of the agency that made it, the appellate court will be strongly inclined to defer, swallowing any doubts it might have.

So what is involved in appellate review is, at bottom, simply confidence or lack thereof in another person's decision. That is an intuitive response informed by experience with similar decisions. It is not rule- or even standard-driven, except in the clearest cases, but it is not mindless guesswork either.

Emphasis on the role of the unconscious in judicial decision making exposes the efforts to eliminate or compress judicial discretion by means of comprehensive theories as quixotic. In a study of *Lochner*-era jurisprudence we read that "the Justices were by and large motivated by a principled commitment to the application of a constitutional ideology of state neutrality" as opposed to "basing decisions on a blind adherence to laissez-faire or on a desire to see members of their class win specific lawsuits or on an interest in imposing their idiosyncratic policy preferences

47. See, for example, William N. Eskridge, Jr., and Lauren E. Baer, "The Supreme Court's Deference Continuum: An Empirical Analysis (from *Chevron* to *Hamdan*)" (forthcoming in *Georgetown Law Journal*).
48. Id.

on the country."[49] If those are the choices, then "a principled commitment to the application of a constitutional ideology of state neutrality" is indeed attractive, even though it is a political ideology unanchored in the text of the Constitution. But if unconscious forces, perhaps heavily salted with class bias, are likely to be the motivation for the "principled commitment," and if the alternative is not willful judging but an honest if unself-conscious and not entirely successful effort to play the judicial game by its rules, "principled commitment" begins to lose its luster, perhaps even its meaning, and the "constitutional ideology of state neutrality" begins to seem like a rationalization for small-government conservatism.

Notice how the approach that I have just been sketching inverts the normative evaluation of the unconscious offered by Adorno, Allport, and Frank, all of whom thought it a malign influence on people's behavior, necessitating psychiatric therapy. But we must not go to the opposite extreme and suppose intuition always a reliable guide to sound decision making, ignoring the value of algorithmic techniques in pushing a decision maker to bring to the conscious level and integrate the full range of factors relevant to a sound decision.[50] Judges already have, however, if not formal algorithms designed to prevent blindsiding, at least crude surrogates in the form of the adversary process and the right of dissent.[51] The lawyer on each side of a case has a strong incentive to bring to the court's attention any consideration that favors his side—and likewise a dissentient judge.

The danger of blindsiding remains, however, and is an argument for a

---

49. Howard Gillman, *The Constitution Besieged: The Rise and Demise of Lochner Era Police Powers Jurisprudence* 199 (1993).

50. See, for example, Dawn Lamond and Carl Thompson, "Intuition and Analysis in Decision Making and Choice," 32 *Journal of Nursing Scholarship* 411 (2000); Willard Zangwill and Michael Lowenthal, "Decision Breakthrough Technology" (University of Chicago, Graduate School of Business, May 2006). Lamond and Thompson, above, at 413, explain that "for ill-structured tasks, with a large number of cues and very little time, intuition is the most appropriate cognitive mode to use. In well-structured tasks, with few cues and a lot of time, then analysis is the favoured cognitive mode. However, most tasks are a mixture of ill and well structured."

51. Cf. Paul Woodruff, "Paideia and Good Judgment," in *The Proceedings of the Twentieth World Congress of Philosophy* 63, 73 (David M. Steiner ed. 1999), noting that "the best defense against error is to give full play to opposing arguments and to sift them carefully for potential defeaters of the conclusion you are inclined to accept. A person of good judgment . . . should be capable of constructing arguments on both sides of an issue."

diverse judiciary. The broader the range of experiences found in an appellate panel, the less likely it is that relevant considerations will be overlooked. Conversely, the more homogeneous the judiciary, the more likely it is that the judges' intuitions will coincide. That will impart stability to the law, at the price of epistemic weakness, as the judges' intuitions will rest on a narrower base of unconscious knowledge. Yet disagreement in even a heterogeneous judiciary will usually be kept within tolerable bounds by a combination of voting and hierarchy: majority vote decides cases at each level, with majority vote at the highest level controlling the lower levels. Unlike intellectual diversity, hierarchy is not an epistemic merit; it is the opposite. Voting and superiors' orders are ways of overcoming disagreement, not dispelling it by reasoning to an agreed-upon conclusion. With voting, a minority does not have to be convinced that it is wrong, but only that it is indeed a minority. The rather rigid structure of the judiciary, with its reliance on votes and seniority, presupposes persistent disagreement that is unresolvable by "rational" means such as logical demonstration or experimentation—and so presupposes the inadequacy of legalism.

The kind of telescoped reasoning that I have been discussing is called by Dan Kahan and Donald Braman "cultural cognition." They point out that "cultural commitments are prior to factual beliefs on highly charged political issues . . . Based on a variety of overlapping psychological mechanisms, individuals accept or reject empirical claims about the consequences of controversial policies based on their vision of a good society."[52] These mechanisms (political preconceptions by a different name) are powerful in the case of educated people such as judges only when empirical claims cannot be verified or falsified by objective data. But the empirical claims made in judicial proceedings—for example, claims concerning the deterrent effect of capital punishment or the risk to national security of allowing suspected terrorists to obtain habeas corpus—often are unverified. So judges fall back on their intuitions, because the empirical challenges to their intuitions do not have the force required to dislodge those intuitions.

Cultural cognition includes common sense, which resembles intuition. Common sense is what "everyone knows" without having to think

---

52. Dan M. Kahan and Donald Braman, "Cultural Cognition and Public Policy," 24 *Yale Law and Policy Review* 149, 150 (2006). See also Douglas and Wildavsky, note 7 above.

hard about a subject. So it is elliptical, like intuition.[53] And it is culturally specific. But within a culture it is a valid though flawed source of knowledge. It operates in judicial decision making as a set of policy judgments that everyone agrees on and so are not thought political at all. A lawyer's position in a case in the open area that violates common sense is a strong candidate for rejection. The doctrine that a literal reading of a statute is to be rejected when it would lead to an absurd result illustrates the use of common sense as a judicial technique.

Appeals to common sense are a familiar rhetorical technique, which should remind us that "rhetoric" has a meaning other than windy oratory. In Aristotle's conception, rhetoric is the set of rational methods used to persuade in situations in which the techniques of logic and other methods of exact inquiry are unusable. Cases in the open area present such situations, and the methods to which lawyers and judges resort in such cases are rhetorical in Aristotle's sense; they do not define a distinctive method of legal reasoning that can make a plausible claim to intellectual rigor.

Another cousin of intuition and another major factor in judicial decisions in the open area is "good judgment," an elusive faculty best understood as a compound of empathy, modesty, maturity, a sense of proportion, balance, a recognition of human limitations, sanity, prudence, a sense of reality, and common sense.[54] It is different, despite my reference to maturity, from experience, because some highly experienced people have poor judgment and some young and inexperienced people have excellent judgment. It is another of the means that people have for maneuvering in situations of uncertainty. If law were logical, "good judgment" would not be an admired quality in judges—as it is even by legalists. Not that good judgment is a guarantor of good decisions, any more than intuition, common sense, or emotion (including righteous indignation) is. As much as any human being, a judge is merely "a choosing organism of limited knowledge and ability."[55]

Let me bring this chapter to a close by adverting briefly to its implica-

53. Charles Antaki, "Commonsense Reasoning: Arriving at Conclusions or Traveling towards Them?" in *The Status of Common Sense in Psychology* 169 (Jürg Siegfried ed. 1994).

54. See Michael Boudin, "Common Sense in Law Practice (or, Was John Brown a Man of Sound Judgment?)," 34 *Harvard Law School Bulletin*, Spring 1983, p. 22.

55. Herbert A. Simon, "A Behavioral Model of Rational Choice," 69 *Quarterly Journal of Economics* 99, 114 (1955).

tions for the training of judges and the practice of law. Apart from brief orientation sessions and occasional continuing legal education seminars, judges in our system are not actually "trained," which is an interesting commentary on the methodological rigor, or rather the lack thereof, of judging. Judicial "training" is learning by doing—a further clue to the largely tacit character of judicial reasoning.

There are occasional proposals to subject judges to formal training of one kind or another. Jerome Frank's proposal that judges undergo psychoanalysis, as he had done, was of that character, though ridiculous. Apart from the time and expense involved, there is no basis for the claim that psychoanalysis has nontherapeutic value—for example, that it can improve the judgment of a normal person. But Frank's underlying emphasis on the psychological dimension of judging was not ridiculous. As Frederick Schauer explains, Frank's version of legal realism can be understood as "an attempt to lessen the distance, descriptively and prescriptively, between how a judge as a human being and that same human being clothed in judicial robes would resolve a controversy."[56]

Dan Simon suggests, more sensibly than Frank, applying techniques of debiasing to judges.[57] But they sound a little ominous, like brainwashing, and would be strongly resisted by judges. Here is a simpler suggestion, directed at the trial and appellate bar: since judges in our system are legislators as well as adjudicators, lawyers should make a greater effort to present facts to judges—not so much the facts of the case, the adjudicative facts, which most lawyers do emphasize, but rather the background or general facts that influence a legislative decision ("legislative facts," in the conventional and in this instance useful terminology). I have pointed to life experiences as a factor shaping judicial choices in what I call the open area. Those experiences include encounters with large, brute facts. Who would deny the impact on judicial thinking of such unignorable facts as the civil rights and women's movements, the ignominious collapse of communism, the spread of free markets, deregulation and privatization, the increased menace of terrorism, and the emergence of homosexuals from the closet and the resulting discovery

---

56. Frederick Schauer, "The Limited Domain of the Law," 90 *Virginia Law Review* 1909, 1923 (2004). See also Andrew S. Watson, "Some Psychological Aspects of the Trial Judge's Decision-Making," 39 *Mercer Law Review* 937 (1988).

57. Dan Simon, "A Psychological Model of Judicial Decision Making," 30 *Rutgers Law Journal* 1, 138–140 (1998).

that they are really quite like other people? More attention to legislative facts, such as what economists have learned about competition and labor markets and what criminologists have learned about criminal behavior and punishment, would influence judicial decisions for the good. Rather than beating appellate judges over the head with cases, which is the standard technique of appellate advocacy, appellate lawyers would be more effective if, recognizing the essentially legislative character of much appellate adjudication and the essentially pragmatic disposition of most American judges, they emphasized instead the practical stakes in their cases and how the stakes would be affected by the court's deciding those cases one way rather than another.[58]

We need not worry that such background facts are bound to be pallid compared to the equities of the individual case, so that the nonlegalist judge will find himself rendering shortsighted justice. One value of a system of precedent is that it invites judges to think about the impact of their decisions on future litigants. (Notice that by doing this it fosters pragmatic thinking by directing judges' attention to the consequences of their decisions.) Moreover, most judges are (surprisingly to nonjudges) unmoved by the equities of the individual case, as most legal realists, other than Jerome Frank, realized.[59] Of course there are exceptions; Justices Douglas and Blackmun come first to mind. And perhaps few judges are fully inoculated against the siren song of an emotionally compelling case. Nevertheless, as Hamlet said, "The hand of little employment hath the daintier sense."[60] Just as doctors tend to be callous about sick people, judges tend to be callous about pathetic litigants because they have seen so many of them. This is true of liberal as well as conservative judges, because setting aside one's natural sympathies is a big part of playing the judicial game. Judges really do internalize the slogan "Hard cases make bad law," and they do not want to make bad law.

Jerome Frank pronounced Oliver Wendell Holmes the "completely adult jurist."[61] He meant by this that Holmes recognized, as the Justice himself put it, that "certitude is not the test of certainty."[62] This

58. See, for example, Matthew A. Edwards, "Posner's Pragmatism and *Payton* Home Arrests," 77 *Washington Law Review* 299 (2002), or any issue of the *Journal of Empirical Legal Studies*.

59. Leiter, note 44 above, at 21–30.

60. William Shakespeare, *Hamlet*, act 5, sc. 1, l. 66.

61. Jerome Frank, *Law and the Modern Mind* 270–277 (1930).

62. Oliver Wendell Holmes, "Natural Law," 32 *Harvard Law Review* 40 (1918).

was his famous detachment, thought callous by his detractors. He may have been callous. Indifference, lack of passion or even of empathy, may be positively correlated with detachment. But the relevant personality trait of Holmes may be different. I conjecture that Holmes—surprisingly given his distinguished lineage, his professional success, his commanding presence, and his wartime prowess—did not take himself very seriously. He was a wit, and wit implies a sense of incongruity, including the incongruity between one's pretensions and one's achievements. If you do not take yourself very seriously you are unlikely to fool yourself into thinking that you have all the answers. A judge who, like Holmes, does not think he has all the answers is less likely to challenge the decisions of the other branches of government than a know-it-all judge. Frank, writing at a time when the Supreme Court was quick to invalidate just the kind of social legislation that he favored, wanted judges to be more deferential, more modest he thought, more adult, but I am content to say more self-aware. He probably was right to sense that overweening confidence in the correctness of one's beliefs (as in the phrase "often in error, never in doubt") goes along with the embrace of a thoroughgoing legalism, and that such a joinder is most attractive to an authoritarian personality. But overconfidence is an occupational risk of all judges, because one doesn't have to be an authoritarian to derive utility from believing that one is right; it is a general human trait.[63] Overconfidence is related to the possession of preconceptions, which, especially when unconscious, generate a sense of rightness even when the evidence gathered in inquiry is weak, and a tendency to interpret the evidence as confirming the inquirer's priors.[64]

Greater recognition of the role of the personal, the emotional, and the intuitive in judicial decisions would not weaken the force of these factors in judicial decision making, because there are no adequate alternatives and judges have to decide their cases with the tools at hand. But I disagree with Scott Altman that introspection would make judges feel free to vote their prejudices because they would no longer think them-

63. Kfir Eliaz and Andrew Schotter, "Experimental Testing of Intrinsic Preferences for Noninstrumental Information," 97 *American Economic Review Papers and Proceedings* 166 (May 2007). On the egocentric biases of judges, see Guthrie, Rachlinski, and Wistrich, note 11 above.

64. See, for example, Charles G. Lord, Lee Ross, and Mark R. Lepper, "Biased Assimilation and Attitude Polarization: The Effects of Prior Theories on Subsequently Considered Evidence," 37 *Journal of Personality and Social Psychology* 2098 (1979).

selves penned in by "the law."[65] They would keep on playing the judicial game as they have always done. A few might become more hesitant to impose their views on the community in the name of law, realizing the tenuous foundations of some of those views. But only a few. For one cannot preach introspection with much success. Nor is introspection the same thing as self-knowledge. We use introspection to acquit ourselves of accusations of bias, while using realistic notions of human behavior to identify bias in others.[66] We are predisposed to an exaggerated confidence in the soundness and coherence of our beliefs even when we cannot defend them.[67] To paraphrase the criticism of King Lear by one of his bad daughters, most judges have ever but slenderly known themselves.[68] That is unlikely to change.

65. Scott Altman, "Beyond Candor," 89 *Michigan Law Review* 296 (1990). The issue of introspection is related to the much-debated issue of whether judges should be candid with their public. See Micah Schwartzman, "The Principle of Judicial Sincerity" (University of Virginia Law School Public Law and Legal Theory Working Paper Series, Paper No. 69, 2007), http://law.bepress.com/uvalwps/uva_publiclaw/art69 (visited June 25, 2007), and references therein. If judges are not introspective, their candor will not illuminate the actual springs of their decisions.

66. Joyce Ehrlinger, Thomas Gilovich, and Lee Ross, "Peering into the Bias Blind Spot: People's Assessments of Bias in Themselves and Others," 31 *Personality and Social Psychology Bulletin* 680 (2005). See also Emily Pronin, Jonah Berger, and Sarah Malouki, "Alone in a Crowd of Sheep: Asymmetric Perceptions of Conformity and Their Roots in an Introspection Illusion," 92 *Journal of Personality and Social Psychology* 585 (2007).

67. That is the theme of Dan Simon's article, note 57 above.

68. William Shakespeare, *King Lear,* act 1, sc. 1, ll. 295–296.

II

The Model Elaborated

5

The Judicial Environment:
External Constraints on Judging

I have argued that even judges who have more or less complete freedom to decide a case any way they want are constrained by concerns for their reputation among people whom they respect but even more by their having internalized the norms and usages of the judicial "game." We might think of these as "internal" constraints on judicial willfulness or errancy. But even in our legal system there are external constraints as well, though fewer than in most other legal systems. The external constraints are the subject of this and the next chapter.

The felt need for such constraints is illuminated by the economic concept of "agency costs," which is fundamental to understanding labor markets, including the judicial labor market. A principal hires an agent to do a job that the principal could not do as well or as cheaply himself. The principal wants the agent to do the best possible job at the lowest possible cost. In other words, he wants the agent's incentives to coincide with his own. But the agent is a self-interested person, just like the principal. Unless the principal can accurately evaluate the agent's performance and adjust his compensation accordingly, and if need be fire him for underperforming, the agent is unlikely to be perfectly faithful.

When the principal is the government and the agent a judge employed by it, the problem of agency costs is acute because the government lacks the usual levers by which to procure an agent's fidelity to the principal's interests. Judicial performance is difficult to evaluate, and trying to proportion compensation to it would undermine the independence of the judiciary (for who would be making the evaluations, and what criteria would they use?), which as we know is a valuable social asset. The judge must be guaranteed unusually strong job security.

A related question is who a federal judge's principal is, or indeed whether there is one in a meaningful sense. Is it the judges of a higher court—but then who are the principals of the judges of the highest court? If the principals are not other judges, are they the members of Congress? The President who appointed the judges? The current President? The American people? The framers of the Constitution? The Constitution itself, or statutes and precedents? But can documents be principals? "The law"?

Whatever the answers, no society leaves its judges completely at large. But there are major differences in the external constraints imposed in different judicial systems, and we can expect judicial behavior to differ across judicial systems accordingly, and also within systems that impose different constraints on different classes of judge. We can also expect the criteria of judicial performance to vary with the constraints on judicial behavior. In some judicial systems a judge's reversal rate might be a critical performance criterion, while in another more weight might be placed on how often a judge's opinions are cited by other courts or even on the political acumen exhibited by the judge in his opinions.

But though correlated, judicial discretion and agency costs are not identical. The studies that find that the political party of the appointing President is a good predictor of a judge's votes are consistent with the judge's being a faithful agent of the President who appointed him and even, to the extent that political preferences are legitimate factors in adjudication, with his being a faithful agent of "the law." The problem of judicial agency costs arises only when the looseness of the principal's control over the judge enables the latter to base his decisions on a preference that is too personal, too idiosyncratic, to be acceptable.

Similarly, the fact that judicial decisions are sometimes influenced by the race, religion, gender, or other personal characteristics of the judge need not be a consequence of disloyalty. It may just reflect the fact that people of different backgrounds bring different priors to their resolution of factual issues and have different policy preferences. Agency costs are triggered not only by disloyalty but also, and perhaps especially in the case of American judges, by uncertainty. When the agents are judges and the principal is the United States, the agents have trouble figuring out what their principal wants them to do.

The problem of agency costs is acute in many other domains besides judging, and employers' responses involve a mixture of inducing and enhancing internal constraints and imposing external ones. Take medicine. Because patients have difficulty evaluating medical services, a variety of mechanisms have evolved for nevertheless constraining doctors to be loyal and competent agents of their patients. These mechanisms include ethical rules (such as the Hippocratic oath), board certification, malpractice liability, monitoring by liability insurers, limits on sharing fees, and, of particular interest, the excessively demanding character of medical training, which has aspects of hazing. The training is an effective filter, screening out of the medical profession persons who may have the skills to be good doctors but lack the passion for becoming a doctor that is required to overcome the hardships of the training. Apart from its effect as a filter, arduous training builds commitment to the institution; an external constraint creates an internal one (a standard objective of hazing—think of Marine training or even fraternity hazing). Legal education has similar but, especially with the decline in professorial bullying and the abandonment of public ranking of students by grades, much weaker effects. The filtration at the judicial appointment stage is particularly weak, though it has grown stronger as the process of appointment and confirmation has become increasingly arduous as a result of increased paperwork requirements and more frequent confirmation battles.

I want to consider how judges are likely to respond to several familiar packages of external constraints. I begin with private judges (that is, arbitrators) and continue with judges in career judiciaries such as one finds in most countries other than those whose legal systems derive ultimately from England; elected judges, as one finds in most state courts in the United States; and federal trial judges, federal intermediate appellate judges, and finally U.S. Supreme Court Justices. In the next chapter I consider the likely effects of altering the judicial environment of federal judges by imposing term limits or raising salaries.

Arbitrators are selected by or with the consent of the litigants. An arbitrator who gets a reputation for favoring one side in a class of cases—such as cases of employment termination, or disputes between investors and brokers or between management and unions—will be unacceptable to one of the parties in any future such dispute, and so the demand for his services will wither. We can therefore expect arbitrators to tend to "split the difference" in their awards—that is, to try to give each side a partial victory (and therefore a partial defeat).[1] For this makes it difficult for parties on either side to infer a pattern of favoritism. Risk-averse disputants like the split-the-difference approach because it truncates both the upside and the downside risks of the dispute-resolution process and thus helps to differentiate arbitration from adjudication. Differentiation is essential to the demand for arbitration as an alternative to adjudication because adjudication is subsidized by the government and arbitration is not; the arbitrators' fees, expenses, and facilities must be paid for by the disputants. The public subsidy of the courts places arbitrators at a cost disadvantage. One way to overcome it is to offer a service unavailable from the courts, and split-the-difference decision making is such a service.

Arbitration may seem to offer something else attractive to risk-averse disputants: a lower error rate than trial by jury. Arbitrators, when they are not lawyers, are businesspeople who have experience relevant to the case at hand. And arbitrators who get a reputation for making mistakes will find it hard to get selected for future cases. This is not because disputants care about the competence of the dispute resolver as such but because the disputant with the stronger case will always veto the selection of an incompetent arbitrator, since an incompetent arbitrator is more likely than a competent one to rule for the party with the weaker case.

The arbitrator's accuracy advantage is at least partially offset, however, by the fact that arbitration awards are not appealable. The reasons are to reduce the cost of arbitration and thus the cost advantage of the courts, and to accelerate the final resolution of the dispute and thus create another advantage of arbitration over judicial dispute resolution. Arbitration awards can, however, be challenged in court, albeit on narrow grounds. This is another reason to think arbitrators more accurate than

1. "Courts and juries are viewed as more likely to adhere to the law and less likely than arbitrators to 'split the difference' between the two sides, thereby lowering damages awards for plaintiffs." Armendariz v. Found. Health Psychcare Services, Inc., 6 P.3d 669, 693 (Cal. 2000). See Donald Wittman, "Lay Juries, Professional Arbitrators, and the Arbitrator Selection Hypothesis," 5 *American Law and Economics Review* 61, 81 (2003); Estelle D. Franklin, "Maneuvering through the Labyrinth: The Employers' Paradox in Responding to Hostile Environment Sexual Harassment—A Proposed Way Out," 67 *Fordham Law Review* 1517, 1565 (1999); Robert Haig, "Corporate Counsel's Guide: Legal Development Report on Cost-Effective Management of Corporate Litigation," in *Federal Pretrial Practice, Procedure and Strategy,* 610 *PLI/Lit* 177, 186–187 (PLI [Practicing Law Institute] Litigation and Administrative Practice Course Handbook Series No. 610, 1999).

judges or jurors. Arbitrators whose awards are repeatedly vacated by the courts will lose business because judicial invalidation of an award creates added delay, uncertainty, and expense for the parties, who, remember, bear the entire cost of arbitration. Besides the absence of the normal right of appeal, the accuracy of arbitration is compromised by the fact that arbitrators usually do not write an opinion and so arbitration lacks that check on the errors to which intuitive decision making can be prone. Because the net accuracy advantage of arbitration over adjudication is unclear and may indeed be nonexistent,[2] I am inclined to stress the split-the-difference character of arbitration in explaining the attractiveness of this adjudication substitute, as well as in elucidating the behavioral effects of privatizing judging.

At the opposite end of what might be called the spectrum of judicial professionalism from arbitration are the career judiciaries found in almost all countries whose legal systems do not have an English origin. As the term "career judiciary" implies, they are systems manned by lawyers who make an entire career of being a judge.[3] In contrast, most Anglo-American judges become judges only after a career in another branch of the legal profession. The average age of appointment to the federal district court has, since Harry Truman's Presidency, varied from 49 to 53, and to the circuit court from 50 to 56.[4] Obviously a lawyer first appointed to a judgeship in his 40s or 50s is embarking on a second career.

Unlike our lateral-entry, second-career judiciary, a career judiciary is a part of a nation's civil service. Appointment and promotion are by merit. Promotion is a critical feature of a career judiciary because a fresh law school graduate will naturally occupy the lowest rung of the judicial ladder and want to progress to more responsible positions as he gains experience. There is so little difference between a career judiciary and other professional civil services that the analysis of judicial behavior in a ca-

2. Theodore Eisenberg and Geoffrey P. Miller, "The Flight from Arbitration: An Empirical Study of Ex Ante Arbitration Clauses in the Contracts of Publicly Held Companies," 56 *DePaul Law Review* 335 (2007).

3. See, for example, Martin R. Schneider, "Judicial Career Incentives and Court Performance: An Empirical Study of the German Labour Courts of Appeal," 20 *European Journal of Law and Economics* 127 (2005); Nicholas L. Georgakopoulos, "Discretion in the Career and Recognition Judiciary," 7 *University of Chicago Law School Roundtable* 205, 205–206 (2000); J. Mark Ramseyer and Eric B. Rasmusen, "Judicial Independence in a Civil Law Regime: The Evidence from Japan," 13 *Journal of Law, Economics and Organization* 259 (1997).

4. Albert Yoon, "Love's Labor's Lost? Judicial Tenure among Federal Court Judges: 1945–2000," 91 *California Law Review* 1029, 1047–1048 n. 70 (2003).

reer judiciary should be like that of public bureaucratic behavior in general, which should in turn resemble, though not be identical to, the behavior of employees in a large business firm.

The economic difference between an employee and an entrepreneur, in the sense of an independent businessperson, is that the employee does not sell his output; instead he rents his labor to the employer. The employer tries to value each employee's output in order to make decisions on compensation and retention; but because the output of a firm is a team effort, only rough estimates are possible. That roughness gives rise to agency costs. (Those costs can also be a serious problem when the agent is an independent contractor, rather than an employer, of his principal, as in the doctor-patient setting.) The more costly it is to evaluate an employee's output, the more inclined the employer will be to substitute evaluation of the employee's inputs, such as credentials (as indicative of ability), hours, and care. It is a costly as well as an imperfect substitute, and on both accounts one expects there to be agency costs, for example in the form of shirking. Leisure and avoidance of hard work are common personal objectives, and an employer unable to monitor his employees' performance must gamble that his criteria for hiring have succeeded in distinguishing between applicants who have a work ethic and those who do not.

Because it is much harder to value the output of a public bureaucracy than that of a business firm and therefore to determine the value contributed by an individual bureaucrat, bureaucrats have a greater scope for pursuing their private objectives than employees of business firms have, and so agency costs are likely to be higher. Another difference arises from the ideological character of the missions of many government agencies, in contrast to the business firm's single goal of profit maximization. The result is that agency costs in a government bureaucracy take the form not only of shirking but also of sabotage in the form of employees' attempting to redefine the agency's mission to coincide with their own ideology or, more commonly, to resist a redefinition of that mission. Many people hold "intense preferences" concerning the role of government in controversial areas, and "professionals seeking employment with the government are often attracted to a particular agency because of its stated mission."[5] Once ensconced in the agency,

5. Ronald N. Johnson and Gary D. Libecap, *The Federal Civil Service System and the Problem of Bureaucracy: The Economics and Politics of Institutional Change* 167–168 (1994). See also John Brehm and Scott Gates, *Working, Shirking and Sabotage: Bureaucratic Response to a Demo-*

they may become powerful opponents of efforts to change the mission. Judges may have the same tendency, given the ideological dimension of adjudication—particularly career judges. Like any civil service, a career judiciary is, to an extent anyway, a self-perpetuating oligarchy, because promotion to the higher ranks in the judiciary will largely be determined by the judges currently occupying those ranks. This will make mission change more difficult than in a judiciary in which there is lateral entry ("fresh blood") at high levels.

Government is not wholly bereft of means for checking judicial agency costs, especially when dealing with a career judiciary. On the input side, credentials are one thing the government can look at in deciding whom to hire as a judge. Grades in law school are a proxy, though an imperfect one, for ability to perform well as a judge, which is one factor in the likelihood of a judge's actually performing well, because people who have shown themselves able to do well at a particular type of work are likely to want to do that work. But note that those who ace tests of the skills important to the legalist dimension of judging may actually subvert legalism. Their skills will enable them to perceive its limitations and circumvent them through imaginative distinguishing of precedents and imaginative interpretation of statutory and constitutional texts.

On the output side, some monitoring of judicial performance is possible. The quality of a judge's performance is reflected, if often only dimly, by such observables as backlog, reversal rate (the monitoring of which limits a judge's ability to minimize his backlog by excessive haste in deciding cases), judicial demeanor, and complaints by litigants and lawyers; we shall consider methods of judicial evaluation later in this chapter. Importantly, in a career judiciary the quality of a judge's rulings is evaluated by his superiors in the judicial bureaucracy as a basis for deciding whether or how fast to promote him. Even when individual performance is difficult to measure, an ordinal ranking may be feasible—it may be obvious that Judge X is better than Judge Y, though how much better, and indeed whether either is good, may be unknowable.

Bureaucracies minimize agency costs by laying down detailed rules for the bureaucrats to follow, since conformity to a rule is easier to verify than whether the bureaucrat is creative, imaginative, energetic, flexible, or forward-looking. Being able to verify compliance with performance

---

cratic Public (1997); Lael R. Kaiser, "The Determinants of Street-Level Bureaucratic Behavior: Gate-Keeping in the Social Security Disability Program" (National Public Management Research Conference, Georgetown University, 2003).

norms is important not only for minimizing agency costs directly but also for enabling promotions to be based on objective criteria, which has an indirect effect on agency costs: judges compete for promotion by trying to please their superiors. It is no accident that legal systems that have career judiciaries and therefore rely on promotion decisions as a management tool tend also to rely on detailed legal codes to guide judges rather than on the looser standards characteristic of common law systems. (I do not know whether codification precedes, follows, or co-evolves with a career judiciary.) A code that sets forth a legal rule with specificity makes it easy to determine whether the judge is applying the rule correctly. And the more precise and detailed the code, the less scope the judge has to indulge his political or other personal preferences. So sabotage is less of a danger, and the injection of politics into the evaluation and promotion of judges is also less likely.

Another device found more in career judiciaries than in a U.S.-style judiciary is specialization, which enables a legal system to have more judges. This enables more of the responsibility for litigation to be shifted to judges from lawyers, because as specialists the judges know (almost) as much as the lawyers. Our generalist judges know less about any given field of law than they would if they were specialists (if they were labor judges, antitrust judges, etc.) and thus more naturally adopt an umpireal role. Specialization preserves variety in the long judicial careers found in career judiciaries (because the judges rotate among the specialized courts) but also facilitates evaluation of judges by their superiors because of each specialist judge's narrower range. Specialization is thus a natural adaptation of a career judiciary.

Emphasis on following rules as the condition for being promoted is a reason to expect a career judiciary to be legalist rather than pragmatic. Another reason is that promotion in a career judiciary, as in any other branch of the civil service, depends ultimately on performing to the satisfaction of one's superiors, and it is difficult to see how the supervisors in a career judiciary would benefit in their own careers from having bold, intellectually challenging, experimentally inclined subordinates. A career judiciary is not like a business firm. There a division head's hard-driving, innovative subordinates may produce increases in revenues and profits that will redound to his credit for having selected and encouraged those subordinates. A junior judge who discovered a new way of minimizing judicial backlogs would be commended, but that would probably be the limit of tolerated nonconformity. Yet no legal code, however detailed, can anticipate and provide for all the cases that arise; and so there is plenty of interest-balancing—which is to say, policy-oriented, legislative-type—adjudication even in civil law systems.[6]

No doubt, as in any large organization, career judiciaries are rife with office politics ("influence activities," as the organizational economists say). It would be naïve to think all promotions based strictly on merit. But office politics is likely to reinforce the inherent tendency toward conformist behavior as judges move up the career ladder.

Because of these factors, the output of a career judiciary can be expected to exhibit low variance, to be of acceptably professional quality, and to be uncreative.[7] One consequence is that law professors in nations that have career judiciaries tend to be regarded not merely as commentators on the law, as in Anglo-American legal systems, but as actual sources of law,[8] the judges being impeded by the structure of their career from playing that role. We should also expect that with judges' legislative role diminished in such systems, legislatures perform the legislative chores that judges perform in a common law system. Indeed, there is a deep incompatibility between common law decision making and a career judiciary. To entrust judges in a career system with common law rulemaking responsibilities would disrupt the system's smooth operation by making the design and implementation of objective promotion

6. James L. Dennis, "Interpretation and Application of the Civil Code and the Evaluation of Judicial Precedent," 54 *Louisiana Law Review* 1, 8–14 (1993). The author is a justice of the Louisiana Supreme Court. Louisiana is the nation's only civil law state.

7. "[The civil law judge] is a kind of expert clerk. He is presented with a fact situation to which a ready legislative response will be readily found in all except the extraordinary case. His function is merely to find the right legislative provision, couple it with the fact situation, and bless the solution that is more or less automatically produced from the union. The whole process of judicial decision is made to follow the formal syllogism of scholastic logic. The major premise is in the statute, the facts of the case furnish the minor premise, and the conclusion inevitably follows." Richard O. Faulk, "Armageddon through Aggregation? The Use and Abuse of Class Actions in International Dispute Resolution," 37 *Tort and Insurance Law Journal* 999, 1011 (2002), quoting John Henry Merryman, *The Civil Law Tradition: An Introduction to the Legal Systems of Western Europe and Latin America* 36 (2d ed. 1985). See also Merryman, "The French Deviation," 44 *American Journal of Comparative Law* 109, 116 (1996); J. Mark Ramseyer, "Not-So-Ordinary Judges in Ordinary Courts: Teaching *Jordan v. Duff & Phelps, Inc.*," 120 *Harvard Law Review* 1199, 1205–1206 (2007); Georgakopoulos, note 3 above, at 212.

8. See, for example, Eugen Ehrlich, *Fundamental Principles of the Sociology of Law* 365 (Walter L. Moll trans. 1936 [1913]). Chapter 12 of Ehrlich's book contains an interesting discussion of the contrast between the common law and civil law systems.

criteria much more difficult. In addition, career judges, living a cloistered professional life, tend to be insufficiently worldly to be effective as
occasional legislators. They know more about their specialized fields,
but what they know is the legal doctrines, not the relation of those doctrines to the activities that the doctrines regulate.

In contrast to the effect of promotion in constraining the behavior of
judges in career judiciaries, promotion (as carrot, denial of promotion as
stick) is of limited significance in an Anglo-American lateral-entry judiciary. Partly because judges in such a system are appointed at a mature
age, partly because there are very few rungs on the judicial ladder in
most Anglo-American judiciaries, and partly because previous judicial
experience is not required for appointment to even the highest rung,
most judges are not promoted at all. In the 1990s, the probability that a
federal district judge would be promoted to the court of appeals was
only 6 percent.[9] And the salary and prestige differences between federal
trial and appellate judges are modest, though the workload generally is
somewhat lighter in the appellate court.

Although all the current Supreme Court Justices were federal circuit
judges previously, there are so few Justices, and they serve for such
a long time, that the percentage of federal court of appeals judges who
become Supreme Court Justices is minuscule. And it is growing ever
smaller, since the number of circuit judges increases with the workload,
while the number of Supreme Court Justices has long been frozen at
nine and turnover on the Court is decreasing because of increased longevity. Furthermore, although merit is not irrelevant to promotion in the
federal court system (even promotion to the Supreme Court,[10] where political criteria dominate), it is not the dominant factor. In particular, unlike the case of a career judiciary, the higher judges do not decide who
among the lower judges shall be promoted. Politicians decide. Politics
thus excludes many judges from having any shot at promotion, while
it grooms others for promotion who lack bright prospects for distinguished service as court of appeals judges. We must look elsewhere than
promotion for the external constraints on the behavior of federal judges.

The elected judiciaries of the states—and all but 12 of the states use

9. Daniel Klerman, "Nonpromotion and Judicial Independence," 72 *Southern California
Law Review* 455, 461 (1999).

10. Lee Epstein et al., "The Role of Qualifications in the Confirmation of Nominees to the
U.S. Supreme Court," 32 *Florida State University Law Review* 1145 (2005).

some form of election to choose all or most of their judges—operate in an environment remote from that of both the U.S. federal judiciary and the career judiciaries of foreign nations. A judge who is elected for only a limited term and therefore must stand for reelection is subject, as a tenured federal judge is not, to a form of performance review. By the same token he has to be more sensitive to public opinion than a judge whose tenure does not depend on the electorate's whim. Only a handful of cases, primarily those involving notorious crimes, will interest a significant portion of the electorate. But in those cases a systematic bias can be expected to creep into the judicial process. Consider a state that has capital punishment. Because only the most egregious murderers are eligible for such punishment, elected judges may lean against the defendants in such cases.[11] They can also be expected to lean more than appointed ones in favor of a litigant who is a resident of the judge's state, if the opposing party is a nonresident.[12]

The judge or judge aspirant in an elected judiciary has also to be able to raise money to conduct his electoral campaign. The donors are mainly lawyers who litigate in the court to which the candidate aspires. If the lawyers on both sides in the principal practice areas—such as lawyers for medical malpractice patients and lawyers for medical malpractice defendants—gave equal amounts of money to a judicial candidate,

11. Herbert M. Kritzer, "Law Is the Mere Continuation of Politics by Different Means: American Judicial Selection in the Twenty-first Century," 56 *DePaul Law Review* 423, 461–464 (2007); Stephen B. Bright and Patrick J. Keenan, "Judges and the Politics of Death: Deciding between the Bill of Rights and the Next Election in Capital Cases," 75 *Boston University Law Review* 759, 792–796 (1995). Consistent with this conjecture, the shorter the average term of judges in a state, the more likely they are to impose the death penalty. Paul R. Brace and Melinda Gann Hall, "The Interplay of Preferences, Case Facts, Context, and Rules in the Politics of Judicial Choice," 59 *Journal of Politics* 1206, 1221, 1223 (1997). In another article, Hall finds that there is not much difference in behavior between elected and appointed state judges, but that the ideological distance between a judicial candidate and the electorate, and an increase in the murder rate while he was a judge, do have the predicted influence on judicial elections, especially partisan judicial elections. "State Supreme Courts in American Democracy: Probing the Myths of Judicial Reform," 95 *American Political Science Review* 315, 325–327 and tabs. 9–11 (2001).

12. For evidence, see Eric Helland and Alexander Tabarrok, "The Effect of Electoral Institutions on Tort Awards," 4 *American Law and Economics Review* 341 (2002); Tabarrok and Helland, "Court Politics: The Political Economy of Tort Awards," 42 *Journal of Law and Economics* 157 (1999). The first-cited article, incidentally, in finding that this effect is not operative in federal diversity cases, provides support for the traditional argument that the diversity jurisdiction protects nonresidents against bias in favor of residents of the state in which the case is litigated.

the situation would be much like that regarding arbitrators: the judge would have an incentive to steer a middle course in his rulings. But the stakes in particular practice areas are often systematically asymmetrical, and in that event an elected judiciary is likely to exhibit a systematic bias.

Sometimes it should. If equality of campaign contributions induced judges to treat both sides of every legal issue equally—labor and management, class action plaintiffs and class action defendants, tort plaintiffs and insurance companies, debtors and debt collectors, and so forth—the balance struck by the law between the opposed groups would not change even if it should. But there is no reason to think that altering the law in the direction indicated by the ratio of campaign contributions pro and con the change would usually be an improvement. For even if an alteration would be efficient in the sense of generating greater benefits than costs, the potential beneficiaries might not be able to raise money to donate to judicial campaigns or otherwise exert political pressure as effectively as the potential losers. They might be a more diffuse group than their opponents and therefore afflicted by more serious free-rider problems. Such disparities in political effectiveness are of course common, as otherwise there would be a great deal more efficient legislation than there is.

But the fact that elected judges are less independent politically than appointed ones, especially appointed judges with lifetime tenure,[13] is not *necessarily* a bad thing. This is not only because of the spur to effort that denial of job security imparts but also because the decisions of elected judges tend to be more predictable than those of appointed ones.[14] This finding is consistent with—maybe even entailed by—the fact that elected judges are less independent. The independent judge is likely to have a more complex decision calculus because he does not want merely to put his finger to the political wind. And as long as the populist element in adjudication does not swell to the point where unpopular though innocent people are convicted of crimes, or other gross

13. Additional evidence of this is presented in Brace and Hall, note 11 above. See also references in F. Andrew Hanssen, "Is There a Politically Optimal Level of Judicial Independence?" 94 *American Economic Review* 712, 717 (2004).

14. F. Andrew Hanssen, "The Effect of Judicial Institutions on Uncertainty and the Rate of Litigation: The Election versus Appointment of State Judges," 28 *Journal of Legal Studies* 205 (1999).

departures from legality occur, conforming judicial policies to democratic preferences can be regarded as a good thing in a society that prides
itself on being the world's leading democracy.

This is just to say that judicial independence is inverse to judicial accountability.[15] If (perhaps a big if) the existence of an elected judiciary is
taken to signify a legitimate democratic preference for aligning judicial
and popular attitudes more closely than is possible in a nonelective system, then a judge who defies public opinion is not only unlikely to be reelected; he is, it can be argued, paradoxically a bad, even a usurpative,
judge. The other side of this coin, however, is that the more uniform
public opinion is, the more important judicial independence is for safe-
guarding minority rights.

A further paradox is that although an elected judiciary is more democratic than an appointive one in the Anglo-American setting, it is not
more democratic than a career judiciary in a legal system that makes
heavy use of detailed legislative codes. The more detailed the code that a
judge interprets and applies, the more likely he is to enforce the code "as
written" rather than using it as merely the starting point for the development of legal standards. The democratic legislature is calling the legal
shots and the judges really are just executing the decisions made by a
democratic process.

One of the worst effects of an elected judiciary, besides the distorting
effect of lawyers' campaign contributions on the evolution of law, is that
it greatly curtails the field of judicial selection. Most people are tempera-
mentally unsuited for electoral politics and in any event not good at it,
though they may have just the suite of abilities required in an excellent
judge. The number of people who have both political and judicial talent
is small. There may even be a degree of incompatibility between the two
kinds of talent, or perhaps the two kinds of personality: judging, especially at the appellate level, is an introvert's profession, politics an extro-
vert's, although the number even of federal judges who held elected office before being appointed to the bench is considerable.[16] Even if there

15. Eric Maskin and Jean Tirole, "The Politician and the Judge: Accountability in Government," 94 *American Economic Review* 2034 (2004); Stephen B. Burbank and Barry Friedman,
"Reconsidering Judicial Independence," in *Judicial Independence at the Crossroads: An Interdisciplinary Approach* 9, 14–16 (Burbank and Friedman eds. 2002).

16. In a large sample of judges, 27 percent of the federal judges and 28 percent of the state
judges had held an elected office; 40 percent and 35 percent, respectively, had held a political
office that was either elected or appointed; and 11 percent and 10 percent, respectively, had

is some incompatibility between political and judicial aptitudes, we cannot be certain that elected judges will on average be less able than appointed ones, because the former have the spur of competition. There is some evidence that appointed judges are abler.[17] But there is contrary evidence in a recent study that finds, after correcting for other variables, that state supreme court justices receive *more* citations in judicial opinions from judges in other states the *less* secure their tenure is.[18]

No state judges have tenure as secure as that of federal judges. Life tenure, while it is likely to have a debilitating effect on effort, at the same time is a highly valuable perquisite and so increases the real income of federal judges relative to state judges. This in turn contributes to making a federal judgeship a more coveted job (as does the fact that federal law is more prestigious than state law) and so broadens the applicant pool. Life tenure would be profoundly inconsistent with the democratic pretensions of an elected judiciary, since, even if originally elected, an official with life tenure is no one's idea of an official in a democracy. And state government is more democratic than our federal government— elections are more frequent, more officials are elected (the only executive officials elected at the federal level are the President and the Vice President, and of course no federal judges are elected), and states that allow referenda, initiatives, and recall (recall of officials—in effect, im-

---

sought political office unsuccessfully. Louis Harris and Associates, Inc., "Judges' Opinions on Procedural Issues: A Survey of State and Federal Trial Judges Who Spend at Least Half Their Time on General Civil Cases," 69 *Boston University Law Review* 731, 755–756 and tab. 9.1 (1989). This no doubt reflects the fact that politicians—the President and the Senators— appoint federal judges, and politicians know other politicians.

17. See, for example, Kermit L. Hall, "Progressive Reform and the Decline of Democratic Accountability: The Popular Election of State Supreme Court Judges, 1850–1920," 1984 *American Bar Foundation Research Journal* 345 (1984).

18. Stephen J. Choi, G. Mitu Gulati, and Eric A. Posner, "Professionals or Politicians: The Uncertain Empirical Case for an Elected Rather Than Appointed Judiciary" (New York University, Duke University, and University of Chicago law schools, Aug. 2007). On the validity of "other states" citations as a performance measure, read on. The appointed judges receive more citations per opinion, but the elected judges write more opinions, and the relative number of opinions is greater than the relative number of citations per opinion. The greater amount of opinion writing by elected judges may be due to the fact that the number of opinions, though obviously a crude measure of value of output, is apparently a talking point in judicial election campaigns. See "Pemberton Tops in State for Appeals Opinion Productivity" (campaign ad for Texas appellate judge), www.bobpemberton.com/2006/09/20/appeals_opinion_productivity/ (visited Aug. 18, 2007).

peachment by voters) add a modicum of direct democracy to representative democracy.

Twenty states plus the District of Columbia are trying to help their electorates make better informed decisions about judicial candidates.[19] Most of these judicial accountability programs are found in "Missouri Plan" states, where judges are appointed by a merit selection board and later stand for retention in elections in which there is no opposing candidate. Independent commissions publish evaluations of each judge standing for retention. The evaluations are based on interviews, on public comment and lawyers' confidential comments, on statistical measures of judicial performance (such as the speed with which the judge decides cases), and even, in some states, on the judge's opinions. Bar groups and newspapers also do evaluations of judicial candidates.

When we turn from arbitrators, career judges, and elected judges to U.S. federal judges, we enter a realm in which the external constraints on judicial behavior are severely attenuated.[20] The absence of good promotion opportunities is especially troublesome from the standpoint of trying to minimize agency costs. It may be impossible to measure individual performance yet be apparent who is the best performer, and so each ambitious employee works hard to prove that he is the best so that he will be promoted. Promotion need not be internal. There can be "promotion" to a job with another employer; civil servants are often "promoted" to a better job in the private sector. But this carrot too is largely missing from the federal judicial setting. A federal judge is (we shall see in the next chapter) unlikely to resign and enter the practice of law or some other line of work before he reaches retirement age. And when he reaches that age he is much more likely to take senior status—continuing to judge part-time yet receiving his full salary—than to retire from judging completely and take another job.

The stick is as etiolated as the carrot. (And even in jobs in which there is a fat carrot, a stick is necessary so that underperformers incapable of responding to the offer of the carrot can be replaced.) Apart from the

19. Rebecca Love Kourlis and Jordan M. Singer, "Using Judicial Performance Evaluations to Promote Judicial Accountability," 90 *Judicature* 200 (2007). See id. at 204 for a good summary of the different state programs.

20. I confine my discussion to Article III judges—district judges, court of appeals judges, and Supreme Court Justices. There are other federal judicial officers, primarily magistrate judges, bankruptcy judges, and administrative law judges. I discuss magistrate judges and bankruptcy judges briefly in chapter 6.

protection of tenure and the fact that the judicial salary is the same for all federal judges at the same level—there are no bonuses for outstanding performance or pay cuts for substandard performance—a judge's ability to cash in on his judicial reputation by moonlighting as a teacher or lecturer is very limited. There are low caps on outside earned income other than book royalties, oddly classified as unearned income, like dividends or oil and gas royalties—in short, investment income. And though there are no caps on a judge's income that is classified as unearned, only Supreme Court Justices land lucrative book contracts.

The more secure judicial tenure is and hence the more difficult it is to control judges' behavior, the more carefully candidates for judgeships should be screened. And in fact candidates for federal judgeships are very carefully screened. There is also lively competition for federal judgeships, which widens the field of selection and thus enables a finer mesh in the screen. The mature age of the candidates makes the screening still more effective. Because people have generally stable preferences and behavior has a strong habitual element, the older a person is when he is appointed to a job, the more predictable his performance in it will be. A lawyer who has performed successfully for many years in private or government law practice or in teaching and scholarship, demonstrating qualities of sobriety, good judgment, integrity, and other attributes that are important in a judge, is likely to continue to exhibit those qualities even when the carrots and sticks of a legal practice are withdrawn. It is like firing a gun: the position and rifling of the gun's barrel impart direction to the bullet, but momentum takes over in guiding the bullet once it leaves the barrel, though wind may deflect it slightly from its initial path.

Furthermore, the absence of strong incentives and constraints creates a space for weak ones to influence behavior. People care about their reputation even when it is not a potential source of tangible rewards. Rank orderings and prizes have psychological effects distinct from any career effects of being singled out from one's fellows. One is apt to care even more about one's reputation as a good worker if unable to point to a large income as proof of the quality of one's work. Many federal district judges are sensitive about the quarterly statistics compiled by the Administrative Office of the U.S. Courts that show how many cases a judge has had under advisement for more than a specified length of time—so sensitive that a judge will sometimes dismiss a case at the end of a reporting period, with leave to reinstate it at the beginning of the next period, in order to improve his statistics. Yet there is no sanction, other than a very slight reputational one limited to the judges of one's circuit, for having bad statistics.

District judges also do not like to be reversed.[21] Even though a reversal has no tangible effect on a judge's career if he is unlikely to be promoted to the court of appeals in any event—and little effect even then[22]—it can imply criticism rather than merely disagreement, and no one likes a public rebuke. Because judges are sensitive to both backlog and reversal, they will not, by making precipitate rulings, allow their backlogs to grow to inordinate length merely to reduce the probability of reversal, or their reversal rates to soar merely to eliminate their backlogs. So they are constrained to exercise a kind of care that is analogous to that of judges in a career judiciary.

District judges often have heavy dockets; a single judge in an urban district will have several hundred cases pending before him. Most of these will be settled or abandoned without the judge's intervention. But enough will remain that require court action to induce the judge to attend to them lest his backlog become unmanageable. He cannot be cavalier in disposing of these cases, as then his reversal rate would rise to an embarrassing level. So backlog pressure keeps him working hard and reversal threat keeps him working carefully—though an alternative strategy is to push the parties to settle, since settlements reduce backlog without risk of reversal.[23]

I may have been too quick to dismiss effect on promotion as a factor

21. David A. Hoffman, Alan J. Izenman, and Jeffrey R. Lidicker, "Docketology, District Courts, and Doctrine" (Temple University, May 21, 2007); William J. Stuntz, "The Pathological Politics of Criminal Law," 100 *Michigan Law Review* 505, 541 (2001); Evan H. Caminker, "Precedent and Prediction: The Forward-Looking Aspects of Inferior Court Decision Making," 73 *Texas Law Review* 1, 77–78 (1994); Richard S. Higgins and Paul H. Rubin, "Judicial Discretion," 9 *Journal of Legal Studies* 129, 130 (1980).

22. Higgins and Rubin, note 21 above, find that a district judge's reversal rate has no effect on his chances of promotion. Notice, though, that if district judges are completely insensitive to reversal, appeals can actually weaken their motivation to do a good job; they know their errors will be corrected without their being punished for having made them. Aspasia Tsaoussis and Eleni Zervogianni, "Judges as Satisficers: A Law and Economics Perspective on Judicial Liability" 10 (ALBA Graduate Business School, Athens, Greece, and University of Piraeus, Greece, Sept. 2007).

23. On district judges' interest in promoting settlement, see Hoffman, Izenman, and Lidicker, note 21 above.

in the behavior of a district judge. Although the tangible benefits of promotion to the court of appeals are very modest and the more cloistered, more intellectual character of appellate judging is not to the taste of everyone who seeks, is qualified for, and obtains a district judgeship, just the fact that appointment of a district judge to the court of appeals is a "promotion" to a "higher" court makes it attractive to many district judges. Moreover, that only 6 percent of district judges are promoted exaggerates the odds against promotion. Many district judges are too old to have realistic prospects of being promoted, would refuse promotion, or for political reasons are extremely unlikely to be promoted. Suppose, though this is just a guess, that only 20 percent of district judges had a chance of being promoted. Then each of the judges in that pool would have a one-third chance ($.20 \div .06 = .33$) of promotion, and those might be short enough odds to induce a judge to do whatever he could to rise within the pool. Such a judge would have a greater incentive than most other district judges to exert himself to be the best judge he could be, because merit is a factor in promotion to the court of appeals. But it is not the only factor. The promoting authorities—the President and the Senate—are politicians, and angling for their approval may influence the small fraction of the judge's decisions that might interest politicians, making those decisions more political than they would otherwise be.

Appellate review might be thought an effective method of controlling judicial agency costs.[24] The problem is that appellate judges, whether they are court of appeals judges or Supreme Court Justices, are not principals; they are agents enjoying great independence from their principal, the government of the United States. Appellate review in the federal system operates to conform the behavior of the district judges to that of the appellate judges rather than to reduce agency costs.

Because a federal district judge has more decisional freedom than judges in career judiciaries, personal factors—including the kind of intellectual laziness that consists of acting prematurely on intuition rather than (also) on analysis and evidence, and even the delights of tormenting the lawyers who appear before the judge—are likely to play a larger role in his behavior than in that of his counterparts in career judicia-

---

24. See Steven Shavell, "The Appeals Process and Adjudicator Incentives," 35 *Journal of Legal Studies* 1 (2006).

ries.[25] Perhaps *especially* tormenting the lawyers, because that affects neither the judge's reversal rate nor his backlog, but on the contrary reduces his backlog by inducing more settlements.

The environment of federal court of appeals judges differs in four main respects from that of district judges. First, the dual constraints imposed by backlog pressure and reversal threat are attenuated. The caseloads of circuit judges are lighter than those of district judges and so the threat of an unmanageable caseload looms less ominously. And once a case has been argued there will be no further activity in it until it is decided, which means that the size of the backlog does not affect the judge's workload, as it does in district courts. In addition, so few court of appeals decisions are reviewed by the Supreme Court (currently less than 1 percent) that the threat of reversal cannot be much of a constraint on court of appeals decision making. Also, many of these reversals reflect ideological differences, rather than error correction and therefore implicit criticism. That is less true of reversals of district court decisions.

Second, because appellate judges sit in panels rather than by themselves, there is a premium on cooperative behavior.[26] The downside is the risk of factions and (though I believe this is quite rare in the federal judiciary) of logrolling (vote trading). Legislators can logroll with a good conscience because they are representatives and logrolling enables them to maximize their constituents' welfare. Judges cannot offer such a justification. So logrolling violates the rules of the judicial game, but with the qualification that the most persuasive explanation for the panel-composition effect discussed in chapter 1 involves something akin to logrolling.

Third, federal court of appeals judges have a greater opportunity to influence the law, on the model most famously of Learned Hand, than federal district judges do. Appellate adjudication focuses far more than adjudication at the trial level on general issues of law rather than on factual or procedural issues specific to the particular case. And not only does the Supreme Court review only a minute percentage of court of appeals decisions, but the cases it does review are not a representative sample of judicial activity in the different fields of federal law. The Court is heavily

25. See, for example, Steven Lubet, "Bullying from the Bench," 5 *Green Bag* (2d ser.) 11 (2001).

26. Harry T. Edwards, "The Effects of Collegiality on Judicial Decision Making," 151 *University of Pennsylvania Law Review* 1639 (2003).

invested in constitutional law and leaves many other fields largely to the courts of appeals to shape.

Many court of appeals judges are not ambitious to influence the direction in which the law will evolve and do not seek to acquire the kind of reputation that judges such as Learned Hand and Henry Friendly acquired. And because the risk of reversal is small, we can expect unambitious appellate judges to weight leisure more heavily, and to vote their personal preferences more often, than district judges do. The risk of reversal is much greater, and the reward for creative legal thinking much less, at the district court level.

Appellate judges in our system often can conceal the role of personal preferences in their decisions by stating the facts selectively, so that the outcome seems to follow from them inevitably, or by taking liberties with precedents. Yet the doctrine of precedent exercises some constraint even on the minority of appellate judges who are ambitious to place their own distinctive stamp on the law.[27] A judge's influence depends on his decisions' being treated as precedents by other judges. If he is cavalier about adhering to precedent in his own decisions, he weakens the doctrine of precedent and hence the likelihood that his own decisions will be followed by other judges.[28] A judge who notices that other judges do not adhere to precedent will wonder why he should bother to do so. And if most of the judges on the court favor adhering to precedent, they will (if necessary by en banc proceedings, which enable a panel decision to be reversed) rein in the mavericks.

But probably the main force behind the doctrine of precedent is that in a system of case law, adherence to precedent is necessary to create the kind of stability that one would have in a system in which law was codified. In a code system it would not matter greatly if judges did not adhere to precedent, because decisions would not create rules but merely apply preexisting rules—the rules laid down in the code. So it is no surprise that judicial decisions have much less force as precedents in

---

27. Their ambition—which may not be to influence the law but may instead be to become a Supreme Court Justice or just to be well regarded—is manifested in the ferocity of their competition to obtain the ablest law clerks. On that competition, see Christopher Avery et al., "The Market for Federal Judicial Law Clerks," 68 *University of Chicago Law Review* 793 (2001); Avery et al., "The New Market for Federal Judicial Law Clerks," 74 *University of Chicago Law Review* 447 (2007).

28. Eric Rasmusen, "Judicial Legitimacy as a Repeated Game," 10 *Journal of Law, Economics and Organization* 63 (1994).

such systems than in our system.[29] But not zero force. The influential civil law doctrine of *jurisprudence constante* accords precedential significance to a line of consistent precedents, though not, as in common law systems, to the first precedent.[30] Thus the civil law judge in the second case to arise concerning some legal issue will give no weight to the decision in the first case as authority. But if he and a few other succeeding judges agree with the first decision, and none during this period of crystallization of judicial views disagrees, the set of decisions will acquire precedential authority.

Our judges are strongly motivated to adhere to precedent, not only because they want to encourage adherence to the precedents they create, but also—and this is more important to most judges—because they want to limit their workloads. Adherence to precedent does this both directly, by reducing the amount of fresh analysis that the judges have to perform, and indirectly, by reducing the number of appeals, since the more certain the law, the lower the litigation rate. The doctrine of precedent has the further value, which I mentioned in chapter 1, of making judges more thoughtful about the consequences of their decisions, although this factor is in some tension with the time-saving benefits of precedent.

Another distinctive subset of court of appeals judges consists of those who by reason of ideology, prominence, political connections, race, gender, ethnicity, or other factors have a real shot at being promoted to the Supreme Court. (This corresponds to the pool of district judges who have a good shot at being promoted to the court of appeals.) With rare exceptions, the probability that a given court of appeals judge, however well-placed he seems to be in the competition to be appointed to the Supreme Court, will actually be appointed is low because there are so many aspirants for so few vacancies and so many unpredictable political elements in appointments to the Court. That is why I said "real" shot rather than "good" shot (some district judges really do have a good shot at promotion to the court of appeals). But if a judge attaches enormous value to being a Supreme Court Justice, the expected utility of such an

29. See, for example, Eva Steiner, *French Legal Method* 80–81 (2002); Dennis, note 6 above, at 14–17.

30. See, for example, Vincy Fon and Francesco Parisi, "Judicial Precedents in Civil Law Systems: A Dynamic Analysis," 26 *International Review of Law and Economics* 519 (2006); Dennis, note 6 above, at 15.

appointment (most simply, the utility of the appointment multiplied by its probability) may influence his behavior. After Robert Bork's nomination to the Supreme Court failed, in part because of his extrajudicial writings (the largest component of the "paper trail" that did him in), the publication rate of court of appeals judges declined precipitately.[31] Moreover, his resignation, and much later that of Michael Luttig, both after their once-bright chances of appointment to the Supreme Court had faded, suggest that some judges may be willing to invest years in a job that does not much grip them if they think it will give them a shot at a Supreme Court appointment.

The fourth distinction between circuit and district judges is that professional criticism of judicial decisions can be expected to place a sharper check on extravagant exercises of judicial discretion at the appellate level than at the trial level. The main public product of appellate judges is judicial opinions, which are self-contained (or at least appear to be self-contained) texts readily accessible to professional critique. But we shall see in chapter 8 that professional criticism of judicial opinions is so heavily discounted by most judges as to have little influence on their behavior. And anyway, so mesmerized are academic commentators (including students who write for law reviews) by Supreme Court decisions, and so numerous are the decisions of the courts of appeals, that the fraction of court of appeals decisions that receives academic notice is slight.[32] The irony is that Supreme Court Justices pay even less attention to academic criticism than lower-court judges do, though more to the reactions of legislators, the general public, and the media.

Of potential significance in constraining federal judicial behavior is the development, mainly by law professors but also by court administrators, of quantitative criteria of federal judicial performance. These overlap with the more eclectic evaluations, mentioned earlier, of elected state judges. Those evaluations, in turn, resemble the evaluations of federal magistrate judges and bankruptcy judges, who are appointed (magistrate judges by the federal district courts, bankruptcy judges by the

31. S. Scott Gaille, "Publishing by United States Court of Appeals Judges: Before and after the Bork Hearings," 26 *Journal of Legal Studies* 371 (1997).

32. Treatises cite many cases, but rarely critically, as the emphasis of a legal treatise is on what the law is, not on what it would be were it not for a lot of decisions with which the treatise writer disagrees. If those decisions are likely to be followed, they are "the law," at least from the practitioner's perspective, and it is to practitioners that legal treatises are mainly directed.

courts of appeals) for fixed, renewable terms. Because district judges and court of appeals judges have life tenure, evaluations of them have less bite, but conceivably could shame some of them into performing better and, probably more important, provide information on the kind of credentials that accurately predict judicial performance.

Quantitative criteria of judicial performance are less likely than the common verbal criteria—"restrained," "activist," "scholarly," "result oriented," and the rest—to be dismissed by judges as politically motivated. They also are more economical, because statistics can compact vast amounts of information as discursive critique cannot. But a number of qualifications must be noted. One is that the criteria of judicial performance should not be uniform across courts and judges. I noted earlier that criteria such as backlog and reversal rate should play a larger role in the evaluation of district judges than of circuit judges. And even good performance criteria may not be useful for determining whether a judge should be promoted. (I will explain this shortly.)

Any numerical ranking system presents a danger that the competitors will be able to game it,[33] as I noted with respect to backlog statistics. And as illustrated by such criteria for evaluating the performance of circuit judges as citations by judges in other circuits,[34] or the more inclusive quantitative ranking scheme developed by Professors Choi and Gulati,[35] the choice of criteria depends on assumptions about the attributes of an outstanding appellate judge. The criteria used so far measure primarily influence and prominence. Besides out-of-circuit citations (the idea behind this measure being that because citing a case in another circuit is optional—a case is not authoritative outside its circuit—an out-of-

33. For striking examples, see Wendy N. Espeland and Michael Sauder, "Rankings and Reactivity: How Public Measures Recreate Social Worlds" 1 (2007), *American Sociological Review*), 113, discussing *U.S. News & World Report*'s influential rankings of law schools.

34. The most complete study is William M. Landes, Lawrence Lessig, and Michael E. Solimine, "Judicial Influence: A Citation Analysis of Federal Court of Appeals Judges," 27 *Journal of Legal Studies* 271 (1998). On the application of the methodology to a foreign court, see Mita Bhattacharya and Russell Smyth, "The Determinants of Judicial Prestige and Influence: Some Empirical Evidence from the High Court of Australia," 30 *Journal of Legal Studies* 223 (2001). Citation counting has become a commonly used tool for evaluating the scholarship of candidates for academic appointments and promotions. See Richard A. Posner, *Frontiers of Legal Theory*, ch. 13 (1991), and references cited there.

35. Stephen J. Choi and G. Mitu Gulati, "Ranking Judges according to Citation Bias (as a Means to Reduce Bias)," 82 *Notre Dame Law Review* 1279 (2007); Choi and Gulati, "A Tournament of Judges?" 92 *California Law Review* 299 (2004).

circuit citation is an unforced acknowledgment of the helpfulness of the cited opinion), one of Choi and Gulati's performance criteria is the number of times a judge is mentioned by name in opinions.[36] Another study ranks judges by how many of their opinions are published in casebooks.[37] Such criteria implicitly treat judicial creativity as the only, or at least the most important, attribute of a circuit judge. Legalists will blanch at this implication.

A related concern is that, as critics of *U.S. News & World Report*'s rankings of law schools emphasize, numerical rankings are questionable when they are multidimensional (composite). The weighting of the different dimensions influences the ranking—and is likely to be arbitrary.[38] The problem is as serious with respect to the ranking of judges as it is with respect to the ranking of law schools, because in neither case is there agreement on the weights to be applied to the different factors. If you happen to think lucidity an extraordinarily important virtue in a judicial opinion, this will affect your weighting relative to that of an observer who thinks that explaining carefully to the losing party why he lost, or discussing even minor issues, or stating the facts in comprehensive detail, or avoiding reversal by never going out on a limb is a more important virtue in a judicial opinion. Not all competent students of the federal court of appeals would place creativity high on the scale of judicial virtues; some would decry the "creative" judge as a destabilizing force.

Also, ranking is an ordinal rather than a cardinal evaluation tool. It does not indicate differences in quality between ranks. If those differences are small, even large rank differences may not signify large differences in the quality of judicial performance. Ranking judges disvalues diversity of judicial approaches, styles, and perspectives by simplifying the criteria of quality; it is like a college's basing admission decisions solely on the applicants' grades.

Choi and Gulati do not use reversal rate as a performance criterion for circuit judges. That may seem a surprising omission. But reversal rate and creativity are likely to be positively correlated, since a judge who is

---

36. See also David Klein and Darby Morrisroe, "The Prestige and Influence of Individual Judges on the U.S. Courts of Appeals," 28 *Journal of Legal Studies* 371 (1999).

37. G. Mitu Gulati and Veronica Sanchez, "Giants in a World of Pygmies? Testing the Superstar Hypothesis with Judicial Opinions in Casebooks," 87 *Iowa Law Review* 1141 (2002). Klein and Morrisroe, note 36 above, attempt to measure judicial prestige quantitatively.

38. I stress this point in my article "Law School Rankings," 81 *Indiana Law Journal* 13 (2006).

creating precedents rather than just following them can be expected to be reversed more often than an unadventurous judge,[39] just as home-run hitters tend to strike out more often than singles hitters. And the effect of reversals is captured automatically in one of the performance criteria that Choi and Gulati do use—frequency of citation to a judge—because a decision is unlikely to be cited after it has been reversed. There is, however, a case for using the Supreme Court's occasional summary reversals as a measure of the performance of courts of appeals, because such reversals are more likely to rest on a determination that the lower court clearly erred than on a disagreement over the resolution of an arguable issue. A similar if slightly weaker case can be made for using unanimous reversals by the Supreme Court as a measure of errors by the lower courts. A study using both measures supports the widespread impression of the Ninth Circuit as the worst-performing federal court of appeals.[40]

Apart from concerns about the accuracy or utility of the specific metrics that are available for evaluating judges, we need to be concerned with what sociologists call "reactivity"—the propensity of "individuals [to] alter their behavior in reaction to being evaluated, observed, or measured."[41] Ranking magnifies differences by implying that, as in an athletic contest, the important thing is not how well you perform in absolute terms but how well you perform relative to others. This in turn may induce the ranked to change their behavior in order to move up the ladder. That is distinct from "gaming" in the sense of manipulating statistics, though similarly motivated. Judges tend to be competitive people, so efforts to rank them, whether directly or by means of measures that being quantitative are readily converted to ranks, could impair judicial quality unless the measures gauge performance accurately; and they may not.

This is the gravest problem with subjecting judges to performance measures. Many important judicial activities go on below the radar, in the sense that it would be difficult to develop performance measures for them. Think of such activities of appellate judges as carefully reading and commenting on the circulated draft of another judge on the panel,

39. Thomas J. Miceli and Metin M. Cosgel, "Reputation and Judicial Decision-Making," 23 *Journal of Economic Behavior and Organization* 31 (1994).

40. Posner, note 34 above, at 413–417.

41. Espeland and Sauder, note 33 above, at 10.

supervising the preparation of unpublished orders (as distinct from published opinions) that dispose of cases that are not orally argued, deciding motions, screening appeals to determine which should be orally argued and for how long (in circuits that use screening panels, as most do), carefully reading all petitions for rehearing, serving on court committees and committees of the Judicial Conference of the United States, and serving as chief judge of their courts. If these activities cannot be subjected to meaningful performance measures, the use of performance measures for those judicial activities that can feasibly be measured may induce judges to slight the unmeasured activities in order to increase their rank in the evaluative hierarchy.

I conclude that it would be premature to embrace performance measures as a method of incentivizing or constraining judges. It would be downright absurd to suggest (nor does anyone suggest) that they should be used as the basis for awarding bonuses to judges who score well on them!

When we turn from the environment of the federal courts of appeals to that of the Supreme Court, the picture changes once again. Reversal risk falls to zero, but there are still constraints—from precedent; from the possibility of political retribution in the form of "Court-curbing" legislation[42] or constitutional amendments (in the case of constitutional decisions) nullifying an unpopular decision;[43] from low-level harassment by congressional budget committees;[44] and from the prospect of the appointment of new Justices, when vacancies arise, who will be antagonistic to the existing ones because they are selected in the hope that they will alter the Court's direction. Indeed, because of the high visibility of the Court's decisions, the political constraints on the Justices are greater than those that operate at the lower levels of the federal judiciary. The public is barely aware of most decisions of lower courts. But it is aware of many Supreme Court decisions, and its response to them, if

42. Tom S. Clark, "Institutional Hostility and the Separation of Powers" (Princeton University, Department of Politics, Apr. 25, 2007).

43. William N. Eskridge, Jr., "Overriding Supreme Court Statutory Interpretation Decisions," 101 Yale Law Journal 331 (1991). For a contrasting view, see Frank B. Cross and Blake J. Nelson, "Strategic Institutional Effects on Supreme Court Decision Making," 95 Northwestern University Law Review 1437, 1451–1457 (2001).

44. Eugenia F. Toma, "A Contractual Model of the Voting Behavior of the Supreme Court: The Role of the Chief Justice," 16 International Review of Law and Economics 433 (1996).

sufficiently intense and widespread, can precipitate a political challenge to the Court.[45]

The combination of those constraints with the lack of guidance that conventional legal materials provide in novel cases, which bulk disproportionately large in the Court's docket, makes the Supreme Court truly a political court,[46] so that analysis of the behavior of the Justices, especially in constitutional cases, should parallel that of the behavior of conventional political actors.[47] Not perfectly, because a rational Justice will give greater weight to precedent than a legislature would do[48] and will be freer from effective threats of political retaliation than a legislator who was not a lame duck would be. But given the Court's inescapably political character, it is not a valid criticism of a Supreme Court Justice that he (or she—Justice O'Connor being widely regarded as the most politically astute of recent Justices) has and uses political smarts. Indeed, it is a legitimate criticism of the current Court that the aggregate political experience of its members is zero.

This analysis places a cloud over Choi and Gulati's proposal[49] that Supreme Court Justices be chosen by a "tournament" of federal court of appeals judges.[50] Just as the best appellate judge in a foreign career judiciary might very well not be the best choice for a U.S. court of appeals, so a court of appeals judge might not be the best choice for the Supreme

45. For evidence that the Court's constitutional decisions are influenced by the political balance in Congress, see William Mishler and Reginald S. Sheehan, "Public Opinion, the Attitudinal Model, and Supreme Court Decision Making: A Micro-Analytic Perspective," 58 *Journal of Politics* 169 (1996); Anna Harvey and Barry Friedman, "Pulling Punches: Congressional Constraints on the Supreme Court's Constitutional Rulings, 1987–2000," 31 *Legislative Studies Quarterly* 533 (2006); Barry Friedman and Anna Harvey, "Electing the Supreme Court," 78 *Indiana Law Journal* 123 (2003).

46. Chapter 10 develops this theme. See also Richard Hodder-Williams, "Six Notions of 'Political' and the United States Supreme Court," 22 *British Journal of Political Science* 1 (1992); Martin Shapiro, *Law and Politics in the Supreme Court: New Approaches to Political Jurisprudence* (1964).

47. See, for example, Jeffrey A. Segal and Albert D. Cover, "Ideological Values and the Votes of U.S. Supreme Court Justices," 83 *American Political Science Review* 557 (1989).

48. For evidence, see Youngsik Lim, "An Empirical Analysis of Supreme Court Justices' Decision Making," 29 *Journal of Legal Studies* 721 (2000).

49. See note 35 above.

50. Steven Goldberg, "Federal Judges and the Heisman Trophy," 32 *Florida State University Law Review* 1237 (2005).

Court.[51] One must not forget the "Peter Principle"—the tendency to promote a person beyond the level of his competence.

The best way to study the tournament proposal would be to apply Choi and Gulati's criteria to the federal court of appeals judges who have become Supreme Court Justices and see whether the criteria are predictive of the judges' performance as Justices.[52] (The criteria can easily be extended to judges of other courts, to bring Holmes, Cardozo, O'Connor, and others who came to the Court from state judgeships into the sample tested.[53]) But this would require developing good performance measures for Supreme Court Justices.

The difficulty of developing judicial performance measures underscores the weakness of the external constraints on the behavior of federal judges. That weakness, however, is the obverse of judicial independence, and there is *some* evidence that this is a good swap—that the Anglo-American–style judiciary, which maximizes independence by minimizing external constraints (at least in the federal judiciary), is more conducive to economic growth than the European-style career judiciary.[54] But note the emphasis on "some"; the evidence is not very strong.[55] As

---

51. Other reservations concerning the adequacy of Choi and Gulati's methodology for selecting Supreme Court Justices are expressed in Daniel A. Farber, "Supreme Court Selection and Measures of Past Judicial Performance," 32 *Florida State University Law Review* 1175 (2005).

52. James J. Brudney, "Foreseeing Greatness? Measurable Performance Criteria and the Selection of Supreme Court Justices," 32 *Florida State University Law Review* 1015 (2005).

53. For example, in my book *Cardozo: A Study in Reputation* (1990), I used out-of-state citations, as well as other numerical criteria, in an effort to determine Cardozo's standing among state judges. Id., ch. 5, especially p. 85 (tab. 5).

54. Simeon Djankov et al., "Courts," 118 *Quarterly Journal of Economics* 453 (2003); Djankov et al., "Debt Enforcement around the World" (World Bank, Dec. 2006); Edward L. Glaeser and Andrei Shleifer, "Legal Origins," 119 *Quarterly Journal of Economics* 1103 (2002); Michael L. Smith, "Deterrence and Origin of Legal System: Evidence from 1950–1999," 7 *American Law and Economics Review* 350 (2005); Daniel Klerman and Paul G. Mahoney, "The Value of Judicial Independence: Evidence from Eighteenth Century England," 7 *American Law and Economics Review* 1 (2005); Rafael La Porta et al., "The Quality of Government," 15 *Journal of Law, Economics and Organization* 222 (1999); La Porta et al., "Law and Finance," 106 *Journal of Political Economy* 1113 (1998).

55. As argued in Kenneth W. Dam, *The Law-Growth Nexus: The Rule of Law and Economic Development* (2006). See also Aristides N. Hatzis, "Civil Contract Law and Economic Reasoning—An Unlikely Pair?" in *The Architecture of European Codes and Contract Law* 159 (Stefan Grundmann and Martin Schauer eds. 2006); Daniel Klerman and Paul G. Mahoney, "Legal Origin?" (USC Legal Studies Research Paper No. 07–3, n.d.); Gillian K. Hadfield, "The Many Legal Institutions That Support Contractual Commitments," in *Handbook of New Institutional Economics* 175, 197–198 (Claude Ménard and Mary M. Shirley eds. 2005); Katharina Pistor et al.,

pointed out by Paul Mahoney,[56] the hostility of the Anglo-American political culture to government bureaucracy may be the cause of both the nonbureaucratic structure of the Anglo-American judiciaries[57] and the greater hospitality of the political culture to commercial endeavors. Moreover, although an independent judiciary is uncontroversially a social good (as I noted in chapter 2), there is a difference between an independent judiciary and independent judges. A career judiciary can in principle be as independent of the other branches of government as Anglo-American judges are even if the career judges are less independent from their judicial superiors. But this is in principle, and perhaps not in actuality. Common law systems give judges the power to make law. This makes them more powerful than civil law judges, and power augments independence.[58] Our judges may have a legislative role because they are trusted by the other branches of government—or perhaps they are trusted because they are independent.

If the principal effect of a career judiciary is, therefore, to shift legislative power from the judges to the legislators, this need not reduce the quality of a nation's laws if the nation has a parliamentary system, unlike our presidential system. In a parliamentary system, politics is a career, parties are disciplined, and the legislature is integrated with the executive and effectively unicameral. Lateral-entry judges, having a wider experience of the world outside the courtroom than career judges, are better equipped to play the occasional-legislator role. But they may not be better legislators than the official legislators in a parliamentary system. The latter may have the time, the experience, the discipline, and the streamlined procedures to enable them to perform the legislative functions that judges perform in our system because our legislative pro-

---

"The Evolution of Corporate Law: A Cross-Country Comparison," 23 *University of Pennsylvania Journal of International Economic Law* 79 (2002); Brian R. Cheffins, "Does Law Matter? The Separation of Ownership and Control in the United Kingdom," 30 *Journal of Legal Studies* 459, 483 (2001). The standard comparisons of "common law" and "civil law" systems are derided as simplistic by Gillian Hadfield, "The Levers of Legal Design: Institutional Determinants of the Quality of Law" (USC Center in Law, Economics and Organization Research Paper No. C07-8, May 2007).

56. Paul G. Mahoney, "The Common Law and Economic Growth: Hayek Might Be Right," 30 *Journal of Legal Studies* 503 (2001).

57. Richard A. Posner, *Law and Legal Theory in England and America* 28 (1996) (tab. 1.1).

58. Frank B. Cross, "Identifying the Virtues of the Common Law" (University of Texas School of Law, Law and Economics Research Paper No. 063, Sept. 2005).

cesses are so cumbersome and impacted. Legal codes in a parliamentary system of government may take the place of case law in our system.

The English created their independent judiciary in the early eighteenth century, and our judicial system derives from it. In point of weakness of external constraints, the English judiciary and our federal judiciary are similar. Yet it was not always so. The English worried a great deal about judicial discretion and employed three techniques for minimizing it. One was a rather rigid adherence to precedent (though softened by "distinguishing," of which more in subsequent chapters). Until 1968, English judges adhered to *stare decisis* (standing by what has been decided—in other words, the doctrine of precedent) in almost a literal sense that enabled a judge to say, "Look, I am not being willful. I do not make law. I simply follow what has been laid down by previous judges." This placed the law on the weak foundation of the first generation's willful judges. But they were not really willful because they had no choice but to be creative—there were no precedents for *them* to follow.

Transposed to the U.S. constitutional arena, rigid adherence to precedent would enable a Supreme Court Justice to say, "I have to interpret two things. I have to interpret the document itself, which is old and vague, but fortunately I have as well the easier task of interpreting decisions by my predecessors, to which I am bound, and so mine is a genuinely interpretive, rather than a creative or innovative or discretionary, judicial activity." Our Justices cannot say this because they feel free to overrule previous decisions. They have to have that freedom because the Constitution is so difficult to amend to adapt it to changed conditions or fresh insights. There are decisions that are seen as profoundly wrongheaded from the outset and decisions that while defensible when made have been rendered obsolete by changes in the social, political, or economic environment. The latter decisions can be distinguished in subsequent cases; the former not, and so must be overruled to prevent them from continuing to do mischief. Rigid adherence to precedent would magnify the consequences of a mistaken or deeply regretted decision enthroned as a precedent. It would also exert great pressure on judges to write judicial opinions very narrowly so that they controlled as little of the future as possible.[59] This would reduce the value of precedent as a

59. It would be interesting to correlate the average number of citations per opinion with a court's propensity to overrule. The less inclined a court is to overrule its precedents, the narrower the court's opinions will tend to be and so, one would expect, the less frequently they will be cited.

source of guidance in future cases. The Justices would have to decide more cases in order to create a rule.

The second device the English used to rein in judges was the principle of "orality," which meant that judges had to do everything in public. They had no staff, read no briefs (there were no briefs), knew nothing of the case when it was presented to them, and did not discuss the case with each other at any stage in the litigation. Oral argument in an appeal might last a week because the judges would be sitting at the bench reading the statutes, cases, and other authorities handed up to them by the lawyers to read on the spot. The idea was that since the judges were doing nothing that was not visible to the public, the public could monitor their performance effectively. Britain has had to abandon this system because of workload pressures, as well as having to abandon its severe conception of *stare decisis*.[60]

The third and most important constraint on English judges (though this too is eroding[61]) was that the judges were picked from a tiny, homogeneous social and professional sliver of the nation. They were the senior barristers, and one was unlikely to become a barrister unless one was a member of the upper class, because it was almost impossible to earn a living until one had established oneself in practice, as firms of barristers were forbidden. Judges who come from the same social and professional background are likely to think alike.[62] So when they disagree they will be arguing from shared premises. Arguments from shared premises can lead to objectively verifiable conclusions—which is not to say that the conclusions are correct. Conclusions that follow logically from incorrect premises have no warrant of correctness.

The pool from which our judges are chosen is not homogeneous, though neither is it fully representative; it is limited as a practical matter to upper-echelon lawyers, almost all of whom are well-socialized, well-behaved, conventionally minded members of the upper middle class. The other limitations on judicial discretion that the British invented and long applied are also missing from our system. Nor do we have a career judiciary. In sum, at the federal level at least, we lack a good set of checks on judges' exercising a degree of discretion that frightens many people, especially those who lose out when the exercise of discretion

---

60. Gary Slapper and David Kelly, *The English Legal System* 81 (8th ed. 2006).

61. See id. at 239–240.

62. Brian Simpson, "The Common Law and Legal Theory," in *Legal Theory and Common Law* 8 (William Twining ed. 1986).

goes against them. Hence our confirmation battles. (There is no confirmation of British judges.) It is one of the few occasions for a populist injection into the process of federal judicial selection.

Yet the framers of the Constitution did build in checks on federal judicial power. This is something that federal judges, taking judicial independence a bit too seriously, tend to forget—that the Constitution limits *every* branch of the federal government by placing every branch in a competitive relation with every other. The Constitution gives the Supreme Court an appellate jurisdiction but subjects that jurisdiction to such exceptions and regulations as Congress may decide to impose. It gives Congress control over the budget of the federal courts, including judicial salaries (though Congress cannot lower them), which is important because it would be dangerous for any branch of government to have complete control over its resources. Congress determines the number of judges, and could show its displeasure with Supreme Court decisions by increasing the number of Justices if it thought the new appointments would alter the political balance on the Court. Franklin Roosevelt tried to persuade Congress to do that in the 1930s. He failed, but earlier efforts had succeeded.[63] The Constitution creates strong protections for the right to a jury trial even in civil cases; this limits judges' power by dividing judicial power between them and the citizenry. Judges are also denied the power to enforce their judgments—that is an executive branch prerogative. And they can decide only cases that someone chooses to file; because Article III of the Constitution limits the judicial power of the United States to cases or controversies, judges cannot declare a statute unconstitutional as soon as it is enacted but must wait for a case challenging its constitutionality. And without directly challenging the courts Congress often can use its legislative authority to pull the sting of constitutional rulings that it does not like, as by defunding abortion clinics, starving legal aid clinics and criminal defenders of funds, curtailing statutory procedural rights, and increasing the severity of criminal penalties, which encourage criminal defendants, in exchange for a sentencing break, to waive the constitutional procedural rights bestowed on them by the Supreme Court. Thus, powerful as the Court is, it does not control enough of the levers of power to overawe the other branches of government even in areas in which it has been particularly

63. Jean Edward Smith, "Stacking the Court," *New York Times*, July 26, 2007, p. A19.

aggressive in creating new rights in the name of the Constitution. Its bark is worse than its bite.[64]

Alexander Hamilton in *Federalist No. 78* claimed that the independence of federal judges would be harmless for a different reason, a reason based on internal rather than external constraints: they would be exercising judgment and not will. Hamilton was not naïve; was he being disingenuous? Not necessarily. The Bill of Rights postdated the original Constitution of 1787 and the publication of the *Federalist Papers*. The 1787 Constitution created few justiciable rights. The Bill of Rights (and later the Fourteenth Amendment) created a host of such rights in language so vague that Learned Hand thought most of its provisions should be nonjusticiable because judges had used them to create constitutional law out of whole cloth.[65] Yet even before the Bill of Rights was promulgated, concern had been expressed, notably by the pseudonymous antifederalist "Brutus," against whom Hamilton was writing, that the Justices of the Supreme Court would become tyrants by deciding cases in accordance with their conception of the "spirit" of the Constitution.[66] With the Constitution and its amendments becoming ever less directive as the passage of time transforms the conditions and understandings on which they were based, there is little to limit judicial discretion in constitutional law except confirmation battles and other manifestations of public opinion, such as the wave of indignation set in motion by the *Kelo* decision, which I discuss in chapter 10. These and the other external constraints do set bounds, but they are capacious bounds.

64. Consider the extraordinary difficulty the Supreme Court experienced in attempting to secure compliance by the southern states with the Court's rulings in civil rights and related criminal cases until the civil rights revolution of the 1960s. This story is well told in Michael J. Klarman, *Unfinished Business: Racial Equality in American History* (2007).

65. Learned Hand, *The Bill of Rights* (1958).

66. "Essays of Brutus," Jan. 31, 1788; Feb. 7, 1788; Feb. 14, 1788, in *The Complete Anti-Federalist*, vol. 2, pp. 417–428 (Herbert J. Storing ed. 1981). See Shlomo Slonim, "Federalist No. 78 and Brutus' Neglected Thesis on Judicial Supremacy," 23 *Constitutional Commentary* 7 (2006).

6

Altering the Environment:
Tenure and Salary Issues

We can learn more about judicial behavior by considering the likely effects on it of two proposals that would alter the federal judicial environment: imposing term limits on federal judges,[1] which would require a constitutional amendment, and increasing their salaries substantially, which would not.

Whether in the academy or in the judiciary, life tenure guarantees independence but also invites abuse because it eliminates any penalty for shirking. More precisely, it reduces the penalty, because if salary can vary, the employer can penalize the tenured employee by denying him raises, though reducing his salary would presumably violate the terms of the tenure contract. The federal judicial salary structure makes dealing with shirkers impossible. Judges do not receive merit raises; when the judicial wage is raised, it is raised for all. Rightly so—performance-based criteria for judicial compensation would compromise judicial independence because of the absence of objective performance measures.

So would a fixed but renewable term. Granted, this is the approach that has been taken, with no untoward results as far as I know, with respect to federal magistrate judges and bankruptcy judges. They are appointed for 8-year and 14-year renewable terms, respectively. But, as I noted in chapter 5, they are appointed by judges rather than by political officials. In any event, a *nonrenewable* fixed term would not compromise judicial independence. A term of, say, 10 years would limit the length of

1. A perennial proposal, but one receiving new attention, though only at the academic level. See *Reforming the Court: Term Limits for Supreme Court Justices* (Roger C. Cramton and Paul D. Carrington eds. 2006).

service of the shirkers and also create an incentive for good performance because the judge would want to secure a good job after his judicial term expired. But there are serious drawbacks, illuminated by the literature on term limits for legislators.[2] Judges would be distracted by having to make arrangements for another job at the expiration of their terms; their decisions might be distorted by the desire to curry favor with potential future employers; and more rapid turnover of judges would reduce legal stability. The first two tendencies illustrate what economists call the "last period" problem. When a worker knows that he is soon to retire or quit, his commitment to his job may dwindle. Yet none of these concerns might be decisive were it not that candidates for federal judgeships are carefully screened, which eliminates from the appointment pool the candidates most likely to shirk. An additional effect of fixed terms would be to increase the President's power to change the political composition of the federal judiciary;[3] as we saw in chapter 1, judges tend to time retirement in such a way that their successors are of the same party.

Senior status is an ingenious carrot-stick response to the problem of shirking. It allows judges, after they become eligible to retire, to continue working, at no reduction in pay, provided they are willing to shoulder at least one-third of an active judge's workload. This is an attractive offer, and most eligible judges accept it when, or within a few years after, they become eligible. But part of the deal is that a senior judge can be barred (though with no diminution in pay) from judging by the chief judge of his court subject to review by the court's judicial council. Senior status is thus a variant of the buyout schemes by which universities and other employers forbidden by law to fix a mandatory retirement age try to induce retirement.

The case for term limits for Supreme Court Justices is stronger than that for judges of the lower federal courts. If I am right that it is a politi-

2. See, for example, Rebekah Herrick and Sue Thomas, "Do Term Limits Make a Difference? Ambition and Motivations among U.S. State Legislators," 33 *American Politics Research* 726 (2005); Edward J. López, "Term Limits: Causes and Consequences," 114 *Public Choice* 1 (2003); Linda Cohen and Matthew Spitzer, "Term Limits," 80 *Georgetown Law Journal* 477 (1992); Gary S. Becker, "Reforming Congress: Why Limiting Terms Won't Work," *Business Week*, Aug. 6, 1990, p. 18.

3. Charles H. Franklin, "Behavioral Factors Affecting Judicial Independence." In *Judicial Independence at the Crossroads: An Interdisciplinary Approach* 148, 157 (Stephen B. Burbank and Barry Friedman eds. 2002).

cal court, the absence of term limits is an affront to democratic theory; conferring life tenure on politicians is profoundly undemocratic. Moreover, the Justices are ineligible for senior status; that is, they cannot sit part-time on the Supreme Court after retiring, though they can if they want sit in the lower federal courts. So they do not have the same incentive that lower-court judges do to semiretire. With increasing longevity, Justices are likely to be serving very long terms into very old age.

We can gain insight into the tenure issue from the literature on constitutional courts in other countries. Ferejohn and Pasquino argue that the limited, nonrenewable terms (usually 10 or 12 years) of the judges of these courts are one reason such courts are less controversial than our Supreme Court,[4] despite lacking the protective coloration that our Court gets from having a nonconstitutional jurisdiction as well as its constitutional one and deciding "real" cases in the standard manner (opposing parties, briefs, oral argument). Shorter terms mean that judicial appointments are less consequential and therefore attract less public attention and controversy.[5] And foreign constitutional courts usually operate without oral arguments, signed opinions, or published dissents, so there is less opportunity for the judges to play to the gallery than there is for our Justices to do so.[6] Our gallery, however, is the court of public opinion, and its participation in constitutional controversies injects a democratic element into constitutional adjudication. It makes the Supreme Court a little more democratic—and a little less like a real court, the judges of which are proudly indifferent to public opinion. Not that they should brag about that; their indifference to public opinion is the mirror of the public's indifference to them.

What is not a good argument for judicial term limits is that elderly people tend to experience diminished mental acuity. They do; but there are a few professions, such as history, theology, literary criticism and scholarship, and philosophy, in which the negative correlation between age and performance is weak.[7] Judging is one of them, though part of the reason is that judges in our system are appointed at relatively advanced ages; this means that early decliners tend to be screened out and judges

4. John Ferejohn and Pasquale Pasquino, "Constitutional Adjudication: Lessons from Europe," 82 *Texas Law Review* 1671, 1702 (2004).

5. Id.

6. Id. at 1692–1700.

7. Richard A. Posner, *Aging and Old Age* 166–174 (1995).

tend not to get bored, or run dry, at the same age at which persons in other fields do who have been in the same line of work for many years.

Even apart from exceptionally able judges, such as Holmes, Brandeis, Learned Hand, and Henry Friendly, who performed with distinction well into their 80s (Holmes served into his 90s, but was fading toward the end), the federal judiciary in general exhibits little age-related decline in quality or (apart from senior status) even quantity of performance.[8] And this is further evidence against an algorithmic model of the judicial process. Were judging highly analytical, we would expect a pronounced aging effect, as in other analytical fields, such as mathematics and physics. It is also an explanation for the legalist character of the foreign career judiciaries. A career judiciary has a lower age profile than a lateral-entry one because the lowest tier of judges consists of recent law school graduates. Young judges have good analytic skills but little experience. Older judges have the experience that younger judges lack, making them abler to play the occasional-legislator role because that role is not algorithmic but depends instead on insight into policy.

The issue of judicial term limits is related to that of judicial salaries, which received renewed prominence when Chief Justice Roberts, in his January 1, 2007, year-end report to Congress on the federal judiciary, urged Congress to raise federal judicial salaries substantially.[9] (The Chief Justice of the United States is the administrative head of the entire federal judiciary.) They have not been increased (except for cost-of-living increases in some, but not all, years in which the cost of living rose),

---

8. Id., ch. 8; Frank M. Coffin, "Transitioning," 8 *Journal of Appellate Practice and Process* 247 (2006); Joshua C. Teitelbaum, "Age and Tenure of the Justices and Productivity of the Supreme Court: Are Term Limits Necessary?" 34 *Florida State University Law Review* 161 (2006); Frank B. Cross, *Decision Making in the U.S. Courts of Appeals* 80–81 (2007). Cross finds that court of appeals judges 70 years of age or older do not vote to affirm district court decisions in a higher percentage of cases than younger judges, as one would expect if the older judges were running down, since it is easier to affirm (one can rely on the reasoning of the lower court) than to reverse a decision.

9. John G. Roberts, Jr., "2006 Year-End Report on the Federal Judiciary," www .supremecourtus.gov/publicinfo/year-end/2006year-endreport.pdf (visited Apr. 20, 2007). Roberts's report was followed up by congressional testimony by two other Supreme Court Justices, Breyer and Alito, at the "Oversight Hearing on 'Federal Judicial Compensation'" before the Subcommittee on the Courts, the Internet and Intellectual Property of the House Committee on the Judiciary, Apr. 19, 2007, www.uscourts.gov/testimony/JusticeBreyerPay041907.pdf (visited May 9, 2007); www.uscourts.gov/testimony/JusticeAlitopay041907.pdf (visited May 9, 2007). For discussion and statistics (through the mid-1990s) concerning federal judicial compensation, see Richard A. Posner, *The Federal Courts: Challenge and Reform* 21–35 (1996).

since a very large raise in 1991—from $89,500 to $125,100 for district judges and from $95,000 to $132,700 for circuit judges. The current salaries of district and circuit judges are $165,200 and $175,100, respectively. Given that average U.S. salaries are higher than average British salaries, it may seem surprising that the salaries of federal judges are a little more than half the salaries of the corresponding British judges.[10] However, the high British salaries may reflect the fact that British judges are recruited almost entirely from the senior ranks of barristers, who have very high incomes.

If low salaries drive many judges to resign, then it is as if these judges had been subject to limits on the length of their terms. If term limits are bad, presumably so are salaries that induce self-termination. But because when salary is the inducer term limits are self-imposed, we must consider which judges are likeliest to resign as the salary gap widens. Judges who have the highest expected income from private practice are likely candidates, certainly—but also judges who derive the least satisfaction from their judgeship, as they may be bad judges because they lack interest in or aptitude for the job. This makes the effect of salary on the quality of the judiciary uncertain (and for a further reason, discussed shortly), though only within limits.

It is not even clear that the judges who have the highest expected income from private practice are the best judges. They may be the ablest lawyers, but that is not always the same thing; and if they yield to the lure of a higher income it may be because they derive relatively little nonpecuniary income from being a judge, which, as I just suggested, is probably positively correlated with not being a very good judge. (It might be possible, by use of the performance measures discussed in the preceding chapter, imperfect as they are, to estimate whether judges who resign, or who retire but then take another job, tend to be of average, below-average, or above-average judicial ability.) The prospect of a high-paying job in the private sector upon resignation or retirement— what I earlier called "external promotion"—would motivate some judges to work harder. But others, rather than work harder, might seek by their rulings to ingratiate themselves with law firms or clients. A high-paying

10. American College of Trial Lawyers, "Judicial Compensation: Our Federal Judges Must Be Fairly Paid" 8 (Mar. 2007).

job in private practice following resignation from the bench would then be in effect the delayed receipt of a bribe.

The Chief Justice's report points out that federal judicial salaries have fallen in real (that is, inflation-adjusted) terms since 1969. But this is misleading. Judicial salaries are raised infrequently except for the occasional cost-of-living increases, and when they are raised it is by a goodly amount. The result is a sawtooth pattern of raises and inflation-adjusted declines. The base year picked by Roberts, 1969, was the year of a big raise (from $33,000 to $42,500 for circuit judges), and afterward inflation ate away at the salary in real terms; likewise after the next big raise, in 1991. Had Roberts picked as his base year 1968 rather than 1969, the picture of decline would have been less dramatic.

What is rather dramatic, however, is that, as his report points out, federal judicial salaries are now well behind those of deans and professors at leading (though by no means all) law schools, whereas they used to be about the same. They are of course far behind the salaries of successful practicing lawyers. But that has always been true, although a novel twist is that judicial salaries are now lower than first-year associates' salaries at New York law firms, when the associates' bonuses are included.

The report warns in crying-wolf fashion that the federal judiciary is facing a crisis because of judges' lagging salaries. It notes that 38 federal judges left the bench between 2000 and 2005 and that 60 percent of newly appointed judges come from the public sector rather than from private practice; the figure used to be only 35 percent. More and more circuit judges are promoted from the ranks of district judges, and more and more district judges come from the lower ranks of the federal judicial hierarchy (bankruptcy judge or magistrate judge) or are appointed from a state court. (This trend, together with dramatic declines in the number of trials and hence in the use of juries, suggests, incidentally, a slight movement in the direction of convergence with the judiciaries of Continental Europe.)

To say that the wages in some job category are "too low" would not make much economic sense if one were talking about a job in the private sector. An employer who has trouble finding workers with the requisite skill and experience at the wage that he is offering will raise the wage or curtail his output and thus his demand for inputs, including labor. Even if there is an unanticipated demand for workers of a particular type, there will be no "shortage"; the limited supply of workers will be allocated to the most urgent demanders, and other employers will substitute other inputs (including workers with less skill or experience) or curtail output. In the public sector, however, there is no automatic equilibrating mechanism, so there may be shortages in particular jobs. The existence of a shortage is a signal that the legislature should raise the wages for those jobs, though the legislature might ignore the signal. No such signal is being emitted in the judicial sector. Rather than a shortage of applicants for federal judgeships, there is a surplus, as is true with regard to many other high-ranking government jobs. But because there are no very definite criteria for appointment to a federal judgeship, it is possible that the queue is dominated by low-quality applicants, just as colleges that have fuzzy acceptance criteria receive many long-shot applications.

Some evidence against this conjecture, however, is the long queues for appointment as a magistrate judge or a bankruptcy judge. Even though these judgeships have less secure tenure, pay less, and are less powerful and prestigious than district and circuit judgeships, there is excess demand for them. Of particular significance is the fact that these are merit appointments. Aspirants for such judgeships who do not have impressive credentials know that they are very unlikely to receive serious consideration. This implies that the applicant pool is of high quality. So if there is a surplus of high-quality applicants for these judgeships, there should be an even greater surplus of high-quality applicants for district and circuit judgeships, unless merit plays a very small role in appointment to such judgeships—and if so, we shall see, steep pay increases may make the situation worse rather than better.

Increased turnover could be a sign of job dissatisfaction due to low wages. But has turnover increased? Roberts gets to the figure of 38 judicial departures only by lumping retirements in with resignations. But the choice between taking senior status and retiring flat out from the judiciary is less likely to be motivated by dissatisfaction with salary than the decision to resign is—and resignations remain rare. In the period covered by the report, only 12 federal judges resigned out of a total of some 1,200 active and senior judges. In the comparable six-year period of 1969 to 1974, when there were only about 60 percent as many federal judges as there are now, 10 of them resigned—a higher percentage than in the period 2000 to 2005. Resignations of circuit judges are especially rare; there have been only 8 since 1981. But with the age of appointment of federal judges dropping,[11] one can expect the rate of resignation to rise somewhat.[12] A judge appointed at 50 may find his interest in the job fading after a decade, but age 60 is a bit old to start a new career, especially as it would mean sacrificing the generous pension to which he will be entitled in 5 years; it is quite different if he was appointed when he was only 40, so that after 10 years he is both young enough for a new career and still 15 years from being eligible to retire from the judiciary with a pension. (The federal judicial pension is a "cliff"; there is no pension if a judge retires a day before his statutory eligibility to retire at full pay.)

With such small samples of federal judges who quit, generalization is perilous. Most of the resignations may be only tangentially related to salary. They may reflect disappointment at not being promoted to the Supreme Court, in the case of a few circuit judges, or to the court of appeals, in the case of a number of district judges; or they may reflect the lure of exciting executive branch jobs at no higher wage. In recent decades two federal judges resigned to become Director of the Federal Bureau of Investigation, another to become Secretary of Education, another to become Secretary of Homeland Security, and three to become Solicitor General of the United States. Salary played no role in the three Supreme Court resignations (James Byrne, Arthur Goldberg, and Abe Fortas). There is also a burnout factor in the district court because of heavy workloads in urban districts and the monotony of a heavy diet of drug trials and sentencing hearings. A higher salary might have deterred some of these resignations. But are disappointed or burnt-out judges likely to do a better job than their eager replacements?

The most serious omission in Roberts's report is any discussion of the other compensation that judges receive besides their salaries.[13] That other compensation is critical to an understanding of the low turnover. Some of it is pecuniary. Most judges who want to can teach part-time at a law school at an annual salary of up to $25,000, the ceiling on

---

11. Albert Yoon, "Love's Labor's Lost? Judicial Tenure among Federal Court Judges: 1945–2000," 91 *California Law Review* 1029, 1050 (2003).

12. The most recent federal district judge to resign (at this writing) was only 48. Letter from U.S. District Judge Paul G. Cassell to President George W. Bush, Sept. 21, 2007, http://sentencing.typepad.com/sentencing_law_and_policy/files/cassell_presidentresign920fix.rtf (visited Sept. 22, 2007).

13. See Yoon, note 11 above, at 1056–1057.

outside income other than investment income and book royalties. It is a low ceiling, given current law school salaries. But this actually benefits judges because it means they need do only a little teaching to justify receiving the maximum permissible law school salary, as $25,000 is an ever-diminishing percentage of a professor's salary. More important, the federal judicial pension is extremely generous; a judge can retire at age 65 with only 15 years of judicial service (or at 70 with 10 years) and receive his full salary for life; nor does he make any contribution to funding the pension. The health benefits are also good.

Even more important are the nonpecuniary benefits of a federal judgeship. The job is less taxing than practicing law, more interesting (though this is a matter of taste), and more prestigious than practice or teaching, except at the highest levels (a firm such as Cravath, Swaine & Moore or a law school such as Harvard). Importantly, it is a better job for a lawyer who wants to work into his old age than either practice or teaching. Partners at major firms usually are forced to retire in their 60s, and most law professors, unlike judges, experience declining productivity and influence with age. Academic tenure removes much of the external pressure to remain active in the profession other than through teaching. Judicial tenure does not, because as long as a judge remains in service, cases keep coming to him for decision. He does not have to initiate projects, as an academic lawyer does.

Judges exercise power, not only over litigants but also (though primarily at the appellate rather than the trial level) in shaping the law for the future; and power is a valued form of compensation for many people. Judges write for publication, and though their audience—lawyers, other judges, and law clerks—is limited and specialized, it does read their writings attentively. Judges also are public figures, even if only locally, to a degree that few even very successful lawyers and law teachers are. And they are not at the beck and call of impatient and demanding clients, as even the most successful lawyers are. Judges receive deference; practicing lawyers do not. Judges also obtain intrinsic satisfaction from being judges, a satisfaction they might not obtain from practicing or teaching law. And if they are lucky, they will continue obtaining that satisfaction long after all their nonjudge contemporaries have retired. Justice Stevens is going strong at 87. For all these reasons there would be little difficulty recruiting first-rate academics for federal judgeships, despite the salary difference.

A further reason for the modesty of the judicial salary is that the judicial labor market is monopsonistic. "Monopsony" denotes the absence of competition on the buying side of a market, as distinct from the absence of competition on the selling side (monopoly). Sellers earn less in a monopsonized market than they would in a competitive one because they lack good alternatives. If you want to be a soldier there is only one possible employer (the government), and so it can and does pay a low wage to soldiers without compromising quality. Similarly, if you want to be a federal judge you have only one possible employer; a state judgeship is not a close substitute for a federal judgeship because the terms and conditions of employment are inferior and the prestige and power that are attached to the judgeship are less.

The competitive picture is changing, however, because of the growth of private judging—that is, of arbitration and particularly mediation. These are highly paid substitutes for working as a "real" judge (especially arbitration, as it involves resolving a suit rather than cajoling a settlement—though district judges do a lot of the latter too). They are close enough substitutes to satisfy even some judges who derive significant nonpecuniary benefits from judging.

Apart from the rise of private judging, the nonpecuniary income of a judgeship is actually growing relative to that of private practice. Private practice is increasingly competitive. That is fine for the clients but not good for the leisure and other nonpecuniary income of the lawyers who serve them. Competition maximizes consumer welfare, not the welfare of the sellers. Partners in law firms today have less leisure, less control over their work, and, above all, less job security (quite apart from being subject to compulsory retirement) than they used to have. Although they are still called "partners," their partnership agreements reduce most of them to the de facto status of employees by denying them any claim on the firm's profits and subjecting them to being fired or "de-equitized" (demoted by being expelled as equity partners) as if they were employees at will.[14]

The fact that most federal judges either continue in active service when they reach retirement age or take senior status—in either case preferring working for nothing to retiring or taking a high-paying job in the private sector—suggests that the nonpecuniary income that a federal judgeship yields is high. In an economic sense, indeed, a judge

14. See, for example, Nathan Koppel, "'Partnership Is No Longer a Tenured Position': More Law Firms Thin Ranks of Partners to Boost Profits, Attract, Keep High Earners," *Wall Street Journal*, July 6, 2007, p. B1.

who could increase his total monetary income by retiring is not working for nothing; he is *paying* to continue to be allowed to work as a judge.

A more mundane explanation for this unusual behavior is that the marginal utility of salary income tends to decline with age. By the time a person is in his mid-60s he has Social Security benefits and Medicare and in the usual case reduced expenses (children grown, mortgage paid). And the "cliff" character of federal judicial retirement discourages resignation by judges approaching eligibility for retirement.

All this is not to say that many successful practitioners would be sufficiently motivated by the prospect of a judgeship to exchange their $1 million or $2 million (or greater) annual income for a judge's salary. But enough, out of a national population of a million lawyers, would be willing and even eager to do so to enable the filling of vacancies in the federal courts with such practitioners, especially ones in their 50s who have built up a nice nest egg to supplement the judicial salary, as well as academics. Not that most of the one million American lawyers are actually qualified to be federal judges—the quality of the bar is notable for heterogeneity. But thousands are and that is a large enough pool to fill the 40 or so annual vacancies in the federal judiciary with highly competent lawyers.

So it is unlikely that the increased draw of new judges from the public sector is due to the salary lag. It is due partly to the fact that the federal docket, especially at the district court level, is increasingly dominated by criminal, prisoner, and employment-discrimination cases, none a category of cases congenial to lawyers who have a commercial practice. And partly to the fact that the judicial performance of lawyers who have worked for the government, for example as career prosecutors, or who have served as judicial officers, federal or state, is easier to predict than that of private practitioners, who may never have dealt with public issues, let alone in an adjudicative capacity. This is important in an era in which federal judicial candidates are carefully screened for ideology as well as for competence—and is further evidence that "legalist" is not an accurate description of today's federal judges. Judges appointed from private practice are more likely to be legalist judges than judges appointed from government service or the academy are, because they are less likely to have developed an interest in public issues. A practicing lawyer does not choose his clients and is more likely to think of himself as an agent or technician, as distinct from a principal or policymaker, than a lawyer who chose government service or a teaching career. Whatever the appointing authorities say, they are increasingly concerned with picking judges who will be politically dependable. It is the triumph of the attitudinal school.

Raising salaries, within the bounds of political feasibility, would not do a great deal to attract commercial lawyers to judgeships. A lawyer unwilling to exchange a $1 million income for a $175,000 income is unlikely to be willing to exchange it for a $225,000 income, especially if he does not want to decide criminal and prisoner civil rights cases. Roberts does not name a figure to which he thinks judicial salaries should be raised,[15] but he can hardly expect Congress to raise them by more than a third, so inflation will eat away at the salary increase until the next jump. Moreover, one effect of raising judicial salaries would be to make the job a bigger patronage plum for ex-Congressmen, friends of Senators, and others with political connections, so that the average quality of the applicant pool might actually fall.

Another effect of a much higher salary, having a similar consequence, would be to attract leisure-loving practitioners. A federal judgeship is a less stressful, more leisured job than practicing law. Those judges who work very hard, as many do, do so because they enjoy the work (or perhaps just enjoy working hard), not because they have to work hard in order to remain in good standing with their colleagues. Because of the salary gap, leisure lovers incur a high opportunity cost by exchanging a law practice for a judgeship. The cost would fall if judicial salaries were raised. And so the obverse of the proposition that low judicial salaries drive out dissatisfied judges is that the low salaries operate as a screening device: only lawyers who really want to be judges will accept the financial sacrifice required.[16] If there is a positive correlation between eagerness for the job and quality of the performance in it, raising judicial salaries could reduce the average quality of applicants, which in turn could reduce the average quality of judges if the appointing authorities

15. The American College of Trial Lawyers, note 10 above, suggests that they be doubled. A bill has been introduced in the Senate that would raise the salary of district judges to $247,800, of court of appeals judges to $262,700, and of Supreme Court Justices to $304,500 ($318,200 for the Chief Justice). Federal Judicial Salary Restoration Act of 2007, S. 1638, 110th Cong., 1st Sess. (2007).

16. Paul E. Greenberg and James A. Haley, "The Role of the Compensation Structure in Enhancing Judicial Quality," 15 *Journal of Legal Studies* 417 (1986).

do not (maybe they cannot) make good predictions concerning the judicial performance of members of the applicant pool. If priests were paid high salaries, the Catholic Church would find it difficult to determine which of the aspirants to the priesthood had a genuine vocation for the religious life.

There is some evidence that failure to raise judicial salaries will prompt resignations, even if not necessarily of the best judges. Since 1969, though not over the entire history of the federal judiciary, the number of resignations of federal judges who then entered private practice has been negatively correlated with federal judicial salaries.[17] The erosion of judicial salaries since the big raise in 1969 has coincided with an abnormal increase in the incomes of elite private practitioners, which in turn has pulled up salaries at elite law schools because they compete with the bar in hiring. High expected and actual earnings of graduates of elite law schools have swelled the schools' coffers both with tuition income and alumni donations, and those swollen coffers have ignited bidding wars for prized academics, which have contributed to the soaring incomes of professors at the leading law schools. Even so, judicial resignations remain at so low a level that their net effect on the quality of the federal judiciary may actually be positive, if the existence of good private practice opportunities for judges operates primarily to provide an attractive exit route for judges dissatisfied with their judicial careers and to minimize patronage appointments to the federal bench.

I do not wish to seem too complacent about the possible effects of the lagging federal judicial salaries. Judicial resignations, which may be on the increase, raise two concerns, though of uncertain gravity. First, it can be argued that a federal judgeship should be a terminal job—that the longer a judge serves, and thus the lower turnover is, the better because we value experienced judges (as suggested by the analysis in chapter 4), there is not much of an aging effect, and we do not want our judges to be angling for postjudicial jobs. Resignations have not, however, reached a point at which these should be serious concerns. Indeed, the average length of service of federal judges is increasing.[18] But second, resignations could be a sign that fewer able people find the job attractive and

17. Scott D. Kominers, "The Effects of Salary Erosion on the Federal Judiciary" (Harvard College, June 2007), http://web.mit.edu/scottkom/www/econ/kominers_980a_paper.pdf (visited June 20, 2007).
18. Yoon, note 11 above, at 1050.

therefore that the quality of the applicant pool is diminishing. With as much excess demand for a federal judgeship as there is, however, this should not be a serious concern. A study by Scott Baker finds no significant relation between a federal circuit judge's performance and his opportunity cost (what he would earn if he left the judgeship to become a partner in a law firm in his locale). Since all federal circuit judges are paid the same, judges who have higher opportunity costs are in effect accepting a lower income to be judges. Yet Baker finds that high-opportunity-cost judges are neither worse nor better judges, on average, than others.[19] This suggests that federal judicial performance, and presumably therefore the composition of the applicant pool, is relatively insensitive to judicial salary levels, though this would doubtless change with very large increases or (inflation-caused) decreases in judicial incomes, or, quite apart from inflation, further decreases in *relative* income (and thus further increases in the opportunity costs of remaining a judge). If relative judicial incomes took a big tumble, the applicant pool would become increasingly dominated by single, independently wealthy, older, dual-career, unsuccessful, power-hungry, publicity-seeking, and lazy lawyers. Very low judicial incomes would also reduce public respect for the courts, which would be unfortunate because that respect makes it easier to obtain compliance with judicial rulings with minimum coercion.

One argument for raising judicial salaries, though not an argument that reflects well on the character of judges (but after all they are only human beings, a species with many deficits), is that people who have a great deal of discretion yet feel underpaid may take revenge by underperforming. A judge who works 2,000 hours a year, so that his hourly fee is less than $90, and who feels indignant at being paid so little relative to his peers in private practice who are billing at $500 to $1,000 an hour, may decide to work fewer hours, delegating more work to his staff; to work the same number of hours but with less concentration; or to increase his nonpecuniary compensation by bullying the lawyers who appear before him. He might do these things in unconscious reaction to his resentment at being underpaid.

This argument for raising judicial salaries is unlikely to receive a

---

19. Scott Baker, "Should We Pay Federal Circuit Judges More (or Less)?" (University of North Carolina at Chapel Hill, School of Law, 2007).

warm welcome from Congress, as is the argument that the warnings by Supreme Court Justices that inadequate salaries are driving federal judges from the bench may become a self-fulfilling prophecy. Judges are being told that they are paid too little, that they are bailing out, and that the private sector is beckoning.[20] This may get them thinking.

If current federal judicial salaries are deemed too low, the question becomes by how much they should be raised. Attempting to answer the question presents all the problems that have bedeviled the "comparable worth" movement. There is no "intrinsic" value of work. Any method of setting a salary other than supply and demand is arbitrary. Partners at leading law firms today earn about 10 times as much as federal judges. If that ratio is too high, what should it be?

Federal judicial salaries cannot be cut, but they can be eroded in real (i.e., through inflation) or relative terms. Suppose there are no raises for years and as a result judges' salaries fall in 2007 dollars to $100,000, while average salaries of partners in leading law firms rise to $3,000,000 and of law professors at the elite law schools to $400,000. There will still be excess demand for judgeships. But at that point the applicant pool will be significantly altered and the quality of the federal judiciary will begin to sink. To prevent that decline requires annual cost-of-living increases at a minimum, and more if law firm and law school salaries continue to increase in real terms.

Intermittent large raises, followed by the erosion of their purchasing power by inflation, are a bad method of adjusting judicial salaries. They encourage retirement by judges who, having received the raise, do not anticipate receiving another for many years. Better to have regular annual raises consisting of a cost-of-living component plus an estimate, say 2 percent, of the average growth of incomes in other professional occupations.

A compensation measure that is long overdue and could be effectuated at minimum cost to the federal fisc would be to introduce a cost-of-living differential for federal judges. The cost of living differs greatly among different communities in the United States. Boston's cost of living

20. This was a particular emphasis of Justice Alito's testimony, note 9 above. Breyer, too, "offers a glimpse of the temptations that lurk there [i.e., in the private sector]." Breyer, note 9 above, p. 4. As both Justices pointed out, retired federal judges, mainly district judges, are being hired to do mediation, in effect private judging. Whether that represents a net loss to legal dispute resolution may be doubted.

is 40 percent above the average for the nation; the cost of living in Kankakee, Illinois, is 12 percent below the average; and these are not the extremes. Modest cost-of-living differentials, constituting raises limited to judges in high–cost-of-living areas, would go some distance toward remedying the perceived problem of inadequate judicial pay.

7

Judicial Method:
Internal Constraints on Judging

We saw in Part One that American judges have a great deal of discretionary authority—fact-finding discretion in the case of trial judges, law-making discretion in the case of appellate judges. We saw that it was plausible to suppose that most judges exercise discretion in such a way as to be recognized by themselves and others as "good" judges rather than lazy or willful ones. But we also saw that because an American judge, especially at the appellate level, is an occasional legislator, yet with no constituency to answer to, his judging is likely to be influenced by temperament, emotion, experience, personal background, and ideology (influenced in turn by temperament and experience), as well as by an "objective" understanding of what would be the "best" legislative policy to adopt in order to resolve the issue in the case. Later we saw that American judges, at least federal judges as distinct from elected state judges, are largely free from external constraints on the exercise of discretionary authority. The major exceptions are constraints that actually expand judges' discretionary authority. These are the constraints that define and protect an independent judiciary, such as ethical and professional norms that enjoin strict impartiality on judges and insulate them from effective control by the popular branches of government. (Judges like to describe the other branches as the "political" branches, as if the judiciary were not, to a significant degree, political.) The freer the judge is from the tug of personal interest and other personal concerns, such as promotion, the wider the range of other influences on his decision making is likely to be.

But maybe I am giving up too soon on the internal constraints. Maybe the reason that studies of judicial behavior find strong correlations between judicial outcomes and judges' personal and political characteristics is that there are many bad judges—judges who refuse through willfulness or incompetence to behave as judges are supposed to behave. Maybe the legalist conception of the judge's role is workable even in the American context, provided judges are able and disinterested. Maybe Ronald Dworkin is correct that there is one right answer to every legal question and that it is at once mandatory and feasible for every American judge to seek and find that answer.

At issue are two concepts of law. In one, which can actually span the considerable distance between the philosophies of adjudication of Antonin Scalia and Ronald Dworkin, law is distinct from politics and policy; it is the realm of rules, rights, and principles. In the other, law, at least insofar as the study of judges is concerned, is whatever judges do in their official capacity unless they go wild and court impeachment for being usurpative. I shall continue to call the first concept of law legalism and the second pragmatism, though it is a stretch to call Dworkin a legalist, for really what he has done is relabel his preferred policies "principles" and urged judges to decide cases in accordance with those "principles" and ignore (other) "policies," which are consigned to the legislature.[1] We shall see that Scalia's commitment to legalism is also in doubt.

Legalism consists of techniques for evaluating evidence; interpreting legally operative texts such as statutory and contractual provisions; applying rules to the facts of a case (which may mean applying a rule in a new, unforeseen situation); choosing between governing an area of law by a broad rule, which lawyers call a "standard," or by a narrow or specific rule (a "rule" in contrast to a standard); and drawing analogies and distinctions between precedents and the case at hand (following or distinguishing precedents). The use of precedent in a new case is central to

---

1. Bernard Williams, "Realism and Moralism in Political Theory," in Williams, *In the Beginning Was the Deed: Realism and Moralism in Political Argument* 1, 12 (Geoffrey Hawthorne ed. 2005), pertinently remarks "the intense moralism of much American political and indeed legal theory, which is predictably matched by the concentration of American political science on the coordination of private or group interests: a division of labour which is replicated institutionally, between the 'politics' of Congress and the principled arguments of the Supreme Court . . . a Manichaean dualism of soul and body, high-mindedness and the pork barrel, and the existence of each helps to explain how anyone could have accepted the other."

our case law system, and is the domain, in legalist analysis, of "reasoning by analogy."

The legalist techniques give judicial decision making an appearance of intellectual rigor. But in many instances it is just an appearance. I will be discussing mainly the interpretation of legislative texts and the handling of precedent, but I want first to touch on the other items in my list of judicial techniques. The rules of evidence (rules concerning hearsay evidence, expert testimony, cross-examination, the balancing of the probative value of a given piece of evidence against its likely prejudicial effect on a jury, jury instructions, jury selection, the authentication of documents, and so forth) have undoubted value in eliminating from litigation the most spurious and otherwise least helpful evidence that a litigant might want to present. The rules go far toward making trial by jury a rational method of resolving legal disputes. They also deter much litigation and enable much other litigation to be disposed of by the judge's granting summary judgment before, and thus averting, a trial. But often the rules fail to close the deal because after the worthless evidence is excluded there is still irreducible uncertainty concerning the true facts of the case. And then the judge or jury is at large, bereft of useful guidance from "the law."

The application of a rule to facts is problematic when the facts are incurably uncertain. But when they are certain, it might seem that applying a rule would involve a simple comparison between rule and facts, as when a driver admits that he was driving more than 60 miles per hour on a highway though the speed limit was 50. Examples such as this lead some judges and academics to tout the advantages of rules over standards because the latter are less certain; it is easier to determine whether a driver was exceeding the speed limit when he collided with another car than whether he was driving negligently.[2] But the certainty of a rule is bought at a price. By excluding considerations potentially relevant to its purpose (such as safe driving), the rule may generate a misfit between purpose and application. And while a posted speed limit is a rule that ev-

---

2. The trade-offs between rules and standards are the subject of an extensive literature. See, for example, Russell B. Korobkin, "Behavioral Analysis and Legal Form: Rules vs. Standards Revisited," 79 *Oregon Law Review* 23 (2000), and articles cited there. Note also that there are all sorts of methods of canalizing judicial discretion that are intermediate between "rules" and "standards," such as presumptions, factors, and advisory guidelines (which we'll meet in chapter 10). For a useful taxonomy, see Cass R. Sunstein, "Problems with Rules," 83 *California Law Review* 953 (1995).

ery user of the highway will learn, most rules of law are not "posted," so unless they are intuitive laypeople will violate them inadvertently. Standards are more likely to conform to lay understandings—which means that despite their greater vagueness they may provide better guidance to compliance with the law. Also, by virtue of being formulated in general terms ("negligence," "possession," "due diligence," and so forth), standards readily embrace unforeseen situations. Rules do not, and that creates arguments over their boundaries and, what is closely related, pressure for exceptions. Often, therefore, the real comparison is between a standard on the one hand and a rule plus exceptions and boundary issues on the other. Clarity may not favor the rule.

To illustrate, the equitable doctrine of laches requires that a suit be brought within a reasonable time after the injury sued on, where what is "reasonable" depends on the diligence of the plaintiff and the prejudice if any to the defendant caused by a delay in suing. Statutes of limitations fix definite deadlines but the judges then fuzz them up with doctrines such as the discovery rule, equitable estoppel, and equitable tolling, which in many cases allow a suit to be brought after the deadline has passed. Or consider "forum analysis" in free-speech cases. Judges tie themselves in knots trying to distinguish among "traditional public forums," "designated public forums," "nonpublic forums," and "limited designated public forums," also called "limited public forums" or "limited forums"[3] (or, in faux elegant terminology, "fora"), because each is the domain of a different rule regulating the government's right to limit freedom of speech.

A rule is like a precedent, in the sense of purchasing certainty (in both cases, though, an often delusive certainty) at the price of forgoing an opportunity to obtain potentially relevant information from experience with new cases. Both rules and precedents illustrate the backward-looking nature of legalist decision making because both reflect the state of knowledge when they were promulgated and are not open to new knowledge. Standards enable information obtained after promulgation to be incorporated into the law without need for further rule making. The point is general. When, for example, Congress passes a vague statute, thus leaving it to the judges enforcing the statute to fill in the details, in effect the judges are enlisted in the legislative process; thus the per se rules of anti-

3. See, for example, Gilles v. Blanchard, 477 F.3d 466 (7th Cir. 2007).

trust laws are judge-made rules that supplement the general directives in the antitrust statutes. Whereas standards permit and indeed invite a judge or jury to use information of which the judges or legislators who promulgated the standard could not have been aware, adjustment to the new in a regime of rules and precedents requires judges to carve exceptions to the rules and distinguish the precedents. These maneuvers, which reduce the predictability of rule-based and precedent-based law, are elided in a regime of standards.

The essence of a rule is that it limits the range of admissible facts. All manner of facts bear on whether a driver's speed is safe, such as road, weather, and traffic conditions; skill and attentiveness; vision and reflexes; and the design, equipment, and condition of the vehicle. A speed limit eliminates from consideration all but the driver's speed. That is fine, but only because there are expert institutions, separate from the courts, for regulating the safety of roads, vehicles, and drivers. In contrast, in *New York Times Co. v. Sullivan*[4] the Supreme Court ruled that a public figure cannot obtain damages for defamation unless the defendant knew, or had been reckless in failing to discover, that the libel or slander was false. This was a rule in the form of a precedent, which halted in its tracks the evolution of a legal regime for regulating defamation of public figures. Had the Court ruled merely that defamation must not be used to stifle criticism of public officials (the situation in *New York Times Co. v. Sullivan*), the lower courts would have been able to develop, in light of the facts of new cases, a more nuanced code of rules and principles to govern this subfield of constitutional law.

An example of successful rule making, oddly parallel to speed limits, is (or perhaps was, in light of developments discussed in chapter 10) the federal sentencing guidelines. Before their promulgation, the choice of the sentence to impose on a defendant between the statutory minimum and maximum sentences prescribed by Congress (often a very broad range) was in the unguided discretion of the sentencing judge. The sentences imposed by different judges varied widely and the variance could not be explained by reference to penological principles; they seemed arbitrary. The United States Sentencing Commission, which drafted the guidelines, drew on the knowledge of criminologists, federal probation officers, and other experts, though the guideline sentencing ranges es-

---

4. 376 U.S. 254 (1964).

tablished by the Commission mostly tracked what had been average judicial sentencing practice before the guidelines. In contrast to the work of the Commission, when the Supreme Court and other appellate courts lay down rules, it is rarely on the basis of expert knowledge.

But the key point about the choice between rules and standards, so far as understanding judicial behavior is concerned, is that judges typically lack the information they would need in order to make an objective choice between the two regimes. Some judges are more comfortable with rules, others with standards, and the reasons may be largely temperamental—may in fact be related to the difference between the authoritarian and the nonauthoritarian personality (see chapter 4), which in turn is correlated, though perhaps only weakly because much more than personality influences a judge's behavior, with the judge's preference ordering of legalism and pragmatism. The legalist loves rules because they promise (though it is a promise frequently broken in application) to curtail judicial discretion by confining judges to determining a handful of prespecified facts.

Although I have been emphasizing the limitations of rules, often it is reasonably clear that they are superior to standards even from a pragmatic standpoint. Statutes of limitations, though not as clear as they look, are preferable to relying solely on the vague concept of laches, which would leave a potential defendant in the dark as to when the deadline for a suit against him had passed so that he could go about his business without the threat of liability hanging over his head and so without having to preserve evidence and take other protective measures against a possible suit. And it is sensible to have speed limits. But the legalists' *general* preference for rules over standards has never been shown to be correct. No responsible person favors a legal regime of just rules or just standards, but there is a large middle range in which the choice of a rule over a standard depends on a policy judgment rather than on an exercise of logic. It would be absurd to think that the per se rules of antitrust law had been derived from the text of the Sherman Act by a process of or akin to deduction. They are judge-made regulatory accretions to the Act. No more can the elaborate rules that the Supreme Court has concocted for regulating searches and seizures, restrictions on free speech and on the public recognition and support of religion, and capital punishment be thought deduced or deducible from the language of the Constitution.

Among legalists' most interesting methods of reasoning are reasoning by analogy in case law and interpretation in constitutional and statutory law. We can approach the former through *Legal Reason: The Use of Analogy in Legal Argument,* by Harvard law professor Lloyd Weinreb. His book argues that reasoning by analogy is at once the essence of legal reasoning in a case law system and a methodology unrelated to economic, policy, or pragmatic analysis (approaches that he treats as interchangeable)—or even to the application of rules—and that other people who have written about reasoning by analogy, such as Weinreb's colleague Scott Brewer,[5] have it wrong.

Weinreb might seem to be driving a spear into legalism's midriff by celebrating reasoning by analogy. For whatever exactly it is, it is not the application, by means resembling deduction, of clear, preexisting rules to found facts. The more that the legalist is forced to resort to reasoning by analogy to decide cases, the farther away he is pushed from the model of law as the application of preexisting rules; faced with a rule squarely applicable to the case before him, he has no need to gauge the similarity of his case to some other case. But Weinreb's project, if successful, would support an alternative conception of legalism—legalism not as deductive reasoning but as a set of techniques for deciding cases without recourse to policy, techniques that presuppose that law is an autonomous field of knowledge, walled off from the social sciences and uncontaminated by concern with policy or consequences.

Weinreb's leading example of reasoning by analogy is an old case called *Adams v. New Jersey Steamboat Co.*[6] The issue was whether a Hudson River steamboat operator owed a passenger who had occupied one of its staterooms the same very high duty of care that courts had held in previous cases an innkeeper owed his guests, or merely the lower duty of care that a railroad had been held to owe passengers who slept in the open berths of its sleeping cars. The court analogized the steamboat company to the innkeeper (it called the steamboat "a floating inn") rather than to the railroad, and so concluded that the steamboat company owed the higher duty of care to the plaintiff. As a result the company was liable to the plaintiff for the theft of $160 by an intruder who

---

5. Scott Brewer, "Exemplary Reasoning: Semantics, Pragmatics, and the Rational Force of Legal Argument by Analogy," 109 *Harvard Law Review* 923 (1996).

6. 45 N.E. 369 (N.Y. 1896).

had pried open the locked window of the plaintiff's stateroom and stolen the money from the plaintiff's clothing that he found there.

The case indeed illustrates what in legal parlance is called "reasoning by analogy." But what exactly is the mental operation that the term denotes? Could it be merely the starting point for policy analysis? These are important questions because reasoning by analogy enjoys canonical status in most discussions of legal reasoning. If, as I believe with only slight exaggeration, there is nothing to reasoning by analogy, this is a clue that the gap between ordinary, everyday reasoning and "legal" reasoning may be slight.

Analogies can be suggestive,[7] like metaphors, similes, and parallel plots in literature—devices that analogies resemble. (Think of the three son-father revenge plots in *Hamlet,* and how the two involving revengers other than Hamlet—Fortinbras and Laertes—provide analogies to Hamlet's situation.) But analogies cannot resolve legal disputes intelligently. To say that something is in some respects like something else is to pose questions rather than answer them. At a conference I once heard it suggested in all seriousness that torture in desperate situations might be justified by analogy to the right of self-defense recognized by tort law if one is assaulted. And yes, an impending terrorist attack and a threatening gesture have something in common—both create an imminent risk of harm to a victim or victims—and self-defense and the torture of a suspected terrorist also have something in common—they are designed to prevent an attack or limit the damage caused by it. One might dress up the comparison by reference to proportions: A is to B as C is to D, where A is a threatening gesture, B self-defense by the victim, C a threatened terrorist attack, and D torturing the terrorist suspect or an accomplice. But to read off a right to torture from such a bit of formal analysis would be hasty, to say the least.

Brewer's answer to the question what is legal reasoning by analogy is that a novel case incites a search for a rule that might cover it. The similarity between innkeepers and steamboat operators as providers of sleeping accommodations for travelers makes the rule that governs innkeepers a likely candidate for a rule to govern steamboat operators. But what is the innkeeper rule? Is it that a contract for sleeping accommodations

---

7. A famous example is how Wilbur and Orville Wright, bicycle makers, discovered how to stabilize a flying vehicle by considering analogous problems of stabilizing a bicycle. See the splendid account in Philip N. Johnson-Laird, *How We Reason,* ch. 25 (2006).

includes an implicit guarantee of safety—that it is one of the things the customer is paying for and so he is excused from having to take any unusual precautions to secure his property? For remember that Adams had locked the window of his stateroom. But this rule, while it covers the steamboat case, must be too broad, because it would require the railroad to extend the same high level of care to its sleeping berth customers. The railroad case is better understood as an exception to the general rule. Because the sleeping berths are open to anyone who happens to be in the car, the railroad cannot feasibly protect each sleeper against all thefts of his property.[8] Knowing this, the passenger implicitly agrees, as part of his contract with the railroad, to take some responsibility for securing his property himself; in the jargon of economic analysis of law, he is the "cheaper cost avoider." The exception is not applicable to the steamboat case. That case involved a stateroom, which is a closed compartment, just like a room in an inn so far as the proprietor's ability to protect the customer's property is concerned. The case is therefore covered by the same rule that governs the innkeeper's liability.

Rather than speak of rule and exception we could say more simply that the three cases taken together exemplify the standard that a business that provides sleeping accommodations to its customers must take as much care to protect them as is feasible. We could say that instead of a rule or a standard there are two rules—one for inns, steamboats, and closed-compartment railroad sleepers and one for open-berth sleepers. We could say that in *Adams* the court "distinguished" the railroad case— that is, limited its scope. Most simply, we could just say that to consult precedent when trying to decide a new case is to look for policy insights that might be applicable to the new case.[9] All these approaches lead to the same result. None requires a discussion of analogy.

"Reasoning by analogy" is a term that does no work and, worse, that is misleading because it sounds like a search for similarity whereas actually it is a search for difference. The interesting thing about the sequence of

8. "It is quite obvious that the passenger has no right to expect, and in fact does not expect, the same degree of security from thieves while in an open berth in a car on a railroad as in a stateroom of a steamboat, securely locked and otherwise guarded from intrusion." Adams v. New Jersey Steamboat Co., note 6 above, at 370.

9. Criticism of reasoning by analogy is not criticism of the doctrine of precedent. The two techniques are easily confused. The benefits that Emily Sherwin in her article "A Defense of Analogical Reasoning in Law," 66 *University of Chicago Law Review* 1179 (1999), ascribes to reasoning by analogy are for the most part benefits of the doctrine of precedent.

cases that culminates in *Adams* is not the similarity between *Adams* and the inn cases but the difference between it and the railroad case. Two cases dealing with sleeping accommodations are bound to be similar in many respects; what is illuminating in a comparison of the steamboat and railroad cases is that in the railroad case the sleeping accommodations were open, and this pointed to a difference in the carrier's ability to protect the passengers from assaults and thefts. That is a difference related to policy, to the allocation of safety responsibilities between carriers and passengers. To "distinguish" an earlier case, such as the railroad case distinguished in *Adams,* is to enrich the law with a new insight,[10] typically, as in *Adams* itself, an insight into public policy.

Analogy belongs to the logic of discovery rather than to the logic of justification. Whether a judge in a common law case starts with other cases or with some sense of what a reasonable decision on grounds of policy would be, he has to make an initial selection from all possible cases, and all possible policy concerns, of those most relevant to the case at hand. (This assumes that he does not have some overarching analytic framework for the field of law in question that gives him a strong initial intuition about the correct decision.) At this stage, pattern recognition, a deeply ingrained capability of the human mind, plays a useful sorting role. It thus made sense for the court in *Adams* to interrogate the previous cases involving passengers and guests at inns—but to interrogate them for the policy that animated them. If the interrogation reveals inconsistent policies, the court must make a legislative judgment in the new case. What makes no sense is to try to determine which case the new one most closely "resembles" without exploring policy, unless the cases are identical in the sense that the first case declared a rule that the second case is clearly governed by. That is not a matter of resemblance, of analogy, but of subsumption. If the cases are merely similar, the question is not how similar—a meaningless question—but whether the differences make the policy that informs the previous case inapplicable to the new one; whether, in short, the cases are distinguishable.

10. Nicola Gennaioli and Andrei Shleifer, "Overruling and the Instability of Law" (forthcoming in *Journal of Comparative Economics*); Gennaioli and Shleifer, "The Evolution of Common Law," 115 *Journal of Political Economy* 43 (2007). For a comprehensive discussion of the doctrine of precedent, see Julius Stone, *Precedent and Law: Dynamics of Common Law Growth* (1985). Stone sums up by calling the doctrine "not so much a straitjacket as a capacious muumuu." Id. at 229. He is right.

Distinguishing a precedent is a useful pragmatic tool when it is not merely a euphemism for overruling. Judges sometimes distinguish a precedent to death by deciding the new case the opposite way when the only difference between the two cases—the difference the court points to as the basis for distinguishing the earlier case—is something irrelevant to the holding of the first case. They do this to maintain a superficial impression of continuity, at the risk, however, of leaving the landscape of case law littered with questionable cases that not having been formally overruled can be revived at any time to confer a spurious pedigree on a novel ruling. The constructive use of distinguishing is to refine a rule stated in an earlier case by bringing to bear insights gleaned from the circumstances of the current case.

Weinreb rejects any analysis of *Adams* that is based on rules because he does not think there was a preexisting rule of which the result in the cases involving innkeepers was an instantiation and to which the result in open-berth railroad cases was an exception.[11] This does not bother him. He is no more enamored of rules than he is of policy. And it is true that a legal rule may be inchoate, intuited rather than articulated, and vaguely bounded, because a judge has to decide a case even if he is unsure what the rule governing it is or should be. A "rule" declared in such circumstances is really just a stab at creating a rule—the preliminary drawing rather than the completed painting. We could abandon rule talk in the line of cases culminating in *Adams* and ask simply why the innkeeper cases were decided as they were and why the open-berth railroad case was decided as it was. The answer is that customers expect providers of overnight accommodations to protect them securely from theft when it is feasible for them to do so, as it was in the innkeeper cases and likewise in the steamboat case but not in the open-berth railroad case.

The legal realist Max Radin noted a

common way in which judges arrive at their conclusion. The category into which to place the situation presented to them for judgment, does not leap into their minds at once. On the contrary, several categories struggle in their minds for the privilege of framing the situation before them. And since there is that struggle, how can they do otherwise than select the one that seems to them to lead to a desirable result.[12]

11. Lloyd L. Weinreb, *Legal Reason: The Use of Analogy in Legal Argument* 111–112 (2005).
12. Max Radin, "The Theory of Judicial Decision: Or How Judges Think," 11 *American Bar Association Journal* 357, 359 (1925).

That is often the situation facing a judge—but not in *Adams*. The two rules, railroad and innkeeper, could coexist happily, the former fitting the latter as exception to rule. There was no tension between the cases once the animating policies were grasped. All that was required was to draw the boundary between the rules on the basis of their policies. The steamboat case clearly fell on the innkeeper side of the boundary.

Weinreb objects to purposive as well as rule-oriented approaches because both merge reasoning by analogy with policy analysis.[13] The purposive approach does so even more completely than the rule-oriented approach. A rule's wording may make its scope so clear that applying the rule to a new set of facts requires no consideration of purpose; analysis never dips below the semantic level. But if the rule claimed to be applicable does not quite fit the case, the court must determine the purpose behind it in order to decide whether extending it to cover the case would be consistent with that purpose.

Radin was thinking of situations in which the court has to go *beyond* the cases in order to decide. *Adams* illustrates the situation in which the court has to go *behind* the cases. Radin's interest was in freewheeling judicial policy analysis, which is problematic, or at least controversial. *Adams* is unproblematic because the court was simply identifying uncontroversial policies found in previous cases and determining which applied to the present case. Such a judicial activity is more passive, more modest, than Radin wished to emphasize. It is also an example of how nonlegalist analysis can be objective.

The distinction between untethered judicial discretion and judicial reasoning based on policies expressed or implied in previous cases does not interest Weinreb. He thinks that reasoning by analogy is its own kind of thing—that it does not require recourse to policy analysis, even the modest kind that involves merely identifying and applying policies that figured in earlier cases. Endeavoring to hold policy at arm's length, Weinreb notes that reasoning by analogy is pervasive in ordinary life, life unconcerned with rules or public policy. He gives the following example: if your power mower won't start, you might try letting it sit awhile and then try again to start it, by analogy to a procedure that often works if your car won't start. But you wouldn't kick it to make it start, as you might do if it were a donkey. In this example lawn mower replaces

13. Weinreb, note 11 above, at 116–122.

steamboat, car replaces inn, and donkey replaces railroad. Yet no one would think you were applying a rule, or engaged in any sort of analysis other than reasoning by analogy understood as exercising an innate capacity to recognize relevant similarities; and so (Weinreb argues) in *Adams*. Actually the example is consistent with a rule-based, purposive, or policy-saturated approach to *Adams*. The rules that you apply in the lawn mower case are that internal-combustion engines start in a certain way and that people and other animals can sometimes be hurt into doing something. Since the power mower is an inanimate object powered by an internal-combustion engine, the first rule determines your response rather than the second.

Reasoning by analogy belongs to legal rhetoric rather than to legal thought. Weinreb was correct when he said at the beginning of his book that it would be "about the *arguments* that lawyers make in support of their clients and judges make in the course of their *opinions*."[14] (The book's subtitle carries a similar implication.) Reasoning by analogy obscures the policy judgments that should determine the outcome of a case, as illustrated by an example of mine[15] to which Weinreb refers. The example is the choice of a rule of property law to govern oil and natural gas, which being liquid or gaseous do not have a fixed shape. Analogizing to the rule governing property in wild animals—the rule of capture, whereby a property right is not obtained until the animal is caught—courts concluded that because, like animals, oil and gas move (though, unlike animals, not under their own power but purely as an effect of gravitational or other external force), they should also be governed by the rule of capture. But it is not a *relevant* similarity. A rule that would make the rabbits that stray onto your land your property by virtue of that fact, so that if they stray off it and are shot you are entitled to their pelts, is not needed for the sake of encouraging investment in rabbits. Wild rabbits are not a product of investment, and so you are not deprived of the fruits of an investment when your neighbor shoots and eats a rabbit that having wandered onto your land later wanders onto his. Oil and gas are extracted from the earth by expensive drilling equipment after costly exploratory efforts often involving the digging of many dry

14. Id. at 1 (emphasis added).
15. Richard A. Posner, *Overcoming Law* 519 (1995).

holes, the expense of which has to be recouped in the occasional lucky strike. Under the rule of capture, someone who drills a well that taps into an underground pool of oil has an incentive to pump as much oil as fast as he can because he has no claim to the pool as such and so any oil he fails to pump is likely to become the property of a competitor. The race to pump may cause the pool to be exhausted prematurely. The applicable analogy is not to the property rules for wild animals but to the property rules for other extractable natural resources, such as coal. You are allowed to own an entire seam and remove coal from it at your leisure, rather than having to worry that anyone else can remove coal from the seam without compensating you.

Eventually the rule of capture for oil and gas was changed by legislation requiring the "unitization" of oil and gas fields—that is, that they be managed as if under single ownership. A single owner would not worry that a competitor might be pumping oil from the same pool—the single owner by definition owns the entire pool and can exclude others from access to it. He can pump oil at whatever rate is most efficient without worrying that by doing so he will be losing profits to competitors.

In the oil and gas case, as in all cases of reasoning by analogy, a sensible result requires attention to the considerations of policy that align the case at hand with one or another line of precedents. Failure to do that was what led to the mistaken application of the rule of capture to oil and gas.

Weinreb both acknowledges and denies the hovering presence of policy. He acknowledges it when he says that a lawyer's "knowledge of the law" would tell "him that the similarities between [the inn cases and the steamboat case] relate to factors that commonly have a bearing on liability,"[16] and when he says that the choice between analogies "is informed also by a broad understanding of what is relevant to the sort of decision being made";[17] "what is relevant" is the open-ended set of policies on which sensible judicial decisions are based. He even admits that there are "policies latent in the law."[18] But he does not indicate what they are or what policies are out of bounds to judges. And he denies the relevance of policy outright when he says that judges "are not to decide for

16. Weinreb, note 11 above, at 133.
17. Id. at 92.
18. Id. at 118 fn.

themselves what the law is but are to seek it out, to discover and apply it as it is."[19]

But more frequent than either acknowledgment or denial of the role of policy is equivocation, as when Weinreb says that "all the talk in the world with engineers, ecologists, and even economists [to decide what rule of property law should govern oil and gas] is beside the point unless what they have to say is reflected in the law."[20] But cannot the implications *become* reflected in the law by persuading judges to change the existing law? Concern with efficiency should certainly be admissible to determine property rights in oil and gas. So when Weinreb says that a judge "may not engage in social or economic engineering *at large*,"[21] we are desperate to know at what point he thinks social or economic engineering, implicitly permitted by him on a small scale, ceases to be legitimate.

He wants judges to stick to the "law itself" or "law in itself" or "law within itself" or "the law as it is," and he even calls the law a "seamless web,"[22] but he does not say where the web ends and something else begins. In places he suggests that "law" includes "ordinary common sense" and even "moral evaluation"[23] à la Ronald Dworkin, whom elsewhere he disparages. He also says that the most the law can aspire to is "human reasonableness."[24] But what is "humanly reasonable" is conforming law to practical needs and interests, which in turn implies a willingness to bring policy considerations to bear in deciding how to resolve novel issues.

When judges ignore policy, nonsense can ensue, as in the oil and gas cases, or sheer indeterminacy, as in a chain of cases that Weinreb discusses involving copyright in mechanical transmissions of copyrighted works. The copyright on a song or a drama includes the right to "perform" it. In an early case a hotel received broadcasts of copyrighted songs and transmitted them to the rooms in the hotel by wires connected to its receiving set. The Supreme Court held in a wooden opinion

19. Id. at 148 (footnote omitted).
20. Id. at 118 (footnote omitted).
21. Id. at 97 (emphasis added).
22. Id. at 102.
23. Id. at 92, 144 fn.
24. Id. at 161.

(one of Brandeis's least impressive performances) that since the hotel's receiving set did not amplify the sound waves from the radio station that broadcast the music but instead transformed them into electromagnetic waves that were transmitted to the rooms through the wires and there reconstituted as sound waves, the transmission to the rooms was a performance no different from hiring an orchestra to perform copyrighted music, and so required a license from the copyright holders.[25] The Court made no attempt to relate the physics of radio reception and transmission to the purpose of copyright protection. It was an opinion to give reasoning by analogy a bad name.

Many years later, in *Fortnightly Corp. v. United Artists Television, Inc.*,[26] the Supreme Court confronted an ostensibly analogous case and reached the opposite result, again misusing analogy. Cable television operators had obtained copyrighted programming for their subscribers by erecting antennas that, as in the earlier case, received programs broadcast over the air, though broadcast by television stations rather than by radio stations. Cables connecting the antennas to the homes of the cable television subscribers transmitted the programs to those subscribers, just as the hotel in the earlier case had distributed programs that it received over the air from radio stations to its customers by means of wire transmission. Yet contrary to its earlier decision, the Court described what the cable television operators were doing as merely amplifying the broadcast signal, just as when a homeowner puts an antenna on his roof in order to receive signals from distant stations.

To suppose that the cable television case can rationally be decided by determining whether cable television is more like a homeowner's putting up an antenna than it is like hiring an orchestra to perform copyrighted music is absurd. A rational resolution of the issue requires discerning the purpose of giving the owner of a copyrighted work the exclusive right to perform it. The purpose is to prevent the form of free riding that consists of waiting for someone to spend money to create a valuable expressive work and then, by copying the work and selling copies at a price below the price that the work's creator would have to charge to break even, preventing him from recouping his investment.

25. Buck v. Jewell-LaSalle Realty Co., 283 U.S. 191, 199–201 (1931).
26. 392 U.S. 390 (1968).

The copier's break-even price is lower because he does not have to recover the cost of creating the work—he incurred no such cost and so his free riding is profitable.

In the early days of cable television, which was when *Fortnightly* was litigated, the primary use of cable television was to provide television reception to communities that because of topography or remoteness from over-the-air stations could not receive clear broadcast signals. Because of hilly terrain, the people living in Fortnightly's service area could receive the signals of only two television stations over the air. Fortnightly brought them the signals of three other stations by cable. Rather than depriving those stations of any of the advertising revenues that the stations would need in order to be able to pay license fees to the owners of the copyrights on the broadcast programs, Fortnightly increased those revenues by enlarging the audience for television broadcasts that the cable subscribers could not have received over the air.[27] Nor had the cable company stripped the advertising from the programs it transmitted and resold advertising time to other advertisers.[28] That would have amounted to appropriating license fees owed to owners of the copyrights on those programs and would thus have been free riding, which copyright law aims to prevent.

Weinreb finds additional evidence of judicial reasoning by analogy in the sequence of cases from *Olmstead v. United States*,[29] which held that wiretapping was not a search within the meaning of the Fourth Amendment, to *Katz v. United States*,[30] which held many years later that it was. The amendment protects "the right of the people to be secure in their persons, houses, papers, and effects, against unreasonable searches and seizures," and the Court in *Olmstead* based its ruling on the fact that a nontrespassory wiretap does not invade the person (as a physical search of him, or an arrest, would), his house, his papers, or his other physical property (his "effects"). In the later case the Court decided that what was important was that wiretapping is an invasion of privacy.

The choice between the two decisions depends on how one thinks constitutional provisions should be interpreted—strictly or loosely, and

27. Id. at 391–393, 401 n. 28.
28. The significance of this point was noted in the subsequent case of Teleprompter Corp. v. Columbia Broadcasting System, Inc., 415 U.S. 394, 405 n. 10 (1974).
29. 277 U.S. 438 (1928).
30. 389 U.S. 347 (1967).

if the latter whether one likes the idea of imputing to the Fourth Amendment a policy of protecting privacy rather than the more concrete interests actually listed in the constitutional text—and how to balance the interest in privacy against the interest in law enforcement, which is impeded if the police have to obtain a warrant in order to wiretap. The Court has consistently held that they do not have to obtain a warrant to plant an informer in a nest of suspected criminals, even if the informer is "wired" to record any conversations he hears. Law enforcers would strenuously resist, as an impediment to effective enforcement, an extension of the requirement of a warrant to that case. They would likewise much prefer not to have to obtain a warrant to do wiretapping.

Weinreb thinks that reasoning by analogy figured in *Katz* because the Court compared the telephone booth from which Katz made the call that was intercepted to a person's office, both being places in which there is an expectation of privacy. But the analogy related to a peripheral issue in the case—whether, if wiretapping *is* a Fourth Amendment search, there should nevertheless be an exception if what is being tapped is the phone line in a public phone booth rather than in a person's home or office. The principal issue in *Katz* was whether nontrespassory wiretapping is *ever* a Fourth Amendment search, and analogies were irrelevant to resolving that issue and were not employed. It illustrates how little work reasoning by analogy actually does in the law.

My last example of traditional legal reasoning is the interpretation of statutes and constitutions. It is the scene of interminable debate. Traditionally it was a debate between advocates of "strict construction," or its approximate synonym "plain meaning," and of "loose construction" ("construction" meaning "interpretation"). Today it is more commonly a debate between advocates of "textualism" and "originalism," on the one hand, and of "dynamic" or "purposive" interpretation, and the concept of "the living Constitution," on the other hand.

"Strict construction" can mean interpreting statutes (and other documents to which legal significance attaches) narrowly, as in the old "canon of construction" that statutes in derogation of the common law are to be interpreted narrowly so as to minimize their inroads into that law. Or it can mean interpreting statutes and other documents literally, that is, according to the "plain meaning" of their words, without recourse to considerations of legislative history, real-world context or consequences, or other indicia of legislative purpose. Literal interpretations can be astonishingly broad. "Literal when narrow" may be the practical meaning of strict construction. The loose constructionist is a nonliteralist, but he does not necessarily favor broad interpretations of statutes or constitutional provisions, creating new judicially enforceable rights. He could in other words be a practitioner of judicial self-restraint rather than of judicial activism.

"Textualism" is literalism. "Originalism" means giving the words of a constitutional provision (the term is rarely used in relation to any other type of enactment) their original meaning—more precisely, restoring the understanding of the ratifiers. So the two terms are quite close, except when the meaning of crucial terms has changed over time—I give the example of habeas corpus in chapter 10—and except that if the statutory text is ambiguous a strict constructionist will want to construe it against the litigant who is relying on it while the originalist will be guided by the meaning that the text's authors (or ratifiers, in the case of constitutional provisions) would have assigned to the text. Textualism and originalism share with strict construction an antipathy to interpreting a statute or a constitutional provision by reference to its purpose. Semantic rather than pragmatic or policy-oriented methods of interpretation,[31] all three are quintessentially legalistic techniques.

Interpretive issues arise in the domain of precedent as well as in that of legislative texts, usually in the form of judges' attempts to distinguish between the holding of a case, which is the part that has precedential effect, and the language of the opinion that could be detached without changing the holding.[32] Despite its antiquity and its seeming essentiality to the operation of a case law system, the distinction is in practice elusive. It is a sign of the growing influence of pragmatic decision making that judges make less of the distinction than they used to. The practical issue always is simply how much of an earlier case you are going to leave alone, and that depends on a host of considerations (such as the cir-

31. These methods, defended in Richard A. Posner, *The Problems of Jurisprudence*, pt. 3 (1990), license "loose" interpretation because they do not require the judge to stick strictly to the words of the enactment that is to be interpreted. For comprehensive treatments of theories of statutory interpretation, see William D. Popkin, *Statutes in Court: The History and Theory of Statutory Interpretation* (1999); William N. Eskridge, Jr., Philip P. Frickey, and Elizabeth Garrett, *Cases and Materials on Legislation: Statutes and the Creation of Public Policy*, ch. 7 (4th ed. 2008).

32. See, for example, Michael Abramowicz and Maxwell Stearns, "Defining Dicta," 57 *Stanford Law Review* 953 (2005), and references cited there.

cumstances of the earlier case relative to present circumstances, the rule implicit in the earlier case and whether it comports with present circumstances, and the desirability of limiting judge-made rules to factual situations akin to those that gave rise to the rule) that can no more be reduced to a formula than the decision whether to overrule a case can be.

I said in chapter 4 and repeat here that interpretation is a natural, intuitive human activity. It is not rule-bound, logical, or step-by-step. It is possible to *impose* a rule—to say to a judge, we don't *want* you to figure out what the legislature was driving at; we want you to interpret statutes as if you were a newcomer to the culture and had only the literal meaning of the statute to go on. The strict constructionist wants to deduce the outcome of a statutory case from a major premise consisting of a rule of law clearly and explicitly stated in legislation or the Constitution and a minor premise consisting of the facts of the case. Preferring rules to standards and words to activity in the world, he tries to dissolve any interpretive difficulties presented by the often vague or confused wording of statutes by invoking rules of interpretation (the "canons of construction") in an effort to make interpretation a rule-bound activity. If the attempt fails, he decides against the party who is trying to extract a claim or defense from ambiguous statutory wording.

The procedure is spurious. It might make sense if legislators or drafters of constitutions were committed to the canons of construction, but they are not, and if in addition the legalist judge-interpreter felt bound only by substantively neutral canons, such as that the outright expression of one thought excludes the implication of another, related thought (the canon known as *expressio unius est exclusio alterius*); or that the same word is presumed to mean the same thing throughout a statute; or that a statute is presumed to contain no surplusage (that is, no words that do no work), as distinct from substantive canons, such as the rule of lenity in the interpretation of criminal statutes. Yet Justice Scalia, consistent with his self-characterization as a "faint-hearted" originalist,[33] accepts the rule of lenity without suggesting that it has an originalist pedigree, for example a source in the Constitution.[34]

The loose constructionist, in contrast to the strict, is a pragmatist. He wants the enactments he interprets to have sensible consequences,

33. Antonin Scalia, "Originalism: The Lesser Evil," 57 *University of Cincinnati Law Review* 849, 864 (1989).
34. Antonin Scalia, *A Matter of Interpretation: Federal Courts and the Law* 29 (1997).

though not necessarily the consequences *he* would prefer—he is a *constrained* pragmatist (see chapter 9), though he thinks that sensible consequences are usually what the legislators want as well. He tries to correct for the limitations of their foresight, seeking, in Learned Hand's words, to "reconstruct the past solution imaginatively in its setting and project the purposes which inspired it upon the concrete occasions which arise for their decision."[35] He agrees with Justice Frankfurter that "unhappily, there is no table of logarithms for statutory construction. No item of evidence has a fixed or even average weight. One or another may be decisive in one set of circumstances, while of little value elsewhere."[36] The pragmatist wants to use the experience gleaned from cases and other sources of postenactment information to complete the legislative project. He wants to help the legislators achieve their ends.

Some strict constructionists argue that imaginative reconstruction of a legislature's purposes is impossible because there is no such thing as "collective intent"; there is just the intent of the individual legislators who vote for or against a statute.[37] That is the autistic theory of interpretation. It denies the possibility of meaningful interpersonal communication and agreement, of a "meeting of minds." The theory is bad philosophy, bad psychology, and bad law.[38] The natural presumption in interpreting a document is that however many authors it had, it is to be interpreted as if it were the product of a single mind. The presumption can be rebutted, but to suggest that one can never meaningfully ask what Congress was driving at in this or that statutory provision because

35. Learned Hand, "The Contribution of an Independent Judiciary to Civilization" (1942), in *The Spirit of Liberty: Papers and Addresses of Learned Hand* 155, 157 (Irving Dilliard ed., 3d ed. 1960). See also Hand, "How Far Is a Judge Free in Rendering a Decision?" (1935), in id. at 103.

36. Felix Frankfurter, "Some Reflections on the Reading of Statutes," in *Judges on Judging: Views from the Bench* 247, 255 (David M. O'Brien ed., 2d ed. 2004 [1947]).

37. The position is forcefully argued by the political scientist Kenneth A. Shepsle in his article "Congress Is a 'They,' Not an 'It': Legislative Intent as Oxymoron," 12 *International Review of Law and Economics* 239 (1992). He commends the following "plain meaning" approach: "In the circumstances of cases apparently falling in the interstices of a statute, the Court must resist bringing the case under the statute's rubric. It may neither generalize the language of a statute, read intent into its words other than what is explicitly stated, nor forecast what the enacting majority (or some other majority for that matter) might have ruled. If the plain meaning of the statute's language does not cover a circumstance, then the statute is inapplicable." Id. at 253.

38. Lawrence M. Solan, "Private Language: Public Laws: The Central Role of Legislative Intent in Statutory Interpretation," 93 *Georgetown Law Journal* 427 (2005).

Congress is not a collective body is to deny that people can ever share a purpose.

The problem goes deeper. Interpretation *presupposes* an intending author. Suppose one sees scratched in the sand on a beach the words "Call your mother," but you realize that the words were formed by the mindless action of wind and waves. It would be insane if, realizing this, you nevertheless called your mother because that was the "plain meaning" of the words. If there is no intent behind a collectively authored document such as a statute, there is no occasion for interpretation. Originalists cannot deny the possibility of collective intent. They *depend* on there being such intent. The meaning that the ratifiers attached to the Constitution, which is the meaning that originalists deem authoritative, was based on their understanding of what the authors of the document intended.

The danger of loose construction is that it may lapse into shortsighted pragmatism, ignoring the bad consequences of too cavalier an attitude toward the written word. A proper choice between the two styles of interpretation, like the choice between rules and standards, which it resembles—which indeed it illustrates—is relative to circumstances, including institutional factors such as the different motivations and tools of courts and legislatures. These issues have engaged the attention of scholars for many years,[39] but as with the choice between rules and standards there is no closure. Students of public choice, and political conservatives generally, being skeptical about the good faith of legislators, fearing the excesses of democracy, deeming statutes unprincipled compromises, and reluctant to help legislators achieve their ends (these skeptics doubt that most legislation *has* ends worthy of assistance), deny that statutes ever have a "spirit" or coherent purposes that might, by channeling loose construction, limit judges' discretion to make policy. They think loose construction debases language as a medium of communication between legislature and court. They point out that to the ex-

---

39. See, for example, William N. Eskridge, Jr., "Overriding Supreme Court Statutory Interpretation Decisions," 101 *Yale Law Journal* 331, 416 (1991); Susan Freiwald, "Comparative Institutional Analysis in Cyberspace: The Case of Intermediary Liability for Defamation," 14 *Harvard Journal of Law and Technology* 569, 574 (2001); Jonathan T. Molot, "Reexamining *Marbury* in the Administrative State: A Structural and Institutional Defense of Judicial Power over Statutory Interpretation," 96 *Northwestern University Law Review* 1239, 1292–1320 (2002); Cass R. Sunstein and Adrian Vermeule, "Interpretation and Institutions," 101 *Michigan Law Review* 885 (2003).

tent that a statute is a product of compromise, a court that interprets the statute to make it more effective in achieving its ostensible goal may be undoing the legislative compromise—which might make it more difficult to enact legislation in the first place given the importance of compromise to the legislative process. These are sound cautionary points, but do not describe the actual practice of strict constructionists. A careful statistical study concludes that "plain meaning is not at all plain, at least to Supreme Court Justices. They are readily able to find whatever plain meaning suits their ideological proclivities."[40] They realize that a court committed to strict construction may make more work for legislatures by never lending them a helping hand. Conservative judges, however, instead of being troubled by this, rather welcome it.

At the opposite end of the spectrum from the legislation skeptics we find the likes of Henry Hart and Albert Sacks, who along with Guido Calabresi and others urge loose interpretation (carried by Calabresi to the extreme of thinking that courts should be allowed to nullify statutes that have become obsolete). They believe in the public-spiritedness of legislators, who these scholars think welcome a helping hand from judges.[41] But they underestimate the risk that judges will upset delicate legislative compromises, substitute their own poorly informed or politically biased policy judgments for those of better-informed legislators, and empower legislative factions.

Realists about the limited knowledge that Supreme Court Justices and other judges bring to many of their cases—judge skeptics as distinct from legislator skeptics—especially urge judges to hesitate to invalidate statutory and other official action on the basis of constitutional interpretation, whether strict or loose. They think it presumptuous of the Justices, who after all are merely lawyers hired by politicians, to consider themselves competent to take sides on the profoundly contested moral and political issues involved in disputes over such matters as sexual and reproductive rights, capital punishment, the role of religion in public life, the financing of political campaigns, the structure of state legisla-

40. Frank B. Cross, "The Significance of Statutory Interpretive Methodologies," 82 *Notre Dame Law Review* 1971, 2001 (2007).

41. Henry M. Hart, Jr., and Albert M. Sacks, *The Legal Process: Basic Problems in the Making and Application of Law* 1414–1415 (tentative ed. 1958) (now Henry M. Hart, Jr., and Albert M. Sacks, *The Legal Process: Basic Problems in the Making and Application of Law* 1378 [William N. Eskridge, Jr., and Philip P. Frickey eds. 1994]); Guido Calabresi, *A Common Law for the Age of Statutes* (1982).

tures, and national security. They think that courts should intervene in such sensitive and emotional controversies only if utterly convinced of the unreasonable character of the act or practice that they are asked to prohibit in the name of the Constitution.

This is a form of loose construction and standard-based legal reasoning, but should not be taken to imply that realists always oppose rule-based adjudication. Students of economic development, who are realists with no interest in defending legalism as such, sensibly recommend the adoption of precise rules of law (which implies strict construction as the mode of interpretation of statutes, regulations, and other sources of rules) by backward nations with weak legal infrastructures.[42] When law consists of precise rules, rather than standards, the scope of interpretive discretion is curtailed and judicial corruption and incompetence therefore held in check, because it is easier to determine whether a judge is applying a rule properly than whether he is applying a standard properly.

This is an illustration of a point I made in chapter 3—that in particular historical circumstances pragmatism may dictate legalism. Another illustration is Savigny's proposal that the German states (he was writing long before Germany became a nation in 1871) adopt the law of ancient Rome as the law of Germany—a highly formalistic version of Roman law, moreover.[43] Savigny's legalism may well have been right for his time and place. As in developing societies today, the urgent need was for clear, uniform rules that could be applied mechanistically and bind the different German states together. Holmes's rejection of Savigny's legalism[44] may well have been right for *his* time and place, which were very different from Savigny's. By Holmes's time "the American legal system . . . had the suppleness and enjoyed the public confidence to be able to adapt legal principles to current social needs without undue danger of sacrificing legitimacy or creating debilitating legal uncertainty."[45] Thus, "formalism [legalism] as a decision making strategy in statutory interpretation, or for that matter in any other setting, can be justified or

---

42. See, for example, Jonathan R. Hay and Andrei Shleifer, "Private Enforcement of Public Laws: A Theory of Legal Reform," 88 *American Economic Review Papers and Proceedings* 398 (May 1998).

43. See Richard A. Posner, *Frontiers of Legal Theory*, ch. 6 (2001).

44. See Oliver Wendell Holmes, Jr., *The Common Law*, lects. 5–6 (1881).

45. Posner, note 43 above, at 221.

opposed (solely) on the basis of a forward-looking assessment of the consequences of the competing alternatives."[46] "The debate over interpretive formalism turns, most critically, on the structure of the lawmaking system rather than on claims about the nature of communication, democracy, or jurisprudential principles."[47]

The Continental European judiciary, as we know, tends to be more legalist than the American. A career judiciary requires performance criteria that can be used to make objective promotion decisions, and the accuracy of a literal interpretation of a legislative text is easier to evaluate than the soundness of a pragmatic interpretation. Then too, career judges, having little experience of the world outside the courtroom, are more comfortable with semantic than with policy-oriented interpretation (though, as I noted in chapter 5, civil law judges cannot avoid occasional policymaking). And parliamentary government, which is the European form of government, is far more streamlined than presidential government, and therefore less reliant on judges to supplement legislation. Legalism would not be a responsible strategy for American judges, given our tricameral legislative system (tricameral because the veto power makes the President in effect a third house of Congress); our 220-year-old Constitution, whose authors were sages but not seers; our federal system, which lays federal law confusingly over the legal systems of 50 different states; and our weak, undisciplined political parties.

Strict construction, along with its textualist-originalist variants, would place an unbearable information load on our legislatures. It would require them to be able to anticipate not only every quirky case that might arise to exploit ambiguities in statutory language but also every future change in society (such as the advent of the telephone or the Internet) that might make a statute or constitutional provision drafted without awareness of the change fail to achieve the provision's aim. Loose construction, in contrast, shares out the information burden between legislators and judges. Vague constitutional and statutory provisions are translated into broad rules by the Supreme Court, then fine-tuned by the lower courts. Not only are more "legislators" brought into the picture, but the postenactment legislators—the judges—contribute to the revisionary process information to which the original legislators, lacking

46. Sunstein and Vermeule, note 39 above, at 921–922.
47. Id. at 925.

the gift of prevision, had no access.[48] Had we more professional, more disciplined legislative bodies, a constitutional convention in continuous session, a federal commission to revise statutes, a counterpart to the Sentencing Commission for every area of federal law, then judges could take a backseat, as foreign judges do. But none of these conditions for judicial passivity in interpretation is satisfied.

This analysis will not convince those who so distrust interpretive flexibility that they accuse Blackstone of "radical institutional blindness"[49] because he said (repeating a point made by a seventeenth-century legal thinker, Samuel Pufendorf) that a law of Bologna "that whoever drew blood in the streets should be punished with the utmost severity" should not be interpreted to make punishable a surgeon "who opened the vein of a person that fell down in the street with a fit."[50] It would not convince critics of the French court that, in the face of the emphatic French commitment to judicial legalism,[51] refused to read literally a statute that, so read, nonsensically forbade the passengers on a train to get on or off the train when it was *not* moving.[52] Actually, the cases are dif-

48. Thorsten Beck, Asli Demirgüç-Kunt, and Ross Levine, "Law and Finance: Why Does Legal Origin Matter?" 31 *Journal of Comparative Economics* 653 (2003). Cf. Franceso Parisi and Nita Ghei, "Legislate Today or Wait until Tomorrow? An Investment Approach to Lawmaking" (University of Minnesota Law School, Legal Studies Research Paper No. 07–11, June 14, 2006), noting the difficulty that legislatures have in determining the optimal timing for the adoption of new laws, given the need to consider the value of the option of waiting. Loose construction is one solution to the dilemma.

49. Sunstein and Vermeule, note 39 above, at 892. See also Adrian Vermeule, *Judging under Uncertainty: An Institutional Theory of Legal Interpretation* 19–20 (2006). For criticism, see Jonathan R. Siegel, "Judicial Interpretation in the Cost-Benefit Crucible" (forthcoming in *Minnesota Law Review*).

50. William Blackstone, *Commentaries on the Laws of England*, vol. 1, p. 60 (1765). As Blackstone explained, "The fairest and most rational method to interpret the will of the legislator, is by exploring his intentions at the time when the law was made, by *signs* the most natural and probable. And these signs are either the words, the context, the subject matter, the effects and consequence, or the spirit and reason of the law . . . As to the effects and consequence, the rule is, where words bear either none, or a very absurd signification, if literally understood, we must a little deviate from the received sense of them." Id. at 59–60 (emphasis in original). He illustrates the point with the Bologna bloodletting statute.

51. On which see, for example, Julius Stone, *The Province and Function of Law: Law as Logic, Justice, and Social Control: A Study in Jurisprudence* 149–159 (2d ed. 1961). In fact, French legalism, like American legalism, is more rhetorical than real. See Eva Steiner, *French Legal Method*, chs. 3, 4, 7 (2002), and next footnote.

52. Steiner, note 51 above, at 60; Michel Troper, Christophe Grzegorczyk, and Jean-Louis Gardies, "Statutory Interpretation in France," in *Interpreting Statutes: A Comparative Study* 171, 192 (D. Neil MacCormick and Robert S. Summers eds. 1991). "In circumstances where the ap-

ferent, because the text of the French statute probably contained a typographical error.[53] The Bolognese statute involved what is far more common and far more difficult for a legislature to avoid, which is failing to anticipate and make provision for cases that are within the semantic extension of a statute but not within its purpose. The extension of a statement commonly exceeds its intended scope because well-understood qualifications are understood rather than expressed. Suppose you asked a druggist for something to help you sleep and he gave you a sledgehammer. Literalism can be a firing offense, or even grounds for commitment.

Remember the *Olmstead* case? As an exercise in strict construction, it was correctly decided, though no one defends the decision anymore. Read literally, or for that matter naturally or even historically, the Fourth Amendment protects your person, house, papers, and effects from being searched, but not your conversations. Ordinary (that is, nonelectronic) nontrespassory eavesdropping has never been considered a search or a seizure. Nor has following a person about or even erecting surveillance cameras on lampposts. It would be unidiomatic to say "the police searched me by listening to my phone conversations" or "the police searched my house by listening to my phone conversations." Electronic eavesdropping could be said (though only by a lawyer) to "seize" conversations, but conversations are not among the things that the amendment protects from intrusion. In order to bring wiretapping and other electronic eavesdropping within the scope of the Fourth Amendment, a court has to posit a purpose behind the amendment, and this requires speculation fatal to the strict constructionist's desire to banish discretion from interpretation. For what *was* the purpose of the amendment? Was

plication of the literal meaning was likely to result in an absurdity, the judge could look at the legislative intent and 'rectify' the legislative provision by means of interpretation . . . Sometimes, in order to keep up with social change, French courts have departed from the literal meaning of a statute, applying instead a meaning that was not originally intended by the legislator at the time when the statute was passed." Steiner, above, at 60. For extended discussions of the absurd-results principle of interpretation, see John F. Manning, "The Absurdity Doctrine," 116 *Harvard Law Review* 2387 (2003); Veronica M. Daugherty, "Absurdity and the Limits of Literalism: Defining the Absurd Result Principle in Statutory Interpretation," 44 *American University Law Review* 127 (1994).

53. Statutory drafting errors are not a French monopoly; they are found in American statutes as well and provide a major challenge to the formalist. See Jonathan R. Siegel, "What Statutory Drafting Errors Teach Us about Statutory Interpretation," 69 *George Washington Law Review* 309 (2001).

it just to limit trespasses by customs and other government officers? Or was it to limit more generally the occasions for and scope of official investigations? Or did it have both purposes—the narrow and the broad? Strict constructionists do not, or at least should not, regard these as questions that judges are permitted to answer. They should applaud *Olmstead* and denounce *Katz*—for *Katz* is just what legalists deplore: a legislative decision. The Supreme Court in *Katz* disregarded the Fourth Amendment's words and original purpose in order to bring a novel form of criminal investigation under the Constitution.

Advocates of strict construction argue that it strengthens democracy by preventing judges from imposing their policy preferences on society in the guise of interpretation. The other side of this coin, however, is that strict constructionists will not intervene to save legislation from being rendered obsolete or absurd by unforeseen cases (such as that of the hypothetical surgeon of Bologna) or by changed circumstances. The legislature can always step in and eliminate those results for the future, by amendment. But at what cost? The legislative process is inertial, legislative capacity limited, the legislative agenda crowded, and as a result amending legislation is difficult and time-consuming—it has to be or legislation would lack durability.[54] A neglected point is that if amending is feasible, it can be used to cure pathologies of loose as well as of strict construction. Indeed, if amending is feasible, there is no longer a practical argument for strict construction; its effects on the legislative process are the same as those of loose construction. But it is more realistic to assume that amending a statute to correct judges' misinterpretation of it is often infeasible.

The choice between strict and loose statutory construction (which is not really a binary choice, since intermediate choices are possible and indeed attractive[55]), like the parallel choice between rules and standards, is full of uncertainty. Nothing in legalism itself can show that the legalist approach to statutory interpretation—strict construction, or in some versions textualism or originalism—is the right approach. And not enough is known about the trade-offs between strict and loose construc-

---

54. William M. Landes and Richard A. Posner, "The Independent Judiciary in an Interest-Group Perspective," 18 *Journal of Law and Economics* 875 (1975).

55. See, for example, Jonathan T. Molot, "The Rise and Fall of Textualism," 106 *Columbia Law Review* 1 (2006).

tion to enable the legalist approach to be endorsed, or for that matter rejected (though that is my inclination), on practical grounds. With the choice between strict and loose construction thus up in the air, judges must choose on the basis of factors that lie outside the boundaries of "the law" as it is conceived of by legalists. Although legalists defend strict construction as the democratic alternative because it limits judicial legislating, their real motive, one suspects, is hostility to big government, a creation primarily of legislation. To impede legislation is hardly democratic, but that is what legalistic interpretation does. It imposes arbitrary meanings on statutes by reading them literally, and by doing so it makes legislators work harder to achieve their objectives yet fall short because of the inertial forces that impede the enactment of legislative amendments designed to overcome judicial rulings.

Because the correction of absurd results by *constitutional* amendment is especially difficult, yet such results would be a frequent consequence of literal interpretation of so old a document as the Constitution of the United States, strict construction is especially maladapted to constitutional cases. I illustrated with electronic eavesdropping, but that is just the beginning. A strict construction of the equal protection clause of the Fourteenth Amendment is that it forbids affirmative action (unequal benefits) but not the racial segregation of public schools (mere separation); of the Sixth Amendment that it requires jury trials in courts-martial; of the First Amendment that it abolishes the tort of defamation and forbids the criminalizing of criminal solicitations, the legal protection of trade secrets, and the censorship of military secrets; of the Second Amendment that it entitles Americans to carry any weapon that one person can operate, including shoulder-launched surface-to-air missiles; of the Fifth Amendment that it permits evidence obtained by torture to be introduced in federal criminal trials provided the torture was not conducted in the courtroom itself; of the Eleventh Amendment that it permits a person to sue in federal court the state of which he is a citizen, though no other state; and of Article I, section 8, that Congress cannot establish the Air Force as a separate branch of the armed forces or regulate military aviation at all. If this is where strict constitutional construction leads, its adoption would create an agenda of proposed constitutional amendments so long that the amending process would break down.

Good pragmatic judges balance two types of consequence, the case-specific and the systemic.[56] A pertinent example of the latter is the danger of making law too uncertain if judges fail to enforce contracts more or less as written—that is, fail to interpret contractual language strictly. It can be argued that a similar undermining is likely to be the consequence of loose construction of statutes, so that a policy of strict construction with only a narrow exception for interpretations that produce palpably absurd results is superior, all things considered, to a general policy of loose construction. This would be an example of preferring rule plus exceptions to standard, a common choice in law. One could even favor strict construction of contracts and loose construction of statutes and the Constitution, just as one could favor strict construction under one type of legal and political regime and loose construction under another. The point is only that legalism no more requires strict construction than it requires a law made up entirely of rules rather than of rules and standards. These are choices that entail the exercise of legislative-like judicial discretion.

56. Richard A. Posner, *Law, Pragmatism, and Democracy,* ch. 2 (2003). For a good discussion of the pros and cons of pragmatic interpretation, see John F. Manning, "Statutory Pragmatism and Constitutional Structure," 120 *Harvard Law Review* 1161 (2007).

8

Judges Are Not Law Professors

The external constraint on judicial behavior that is most compatible with a judiciary as independent as our federal judiciary is academic criticism, since it is noncoercive. It is potentially a powerful constraint because judges care about their reputation, care about being (and not merely being thought to be) "good" judges, respect the intellect and specialized knowledge of first-rate academic lawyers, and by virtue of their very independence are open to a wide array of influences, including those exerted by criticism, that would have little impact were judges subject to the powerful incentives and constraints of employees who lack the independence of a federal judge. Actually a better word than "criticism" in this context is "critique." Judges would benefit from praise that indicated where they were doing a good job as well as from criticism, and judges who were not praised would learn from the praise of others where they were falling short.

Yet academic critique of judges and judging has little impact these days on judicial behavior.[1] This is not to say that academic *scholarship* has little impact on law, including the law made by judges in their legislative role. But my interest in this book is not in how law professors create knowledge that finds its way into judicial opinions and hence into

---

1. For an acknowledgment and interesting discussion of this point, see Sanford Levinson, "The Audience for Constitutional Meta-Theory (or, Why, and to Whom, Do I Write the Things I Do?)," 63 *University of Colorado Law Review* 389 (1992). See also Barry Friedman, "The Counter-Majoritarian Problem and the Pathology of Constitutional Scholarship," 95 *Northwestern University Law Review* 933, 953 (2001); Robert Post, "Legal Scholarship and the Practice of Law," 63 *University of Colorado Law Review* 615 (1992).

the law; it is in the law professor's role as an evaluator of judicial perfor-mance whom judges take seriously.

There are two reasons that academic criticism does not much affect judicial behavior. One is that although judges indeed care about whether they are doing and are thought by certain others (other judges, for ex-ample) to be doing a good job, they do not care greatly what law profes-sors think of them. The other reason is that law professors are not much interested in evaluating individual judges, except Supreme Court Jus-tices—who are the last judges to care about how they are thought of in the groves of academe. Beneath these specific reasons for the ineffec-tuality of academic critique of judicial performance is a deeper one—the alienation of the elite law professor from legal practice, including judging.[2]

Judicial insensitivity to academic criticism derives in part from the differences between judges and professors in working conditions, incen-tives, constraints, selection, outlook, and social role. Many judges think that academics do not understand the aims and pressures of judicial work and that as a result much academic criticism of judicial perfor-mance is captious, obtuse, and unconstructive. This sense is shared even by appellate judges, engaged in the quasi-scholarly work of opinion writing, including appellate judges appointed from the professoriat.

Apart from the courts of appeals for the Federal Circuit and to a lesser extent the District of Columbia Circuit, the jurisdiction of the federal courts of appeals ranges over virtually the entirety of federal civil and criminal law, and, by virtue of the federal diversity jurisdiction and fed-eral habeas corpus for state prisoners, over virtually the entirety of state law as well, plus bits of foreign and international law.[3] No judge of such a court can be an expert in more than a small fraction of the fields of law that generate the appeals that he must decide, or can devote enough time to an individual case to make himself, if only for the moment (knowledge obtained by cramming is quickly forgotten), an expert in the field out of which the case arises. Unlike the Supreme Court, more-

2. See Harry T. Edwards, "The Growing Disjunction between Legal Education and the Legal Profession," 91 *Michigan Law Review* 34 (1992), and, for an amusing anticipation, William L. Prosser, "The Decline and Fall of the Institute," 19 *Journal of Legal Education* 41 (1966).

3. The principal exceptions to the jurisdiction of the regional courts of appeals are patent law and probate and domestic relations law, though the exception for probate and domestic re-lations is only partial. See, for example, Kijowska v. Haines, 463 F.3d 583 (7th Cir. 2006).

over, the courts of appeals must decide all the dispositive issues presented by a case, however many there are, and a single case may present issues in several different fields of law.

A judge is a generalist who writes an opinion under pressure of time in whatever case, in whatever field of law, is assigned to him. Lack of time and lack of specialization are not problems for the law professor. He writes an article on a topic of his choice in the area of his specialty at a pace that he is comfortable with. He strives to make an original contribution. In contrast, lack of originality is no problem for the judge. He must write the opinion assigned to him whether or not he has an original thought about any of the issues in the case. Especially if he is the presiding judge he may have some choice of which cases to write the majority opinion in, but it is a choice only among the cases that he has been chosen by random assignment to hear as part of a randomly chosen panel of the judges of his court. A law professor does not have to write 25 articles a year (roughly the current minimum number of opinions published by a federal court of appeals judge; some publish many more, and all are responsible for a number—invariably a larger number—of unpublished opinions) on topics not of his choice. The professor can, without losing his academic standing, write just one or two articles a year on the one or two topics about which he has an original thought. But he is expected to write the articles himself, whereas most judicial opinions are drafted by law clerks, though edited, and sometimes extensively rewritten, by the judge.

It is not just that the judge, unlike the professor, cannot be expected to have an original thought in every case because of the volume of cases and the lack of choice and of specialization; originality is far less valued—and valuable—in judicial opinions than in academic books and articles. Stability and continuity are highly valued qualities in any legal system, and judges (in part for that reason) are hemmed in, though not nearly so tightly as legalists believe, by precedents and other authoritative texts. Their freedom of action is also hampered by the need to compromise with other judges who may be less adventurous than they, in order to command a majority. And this point highlights the difference in the audiences for the two types of document. The primary audience for academic writing consists of other academics. The appellate judge, writing what he hopes will be the majority opinion, is writing in the first instance for his fellow judges, with at least a glance over his shoulder at the Supreme Court, with a sense of wanting to be persuasive to judges of other courts who may someday be faced with a similar case, and with a desire to provide guidance to the bar. Academics are at the periphery of his concern.

Deciding a case, moreover, is judging a contest, though, *pace* Chief Justice Roberts, it is not like umpiring a baseball game. A contest, a dispute, does not have the form of an article topic, even when the topic has a binary form. A law review article might take a position pro or con whether intellectual property rights have been construed too broadly and should be cut back. But the abstractness of such an issue would set it apart from a dispute over whether the publication of an unauthorized photograph of a copyrighted Beanie Baby (a "soft sculpture" in copyright jargon) is a "fair use" when the photograph is part of a guide for collectors of Beanie Babies.[4] The judge is wont to ask himself in such a case what outcome would be the more reasonable, the more sensible, bearing in mind the range of admissible considerations in deciding a case, which include but are not exhausted by statutory language, precedents, and the other conventional materials of judicial decision making, but also include common sense, policy preferences, and often much else besides.

One can imagine a law professor's article on the proper scope of intellectual property rights that would have a similarly pragmatic, undertheorized, grab bag character. Indeed, there was a time—a time when the various branches of the legal profession, including the academic and the judicial, were closer to each other than they are today—when the typical law review article was of that character. Law professors used to identify primarily with the legal profession and only secondarily with the university. Hired after several years of practice, on the basis of evidence (often based largely or even entirely on performance on exams as a law student) of possessing superlative skills of legal analysis, the law professor was expected to be a superb lawyer whose primary responsibility would be to instruct generations of law students so that they would become good, and some of them superb, lawyers. He instructed them by precept but also by example, by being a role model, and the role was that of a practicing lawyer despite the limited practical experience of most of the professors. The professor's scholarly work tended to be ei-

---

4. Ty, Inc. v. Publications International Ltd., 292 F.3d 512 (7th Cir. 2002).

ther pedagogical, as in the editing of casebooks, or of direct service to the practicing bar and the judiciary, as in the writing of legal treatises, articles on points of law, and contributions to projects of legal reform exemplified by the American Law Institute's restatements of law.

It was an era, unlike today, in which professors at elite law schools worked closely with judges on the problems of ordinary courts (professors at those law schools were active in the American Law Institute, along with prominent judges such as Cardozo and Hand, and the Institute's principal focus was the common law[5]), not the U.S. Supreme Court. It was an era in which judges were among the intellectual leaders of the legal profession, fully on a par with and highly respected by law professors. Think of Holmes, Brandeis, Cardozo, Frankfurter, Hand, and, at the end of the era, Henry Friendly. What judges such as these said about judging, as about specific legal issues, was taken as seriously by professors as what other professors said, and, to a degree anyway, vice versa. The legal realists of the 1920s and 1930s, and even the legal process school of the 1950s, had a judicial as well as an academic audience.

There was even then a gap between the judiciary and the professoriat, well illustrated by Henry Hart's "time chart of the Justices" (see chapter 10). But it has widened since the 1960s—that watershed decade in modern American history. By the late 1960s the traditional model of academic law that I have described was almost a century old and ripe for challenge. Challenges came from two directions, which though opposite turned out to be complementary in their effect on the traditional model. One, the direction from social science, and in particular from economics, complained that the model failed to articulate concrete social goals for the law and to test legal doctrines against them. It could not tell judges and legislators when, for example, the rule of tort liability should be negligence and when strict liability; or how to decide when a land use should be deemed a nuisance, when a preliminary injunction should be granted and when denied, when solicitations by police to commit a crime should be deemed entrapment, whether a rescuer of a lost item should have a legal claim to the reward posted by the owner though unaware of the offer of the reward, or whether spendthrift trusts should be

---

5. On the decline of the American Law Institute, see Kristen David Adams, "Blaming the Mirror: The Restatements and the Common Law," 40 *Indiana Law Review* 205 (2007); Adams, "The Folly of Uniformity? Lessons from the Restatement Movement," 33 *Hofstra Law Review* 423 (2004).

allowed because they reduce, or forbidden because they increase, the likelihood of bankruptcy. (The list can be extended indefinitely.) Too often decisions were based on invocations of hopelessly vague words such as "fairness" and "justice."

The second challenge was inspired by the left-wing politics that helped to define the late 1960s and early 1970s. The challengers complained that the traditional model was a mask for decisions reached on base political grounds. The critical legal studies movement and its offshoots resurrected the legal realism of the 1920s and 1930s in a form at once more strident and intellectually more pretentious, and rejected the legal process school of the 1950s that had sought to reconcile legal realism with the conventional model through the concept of neutral principles.

These challenges to the traditional conception of the law professor's vocation so far succeeded as to bring about a fundamental change in the character of legal teaching and scholarship and the method of recruitment into academic law. From the challenge mounted by social science came unprecedented emphasis on basing legal scholarship on the insights of other fields, such as economics, philosophy, and history. From the challenge mounted by the left came a reinforcing skepticism about the capacity of the traditional model of legal scholarship to yield cogent answers to legal questions.

The traditional model was largely buried in these twin avalanches, at least in the elite law schools. And with its burial, interest in hiring the masters of the traditional skills of lawyer and judge to teach law waned. The knack (and it is a knack—it is not something that even every very bright person can acquire) of reading cases and statutes creatively, the bag of rhetorical tricks and the professional demeanor that mark the legal insider, and an ineffable sense ("judgment") of just how far one can go as a judge in changing the law (or as a practicing lawyer in advocating a judicial law change) to keep it abreast of changing social and economic conditions, cannot be the entirety of the modern lawyer's or judge's professional equipment, and their inculcation cannot be the entirety of a first-rate modern legal education. The law has become too deeply interfused with the methods and insights of other fields—and law schools *still* have a long way to go to overcome the shameful aversion of most law students to math, statistics, science, and technology. Maybe at the law schools that have the brightest students only half of the instruction should be in the traditional mold. But to reach that level those law schools would have to start hiring teachers who identify more strongly with the practicing profession than they do with academia.

The modern style of academic law, when set against the style, which is not modern, of deciding cases, leaves a gap in the legal profession. In a system of case law, which is the dominant American system even in primarily statutory fields, the principles and rules of law are rarely found clearly stated in written codes. They must be teased out of the codes and out of strings of precedents. Law is more often inferred than positive (i.e., posited), and inferred law is "unwritten" in the significant sense that it is constructed or reconstructed by judges, lawyers, and scholars out of scattered, sometimes inconsistent, and often ambiguous, incomplete, or poorly informed materials, mainly judicial opinions. The messy work product of judges and legislators requires much tidying up, synthesis, analysis, restatement, and critique. These are intellectually demanding tasks, requiring vast knowledge and the ability (not only brains, knowledge, and judgment but also *Sitzfleisch*) to organize dispersed, fragmentary, prolix, and rebarbative materials. Though these tasks lack the theoretical ambition of scholarship in more typically academic fields, they are vital to the legal system and of greater social value than much of today's esoteric interdisciplinary legal scholarship.

They are vital because judges are deciding cases rather than attempting to formulate a code.[6] In explaining a decision they will typically state a rule in the hope of providing guidance for future cases and subsume the case under it. But they cannot see the future clearly, in part because a case system concentrates the judge's attention on the case at hand. So rules keep having to be refined and reformulated as new cases arise. Sometimes they are recast as standards, sometimes precipitated out of standards, and sometimes festooned with exceptions. Early on, for example, the English royal courts held that a threatening gesture is tortious (an assault) even if the person threatened is not actually struck by the threatener.[7] That sounds like a simple, clean rule to guide the decision of future cases. Then came a case in which there was again a threatening gesture: the defendant in an angry confrontation with the plaintiff placed his hand on his sword—but at the same moment he negated the threat by stating, with careful use of the subjunctive, that "if it were not

6. See A. W. B. Simpson, "Legal Reasoning Anatomized: On Steiner's *Moral Argument and Social Vision in the Courts*," 13 *Law and Social Inquiry* 637 (1988).

7. I. de S. and Wife v. W. de S., Y.B. Liber Assisarum, 22 Edw. 3, f. 99, pl. 60 (1348 or 1349).

assize-time, I would not take such language from you." The court ruled for the defendant,[8] thus indicating that the original statement of the assault rule had been too broad. This is an example of legal progress through the distinguishing of prior cases—in other words through refining rules on the basis of knowledge generated by new, unforeseen disputes.

Judges try to keep track of old cases and reformulate the rules of decision making as tested by new, unanticipated ones. But a mature or complete rule is more likely to have been reconstructed from a line of cases than to be found fully and precisely stated and explained in the latest case in the line. It falls to the law professors to clean up after the judges by making explicit in treatises, articles, and restatements the rules implicit in the various lines of cases, identifying outliers, explicating policy grounds, and charting the path of future development. This type of scholarship resembles appellate judging because it is the kind of thing one could imagine the judges themselves doing had they the time and the specialized knowledge. Indeed, judges in their opinions sometimes try to do a preliminary tidying up of an area of law by restating a rule or standard in a way that clarifies, unifies, and perhaps modestly improves the rule implicit in a line of cases.

The type of legal scholarship that I am discussing is no longer in vogue at the leading law schools. No longer are the law professors at those schools appellate judges manqué, or überjudges who codify the implicit judge-made rules, giving them a fixity, an amplitude, and a clarity that an implicit rule could not achieve. They influence law, maybe more so than their more conventional predecessors. But they do so not by shaping the timbers rough hewn by judges but instead by inviting judges' attention to new considerations to take into account in deciding difficult cases. Typically the invitation is indirect. The professors are not writing for judges but for other law professors and to a lesser extent for law students. Still, there is a trickle-down effect, operating through law clerks, sophisticated members of the bar, and judges who are former law professors.

The trickle-down effect is important, for reasons central to this book. In difficult cases, which are so mainly because they are cases in which the orthodox materials of legal decision making cannot produce a satis-

8. Tuberville v. Savage, 1 Mod. Rep. 3, 86 Eng. Rep. 684 (1669).

factory decision (sometimes cannot produce a decision, period), judges are perforce reliant on other sources for their decision. They must find something to move them off dead center, and the modern law professor can help them in their quest. In a number of areas of law, economic analysis has helped move judges from reliance on instinct and semantics to something closer to cost-benefit analysis. This has produced a gain in precision and concreteness that should actually warm a legalist's heart because it reduces the area in which judges make decisions in a fog of emotion and undisciplined intuition.

But apart from the handful of professors who, as I mentioned in chapter 5, are trying to develop quantitative measures of judicial performance, not many law professors at the elite schools are interested in doing critiques of the courts, other than law professors who write about the Supreme Court, typically with reference to the Court's constitutional decisions. Like the Court itself when it is deciding constitutional cases, academic commentary on constitutional decisions is highly politicized—which makes it especially easy for the Justices to ignore. Law professors may express strong reservations about judicial performance in particular fields dominated by the lower courts, such as intellectual property, but it is the field that fascinates them, not what it might be about the judicial institution that is leading judges astray.

Michael Dorf, a well-known professor of constitutional law at Columbia, accusing the new Supreme Court majority of "assert[ing] fidelity to the prior precedents and then ruling the other way," "register[s] a parochial complaint against this particular brand of what is charitably called minimalism: It's going to make it hard to train new students about what it means to reason from or even follow precedent."[9] No, it's going to be hard to keep on teaching constitutional law as if the Justices took precedent as seriously as lower-court judges and common law judges do. It's going to be hard to keep pretending that Justices are like other judges rather than like other legislators. It is high time some realism about judging was injected into the teaching of law. The appointment of political scientists to law faculties—a rarity today—deserves serious consideration.

I have suggested that law professors have been growing apart from

9. "Is It Possible to Teach the Meaning of Precedent in the Era of the Roberts Court?" *Dorf on Law,* July 9, 2007, http://michaeldorf.org/2007/07/is-it-possible-to-teach-meaning-of.html (visited Sept. 24, 2007).

judges, and Dorf's surprise at discovering that Supreme Court Justices play fast and loose with precedent might be taken as a sign of this (for was there ever a time when Justices were scrupulous about precedent?). In this regard there is an illuminating contrast between two works on judging written by law professors a quarter of a century apart. Karl Llewellyn's book *The Common Law Tradition: Deciding Appeals*, published in 1960, is a legal realist summa. A 565-page study of state appellate courts, which tries with some success to reconcile legal realism with the undoubted fact that there is a fair degree of predictability in the common law, Llewellyn's book can be seen as the culmination of a realist tradition that goes back to Holmes and before him to Bentham. I will say more about this tradition, gathering together the scattered remarks I have made so far in this book about legal realism, in the next chapter. Suffice it to say that Llewellyn is on the same wavelength as most judges.

With Llewellyn's book compare Duncan Kennedy's article "Freedom and Constraint in Adjudication: A Critical Phenomenology,"[10] published in 1986. The subtitle is a clue to the difference that a quarter century had made in academic law. Kennedy imagines himself a judge torn between "law" that favors the granting of an injunction against striking workers and the judge's sense of "social justice" that impels him to search for ways in which he can deny the injunction. Judges do not think the way he imagines them to (though they sometimes say they do). They do not think, "This is an awful rule but it is the law, so I have a dilemma—can I get around it?" The business of judges is enforcing the law. If you do not like enforcing the law, you are not going to be a happy judge, which means you are not going to self-select into the judiciary, or if you somehow find yourself a judge (maybe you didn't know what being a judge was like or what you are like), you are likely to quit.

When a judge does bend a rule to avoid an awful result, he does not feel that he is engaging in civil disobedience;[11] he thinks the rule does not *really* compel the awful result. He will have rejected, probably unconsciously (few judges think a great deal about jurisprudential questions such as "What is law?"), the crabbed view of "law" that would if

10. Duncan Kennedy, "Freedom and Constraint in Adjudication: A Critical Phenomenology," 36 *Journal of Legal Education* 518 (1986).

11. Not usually at any rate; for American judges do sometimes engage in civil disobedience, as argued in Paul Butler, "When Judges Lie (and When They Should)," 91 *Minnesota Law Review* 1785 (2007).

adopted make much of what American judges do be classified as lawless. Oblivious to the tension that Professor Kennedy assumes to exist between "law" and "social justice," judges no more identify with Kennedy's imagined judge than they do with Dworkin's fictional "Judge Hercules." This is a damaging criticism of an article about the conscious mind of the judge—an essay in phenomenology, the study of conscious experience from the first-person perspective.

Should it be objected that Duncan Kennedy is outside the academic mainstream, I retreat to Adrian Vermeule, an indisputably mainstream colleague of Kennedy's at the Harvard Law School. I mentioned in chapter 7 his characterization of Blackstone's purposive interpretation of statutes as "institutional blindness." Even legalists such as Justice Scalia accept the "absurdity exception" to the strict construction of statutes.[12] Vermeule does not. He is concerned that false positives (deeming a statutory provision absurd when it is not) may outweigh false negatives (enforcing an absurd provision).[13] He urges judges to abandon purposive interpretation because of this possibility and offers the reassurance that prosecutorial discretion, jury lenity, the pardon power, and other nonjudicial responses to an absurd statutory interpretation can protect us adequately. I find this unconvincing. Let me give an up-to-date example why. The Child Pornography Prevention Act of 1996, which forbids the knowing possession of child pornography,[14] contains no exception for the knowing possession of such pornography by law enforcement officers who seize it for use in prosecuting child pornographers and maintain possession of it until the prosecution is complete, whereupon possession passes to the keepers of judicial archives. According to Vermeule's theory of statutory interpretation, the Act could properly

12. See, for example, Green v. Bock Laundry Machine Co., 490 U.S. 504, 527–528 (1989) (Scalia, J., concurring); City of Columbus v. Ours Garage & Wrecker Service, Inc., 536 U.S. 424, 449 n. 4 (2002) (Scalia, J., dissenting); Antonin Scalia, "Judicial Deference to Administrative Interpretations of Law," 1989 *Duke Law Journal* 511, 515 (1989); John F. Manning, "The Absurdity Doctrine," 116 *Harvard Law Review* 2387, 2391, 2419–2420 (2003). For other judicial endorsements of the doctrine, see, for example, Lamie v. United States Trustee, 540 U.S. 526, 534 (2004); United States v. American Trucking Associations, Inc., 310 U.S. 534, 543–544 (1940); Krzalic v. Republic Title Co., 314 F.3d 875, 879–880 (7th Cir. 2002); United States v. Aerts, 121 F.3d 277, 280 (7th Cir. 1997). Professor Manning himself rejects the doctrine, but reaches many of the same conclusions (including Blackstone's concerning the Bolognese surgeon's case) as those who accept it. See, for example, Manning, above, at 2461–2463.

13. Adrian Vermeule, *Judging under Uncertainty: An Institutional Theory of Legal Interpretation* 57–59 (2006).

14. 18 U.S.C. § 2252A(a)(5)(B).

be read to make all these "knowing possessors" guilty of violating the Act and thus subject to the Act's maximum punishment of 10 years in prison. Of course the prosecution of any of the law enforcers would be unlikely, though not out of the question; for example, the government might suspect, without being able to prove, that one of the investigating officers had stolen some of the pornography from the U.S. Attorney's office in the course of the prosecution. Yet the logic of Vermeule's theory is that if any of these "possessors" were ever asked on an employment form whether he had committed a felony, he would be lying if he failed to say that he had. If this is where Vermeule's theory leads, as it appears to, no judge will follow him there.

Vermeule presents no evidence that the number of false positives (whether weighted by the likelihood of legislative correction or by something else, or unweighted)—cases in which a court errs in thinking that the literal reading of some statutory provision is absurd—outweighs the number of false negatives (similarly weighted). American judges have been engaged in purposive interpretation since before there *was* a United States. There is no basis for thinking it has produced worse results than mindless literalism would have produced—the kind of literalism that would condemn the surgeon in Bologna or the prosecutor in a child pornography trial for possessing pornographic evidence. Statutes often are made overinclusive in order to stop up loopholes. To avoid overreach, the legislature leaves the task of fine-tuning its statutes to judges, and not just to jurors and executive branch officials.

Judges have to be given a better reason to change course 180 degrees than Vermeule gives them. Either he has no insight into what persuades judges, or, more likely, though his book urges a radical change in judicial behavior, this is just a rhetorical trope and judges are not actually a part of his intended audience, which is limited to other professors, who delight in paradox.

Lawyers, legislators, judges, and others seriously engaged with judicial activity, including law professors of the old school, take the interpretive medium—the judiciary—as it is and adjust their arguments, regulations, and so forth to it. For it is what it is, and is unlikely to change at the urging of professors, or of anyone else for that matter. Academics who are not seriously engaged with the judiciary urge judges to change by adopting this or that approach, and usually it is an approach designed to clip judges' wings. Judges are not interested in having their wings clipped, but will happily adopt restraintist approaches as rhetorical tools to persuade others that what looks like judicial assertiveness is obedience. Academics who are serious about wanting judges to change have to appeal to their self-interest. To tell judges, as Vermeule in effect does, that they are so dumb that they cannot even administer the absurdity exception to literal interpretation, and so should give it up, will not strike a responsive chord. It perfectly illustrates the contemporary alienation of the elite academy from the judiciary.

Academics have pointed out consequences of judicial decisions that even not-so-dumb judges did not understand; entire fields of law, such as antitrust law, trust investment law, and conflict of laws, have changed at the urging of law professors and other academics, mainly economists. But to change judges' basic outlook on judging rather than specific doctrines that they administer would require changing the judicial environment—the structure of incentives and constraints that influence judicial behavior. To achieve such change academics would have to address their arguments to the interests of the persons who manage the institutions that can alter the judicial environment, such as Congress, the White House, and the Department of Justice. Lecturing judges on their limitations will not have any effect.

The legal academy has been growing apart from the judiciary for a reason I have not yet mentioned—the growth of specialization in academic law. American judges are still generalists, but law professors increasingly are specialists. This is partly a result of the growth in size of the legal professoriat, because the larger a market (in this case the market for legal scholarship), the more room there is for specialization. It is more the result of the growing intellectual sophistication of law professors, which in turn is related to increased recognition that the social sciences, along with humanities such as history and philosophy, hold many of the keys to understanding and improving the legal system. And therefore the growing apart of the academy and the judiciary since the 1960s, though it has retarded empathy and mutual understanding, need not emasculate academic criticism of judges. This is shown not only by the proliferation of social scientific theories of judicial behavior, canvassed in chapter 1, but also by the quantitative literature on evaluating judicial performance—a form of critique, central to the analysis of judicial behavior and hence to this book, that would not have occurred to the traditional legal academic.[15] But recall its numerous shortcomings: counting citations provides a measure of influence rather than of quality; adjustments must be made for different courts, different length of service, and so forth that affect a judge's ranking independent of his quality; combining various quantitative measures to create a composite evaluation requires an arbitrary weighting of the different measures; rankings are merely ordinal measures (if, for example, the distance between number 1 and number 100 is slight, no specification of rank within that range will convey useful information); and ranking may induce undesirable behavioral changes by the persons ranked.

The limitations of quantitative measures of judicial performance highlight the need for qualitative assessments. It is remarkable how rare they are—which casts further light on the contemporary alienation of the academy from the judiciary. Of course law professors express agreement or disagreement with particular decisions, but that is different from evaluating a judge's overall performance, and it tends to fall on deaf ears because of the judges' sense that law professors do not understand them. Judicial biographies attempt critique, but their emphasis tends to be on producing a narrative of a judge's career and excavating the details, especially the piquant details, of his personal life—and these are to one side of his judicial failures or achievements.[16] If I am right in thinking that the judges in our system have a large measure of discretion, the exercise of which is bound to be influenced by personal experiences, character foibles, and so forth, biographical details may help to explain a judge's decisions. But that too is to one side of evaluating his performance. Noting that two judges disagreed frequently because they had different intuitions as a result of having different experiences, temperaments, and so on does not reveal which judge did better work, though it can provide insights into influences on a judge's decisions.

If academic critique is to alter judicial behavior, we need *critical* studies of judges,[17] as distinguished from biographies[18] on one side and

---

15. An exception, though not a happy one, is Hart's "time chart of the Justices." See chapter 10.

16. On the limitations of judicial biographies, see Richard A. Posner, *Law and Literature* 357–377 (revised and enlarged ed. 1998).

17. See id. at 375–377. I attempted such a study in my book *Cardozo: A Study in Reputation* (1990). See also my article "The Learned Hand Biography and the Question of Judicial Greatness," 104 *Yale Law Journal* 511 (1994). There are, of course, other such studies. See, for example, Ben Field, *Activism in Pursuit of the Public Interest: The Jurisprudence of Chief Justice Roger J. Traynor* (2003); Robert Jerome Glennon, *The Iconoclast as Reformer: Jerome Frank's Impact on American Law*, ch. 5 (1985).

18. Or rather from most biographies. Andrew Kaufman's 735-page biography of Cardozo provides a comprehensive and convincing assessment of Cardozo's judicial opinions. Kaufman, *Cardozo*, chs. 12–22 (1998).

quantitative performance measures on the other. The most illuminating kind of critical study would compare the judge's opinion in some notable case with the opinion of the lower-court judge, the record of the case, and the lawyers' briefs and oral arguments, along with any internal court memoranda written by the judge, his colleagues, or his or their law clerks. The aim would be to determine the accuracy and completeness of the judge's opinion; whether it was scrupulous in its use of precedent; the value it added to the briefs and arguments and the contributions made to the opinion by law clerks and other judges, and thus the opinion's originality; and what if anything it added to academic understanding. The interactions between the judge and his colleagues would be an important focus of study, for, as in team sports, a judge's performance can be decisively affected by his colleagues: Are they supportive or competitive? Do they nitpick his opinions or make helpful suggestions? Is he treated fairly by the opinion-assigning judge? Are his colleagues on the same political and methodological wavelength as he is? To what extent are his opinions really a group product?

A series of critical judicial studies would yield insights into the methods as well as the quality of the judge. A study expanded to consider judges serving on the same court at approximately the same time, and thus correcting for court-specific and time-specific differences between judges, would further sharpen judicial evaluation.

There are fruitful possibilities for combining quantitative assessments of judges with critical studies. Being unschooled in statistical methodology, judges are skeptical about quantitative measures of judicial performance. When they see a judge whom they do not recognize as one of the most distinguished members of the judiciary being ranked high by such a measure, they are more likely to reject the measure than to revise their opinion of the judge. A useful project would be to compare qualitative and quantitative assessments and seek to explain any discrepancies by a critical study of the opinions of judges whose quantitative and qualitative assessments differ substantially. We would gain insight into the strengths and limitations of the quantitative assessments.

Ours remains a case law system, and judges are central players in such a system. But because few law professors are interested any longer in trying to understand what makes judges tick or in trying to improve the judicial ticker—except in the case of Supreme Court Justices—academic discussion of judicial opinions rarely even identifies the judges whose opinions are being discussed, as if to say that legalism reigns and judges, being in effect just calculating machines, are fungible. Academic critique thus perpetuates a false notion of judicial behavior. This disserves the bar as well as the judiciary. Law students do not learn much about judges (most law teachers do not reveal to students the extent to which the cases the students read in casebooks are ghostwritten by law clerks). As a result, few lawyers, apart from those who have clerked for judges, or at least for those judges who are open and candid with their clerks, know how best to brief and argue cases.

Academic lawyers are terrific at taking apart the formal grounds of a judicial decision, and those are the grounds that take up most of the space in most opinions. But the academics have (or express) little understanding of how cases are actually decided, where the judges who decided a case were coming from, and what *really* made them alter existing doctrine as distinct from what they said made them change it. The academic emphasis on the formal grounds of a decision conveys to law students and the bar the impression that every judge is a thoroughgoing legalist who can therefore be "reached" only by ceaseless iteration of legalist slogans such as "plain meaning" and by barrages of case citations. Misled by the legalistic style of judicial opinions—mistaking style for substance, the logic of exposition for the logic of the decision itself—and unaided by a realistic scholarly literature on judicial decision making, lawyers tend in briefing and arguing cases to stop with the language of statutes and cases. Old-style law teaching adopted the standpoint of the litigating lawyer and so taught the student agility in argument, how to clear away the debris of precedent, and how to interpret legal texts imaginatively, because if you're litigating you have to master these sometimes dark arts. But the old-time teachers offered nothing in place of the debris; they did not teach policy. Modern teaching supplies the substance missing from the old style, but downplays the debris-clearing function, and as a result students are too respectful of precedent and statutory language. Nor can economic talk be automatically ported to the courtroom; students sense this but are not given a rhetoric in which to feed economic policy to hungry judges.

A sense of the audience is the key to rhetorical effectiveness, and so the key to effective appellate advocacy is the advocate's imagining himself an appellate judge. If he does that he will see immediately that appellate judges labor under the immense disadvantage of having very little time to spend on each case and, in addition, of lacking specialized knowledge of most of the cases that come before them. The judges are badly in need of the advocate's help, yet the working assumption of most of the lawyers who argue before appellate courts is that the judges have the same knowledge and outlook as the lawyers.

Rarely is it effective advocacy to try to convince the judges that the case law compels them to rule in one's favor. For if that were so, the case probably would not have gotten to the appellate stage (unless it is a criminal case—criminal cases tend to be appealed regardless of the merit of the appeal, because normally the appellant is not bearing the cost of the appeal). And so the second-biggest mistake that appellate advocates make, after exaggerating how much the judges know about, or are willing to devote time to learning about, the circumstances behind the appeal, is to think they can win by rubbing the judges' noses in the precedents. In a case that is not controlled by precedent, the task of the advocate is to convince the judges that the position for which he is contending is the more reasonable one in light of all relevant circumstances, which include but are not exhausted in the case law, the statutory text, and the other conventional materials of legal decision making.

The most effective method of arguing such a case, as should be clear from the discussion of case-based reasoning in chapter 7, is to identify the purpose behind the relevant legal principle and then show how that purpose would be furthered by a decision in favor of the advocate's position. Having done this, he will have to show that the position does not violate settled law, and this will require a further discussion of the cases. So precedent will enter at two stages in the argument: as a source of governing principles, and as a constraint on efforts to realize those principles in the novel setting of the case at hand. At neither stage, however, will the good advocate be arguing that the result for which he is contending is already "in" the law.

These simple principles should be at the heart of a legal education. Law students could learn something about them from reading what judges have written about judging, as we shall see in the next chapter, and indeed from reading Llewellyn's book. But these writings are not taught. It would also be helpful to law students if casebooks sometimes published not only the judicial opinion in a case but also the lawyers' briefs, so that the student could see how close to or (more likely) far from the judge's conception of the case the lawyers' conceptions were; how the lawyers failed or succeeded in communicating effectively with the judge; and how different the judge's concerns were from the lawyers'. It would be an eye-opener.

Problems of communication are typically and in this instance two-way. Judges are not good at telling lawyers what they expect from them. This is an aspect of the curious institutional passivity of the judges in our system. One thing judges and umpires really do have in common is that just as umpires don't try to tell players how to play better, judges are disinclined to tell lawyers how to brief and argue cases better. The difference is that judges, but not umpires, change the rules from time to time, and do so in response to the urging of contestants. They are not passive observers, but they often act as if they are, watching lawyers drone their way to defeat.

The failure of law professors to come to terms in their teaching and writing with the ghostwriting of judicial opinions by law clerks is especially damaging to a realistic understanding of adjudication. The failure may be rooted in embarrassment at teaching as the law the writings of neophyte lawyers who a year or two before were students, or in a desire not to make impressionable students prematurely cynical about judges. Whatever the cause, the effect is to obfuscate the judicial process. Why, in the aftermath of legal realism, the legal process school, the findings of the attitudinalists, and the analysis of the judicial process in books such as this, are judicial opinions on average as legalistic as they were a century ago and more legalistic than they were a half century ago? Because today most judicial opinions are written by law clerks, which was not true a century ago, when very few judges even *had* law clerks (some had "legal secretaries," but most of their duties were indeed secretarial), and was less true decades ago, when judges had fewer law clerks and law still had a writing culture. Students are taught to approach judicial opinions as if every word were written by the nominal author—that is, the judge—and the effect is to imbue them with a legalistic outlook, an effect reinforced by their youth (to which, as I suggested in chapter 6, algorithmic thinking as distinguished from pragmatic or legislative thinking is more congenial than it is to older persons) and by an understandable desire to believe that their steep law school tuition is buying them a set of powerful analytic tools. When they become law clerks it is natural for them to write opinions designed to provide legalistic justifications for their judges' votes. They thus contribute to the mystification of the next student generation.

If after all this you still doubt the alienation of the elite legal professoriat from the courts, I ask you to consider the participation of a number of those professors in the litigation that culminated in the Supreme Court's 8–0 decision in *Rumsfeld v. Forum for Academic & Institutional Rights, Inc. (FAIR)*.[19] The decision, which involved the response of law schools to military discrimination against homosexuals, was neither momentous nor unexpected (a decision the other way would have been both), but the suit was in effect an academic project from which we can learn something about the relation between judges and law professors.

As a result of the compromise in 1993 between the Defense Department and President Clinton that created the "don't ask, don't tell" policy, homosexual orientation is no longer a bar to serving in the armed forces unless manifested by homosexual "conduct," broadly and somewhat oddly defined as a homosexual act, a statement that the person is homosexual, or a marriage or attempted marriage to someone of the same sex.[20] Military recruiters no longer ask applicants what their sexual orientation is. But members of the armed forces who disclose a homosexual orientation are liable to expulsion even if they are not known to engage in homosexual acts and do not flaunt their homosexuality, as by attempting a homosexual marriage.

The response of most law schools to military discrimination against homosexuals, beginning in the 1970s and undeterred by the "don't ask, don't tell" compromise, was to deny Judge Advocate General (JAG) recruiters the same assistance in recruiting law students that the schools' career placement offices provide to law firms and other potential employers who promise not to discriminate against applicants for employment on the basis of their sexual orientation. Not that the law schools single out military recruiters. The denial of assistance applies to all employers who refuse to hire homosexuals. Nor are JAG recruiters (or other discriminators) banned from law school campuses. But they are denied the extensive assistance that law schools offer recruiters who, so to speak, take the pledge—assistance that includes "recurring 'meet the employer nights,' or gatherings on campus at which students and em-

---

19. 126 S. Ct. 1297 (2006). Justice Alito did not participate.

20. "Policy on Homosexual Conduct in the Armed Forces," Memorandum from Secretary of Defense Les Aspin to the Secretaries of the Army, Navy, and Air Force, and to the Chairman of the Joint Chiefs of Staff (July 19, 1993), http://dont.stanford.edu/regulations/lesaspinmemo.pdf (visited Sept. 24, 2007). The policy was codified by Congress in 10 U.S.C. § 654(b).

ployers' representatives can meet in a cordial, low-pressure, event that is more like a cocktail reception than an interview or meeting."[21]

Congress riposted with a law known as the Solomon Amendment, which in its present form denies federal funding to any institution of higher education any component of which prevents military recruiters "from gaining access to campuses, or access to students . . . on campuses, for purposes of military recruiting in a manner that is at least equal in quality and scope to the access to campuses and to students that is provided to any other employer."[22] Law schools reluctantly complied lest their universities lose federal funding. But a coalition of law schools and law professors—the Forum for Academic and Institutional Rights (FAIR)—challenged the constitutionality of the law, arguing that it imposes an unconstitutional condition on the receipt of federal funds: to obtain them a law school must mute its opposition to discrimination against homosexuals by providing the same hospitality to military recruiters that it extends to employers who pledge not to discriminate. FAIR lost in the district court, won in the court of appeals,[23] and lost again in the Supreme Court.

An amicus curiae brief filed on behalf of a large number of Harvard Law School professors opposed the government on a different ground from FAIR's—that there is no violation of the Solomon Amendment as long as a law school, rather than singling out military recruiters, denies placement assistance to all employers who refuse to promise not to discriminate against homosexuals. The brief argues *against* holding the Solomon Amendment unconstitutional because that "could encourage attempts by discriminatory employers, educational institutions or other groups to evade compliance with various pieces of federal civil rights legislation . . . by asserting that granting equal treatment without regard to race or sex would send a 'message' with which they disagree."[24]

The Supreme Court rejected the suggested interpretation, which bordered on the absurd. As the Court pointed out (and remember that eight Justices, including the four liberal Justices, agreed), the interpretation

21. Brief of NALP et al., 2005 U.S. S. Ct. Briefs LEXIS 622, at n. 12 (Sept. 20, 2005) (footnotes omitted).
22. 10 U.S.C. § 983 (Supp. 2005).
23. 390 F.3d 219 (3d Cir. 2004).
24. Brief of Professors William Alford et al., 2005 U.S. S. Ct. Briefs LEXIS 630, at n. 22 (Sept. 21, 2005) (footnote omitted).

would defeat the purpose of the Solomon Amendment because it would allow law schools to continue without any change at all their policy of excluding military recruiters, as what law school would permit *any* employer that discriminated against homosexuals access to recruitment favors? Congress would have achieved nothing by its law. Nullification is not an accepted method of statutory interpretation.

Concerning the constitutional issue—the issue pressed by FAIR and decided in its favor by the court of appeals—the Supreme Court said that "the Solomon Amendment neither limits what law schools may say nor requires them to say anything. Law schools remain free under the statute to express whatever views they may have on the military's congressionally mandated employment policy, all the while retaining eligibility for federal funds."[25] To the argument that the assistance that law school placement services render compliant employers includes compelled speech in the form of "send[ing] e-mails or post[ing] notices on bulletin boards on an employer's behalf," the Court responded that Congress "can prohibit employers from discriminating in hiring on the basis of race. The fact that this will require an employer to take down a sign reading 'White Applicants Only' hardly means that the law should be analyzed as one regulating the employer's speech rather than conduct."[26]

Just as no one would suppose that the racist employer had had a change of heart, so no one reading the notices sent to students or employers by law school placement offices would think the law schools were expressing agreement with the policies of prospective employers. Law firms that represent cigarette companies or pornographers, the law departments of giant corporations that pollute the atmosphere or sell munitions to Third World dictators or abuse experimental animals or buy gold from slave labor mines in the Congo, the offices of the general counsel of the CIA and the Defense Department, right-wing and left-wing public interest firms—all are welcome to "meet the employer" nights. (This raises the question why only discriminators against homosexuality are turned away. The answer is that the grievance of homosexual law students is "available," in the cognitive psychologists' sense, to law school faculty in a way that other questionable conduct of potential employers is not.) No one, least of all the law schools themselves, thinks

25. 126 S. Ct. at 1308.
26. Id.

that by extending this welcome the law schools or their faculties endorse the policies of their employer guests. All that a law school is "express-ing" by its hospitality gestures to prospective employers of its students is its desire to help the students get good jobs, for the law school's sake as well as the students'. (Successful graduates tend to be loyal and gener-ous alumni.) A law school can if it wants make emphatically clear that it is playing host to JAG recruiters only because it must do so or cost its university federal money. The Court pointed out that it had "held that high school students can appreciate the difference between speech a school sponsors and speech the school permits because legally required to do so, pursuant to an equal access policy. Surely students have not lost that ability by the time they get to law school."[27]

The other seven Justices who participated in the decision all joined the Chief Justice's rebuke of the legal professoriat for overreaching: "In this case, FAIR has attempted to stretch a number of First Amendment doctrines well beyond the sort of activities these doctrines protect."[28] FAIR "plainly overstates the expressive nature of [the law schools'] ac-tivity and the impact of the Solomon Amendment on it, while exaggerat-ing the reach of our First Amendment precedents."[29]

The Harvard professors (who did their stretching on the principles of statutory interpretation) were right that invalidating the Solomon Amendment would foster other discrimination by educational institu-tions by curtailing the government's authority to use its spending power to prevent discrimination. It would empower conservative law schools to refuse to assist employers who refused to promise *not* to hire homo-sexuals. But the professors' solution was so far-fetched as to raise a ques-tion of academic integrity. A lawyer whom you hire to represent you can in perfect good faith make any argument on your behalf that is not frivo-lous. But the professors were not parties to *Rumsfeld v. FAIR* and so a reader of their amicus curiae brief might expect the views expressed in it to represent their best professional judgment on the meaning of the Sol-omon Amendment. The brief identifies them as full-time faculty mem-bers of the Harvard Law School rather than as concerned citizens, and one expects law professors, when speaking ex cathedra as it were, to be expressing their true beliefs rather than making any old argument that

27. Id. at 1310.
28. Id. at 1313.
29. Id.

they thought had a 1 percent chance of persuading a court. It is hard to believe that all of the professors who subscribed to the Harvard brief actually thought that interpreting the Solomon Amendment as a nullity was the best interpretation, or that they are interpretive nihilists who believe that the meaning of a text is *entirely* in the eye of the beholder.

This criticism of the law professors is inapplicable to law schools themselves and to their association (the Association of American Law Schools, another amicus curiae). Of course a law school (and its university) would prefer to have federal money given to it without strings attached, especially strings that will get it in trouble with students and faculty members strongly hostile to the military's policy on homosexuals. It is hyperbole for the Association of American Law Schools to argue that the price of a law school's retaining its federal funding is to "abandon its commitment to fight discrimination"[30] or that the issue in the case was the right of a university to decide what may be taught.[31] But one understands that this is merely lawyer rhetoric in the service of a conventional client interest.

The same cannot be said for the Harvard professors' amicus brief, or for the brief filed on behalf of a large majority of the faculty of the Yale Law School. That brief restates FAIR's constitutional argument in exaggerated form, saying that the Solomon Amendment "trample[s] upon the [Yale Law School] Faculty Members' academic freedom" by forcing them "to assist the military in telling some Yale Law students that they are not fit to serve in our country's armed forces because of their sexual orientation."[32] No student could think that by virtue of Yale's bowing to the Solomon Amendment, the law school faculty was complicit with the military policy on homosexuals. If the Yale hospital treats a homophobe who has cancer, is the Yale medical faculty signaling its approval of homophobia? That is the logic of the brief.

To bolster its extravagant claim, the Yale brief cites a case in which the Supreme Court held that the First Amendment entitled the NAACP to organize a boycott of merchants who discriminated against blacks:[33] "The Court's decision in *Claiborne* makes it clear that the First Amend-

---

30. Brief for the Association of American Law Schools, 2005 U.S. S. Ct. Briefs LEXIS 637, at n. 16 (Sept. 21, 2005).

31. Id. at n. 29–30.

32. Brief Amici Curiae of Robert A. Burt et al., 2005 U.S. S. Ct. Briefs LEXIS 638, at nn. 2–3 (Sept. 21, 2005).

33. Id. at nn. 13–14, discussing National Association for the Advancement of Colored People v. Claiborne, 458 U.S. 886, 911, 913 (1982).

ment fully protects the Faculty Members' refusal to cooperate with or assist, to disassociate from, and thereby to protest against, the military's discrimination against their gay, lesbian, and bisexual students."[34] But the NAACP was not trying to bite the hand that fed it. The logic of the Yale professors' reading of *Claiborne* is that if the Yale Law School refused to allow the federal government to audit its use of federal funds, on the ground that money saved by the auditors might be diverted to the war in Iraq, the First Amendment would entitle Yale to bar the auditors but keep the money. It is no answer that the government has a legitimate interest in auditing government grants but not in discriminating against homosexuals. The discrimination against homosexuals is legal, and the Yale professors' brief makes no effort to evaluate the reasons for it, which may not be entirely the product of ignorance and malice, as the professors believe. They also fail to note a countervailing First Amendment interest. In discriminating against military recruiters the law schools limit their students' exposure to views concerning military policy that are contrary to the orthodoxy that dominates the law school community. If the Solomon Amendment is censorship, so is the law schools' discrimination against military recruiters.

The Harvard and Yale law professors' amicus curiae briefs are conventional in approach, poorly reasoned, and devoid of constructive content. In all but one instance[35] the professors did not write the briefs themselves but instead hired a law firm to do so. I am told that at least in the case of the Yale professors' brief the intellectual input by the professors was substantial. I would be more comfortable had it been insubstantial. Not only is there nothing in the briefs that distinguishes them from the ordinary product of practicing lawyers, but they make some embarrassingly bad arguments and contain no academic insights.

These law professors, the cream of the current crop, seem to have no clue as to how to help a court decide a case. Their idea of a persuasive brief is one that bludgeons the judges with precedents that though inapt contain some general language helpful to the cause. They think that the only rhetoric that is effective in the Supreme Court is a legalist rhetoric.

34. Brief Amici Curiae of Robert A. Burt et al., note 32 above, at n. 14.

35. Brief for Amicus Curiae the American Association of University Professors, 2005 U.S. S. Ct. Briefs LEXIS 641, at nn. 2–3 (Sept. 21, 2005). This brief states that "a faculty is entitled to make the academic judgment that assisting recruitment by an employer that refuses to hire openly gay students is akin to failing a student in class merely for being gay." Id. at n. 12. That is like saying that teaching evolution to a class that contains believers in biblical inerrancy is akin to flunking a student because he is a fundamentalist Christian.

They do not understand that the distinctive legal academic culture that has evolved in recent decades could, without offense to the norms of appellate advocacy, have made a distinctive contribution to the Justices' consideration of *Rumsfeld v. FAIR*. Missing from the briefs is any discussion of why our armed forces want to continue a ban on homosexuals that has been abandoned by most of the countries that we consider to be our peers, and what effect invalidating the Solomon Amendment would have on the ban, on the quality of the armed forces, and on military justice. Judges are curious about such things. They want to understand the real stakes in a case. They want the lawyers to help them dig below the semantic surface. Maybe the military has reason to believe that lifting the ban on homosexuals all the way would undermine military morale, complicate recruitment, and further strain our already overstretched military. If so, this belief would have to be weighed against the harm to homosexuals[36] (indeed, the harm to the military itself) from the ban. The military perforce recruits heavily from a segment of the population that would be upset at the thought of homosexuals' being entitled to serve with them. And that anxiety—even if no better than an ignorant prejudice—is something that a conscientious Administration would have to weigh, especially when the nation is at war. (I am referring not to the "war on terror," a locution that is both imprecise and misleading, but to U.S. military operations in Iraq and Afghanistan.) But public opinion on homosexuality is in flux. Abolishing the ban might have no more effect on U.S. military morale than abolishing it in Britain, Israel, and many other countries has had on their militaries.

As for the consequences of invalidating the Solomon Amendment—a topic on which academics might be expected to have a unique perspective just by virtue of being academics—one would be that fewer students from elite law schools would be hired by the military because JAG recruiters would not have the same access to those students as other recruiters would. Some of the discouraged students would be homosexual. Homosexuals are not excluded by the armed forces; they are forced to stay in the closet. (The situation was practically though not legally identical before "don't ask, don't tell.") Many homosexuals today are unwilling to remain closeted, but some are willing, even some who attend

---

36. "It is terrible to tell people they are unfit to serve their country, unless they really are unfit, which is not the case here." Richard A. Posner, *Sex and Reason* 321 (1992).

schools such as Harvard and Yale. If they are recruited into a JAG corps, this may hasten the end of the formal ban on homosexuals. But what is more important, as Peter Berkowitz has pointed out, is that most students at such law schools, whatever their sexual orientation, are liberal.[37] The more of them who are recruited for JAG service, the sooner the ban will collapse.

The practical consequences of upholding or invalidating the Solomon Amendment are sociopolitical facts that academics are in a better position to investigate than practicing lawyers. Inquiring into those facts and presenting the results to the courts would be a more useful employment of law professors' time than hiring practitioners to flog precedents. There is a sheeplike character to all these professors signing on to a practitioner's brief (the sheep being led by the goat). One might have thought that some of them would speak in their own voice—express an individual view. Can't a law professor at Harvard or Yale write a brief? Well, maybe not anymore; but he could do the research that only academics can do well, and let the practitioner convey the results in the brief.

Maybe the law professors, or most of them, who signed the amicus curiae briefs were just buckling to student pressure, or demonstrating solidarity with their liberal students, who are in the strong majority in elite law schools. One hopes that that is true and that they can be persuaded to turn their minds to questions fundamental to the judicial process that judges cannot answer, such as the trade-offs between rules and standards or between strict and loose construction. Law professors have better tools for investigating such questions of urgent importance to judges than they used to have, but worse communication with and less insight into the judiciary. The academics' briefs in *Rumsfeld v. FAIR* mirror the lack of realism in the teaching of law students about courts. Both realms treat an appeal as a duel of precedents. Neither understands the judicial mind. Neither acknowledges the politicization of constitutional law and the consequences for effective advocacy. Judges sense a widening chasm between the professoriat and the judiciary. In *Rumsfeld v. FAIR* we glimpse its breadth. If as I suspect the root cause is the increased specialization of academic lawyers, the chasm may be unbridgeable.

37. Peter Berkowitz, "U.S. Military: 8, Elite Law Schools: 0, How Many Professors Does It Take to Misunderstand the Law?" *Weekly Standard,* Mar. 20, 2006, p. 10.

9

Is Pragmatic Adjudication Inescapable?

The word that best describes the average American judge at all levels of our judicial hierarchies and yields the greatest insight into his behavior is "pragmatist"[1] (more precisely, as I shall explain, "constrained pragmatist"). It is not *all* that is left after legalism, extreme attitudinalism, and the compulsion of comprehensive theory are rejected as being inadequately descriptive of judicial behavior. But it is a lot. Brian Tamanaha estimates that more American judges fit the pragmatist label than any other,[2] but it would be more accurate to say that most American judges are legalists in some cases and pragmatists in others; for remember that legalism is a pragmatic tactic, though it need not be only that. And many

---

1. This is an old theme for me; see my books *The Problems of Jurisprudence* (1990), especially ch. 15; *Overcoming Law* (1995), especially ch. 19; *The Problematics of Moral and Legal Theory*, ch. 4 (1999); *An Affair of State: The Investigation, Impeachment, and Trial of President Clinton* 217–230 (1999); *Breaking the Deadlock: The 2000 Election, the Constitution, and the Courts* 169–187 (2001); *Law, Pragmatism, and Democracy* (2003).

2. Brian Z. Tamanaha, "How an Instrumental View of Law Corrodes the Rule of Law," 56 *DePaul Law Review* 469, 490 (2007) ("It is fair to surmise that a greater proportion of contemporary judges are judicial pragmatists . . . Judicial decisions today routinely cite policy considerations, consider the purposes behind the law, and pay attention to law's social consequences"). For interesting recent acknowledgments of the prevalence of pragmatic judging in the Supreme Court, see Nelson Lund, "The Rehnquist Court's Pragmatic Approach to Civil Rights," 99 *Northwestern University Law Review* 249 (2004); Kenneth W. Starr, "The Court of Pragmatism and Internationalization: A Response to Professors Chemerinsky and Amann," 94 *Georgetown Law Journal* 1565 (2006). I discuss the Court's (intermittent) pragmatism in the next chapter. There is a growing literature, illustrated by John R. Tennert, "Administrative Law as Pragmatism," 29 *International Journal of Public Administration* 1339 (2006), on the pragmatic vein in various fields of law, but it would carry me too far afield to discuss that literature in this book.

judges of either inclination encounter cases in which neither set of techniques works—the legalist techniques run out but the consequences of the decision are unknown; or perhaps a strong moral or emotional reaction (maybe indignation aroused by the conduct of one of the parties) overrides both a legalistic response and a concern with consequences. Nevertheless the pragmatic vein in American judging is wide and deep.

It was as a style of philosophizing that the word "pragmatism" first achieved widespread currency in American intellectual circles. Pragmatism was the invention of three American philosophers—Charles Sanders Peirce, William James, and John Dewey—whose lives overlapped and who among them spanned almost a century, from the late 1860s to the early 1950s, although the antecedents reach back to the Sophists and Aristotle and less remotely to Hume, Mill, Emerson, Hegel, and Nietzsche. The views and methods of the classic American pragmatists were diverse (and only Dewey was actually trained as a philosopher), but they had in common a turning away from the traditional philosophical agenda of the West. The agenda had been set by Plato and was concerned primarily with investigating the meaning and possibility of truth, the foundations of knowledge, modes of reasoning, the nature of reality, the meaning of life, the roles of freedom and causality in human action, and the nature and principles of morality. The pragmatists turned away not only from the topics but also from the methodology of the philosophical mainstream, with its emphasis on conceptualism, the a priori, and logical rigor. They advocated a radical empiricism in which propositions would be evaluated by their observable consequences rather than by their logical antecedents—advocated, in other words, an extension of the scientific method into all areas of inquiry. Dewey called his brand of pragmatism "experimentalism," and the word conveys an apt sense of the tentative, antidogmatic, to a degree antitheoretical outlook that characterized (and characterizes) philosophical pragmatism—"an instrumentalist or problem solving approach to ideas and institutions. On a pragmatist view, our ideas, principles, practices and institutions simply are tools for navigating a social and political world that is shot through with indeterminacy."[3]

Pragmatism had been hatched in an informal discussion group in

3. Jack Knight and James Johnson, "The Priority of Democracy: A Pragmatist Approach to Political-Economic Institutions and the Burden of Justification," 101 *American Political Science Review* 47, 49 (2007).

Cambridge, Massachusetts, in the early 1870s. The participants included not only Peirce and James but also, among others, the young Holmes. Precisely what contribution Holmes made to the birth of philosophical pragmatism is unclear. But throughout his life his thought was strongly marked by pragmatism. The pragmatic approach to law was announced in the famous opening sentence of *The Common Law* (1881) ("The life of the law has not been logic; it has been experience") and elaborated in that book and in a later article, "The Path of the Law."[4] In these and other works, and in many of his judicial opinions, Holmes rejected the then orthodox notion that judges could decide difficult cases by a process of or very similar to logical deduction from premises given by authoritative legal texts, or by unquestioned universal principles that inspire and subsume those texts ("natural law"). He argued that judges in difficult cases made law with reference to the likely social and economic consequences of their decisions, and that their intuitions about those consequences, rather than the abstract moral principles and formal legal analysis deployed in conventional judicial opinions, drove legal change and had made the law what it had become. Nor did he think that judges engaged in bloodless policy science. He thought that their political views, such as fear of socialism, were major influences on their decisions.

Philosophical and legal pragmatism coevolved. A celebrated essay by John Dewey drew heavily on Holmes's writings.[5] Published in 1924, just as legal realism was getting under way, the essay urged judges and lawyers to turn from conceiving of legal decisions as the products of deduction from rules taken as given to understanding the practical consequences of legal decisions and shaping the law accordingly. Dewey advocated a forward-looking, empiricist, even *political*—though in a nonpartisan sense—approach, as distinct from the backward-looking syllogistic approach (and other mystifications, such as "legal reasoning by analogy") of conventional legal thinkers. He was in sync with Holmes, who also had a nondoctrinaire, open-minded, experimentalist approach to law and public policy, as when in his judicial decisions he urged that the Supreme Court not cut off in the name of constitutional rights the newfangled social welfare legislation being enacted by

---

4. Oliver Wendell Holmes, "The Path of the Law," 10 *Harvard Law Review* 457 (1897).
5. John Dewey, "Logical Method and Law," 10 *Cornell Law Quarterly* 17 (1924).

states, which he viewed as laboratories for social experimentation that the Court should allow to continue, or when he said anent socialism (which he opposed), "Of course I have no *a priori* objection to socialism any more than to polygamy. Our public schools and our post office are socialist, and wherever it is thought to pay I have no objection except that it probably is wrongly thought."[6]

When Dewey died in 1952, philosophical pragmatism underwent an eclipse from which it emerged twenty years later through the efforts of the philosopher Richard Rorty, who built on work by Wittgenstein, Quine, and Davidson that had strong affinities with the work of the original pragmatists. In the last quarter century philosophical pragmatism has enjoyed a renascence and for the first time has begun to attract a European following, notably in the figure of Jürgen Habermas, who has acknowledged a debt to the American pragmatists. Before Habermas virtually the only European pragmatic philosopher had been F. S. C. Schiller, and his influence had been limited.

Despite the fading of the legal realist movement in the early 1940s, American legal pragmatism continued throughout the period of philosophical pragmatism's eclipse to be a highly influential tendency in legal thought, and so it continues to be. Only recently, however, has it become *self-conscious,* in the sense that advocates of legal pragmatism are endeavoring to define it carefully, to compare it with other schools of legal thought such as economic analysis of law, to situate it in relation to other currents of social thought such as philosophical pragmatism, to apply it to specific legal doctrines and decisions, and to evaluate its strengths and limitations.

I said that philosophical and legal pragmatism coevolved. But it would be a mistake to suppose legal pragmatism identical to or dependent on philosophical pragmatism, so that criticisms of philosophical pragmatism would necessarily be criticisms of legal pragmatism. The case for legal pragmatism is based not on philosophical argument but on the needs and character of American law. I note at the end of this chapter that legal thinking in Continental European judiciaries is less pragmatic than in the United States because of the institutional differences, discussed in

---

6. Letter from Oliver Wendell Holmes to Lewis Einstein, Nov. 24, 1912, in *The Essential Holmes: Selections from the Letters, Speeches, Judicial Opinions, and Other Writings of Oliver Wendell Holmes, Jr.* 66 (Richard A. Posner ed. 1992).

chapter 5, between the American judicial system and the European career judiciaries.

I do not even think that legal pragmatism is strongly derivative from philosophical pragmatism. Its origin is more likely the nineteenth-century loss of faith in natural law, a loss connected with the loss of religious faith that many intellectuals experienced in the wake of Darwin and the ascent of a scientific outlook arising from the growing success of science as a mode of understanding and control. If the common law, which loomed larger in the nineteenth century than it does today, is not the translation of natural law into positive law, or the judicial adoption of immemorial custom as Blackstone and later Hayek urged, then it must be something that judges make up as they go along. It must mean that judges in the Anglo-American tradition really are occasional legislators. That was Holmes's conclusion.[7]

Hayek was a legalist *tout court,* but Blackstone's case is more complicated. There is a sense in which he was a founder of legal pragmatism. His claim that the common law was of Saxon origin was a fiction useful for justifying judicial creativity in terms congenial to eighteenth-century thinking. In effect he licensed judges to justify changing the common law by claiming that by doing so they were restoring its original meaning.[8] This was pragmatism as fake originalism. And we recall that Blackstone, in his response to the Bologna bloodletting statute, adopted a purposive theory of statutory interpretation—a key plank in the platform of legal pragmatism.

Saxon law cannot be our answer to the question, if judges are indeed occasional legislators, what are the sources and content of the legislation they enact in the course of deciding cases? The answer at which Holmes hinted is ideology,[9] and it was the answer given by many of the legal realists of the 1920s and 1930s. Some thought all law was politics in a narrow partisan sense, denounced judges for their reactionary politics, and urged the appointment of liberals to the bench. But this

7. "I recognize without hesitation that judges do and must legislate." Southern Pacific Co. v. Jensen, 244 U.S. 205, 221 (1917) (dissenting opinion).

8. Richard A. Posner, *The Economics of Justice* 25–27 (1981).

9. Holmes, note 4 above, at 466; Oliver Wendell Holmes, Jr., *The Common Law* 1 (1881): "The life of the law has not been logic; it has been experience. The felt necessities of the time, the prevalent moral and political theories, intuitions of public policy, avowed or unconscious, even the prejudices which judges share with their fellow-men, have had a good deal more to do than the syllogism in determining the rules by which men should be governed."

approach seemed to imply that one group of usurpative judges should simply be replaced by another, a thought remote from Holmes's proto-realism and troubling to influential judges such as Cardozo and Hand who agreed with Holmes. Those judges, joined by thoughtful realists such as Felix Cohen, Max Radin, and Karl Llewellyn, wanted the judiciary to be "realistic," practical, think things not words, recognize the epistemic limitations of legalism. But they did not want them to be political in the narrow sense of trying to retard or (a favorite realist project) promote the New Deal.

The realists could have pointed out that even a "politicized" judiciary is not usurpative in a society that is politically homogeneous. Law is shot through with political values, which when endorsed by the public at large provide a neutral background of assumptions and presuppositions rather than being a cockpit of contention. That which is unchallenged seems natural rather than political. (We do not think that our disapproval of cannibalism or infanticide is merely a political opinion.) This is the situation in large stretches of the common law today—for it is false that "the increasingly heterogeneous nature of modern society . . . renders it highly unlikely that a social consensus will exist regarding *any* ethical principle or policy goal that might ground common law adjudication."[10] Contract law, for example, is suffused with the values of capitalism, a political theory and practice. Yet as with property law, tort law, commercial law, corporate law, and antitrust and securities law—among many other fields, both common law and statutory—the basic tenets of contract law are uncontroversial because America is so strongly committed to capitalism. In many areas of law, however, including some of the areas just listed before capitalism vanquished communism in the battle of economic ideologies, there was no consensus when the realists wrote. Where did that leave the judge who could no longer accept that his role was exhausted in the technical task of ascertaining and applying preexisting legal rules? How other than by reference to his political opinions was he to resolve politically consequential issues that could not be re-

10. Jack Knight and James Johnson, "Political Consequences of Pragmatism," 24 *Political Theory* 68, 78 (1996) (emphasis added). Whether consensus *justifies* particular common law rules, as doubted by Knight and Johnson in their criticisms of my defense of legal pragmatism, is not the concern of this chapter. The concern is whether American judges are pragmatists, not whether they should be, except insofar as the normative adequacy of such a judicial philosophy might bear on the plausibility of thinking that American judges have ever actually practiced it.

solved by conventional legal reasoning? The realists thought the answer lay in bringing the methods and insights of the social sciences into law. But either the social sciences were not up to the job or the realists were not up to the social sciences. Not until the law and economics movement gained momentum decades after realism faded would social science make a major substantive contribution to legal pragmatism.

A diversity of moral and political views creates pressure for resolving disputes on the basis of a thin proceduralism, which by avoiding substantive commitments provides a common ground on which persons of antagonistic substantive views can meet.[11] That is what we observe in the legal process school (discussed further in chapter 10), which succeeded legal realism. Judges are adjured by that school to be impartial, of course, but also to deliberate patiently and with an open mind and to base jurisdictional allocations—between judge and jury, trial court and appellate court, court and legislature, and so forth—on relative institutional competence and thus to be respectful of other institutions (especially legislatures and administrative agencies; the legal process school had a Progressive Era and New Deal flavor). Judges are especially adjured to be mindful of the limits of their knowledge and the sources of possible bias and to base their decisions on neutral principles rather than on the consequences for society, or for the litigants, of deciding a case one way or another. But saluting these content-free, technocratic-seeming precepts is to adjudication as spring training is to the baseball season. The precepts are warm-up measures. Closure requires agreement on substance. Without that, the choice of neutral principles is up in the air. No more than legal realism could legal process offer a substitute for legalism on the one hand and politics and emotion on the other.

The idea of neutral principles reflects a confusion between legislation and case law that came naturally to persons who were Progressives or New Dealers and thus products of eras in which legislation, which declares rights and obligations in general language and in advance of implementation, was exalted by advanced thinkers over the common law. Judges imbued with the values and methods of the common law were thought (not without reason) reactionary; the evidence was judicial hostility to labor unions, judicial invalidation of social legislation in the

11. See Bernard Williams, "Modernity and the Substance of Ethical Life," in Williams, *In the Beginning Was the Deed: Realism and Moralism in Political Argument* 40, 48–49 (Geoffrey Hawthorne ed. 2005).

name of "liberty of contract," the perceived inadequacy of tort law as a regime for regulating safety, and the interpretive principle that statutes in derogation of the common law are to be strictly construed. Neutral principles were offered as the antidote to political decision making. But when a court states a new principle in the course of deciding a novel case, more often than not the statement's semantic reach exceeds what is necessary to decide the case. If the court in later cases insists in the name of neutrality on enforcing the principle to the full literal extent of its original statement, come what may, it will be refusing to learn from experience. It will be imitating a legislature, rather than using the knowledge acquired from cases that the legislature did not foresee to fine-tune the legislative rule.

With the increasing intellectual ambitiousness of academic law, comprehensive theories, substantive rather than procedural in character, have been proposed to fill the gap between the orthodox legal materials and the necessity of deciding a case even when those materials do not generate a convincing answer. These theories mainly are normative but their proponents invariably find at least traces of them in case law. Most of the theories have been proposed for constitutional law, that least disciplined area of American law, and so are examined in Part Three. The most important theory that is not limited to constitutional law, though it embraces it, is economics. It is offered to explain legal doctrines and case outcomes in some fields of law, mainly though not only the common law fields, and to guide legal reform in the remaining fields.[12] As a normative theory, economic analysis of law is controversial. A judge's choice to use it to generate outcomes in the open area is an ideological choice except when there is broad agreement that economics should guide the decision; consensus represses ideological conflict. As a positive theory, however, economic analysis of law does well in explaining legal doctrines in a variety of commercial and noncommercial fields of law, including broad swaths of tort, contract, criminal, intellectual property, environmental, labor, and even constitutional law, along with major parts of remedial and procedural law. But it would be odd to describe American judges as "economists," or even as economic analysts of law. Very few of them have a substantial background in economics, and in only a few areas, such as antitrust law, are cases pitched to judges and juries in ex-

---

12. See Richard A. Posner, *Economic Analysis of Law* (7th ed. 2007).

plicitly economic terms. The significance of economics for the study of judicial behavior lies mainly in the consilience of economics with pragmatism.[13] The economist, like the pragmatist, is interested in ferreting out practical consequences rather than engaging in a logical or semantic analysis of legal doctrines.

Legalists object that if judges do not talk economics in their opinions, and they rarely do, they cannot be doing economics.[14] But this confuses semantics with substance. There are parallel vocabularies in which to discuss questions such as when an accidental injury should give rise to a claim for damages. One vocabulary, very old, is legal, and the other, much newer, is economic. The economic study of the common law, and of other bodies of American law as well, has found considerable isomorphism between legal and economic analysis. The continued use of different vocabularies illustrates "contextual convergence": judges continue to employ a traditional vocabulary of rights and duties while gradually investing the words with an economic meaning.[15] This is an echo of Holmes's argument in *The Common Law* and "The Path of the Law" that common law judges use an inherited moralistic vocabulary in a nonmoralistic way.

But can legal pragmatism really do better than legalism (cannot resolve tough cases), legal realism (too vulgarly political in some versions, too lacking in content in others), legal process (too thinly procedural), or comprehensive theories (too controversial and too remote from the judicial mind-set) in explaining the behavior of American judges?

The core of legal pragmatism is pragmatic adjudication, and its core is heightened judicial concern for consequences and thus a disposition to base policy judgments on them rather than on conceptualisms and generalities. But rather than being a synonym for ad hoc adjudication, in the sense of having regard only for the consequences to the parties to the immediate case, sensible legal pragmatism tells the judge to consider systemic, including institutional, consequences as well as consequences of the decision in the case at hand. He thus must consider the effects on

13. See Elisabeth Krecké, "Economic Analysis and Legal Pragmatism," 23 *International Review of Law and Economics* 421 (2004).

14. See, for example, Stephen A. Smith, *Contract Theory* 132–136 (2004).

15. See Jody S. Kraus, "Transparency and Determinacy in Common Law Adjudication: A Philosophical Defense of Explanatory Economic Analysis," 93 *Virginia Law Review* 287 (2007); Nathan Oman, "Unity and Pluralism in Contract Law," 103 *Michigan Law Review* 1483, 1492–1498 (2005).

commercial activity of disregarding the actual wording of a contract or failing to adhere to legal precedents on which the commercial community has come to rely.

Sensible pragmatic judges are to be distinguished from shortsighted pragmatists, blinded by the equities of the case to the long-term consequences of their decision; it is for the latter that the pejorative expression "result oriented" should be reserved. Imagine a judge (there are more than a few) who does not think that the sale or use of marijuana should be outlawed and the sellers of it harshly punished, as they are under federal law today. He might be inclined to go easy on persons charged with marijuana offenses. But the inclination would be offset by the realization that judges would be bound to lose a guerrilla war with Congress over the punishment of drug trafficking, by concern with the possibility of compensatory harshness on the part of judges (and there are many) who favor the application of strict drug laws to marijuana, by respect for the beneficial consequences of the separation of powers, by the advantages of uniform as opposed to ad hoc sentencing policies, and even by disapproval of pleonexia. That was Aristotle's term for trying to get more than your fair share. It is what a person does who commits an acquisitive crime, such as selling drugs, because by doing so he is stealing a march on the law-abiding. The worker struggling to get by without violating the law is justifiably indignant at the spectacle of the drug dealer flaunting his jewelry and fancy cars. And because it is an acquisitive crime, drug dealing can be deterred only by the threat of severe punishment, even if the crime itself seems rather trivial from either a practical (harm to society) or a moral standpoint.

In contrast to pragmatists, legalists tend (or pretend) to give controlling weight to an arbitrary subset of institutional consequences of judicial decisions. They are hypersensitive to the uncertainty that can result from loose construction of statutes and contracts, from seeking out the purpose of a rule to determine the rule's scope and application, from salting doctrine with policy, and from aggressive distinguishing and overruling of precedents. Pragmatists do not see how so one-sided an emphasis on possible negative consequences of pragmatic judging can be sensible. But more interesting is the fact that contemporary justifications of legalism should rest as heavily as they do on its consequences, rather than on claims of what "law" means or requires. So pervasive is pragmatic thinking in the American political culture that legalists are driven to defend the blinkered results to which their methodology of strict rules and literal interpretations tends as yielding better consequences than a fuller engagement with the facts of a case, a greater willingness to knead rules into standards, and a looser interpretation of rules that were created without reference to the situation presented by the new case would do.

Pragmatists believe that the claim that legalism has better social consequences is dogmatic and implausible, rather than being a hypothesis that legalists are willing to see tested. Legalists argue that adjudication should be backward-looking, that judges should not try to keep law up to date but should leave to legislatures in the case of statutory law, and to the amendment process in the case of constitutional law, any needed updating of statutes or the Constitution. But they do not back their argument with facts concerning the ability of legislatures to update legislation in the face of the inertial forces built into the legislative process, or the feasibility of a program of continuously amending the Constitution to keep it up to date. They do not try to show what the state of the law, and of the society, would be today had American judges, beginning with that great loose constructionist John Marshall, consistently adhered to the legalist creed.

Legalists even accept without demur a vast area of acknowledged indeterminacy of judicial rulings. Anytime the standard of appellate review is deferential—as where findings of fact made by a trial judge are upheld because they are not "clearly erroneous," or a ruling on evidence is upheld because it is not an "abuse of discretion"—the appellate court is implying that it would also uphold the opposite ruling. For it is saying not that the finding of fact or the evidentiary ruling is correct but only that it is within the bounds of the reasonable. Since the ruling and its opposite cannot both be correct, it must be that legalism—which does not question the propriety of deferential appellate review of the types of ruling that typically receive such review—countenances a great deal of error.

Yet legal pragmatism may seem as empty as the legal process approach to which it is a successor, because it does not weight the consequences of a decision or even specify which consequences should be considered. Consequences are facts, and facts have no normative significance in themselves. One cannot derive "ought" from "is." A value must be placed on each consequence. But often the value and its importance are obvious. To deem the consequences of mass murder "harmful" one has to believe mass murder a bad thing. But one does not need an elaborate conceptual apparatus to arrive at or justify the belief. All one needs is to share the basic moral values of one's society.

This means, though, that what counts as an acceptably pragmatic resolution of a dispute is relative to the prevailing norms of particular societies. Pragmatism provides local rather than universal guidance to judicial action. And its local utility depends on the degree to which the society is normatively homogeneous. The more homogeneous, and therefore the wider the agreement on what kind of consequences are good and what kind are bad (and how good and how bad), the greater the guidance that pragmatism will provide. By way of humble analogy, most people in America believe that (with certain qualifications) if a watch is broken it should be fixed. The belief is not inevitable. There might be a society in which people believed it is bad luck to repair a watch. But given the American belief, the fact that a watch is broken is a reason on which almost everyone can agree for fixing it. It is not a conclusive reason, because (these are the qualifications to which I alluded) the owner of the watch might be glad to be rid of it, the watch might cost more to repair than to replace, or it might not have been used to keep time (maybe it was just valued as an antique). But there is enough agreement on the relevant considerations to enable a satisfactory pragmatic judgment on what to do with a broken watch.

Similarly, even in our politically and morally divided society there is convergence on many of the beliefs that undergird legal principles. For example, although we lack the information we would need in order to be able to assess the relative efficiency of rules and standards in general, there are many specific areas in which the better choice is clear. We must not make the best the enemy of the good. Although pragmatic adjudication rarely generates enough information to enable a decision that produces a social optimum, often it produces an approximation that is good enough for the law's purposes.

This possibility is given stylized representation in Figure 1. The marginal benefits (MB) and marginal costs (MC) of a safety measure that would avoid an accident that has given rise to a tort suit are functions of the type and quantity of the precautions that would have averted the accident. The optimal level of precautions (q^*) is given by the intersection of the two functions. To the right, an additional expenditure on safety

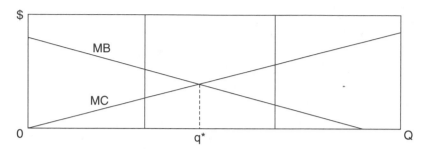

Figure 1. Tolerable Windows

would cost more than the benefit it would confer; to the left, an additional expenditure on safety would cost less than the benefit. Suppose q^* cannot be determined by the methods of litigation. The court may nevertheless know enough about the benefits and costs to be able to create the "window" formed by the two inner vertical lines.[16] At the left side of the window frame the benefits of a further effort to eliminate or prevent the accident comfortably exceed the costs. At the right side the reverse is true. If the judge knows whether the case is nearer the left or the right side of the window, he knows which party has the better case. He does not have to be able to determine the optimal level of precaution in order to make a correct decision.

Legal pragmatism is "thicker" than the approach of the legal process school, the school of thin proceduralism. There is a difference between exhorting judges to be impartial, open-minded, neutral, and so forth and exhorting them to base their decisions on consequences. For then at least they must attend to consequences, and this has significant implications for how a judge approaches a case, what he demands from the lawyers, what research he conducts, and what he discusses in his opinions. Most often a case is difficult because it requires striking a balance between two interests, both of social value, such as civil liberties and national security, intellectual creativity and access to already created intellectual works, a woman's welfare and her fetus's survival, a fair trial and a public trial, privacy and information. There may be no objective method of valuing the competing interests. But analysis can be made

16. Ferenc L. Toth, "Climate Policy in Light of Climate Science: The ICLIPS Project," 56 *Climatic Change* 7 (2003). See also Thomas Bruckner et al., "Methodological Aspects of the Tolerable Windows Approach," 56 *Climatic Change* 73 (2003).

more manageable by pragmatically recasting the question as not which of the competing interests is more valuable but what are the consequences for each interest of deciding the case one way rather than the other. If one outcome involves a much smaller sacrifice of one of the competing interests, then unless the two are of very different value that outcome will probably have the better overall consequences. That was the approach the Supreme Court took in *Roe v. Wade,* in balancing the mother's interest against the state's interest in fetal life, though the approach was executed ineptly.

Moreover, pragmatic analysis will sometimes reveal, as in the *Leegin* case (see chapter 1), that the conflict is a false one, as when consumer and producer interests are mistakenly thought to be in conflict when producers seek to fix minimum retail prices for their goods in an effort to encourage retailers to provide presale services valued by consumers.

The pragmatic judge is less interested in whether the facts of a case bring it within the semantic scope of the rule agreed to govern the case than in what the purpose of the rule is—what consequences it seeks to induce or block—and how that purpose, those consequences, would be affected by deciding the case one way or the other. The advantages of the pragmatic approach are exhibited in a recent case, *Yi v. Sterling Collision Centers, Inc.*[17] The issue was whether the defendant, sued for violating the overtime provisions of the Fair Labor Standards Act, could bring itself within one of the Act's exceptions. The district court had held, in accordance with a long line of cases, that the defendant had not presented "clear and affirmative evidence" of its entitlement to the exception. Because so many cases had recited this formula, it was natural for lawyers and judges to treat it as gospel and ask whether the defendant had presented such evidence. But in doing so they were ignoring Holmes's warning that "to rest upon a formula is a slumber that, prolonged, means death."[18] For what could "affirmative evidence" mean? And since no one believes that to prove a violation of the Fair Labor Standards Act the plaintiff must present "clear and affirmative evidence," why should the defendant have to do so in order to bring itself within an exception to the Act? Why the asymmetry?

The court of appeals in *Yi* traced the formula back to its origin and

17. 480 F.3d 505 (7th Cir. 2007).
18. Oliver Wendell Holmes, "Ideals and Doubts," in Holmes, *Collected Legal Papers* 303, 306 (1920 [1915]).

discovered that it had first appeared in a case decided in 1984, where it had not been explained but had merely been attributed to two earlier cases. One of them had said only that the burden of proving entitlement to an exemption is on the defendant (of course), the other that the defendant "has the burden of establishing the exemption affirmatively and clearly." In support of this proposition the court had cited a case that again without explanation had said that an employer seeking an exemption "has the burden of showing affirmatively that [the employees] come clearly within an exemption provision." Earlier still, another case had offered a variant of this formulation—"the burden is upon the appellant to bring itself plainly and unmistakably within the terms and the spirit of the exemptions"—which had in turn been lifted from a 1945 decision in which the Supreme Court had said that "any exemption from such humanitarian and remedial legislation [i.e., the Fair Labor Standards Act] must . . . be narrowly construed, giving due regard to the plain meaning of statutory language and the intent of Congress. To extend an exemption to other than those plainly and unmistakably within its terms and spirit is to abuse the interpretative process and to frustrate the announced will of the people."[19]

At this point the trail grows cold. But one sees what happened—what so often happens when judges think words not things. The early opinions used "affirmatively" and "clearly" or (equivalently) "plainly" and "unmistakably" merely to indicate that exemptions are to be construed narrowly—this is unquestionably the meaning of the passage in the Supreme Court's opinion (*Phillips*)—and also that the burden of proof is on the defendant, since entitlement to an exemption is an affirmative defense. The phrases were then garbled ("affirmative evidence" implies that there must be a concept of "negative evidence"), the garbled form repeated, and the original meaning forgotten.

Even if understood as merely a clumsy invocation of the familiar principle of statutory interpretation that exemptions from a statute that creates remedies should be construed narrowly, the "clear and affirmative evidence" formula is unsatisfactory because the underlying principle is mysterious. Why should one provision in a statute take precedence over another? It shouldn't. But if you go back to the origin of the formula in the *Phillips* opinion—"to extend an exemption to other than those

19. A. H. Phillips, Inc. v. Walling, 324 U.S. 490, 493 (1945).

plainly and unmistakably within its terms and spirit is to abuse the interpretative process and to frustrate the announced will of the people"—you will see that the Court was merely cautioning that an exemption should not be interpreted *so* broadly as to render the statutory remedy ineffectual or easily evaded.

Many appellate cases, one might even say the typical such case, involve a dispute over the scope or application of a rule; in *Yi* it was the rule governing the defendant's burden of proving entitlement to an exception from a statutory duty. The scope or application is likely to be uncertain; otherwise the case would probably not have been brought, or if brought probably would not have reached the appellate level.[20] There are two ways to determine whether a new case fits under a rule. The first is to examine the extension of the rule—that is, to determine what instances fall within its meaning (as you would gather meaning, knowing nothing about the context, from a dictionary plus the rules for constructing English sentences), and then to determine whether the facts of the case at hand correspond to one of those instances. The second method, which is the pragmatic, is to determine the purpose of the rule—almost always there is a discernible purpose—and then pick the outcome that will accomplish that purpose. A purpose having been identified, the rule can be restated in practical rather than legalistic terms. The search for the purpose carries the judge beneath the verbal surface of the law to the social reality that the law is trying to shape. He must of course try not to exaggerate the thrust of the statute by ignoring a legislative compromise that may have blunted that thrust. He must save the legislation from being undone by unforeseen contingencies rather than improve it.

The question in *Yi* was whether the defendant was within an exemption for employers who pay their employees on a commission rather than a salary basis. The answer required identifying the purpose of such an exemption and then determining whether the defendant's method of compensating its employees accomplished that purpose. Neither step was particularly controversial for the politically diverse panel (two judges appointed by Republican Presidents, one by a Democratic President).

Many areas of consensus in the law today are ones in which economic

20. This is less true in criminal than in civil cases because in most criminal cases the defendant is the appellant and is not paying for his lawyer, so he is under no economic pressure to forgo a long-shot appeal.

analysis provides a good account of what judges are doing, whether or not they are conscious that what they are doing is economics. Cost-benefit analysis—the economist's method of determining what course of action to follow—is simply a disciplined way of weighing the consequences of alternative courses and choosing the one that is likely to produce the largest surplus of good over bad consequences. Remember that when cases are difficult to decide it is usually because the decision must strike a balance between two legitimate interests, one of which must give way. Pragmatism is a better description of judicial behavior in these areas than economics only because judges are more likely to recognize themselves in a description of a pragmatist than in a description of an economist, pragmatism being so deeply ingrained in American popular and political culture.

Just as legal pragmatism incorporates economic analysis of law as one of its methods, so, we must not forget, it incorporates legalism as another. An example is insistence on jurisdictional niceties, such as that a federal court must not adjudicate a case unless the case meets exacting and sometimes quite arbitrary requirements concerning deadlines for filing (for example, the requirement that in an appeal to a federal court of appeals in a civil case to which the federal government is not a party, the notice of appeal must be filed within 30 days of the final judgment by the district court); that the parties must have a particular type of stake in the case for it to be justiciable (the "standing" requirement); that it be "ripe" and not "moot"; and so forth. The effect of the concepts of standing, ripeness, mootness, and other legalist obstacles to decision on the merits of a case is to delay judicial intervention in the affairs of the nation, thus creating space for social experimentation. It would be unpragmatic for a court to invalidate a program as unconstitutional or otherwise unlawful before the program had a chance to prove its worth empirically.

A related point is that the pragmatic judge is likely to favor narrow over broad grounds of decision in the early stages of the evolution of a legal doctrine. Deciding a case on a narrow ground is a corollary of an empiricist or experimentalist orientation. The narrower the ground, the less the judges are interfering with the challenged activity. The broader the ground, the less scope the judges will have for obtaining from future cases additional information bearing on the consequences of the activity, because the decision will be a precedent that until overruled or distinguished will rule new cases within its semantic domain, which may be vast.

This last point underscores the difference between the pragmatist and legal process approaches. The latter insists on the disciplining effect of neutral principles—of the judge's committing himself to a position that will prevent him from deciding future cases in accordance with his political preferences. (So a broad precedent is an example of a neutral principle.) Legal process is thus another example of legalism in the service of pragmatism. The pragmatist who rejects the legal process approach accepts the value of neutrality and of the doctrine of precedent but worries about premature commitment to a position with unforeseeable consequences. He therefore commends not only the distinguishing of precedents as a way of reaping the fruits of knowledge gained from fresh facts revealed by new cases but also the refusing to cut off further inquiry by laying down a broad principle in the first case in a line of cases. Would it have been wise for the Supreme Court in *Brown v. Board of Education* to have ruled flatly that the Constitution is colorblind and race therefore may never be used by a public institution as a basis for action, thus ruling out affirmative action by such institutions before it had been proposed, let alone implemented? Wise or unwise, it would have been unpragmatic.

Neutral principles are a legalist trace in a school (the legal process school) that thought it had turned its back on legalism and was merely tempering legal realism. With neutral principles as with originalism, the past is allowed to rule the present and future. The neutral principle is laid down on the basis of what is known today but establishes a commitment for tomorrow, when much more may be known. Since the consequences of a decision always lie in the future, legal pragmatism is forward-looking. Adherence to precedent performs important functions, but ultimately precedent, and thus the past, is servant rather than master to the pragmatist. The value to him of the study of history lies less in directing judgment than in identifying rules that have nothing to validate them but a pedigree. Like the weakened descendants of overbred aristocrats, such rules are candidates for a critical reexamination that may lead to their supersession. Pragmatic judges thus are historicist in the counterintuitive sense of being alert to the possibility that a current legal doctrine may be a mere vestige of historical circumstances and should be discarded. Historical inquiry is like distinguishing; it is a search for differences rather than for similarities.[21]

A key tenet of legal pragmatism is that no general analytic procedure distinguishes legal reasoning from other practical reasoning. Law has a special vocabulary, special concerns, special traditions. But the analytical methods used by judges are those of ordinary, everyday reasoning, which is concerned with practical benefits and costs. *Yi* shows judges moving beyond semantics to engage with the concrete interests presented by a case. At a deeper level legal pragmatism asks litigants and their lawyers, along with judges and their law clerks, to go beyond argument—beyond "rhetoric" in the pejorative sense of verbal jousting ungrounded in facts—to data: statistics, precise measurements, photographs, diagrams.

Judges are lawyers and bring to their judging the lawyer's habitual exaggeration of the power of argument, and thus of words, to resolve disagreements. But they are less mesmerized by words than lawyers are[22] because they have to choose between competing arguments that may be finely balanced. They are not judging a debate, moreover; they are looking for a sensible resolution and this pushes them to look beyond the bickering of the lawyers to the concrete interests at stake.

Lawyers are like mathematicians in wanting to manipulate symbols, albeit verbal instead of mathematical ones, rather than to investigate the relevant phenomena, which are the social interactions that law regulates. The greater the separation between legal language and the language in which nonlawyers discuss social and personal issues, the easier it is for lawyers and judges to think that their business is indeed to manipulate symbols rather than to engage with social reality. Bryan Garner's invaluable *Redbook* is a reminder—in its lists of "stuffy" words, plethoric phrases, doublets (such as "cease and desist," "free and clear"), dispens-

21. I amplify this concept of legal historicism in chapter 4 of my book *Frontiers of Legal Theory* (2001).

22. Coffey v. Northeast Regional Commuter Railroad Corp., 479 F.3d 472, 478 (7th Cir. 2007), remarks "the curious and deplorable aversion of many lawyers to visual evidence and exact measurements (feet, inches, pounds, etc.) even when vastly more informative than a verbal description. We have noted this aversion in previous cases, *United States v. Boyd,* 475 F.3d 875, 878 (7th Cir. 2007); *Miller v. Illinois Central R.R.,* 474 F.3d 951, 954 (7th Cir. 2007); *United States v. Barnes,* 188 F.3d 893, 895 (7th Cir. 1999)—once remarking [in the *Barnes* case] that some lawyers think a word is worth a thousand pictures."

able legalese ("arguendo," "gravamen," "instant case," "simpliciter," "nexus," and the rest), and common words that bear a special meaning in law (such as "appearance," "consideration," "constructive,"[23] "presumption," "servant," etc.)[24]—of how easy it is to lose sight of reality in a welter of verbiage.

I must not oversell pragmatism. It is not a machine for grinding out certifiably correct answers to legal questions. It does not dissolve political judging into policy science. It does not transform judges into expert administrators and law into cost-benefit analysis. It acknowledges the inevitability that like cases will often be treated inconsistently not only because different judges weigh consequences differently depending on a judge's background, temperament, training, experience, and ideology, which shape his preconceptions and thus his response to arguments and evidence, but also because, for the same reasons, different judges *see* different consequences. Legal pragmatism accepts the empirical evidence of the attitudinal school. And it sets no higher aspiration for the judge than that his decisions be reasonable in light of the warring interests in the cases, although a reasonable decision is not necessarily a "right" one.

But how, it may be asked, can a judge decide a case on any basis other than belief in what the right decision is? That is the kind of question that a law professor would be apt to ask. It forgets Aristotle's warning against demanding that an inquiry be conducted with a degree of rigor that the type of inquiry does not permit. The judge does not choose his cases or the sequence in which they are presented to him, or contrive a leisurely schedule on which to decide them, unlike law professors, who choose their topics and need not let go of a paper until satisfied that it is right. Legalists place unrealistic demands on judges, who in our system *should* often have the uncomfortable feeling of skating on thin ice without the luxury of being able to defer decisions until certitude descends on them.

Although I am concerned more with pragmatism's descriptive adequacy than with its normative appeal, I cannot ignore the question of its normative adequacy, because were it as repulsive a basis for judicial action as its critics claim, it could not plausibly be imputed to our judges. I disagree with the critics, but not because I think it demonstra-

---

23. That is, "constructed": "constructive possession" means that someone who is not in possession of a thing is treated by the law as if he were.

24. Bryan Garner, with Jeff Newman and Tiger Jackson, *The Redbook: A Manual on Legal Style,* § 11 (2d ed. 2006).

ble that pragmatic adjudication is "right." Consider that most unpragmatic decision, *Clinton v. Jones*,[25] in which the Supreme Court refused to grant President Clinton an immunity from Paula Jones's suit for sexual harassment that would last until his term of office ended. The Justices should have realized that forcing the President to submit to a deposition in a case about his sexual escapades would be political dynamite that would explode and interfere with his ability to perform his duties. That of course is what happened. But one cannot say that the Court was "wrong" to find no basis in Article II of the Constitution for immunizing a sitting President from suits that arise from acts that he committed before he took office. A basic principle of republican government is that officials are not above the law; how far to go in compromising that principle in recognition of political reality is a matter of judgment, not of legal analysis in a conventional sense. So *Clinton v. Jones* was not "wrong." Yet a Court consisting of politically savvy Justices would have decided the case the other way—and that, I am content to argue, would not have been "wrong" either.

Some critics think that legal pragmatism lacks moral earnestness; that it cannot bestow metaphysical cachet or universality or "objectivity" on precious legal values such as freedom of speech.[26] After all, did not Richard Rorty define pragmatism "as a doctrine of the relativity of normative judgments to purposes served"?[27] There is nothing to prevent pragmatic judges from dressing their free-speech decisions in a rhetoric of moral realism if doing so will make the decisions more effective. But critics of legal pragmatism will not be satisfied with this response. They will argue that if the reality of judicial decision making is pragmatic, then however the judge chooses to articulate the grounds of his decision the danger will remain that a pragmatic balancing of competing interests cannot safeguard basic values.

The issue is brought into focus by recent controversies over limiting civil liberties in response to the threat of terrorism, which the attacks of September 11, 2001, taught us is acute. I have argued that the enhanced danger of terrorism in an era of weapons of mass destruction warrants a

25. 520 U.S. 681 (1997).
26. See, for example, R. George Wright, "Pragmatism and Freedom of Speech," 80 *North Dakota Law Review* 103 (2004).
27. Richard Rorty, "Dewey between Hegel and Darwin," in *Rorty and Pragmatism: The Philosopher Responds to His Critics* 1, 15 (Herman J. Saatkamp, Jr., ed. 1995).

curtailment, albeit a modest one, of existing civil liberties.[28] But by thus failing to give civil liberties lexical priority over competing interests, such as national security, the pragmatist cannot resist a gradual curtailment of those liberties that has no fixed stopping point. The pragmatist might reply that if we want to entrench civil liberties against any modification based on safety or other concerns, the proper entrenching tool is a constitutional amendment rather than a judicial interpretation of the Bill of Rights. But issues of delay and feasibility to one side, constitutional entrenchment can be overkill, creating an insuperable barrier to rethinking the proper scope of civil liberties in light of an emergency situation unforeseen when the Constitution was amended.

A better reply is that judges who want to curtail civil liberties have at hand legalist tools as powerful as those used by civil libertarians. The Constitution is full of contradictions and ambiguities, sources of endless contestation. In the case of national security, against arguments based on the language of the Bill of Rights can be deployed arguments based on the language of Article II, which confers on the President primary authority to conduct the nation's foreign affairs, command of the armed forces, and the duty to enforce the nation's laws. Legalism won't resolve such disputes. Trying to banish pragmatism must fail because it cannot be banished. The only effect of trying to banish it would be to make judges even less candid than they are.

But the objection to pragmatism's lack of moral earnestness goes deeper than I have acknowledged. It can be understood sympathetically as distress at the thought that judges often make life-and-death decisions (literally so in capital cases) without warranted confidence that what they are doing is "right" in a strong sense of the word. Pragmatists seem to have a casual attitude toward truth, especially moral truth, as when Holmes said that what is true is simply what he could not help believing or that the test of truth is how well it "sells" in the marketplace of ideas. Jerome Frank was wrong to think that judges' craving for certitude is infantile (see chapter 4); it is the consequence of the natural anxiety that decent people feel when they find themselves exercising power over other people and therefore want very much to think that their exercise of that power is just. But critics of pragmatism lack the tools to allay that

---

28. Richard A. Posner, *Not a Suicide Pact: The Constitution in a Time of National Emergency* (2006).

anxiety. All that they can offer judges is a rhetoric of certitude. (Rhetoric in a different sense—the Aristotelian sense, noted in chapter 3, of the methodology for resolving issues that cannot be resolved by exact inquiry—is congenial to, perhaps even fundamental to, Holmes's pragmatism.[29])

Some critics argue that legal pragmatism breeds cynicism about law that in turn induces intellectual laziness in students, law professors, lawyers, and, most ominously, judges. The legal pragmatist is said to be unwilling to invest significant time and effort in learning the rules of law and the methods of legal reasoning because he regards these things as obstacles to getting to the point, the point being to weigh consequences. That is incorrect. The law student must learn to pay careful attention to the conventional materials, specialized vocabulary, and other resources and techniques developed by the legal profession over millennia. He must learn these things en route to transcending them. But transcend them (or at least begin the process of transcending them) he must. He must be disabused of the notion that "the law" is a set of propositions written down in a book and legal training consists simply of learning how to find the correct place in the book. That is what laypeople think and some judges pretend to think. In our system the law as it is enforced in courts is created by judges, using legal propositions as raw materials. Lawyers must learn how to assist judges in that creative activity. That requires more than beating judges about the head with snatches of legalese (such as "clear and affirmative evidence") taken from statutes and judicial opinions.

Legal pragmatism is said by its critics to allow, invite, or even command judges to decide cases however they want. By loosening the constraints of text and doctrine, the criticism continues, pragmatism turns judges into loose legislative cannons and expands the area of judicial indeterminacy to all cases. Not so. Judges are less likely to be drunk with power if they realize they are exercising discretion than if they think they are just a transmission belt for decisions made elsewhere and so bear no responsibility for any ugly consequences of those decisions. Legalists, sometimes hypocritically, sometimes unconsciously, smuggle their political preferences into their decisions but seek to deflect blame

---

29. Robert Danisch, *Pragmatism, Democracy, and the Necessity of Rhetoric*, ch. 4 (2007).

for any resulting cruelties or absurdities by pleading that the law made them do it.

Legislation reflects the preferences of legislators, and think how those preferences are formed (even setting aside pressure from constituents). They are formed by each legislator's values, temperament, life experiences, and conception of the scope and limits of the legislative function. And likewise in the case of the judge as legislator. But stated as a criticism, this ignores not only the possibility of weighing consequences in a dispassionate and even predictable manner in areas of consensus, but also the material, psychological, and institutional constraints on pragmatic as on other judges (more precisely, on judges when they are being pragmatic). Judges are subject to forcible removal from office for dereliction of duty; their decisions can be nullified by legislative or constitutional amendment; the process of selecting judges tends to exclude those who are the most power hungry, the most "political," the farthest out of the mainstream; and the system of compensation and the rules concerning conflicts of interest subject judges to "flat" incentives—that is, incentives not tied to the outcome of the particular cases they are called upon to decide—so that a powerful potential source of bias is removed. If the judge is a legislator, at least he is a disinterested one.

The good pragmatist judge, we know, is not a shortsighted pragmatist. He is not a philosophical pragmatist. But he *is* a *constrained* pragmatist. We know from previous chapters that judges in our system operate under both internal and external constraints. That is as true of pragmatic judges as it is of legalist judges. There are many consequences of a decision that a pragmatic judge cannot properly take into account. The issue is sharply focused by *Bush v. Gore*.[30] Suppose a Justice thought that Gore had the better of the legal case, but that Bush would be a better President. The Justice might conclude that all things considered, a decision in favor of Bush would have better consequences than a decision in favor of Gore. Yet it would be improper for the Justice to consider the relative merits of Bush and Gore as presidential aspirants. It would violate the rule, basic to corrective justice, that cases must be decided "without respect to persons." The pragmatic judge must play by the rules of the judicial game, just like other judges. The rules permit the consideration of

---

30. 531 U.S. 98 (2000).

certain types of consequence but forbid the consideration of other types. They limit the judge to being, by analogy to rule utilitarianism, a "rule pragmatist."[31]

The difference between a constrained and an unconstrained pragmatist is well illustrated by Jerome Frank in his twin roles as bomb-throwing legal realist and Second Circuit judge. He did not abandon legal realism on the bench, but he curbed it; his judicial opinions are well within the mainstream.[32]

Judge Michael McConnell, the originalist whom we met in chapter 7, claims that "the real points of division [between legalists and pragmatists] relate to how strictly or loosely judges read the constraints [of legalism], and whether in the remaining gray areas they defer to democratic judgment or give play to their own ideological commitments."[33] He is right that "how strictly or loosely judges read the constraints" of legalism is a difference between the legalist and the pragmatist; legalists, for example, are more likely to remain on the semantic surface of a statute than to try to figure out its purpose. But whether "in the remaining gray areas [judges] defer to democratic judgment or give play to their own ideological commitments" is not a real difference. The originalist's tiebreaker is not democracy (see chapter 11). Who except the self-deluded believe that "ideological commitments" play a significantly smaller role in the decisions of legalists, such as the four most conservative Supreme Court Justices, than in those of quasi-pragmatists, such as Justice Breyer?[34]

Even if the objections to legal pragmatism are stronger than I think

31. See Melissa Armstrong, "Rule Pragmatism: Theory and Application to Qualified Immunity Analysis," 38 *Columbia Journal of Law and Social Problems* 107 (2004); Posner, *The Problematics of Moral and Legal Theory,* note 1 above, at 241.

32. See Robert Jerome Glennon, *The Iconoclast as Reformer: Jerome Frank's Impact on American Law,* ch. 5 (1985).

33. Michael W. McConnell, "Active Liberty: A Progressive Alternative to Textualism and Originalism?" 119 *Harvard Law Review* 2387, 2415 (2006), reviewing Justice Breyer's book *Active Liberty,* which I discuss in chapter 11.

34. Rorie Spill Solberg and Stefanie A. Lindquist, in "Activism, Ideology, and Federalism: Judicial Behavior in Constitutional Challenges before the Rehnquist Court, 1986–2000," 3 *Journal of Empirical Legal Studies* 237 (2006), find a slightly higher degree of self-restraint on the part of conservative Justices, but conclude that, in general, "where liberal statutes are challenged, regardless of whether they emerge at the state or federal level, conservatives tend to be more likely to strike down those statutes. The opposite is true for conservative statutes." Id. at 259–260.

they are, there is no alternative in the United States of the twenty-first century. America's judicially enforceable Constitution; its common law heritage; its undisciplined legislatures (a product in part of the weakness of political parties in the United States and in part of bicameralism and the presidential veto, which together make it extremely difficult to enact legislation unless it is left vague); the sheer complexity of the American legal system (the federal Constitution layered over federal statutes and the whole layered over the legal systems of the 50 different states)—all these things compound with the heterogeneity of the judges, and the related fact that judging in the United States is not a career but a position to which middle-aged lawyers are appointed after a career as a practicing lawyer, professor, or prosecutor, to create an immense irreducible domain of discretionary lawmaking. And many judges owe their appointments to political connections, to being at least on the outskirts of politics. Legalism is not a straitjacket that can be put on these worldly judges, and anyway has no resources to guide the making of new law as distinct from the ascertainment of the old, for it denies that lawmaking is a legitimate task of judges.

Lateral entry deserves emphasis not only as a factor contributing to the heterogeneity of the judiciary but also as a reflection of the *fluidity* of American professional and intellectual life, which fosters legal pragmatism—as it does philosophical pragmatism—and helps stamp both as distinctively American movements. The legal profession in the United States is not compartmentalized; lawyers move freely among private practice, government service, law teaching, and judging. Nor is the profession sealed off from the rest of American intellectual life. It is permeable to developments in other departments of social thought, such as economics. John Dewey and other pragmatic philosophers were able to take as the model for *all* inquiry the methods of the natural sciences because American thought is not tightly bulkheaded. The permeability of professional cultures to outside influences is an antidote to the development of a parochial judicial culture in which law is an autonomous system of thought, isolated from the practice of law, the social sciences, and the commercial and political life of the nation.

The heterogeneity of the judiciary encourages a proliferation of varied insights and retards group polarization, and at the same time anchors law more firmly in durable public opinion. This is both cause for and justification of the elaborate screening of judicial candidates for ideological predisposition and ethnic and other group identity, as well as for professional competence. But diversity comes at a price. The greater the judiciary's diversity, the more disagreement, dissent, and distinguishing of cases (and hence the less adherence to precedent and therefore the less legal certainty), and the less uniformity across appellate panels. These costs have to be traded off against the epistemic value of diversity or, equivalently, the costs of confining deliberation to the like-minded.[35]

But all this said, are American judges *really* predestined to be pragmatists? Can we trust Karl Llewellyn (see chapter 8), or was he just finding what he was looking for? The rhetoric of judicial opinions is predominantly legalistic; and the attitudinal school's discovery of a wide political streak in American judging does not make the case, because political judging could be the work of an ideologue rather than a pragmatist.

We can gain some insights into the issue from the critical literature on judges.[36] From it we learn for example that Brandeis's judicial decisions "were not determined by a uniquely 'juristic' set of values, but by generalized articles of social, economic, and political faith that derived as much from the gleanings of literature, history, and social sciences as they did from the study of law,"[37] and that political judging characterized the Second Circuit even under the revered leadership of Learned Hand.[38] From judicial biographies and the expanding list of book-length exposés of the Supreme Court we can learn (if we are so naïve as not to realize it already) that judges at all levels are all too human.

But a neglected literature that I particularly wish to emphasize is writing by judges on judging.[39] In a previous chapter I quoted Learned Hand

35. Harry T. Edwards, "The Effects of Collegiality on Judicial Decision Making," 151 *University of Pennsylvania Law Review* 1639, 1667 (2003). Cass R. Sunstein et al., *Are Judges Political? An Empirical Analysis of the Federal Judiciary* (2006), emphasizes the benefits of diversity in insight and whistle-blowing, and the costs of uniformity in group polarization and ideological amplification—products of overconfidence from being among like-minded people and thus never challenged, never forced to reflect critically on one's beliefs.

36. Exemplified by G. Edward White, *The American Judicial Tradition: Profiles of Leading American Judges* (expanded ed. 1988).

37. Stephen W. Baskerville, *Of Laws and Limitations: An Intellectual Portrait of Louis Dembitz Brandeis* 274 (1994).

38. Marvin Schick, *Learned Hand's Court* (1970).

39. For a comprehensive bibliography of such writings, see *Judges on Judging: Views from the Bench* 305–323 (David M. O'Brien ed., 2d ed. 2004). And for a massive anthology of writings by judges as well as academics about judging, see Ruggero J. Aldisert, *The Judicial Process: Readings, Materials and Cases* (2d ed. 1996). There is also the occasional testimony of former law clerks. See, for example, Stephen L. Wasby, "'Why Clerk? What Did I Get out of It?'" 56

on judging and I have referred to two famous works by Holmes in this one; there is additional evidence of Holmes's judicial pragmatism in other writings of his, including letters and judicial opinions.[40] There are Cardozo's writings about judging, most famously his book *The Nature of the Judicial Process* (1921), "the fullest statement of a jurisprudence of pragmatism that we possess."[41] There is Judge Hutcheson's article on decision by hunch, from which I took the epigraph in the introduction, surprisingly echoed by Supreme Court Justice Anthony Kennedy in a recent interview:

> You know, all of us have an instinctive judgment that we make. You meet a person, you say, "I trust this person. I don't trust this person. I find her interesting. I don't find him interesting." Whatever. You make these quick judgments. That's the way you get through life. *And judges do the same thing.* And I suppose there's nothing wrong with that if it's just a beginning point. But after you make a judgment, you then must formulate the reason for your judgment into a verbal phrase, into a verbal formula. And then you have to see if that makes sense, if it's logical, if it's fair, if it accords with the law, if it accords with the Constitution, if it accords with your own sense of ethics and morality. And if at any point along this process you think you're wrong, you have to go back and do it all over again. And that's, I think, not unique to the law, in that any prudent person behaves that way . . . I think that maybe the qualities for achievement in my field are not different—much different—than any others. Number one: Knowing yourself, and being honest about your own failings and your own weakness. Number two: To have an understanding that you have the opportunity to shape the destiny of this country. *The framers wanted you to shape the destiny of the country. They didn't want to frame it for you.*[42]

There is Jerome Frank's book, *Courts on Trial: Myth and Reality in American Justice* (1949), written after he became a federal court of ap-

---

Journal of Legal Education 411, 426 (2006), remarking that one "litigator's strong belief that 'it is facts more than law which decides cases' really started during his clerkship year, 'when I saw that application of law to facts was much more complex, subtle, and fact-oriented than I had imagined.'"

40. See *The Essential Holmes*, note 6 above, and the references to Holmes in the books cited in note 1 above.

41. Richard A. Posner, *Cardozo: A Study in Reputation* 28 (1990).

42. "Anthony Kennedy Interview," *Academy of Achievement: A Museum of Living History*, Oct. 22, 2006, www.achievement.org/autodoc/page/ken0int-3,int-5 (visited May 16, 2007) (emphasis added).

peals judge but repeating many of the realist heresies of his earlier and better-known book *Law and the Modern Mind* (1930). Frank's distinguished rival on the Second Circuit, Charles Clark, articulated a pragmatic philosophy of judging, remarking that "only by recognizing the lonely responsibility of the judge as a legislator, and the inevitable subjective nature of his perception, can we hope to find ways and means of harnessing that subjectivity to the service of society, present and future."[43] Similar sentiments have been expressed by a host of other distinguished judges, including Walter Schaefer,[44] Henry Friendly,[45] Albert Tate,[46] Roger Traynor,[47] and Frank Coffin.[48] Justice, later Chief Justice, Harlan Fiske Stone said that "within the limits lying between the command of statutes on the one hand and the restraints of precedents and doctrines, by common consent regarded as binding, on the other, the judge has liberty of choice of the rule which he applies, and his choice will rightly depend upon the relative weights of the social and economic advantages which will finally turn the scales of judgment in favor of one rule rather than another. Within this area he performs essentially the function of the legislator, and in a real sense makes law."[49]

I wish our current Justices were as candid as Stone, or as Judge Patricia Wald when she said that "our colleagues are our colleagues as a result of politics. The kind of controlling precedent the Supreme Court

43. Charles E. Clark and David M. Trubek, "The Creative Role of the Judge: Restraint and Freedom in the Common Law Tradition," 71 *Yale Law Journal* 255, 275–276 (1961). See also *Procedure: The Handmaid of Justice: Essays of Judge Charles E. Clark* (Charles A. Wright and Harry M. Reasoner eds. 1965). Clark and Trubek, above, at 267, perceptively remark that Karl Llewellyn exaggerated the degree to which judges can attain certainty in difficult cases by the use of "realist" methods. We shall encounter similar exaggerations in chapter 12 in discussing the realist jurisprudence of David Beatty.

44. Walter V. Schaefer, "Precedent and Policy," 34 *University of Chicago Law Review* 3 (1966).

45. Henry J. Friendly, *Benchmarks* (1967).

46. Albert Tate, Jr., "The Law-Making Function of the Judge," 28 *Louisiana Law Review* 211 (1968); Tate, "Forum Juridicum: The Judge as a Person," 19 *Louisiana Law Review* 438 (1959).

47. Roger J. Traynor, *The Traynor Reader: A Collection of Essays by the Honorable Roger J. Traynor* (1987).

48. See Frank M. Coffin, *The Ways of a Judge: Reflections from the Federal Appellate Bench* (1980), and, even better, Coffin, *On Appeal: Courts, Lawyering, and Judging* (1994), especially chs. 13 and 14.

49. Harlan F. Stone, "The Common Law in the United States," 50 *Harvard Law Review* 4, 20 (1936).

hands down to lower courts reflects the makeup of that court and has been determined, in large part, by the politics of the nomination and confirmation process . . . The values by which judges make choices in areas of discretion will more often than not be in sync with that section of the political spectrum they inhabited in their former lives."[50] Professor David Klein has gathered additional references along these lines,[51] and J. Woodford Howard offers the following judicious summary based on extensive interviews with federal court of appeals judges: "The short of it is that federal intermediate courts tended to attract political lawyers who by vocation and training fused elements of political and legal culture in appellate adjudication."[52]

Judge Friendly's former law clerk and good friend Michael Boudin, himself a distinguished federal court of appeals judge, has listed the elements of Friendly's distinction. He mentions the "experience of a practicing lawyer who had spent three decades addressing real-world problems" and who "rivaled Justice Robert Jackson [a great pragmatic judge] in giving readers the sense that his decisions were grounded in reality."[53] He quotes Friendly's advice that "on the whole it may be better that the [Supreme] Court should plot a few reference points, even on what may be largely an intuitive basis, which can be erased if they prove unwise, before it attempts to project a curve to which all future determinations must conform."[54] He remarks on Friendly's view that "a judge's first take is often an intuitive response" to the "diverse pressures" that a case exerts on a judge—pressures "to conform to precedent, to do justice, to achieve a socially useful result." Boudin sums up the influences that shaped Friendly's judging as "his training as a historian and respect for precedent, a dose of legal realism, a pragmatic interest in outcomes, a re-

50. Patricia M. Wald, "Some Real-Life Observations about Judging," 26 *Indiana Law Review* 173, 180 (1992). Judge Wald unsurprisingly describes herself as a pragmatist. Id. at 181.

51. David E. Klein, *Making Law in the United States Court of Appeals* 15–16 (2002). Klein's excellent book also contains numerous interviews with federal circuit judges, speaking anonymously and presumably therefore with more candor than usual. Another fine book, employing the same methodology, is J. Woodford Howard, Jr., *Courts of Appeals in the Federal Judicial System: A Study of the Second, Fifth, and District of Columbia Circuits* (1981).

52. Howard, note 51 above, at 188.

53. Michael Boudin, "Judge Henry Friendly and the Mirror of Constitutional Law" 11 (forthcoming in *New York University Law Review*).

54. Id. at 17, quoting Henry J. Friendly, *The Dartmouth College Case and the Public-Private Penumbra* 31 (1969).

spect for legal process, an insistence on relative competence, a sense of what is practical, and a concern with judicial overreaching."[55]

This is the portrait of a pragmatic judge sensitive to the institutional as well as the substantive consequences of judicial decision making. And, speaking of Justice Jackson, as Boudin did, recall from chapter 4 Frederick Schauer's redescription of Jerome Frank's brand of legal realism: "an attempt to lessen the distance, descriptively and prescriptively, between how a judge as a human being and that same human being clothed in judicial robes would resolve a controversy." That attempt gets close to the heart of legal pragmatism, as in the following description of Justice Jackson's opinion-writing style: "Jackson never seemed to be searching for the proper 'judicial' stance or tone in his opinions. Instead, he appeared capable of expanding the stylistic range of opinion writing to accommodate his human reactions . . . The distance between judges and mortals was suddenly shortened."[56]

Llewellyn collected many choice examples of judicial self-reflection from different eras. I quote a few: "No precedent is of such force as resoun [right sense]."[57] "Every lawyer knows that a prior case may, at the will of the court, 'stand' either for the narrowest point to which its holding may be reduced, or for the widest formulation that its *ratio decidendi* [reason for deciding] will allow."[58] "What is new in juristic thought today is chiefly the candor of its processes. Much that was once unavowed and kept beneath the surface is now avowed and open. From time immemorial lawyers have felt the impulse to pare down the old rules when in conflict with the present needs. The difference is that even when they yielded to the impulse, it was their habit in greater measure than today to disguise what they were doing, to disguise the innovation even from themselves, and to announce in all sincerity that it was all as it had been before."[59] "In talking to the [state] Chief Justices I [Llewellyn] found only about a third (including, and this gave me comfort, all but one out

55. Boudin, note 53 above, at 23.

56. White, note 36 above, at 232. Chapter 11 of White's book is a superb discussion of Jackson.

57. Karl N. Llewellyn, *The Common Law Tradition: Deciding Appeals* 52 n. 46 (1960).

58. Id. at 117.

59. Id. at 266–267, quoting Cardozo, "Jurisprudence," in *Selected Writings of Benjamin Nathan Cardozo: The Choice of Tyco Brahe* 7, 37 (Margaret E. Hall ed. 1947).

of the youngest third) who could recognize that I was telling truth about what they were doing, daily. There was even one who had been made to see that he 'had been doing, all along, exactly what he didn't want to'; but who guessed, wryly, that he would go on doing it."[60] And here is a quotation for the legalists: "A strong opinion [is] one in which by the employment of pure legal reasoning one arrived inescapably at a conclusion which no layman could possibly have foreseen."[61]

One can even reach back to Justice Joseph Story of the early-nineteenth-century Supreme Court, who, admonishing the lawyer to "accomplish himself for his duties by familiarity with every study," said that the lawyer "will thus be taught to distrust theory, and cling to practical good; to rely more upon experience, than reasoning; more upon institutions, than laws; more upon checks to vice, than upon motives to virtue. He will become . . . more wise, more candid, more forgiving, more disinterested."[62] One can reach across the seas to other Anglo-American judiciaries and find similar sentiments expressed by their judges.[63]

Of particular note is the pragmatist strain in the age of classic American legal formalism, which William Wiecek dates from 1886 to 1937.[64] What I am calling legalism was indeed the official, the establishment, conception of judicial behavior. Yet Brian Tamanaha has compiled a wonderful assortment of contemporaneous statements indicative of a strong undertone of skepticism.[65] We read that "it is useless for judges to quote a score of cases from the digest to sustain almost every sentence, when every one knows that another score might be collected to support the opposite ruling . . . He writes, it may be, a beautiful essay upon the law of the case, but the real grounds of decision lie concealed under the

---

60. Llewellyn, note 57 above, at 392.

61. Id. at 39 n. 31.

62. Joseph Story, *Discourse Pronounced upon the Inauguration of the Author, as Dane Professor of Law in Harvard University* 34–35 (1829).

63. See, for example, E. W. Thomas, *The Judicial Process: Realism, Pragmatism, Practical Reasoning and Principles* (2005); Tom Bingham, *The Business of Judging: Selected Essays and Speeches,* ch. 2 (2000); David Robertson, *Judicial Discretion in the House of Lords* (1998); John Bell, *Policy Arguments in Judicial Decisions* (1983).

64. William M. Wiecek, *The Lost World of Classical Legal Thought: Law and Ideology in America, 1886–1937* (1998).

65. The quotations that follow are from Brian Z. Tamanaha, "The Realism of the 'Formalist' Age" (St. John's University School of Law, Aug. 2007).

statement of facts with which it is prefaced."[66] A judge is quoted as say-ing that "what is called legal sense is often the rankest nonsense,"[67] and the president of the American Bar Association as saying that "our courts can generally find precedents for almost any proposition."[68]

The first of these quotations is from an article published in 1881, the same year that Holmes published *The Common Law*. The novelty of Holmes's criticism of legalism was that he thought it inevitable, and thus not particularly reprehensible, that judges should be occasional legisla-tors rather than full-time rule appliers, though he also thought that if they were more self-conscious about what they were doing they would be more restrained.

The distinction of most of the judges whom I have quoted or men-tioned is notable, but more notable still is that they should confess prag-matism despite the allure of being able to pose as a discerner rather than a creator of law, for that is the less controversial position and also flat-ters the laity's ignorant expectation of what a judge is supposed to do. Judges' writing on judging, as well as what they say in interviews, espe-cially when speaking off the record,[69] is striking for the infrequency of legalist manifestos. There are some,[70] of course, but many of them have an air of embattlement, of swimming against the tide, and sometimes of apology and qualification, as in Justice Scalia's revealingly entitled ar-ticle "Originalism: The Lesser Evil."[71] He confesses himself a "faint-hearted" originalist and assures the reader that he would not counte-nance flogging even though on an originalist construal it is not a cruel and unusual punishment.[72] He made a further confession of faintheart-

66. W. G. Hammond, "American Law Schools, Past, and Future," 7 *Southern Law Review* 400, 412–413 (1881). Hammond was the dean of the St. Louis Law School.

67. Seymour D. Thompson, "More Justice and Less Technicality," 23 *American Law Review* 22, 48 (1889).

68. U. M. Rose, "American Bar Association," 64 *Albany Law Journal* 333, 336 (1902).

69. See note 51 above.

70. See, for example, J. Harvie Wilkinson III, "The Role of Reason in the Rule of Law," 56 *University of Chicago Law Review* 779 (1989); Antonin Scalia, "The Rule of Law as a Law of Rules," 56 *University of Chicago Law Review* 1175 (1989); *Judges on Judging*, note 39 above, chs. 13, 15, 16, 18, 20, 22. I have mentioned Judge McConnell; I discuss his views further, and those of other judges as well, in subsequent chapters.

71. Antonin Scalia, "Originalism: The Lesser Evil," 57 *University of Cincinnati Law School* 849 (1989).

72. Id. at 861, 864—for which he was criticized by Judge Easterbrook, perhaps the least

edness in another article: "We will have totality of the circumstances tests and balancing modes of analysis with us forever—and for my sins, I will probably write some of the opinions that use them. *All* I urge is that those modes of analysis be avoided *where possible.*"[73]

Maybe distinguished judges are readier than others to confess pragmatism (even if it is only occasional pragmatism, as in the case of Justice Scalia) because their distinction insulates them from the criticism that a lesser heretic would invite, or because the distinguished judge is more likely to be an occasional legislator than his less distinguished colleagues and so more likely to realize that judging at its most demanding is a pragmatic activity.

A final question is how well legal pragmatism, which along with constitutional law is *the* distinctive American contribution to jurisprudence (though with English roots—the English philosophical tradition is empiricist; the common law, which we got from England, is pragmatic; and remember Blackstone on statutory interpretation), travels. Perhaps not well, at least outside English-origin jurisdictions.[74] Continental European judges are more legalistic than American or English ones. The European (civil law) legal systems, and the European systems of government more broadly, have been constructed along lines that greatly limit judicial discretion and hence departures from legalism. The judicial career attracts the type of person who is comfortable in a bureaucracy, and it breeds in him once there habits of obedience to directives and other authoritative texts. Bureaucratic administration is government by written rules. Continental Europe does not have the common law and until recently did not have judicial review of the constitutionality of statutes, and so judges' legislative scope was severely truncated.

European governments tend moreover to be highly centralized. Power is concentrated in parliaments that are functionally unicameral and enact legal codes that are clearer than most of our statutes. There are fewer gaps, overlaps, inconsistencies, and ambiguities. Most European courts

---

fainthearted judicial defender of legalism. Frank H. Easterbrook, "Abstraction and Authority," 59 *University of Chicago Law Review* 349, 378 n. 92 (1992).

73. Scalia, note 70 above, at 1187 (emphasis added).

74. Robertson, note 63 above, at 401, argues powerfully that "the ideology" of England's highest court "is one of pragmatism, indeed the sort of pragmatism that is unable to conceive that it is an ideology."

are specialized (labor courts, criminal courts, etc.), and specialists tend to share the premises of analysis and decision, enabling them to derive conclusions by logical processes. Specialist courts also do not have to worry about adapting the rules and principles of one area of law to another. American judges at this moment are wrestling with adapting our normal law of criminal procedure to the special challenges presented by the struggle against international terrorism. They are rebalancing public safety and civil liberties in light of the perceived increase in danger. A European nation can if it wants deal with the problem by establishing a special court for terrorist cases. (We could do that too, but it would be a departure from the American tradition of generalist judges.) The judges of such a court could formulate doctrine for their specialized jurisdiction without having to rethink broader principles.

Because the United States does not have the institutions that make a career judiciary feasible, legalism is not available to us as an overall judicial strategy. Is this a bad thing? That is a huge question. We saw in chapter 5 that our courts protect property rights, a cornerstone of freedom and prosperity, as well as European judiciaries do. Their judges are more disciplined than ours, more closely supervised, but being career judges less comfortable with commercial and other economic issues than our judges are. Specialization may be only a partial cure. The specialized judge who focuses on commercial cases presumably learns a great deal about the subject area in his judicial career, but this learning may not be a perfect substitute for direct participation in the commercial life of the nation as a practicing lawyer.[75] On the other hand, although good statistics are lacking, there is no doubt that the United States spends more money per capita on its legal system than the countries with which we like to compare ourselves. Unfortunately, there are no data that would permit a determination of whether the benefits that our system generates exceed its heavy costs. All that can be said is that if judges are too much alike in background, politics, values, and other personal characteristics that influence judicial decision making in the gaping open area created by our constitutional structure and political culture, pragmatic judgments will rest on a thin base of knowledge and

75. On the pros and cons of judicial specialization generally, see the thorough discussion in Edward K. Cheng, "The Myth of the Generalist Judge: An Empirical Study of Opinion Specialization in the Federal Courts of Appeals" (Brooklyn Law School, May 10, 2007).

insight, while if judges are too different from one another, their decisions will fail to create a stable, intelligible pattern and people will be able only to guess what their legal obligations are. One can hope that the tough screening of federal judicial candidates is truncating the distribution of personality and opinion enough to ensure the necessary minimum of homogeneity but not so much as to eliminate a nourishing variety of opinion and experience.

III

Justices

10

The Supreme Court Is a Political Court

I have suggested that American judges are predestined to be pragmatists. But a more illuminating description of the Justices of the U.S. Supreme Court, particularly when they are deciding issues of constitutional law, is that they are political judges, as I shall argue with reference primarily to cases decided in the Court's 2004 term, the last term before the Court changed direction as a result of the replacement of Rehnquist and O'Connor by Roberts and Alito. But political judges are pragmatists if what is driving them is, as I believe it mainly is, the political *consequences* of their decisions.

I begin with a neglected factor in discussions of the politicization of the Court—the extraordinary growth in the ratio of lower-court to Supreme Court decisions. The Court can no longer control the lower courts by means of narrow, case-by-case determinations—the patient, incremental method of the common law. It must perforce act legislatively. In 2003 the federal courts of appeals decided 56,396 cases, compared to only 3,753 in 1960. State courts of last resort decided more than 25,000 cases in 2002,[1] an unknown but probably substantial percentage of which presented a federal question, if one may judge from the fact that 13 percent of state supreme court decisions in the late 1960s—when constitutional law was not yet ubiquitous—concerned the federal constitutional rights of criminal defendants.[2] State intermediate appellate courts decided more than 130,000 cases in 2003. What percentage

1. Shauna M. Strickland, Court Statistics Project Staff, *State Court Caseload Statistics, 2004* 105 (2005) (tab. 1).
2. Robert A. Kagan et al., "The Business of State Supreme Courts, 1870–1970," 30 *Stanford Law Review* 121, 147 n. 63 (1977).

were final decisions that raised issues of federal law and therefore were reviewable by the U.S. Supreme Court is unknown. So one cannot say how many cases reviewable by the Supreme Court the state courts decided in either period and therefore compute the percentages of those cases in which the Court granted certiorari. But one can compare the percentage of federal court cases in which the Court granted certiorari in 2004—0.11 percent (64 ÷ 56,396)—with the corresponding percentage in 1960—1.6 percent (60 ÷ 3,753). The comparison indicates that the Court reviewed, in relative terms, almost 15 times as many federal court cases in 1960 as in 2004.

Granted, many of the cases terminated in the federal courts of appeals are not even remotely plausible candidates for further review, having been consolidated, abandoned, or dismissed because of obvious jurisdictional defects. If attention is confined to cases that the Administrative Office of the U.S. Courts classifies as terminated "on the merits" or (the corresponding, though not identical, classification in 1959) "after hearing or submission," the figures of 56,396 and 3,753 in the preceding paragraph shrink to 27,009 and 2,705, and this adjustment changes the percentage of federal court of appeals decisions reviewed by the Supreme Court from 0.13 percent and 1.7 percent in 2004 and 1960, respectively, to 0.27 percent and 2.4 percent. Nevertheless the difference remains striking: the Court in 1960 decided, in relative terms, almost nine times as many federal cases as it decided in 2004.

The Court has long emphasized that it is not in the business of correcting the errors, as such, of the lower courts; cases that come to it have already had at least one tier of appellate review. The statistics make plain that the Court is indeed out of the error-correction business, and this is a clue to how far it has departed from the conventional model of appellate adjudication and should prepare us to accept the Court's basically legislative character. If the Court tried to make law the common law way— that is, in tiny incremental steps, which is a form of legislating but one remote from how legislatures proceed—it would have little control over the development of the law; it would be deciding too few decisions to provide significant guidance to the lower courts. So the Court tries to use the few cases that it agrees to hear as occasions for laying down rules or standards that will control a large number of future cases.[3]

3. Frederick Schauer, "Freedom of Expression: Adjudication in Europe and the United States: A Case Study in Comparative Constitutional Architecture," in *European and US Constitutionalism* 47, 60–61 (G. Nolte ed. 2005).

The declining ratio of Supreme Court to lower-court decisions may have another effect—that of feeding the widespread but inaccurate perception that a majority of the cases that the Court decides nowadays are constitutional cases. The percentage of Supreme Court cases that are primarily constitutional has not exceeded 50 percent in recent years. In fact the Court is deciding a smaller percentage of constitutional cases today than it did in the late 1960s and early 1970s.[4] And because it is hearing fewer cases overall, the number of constitutional cases that it is hearing has fallen markedly. But those cases draw much more public attention than the more numerous statutory ones do. They are not only more consequential; they are more controversial even within the Court. In the 2004 term, 80 percent of the Court's primarily constitutional decisions were by split vote, compared to 63 percent of its other decisions.[5] A split decision is more likely to attract attention than a unanimous one, in part by generating more—and more contentious—opinions per case. Thus, although only 38 percent of all the Court's cases in 2004 were primarily constitutional, 44 percent of the Justices' opinions (including concurrences and dissents) were issued in such cases. And the average constitutional decision is more controversial than formerly because of the nation's increased political polarization with respect to just the sorts of issue most likely to get the Court's attention these days, such as abortion, affirmative action, national security, homosexual rights, capital punishment, and government recognition of religion. Why the Court is drawn mothlike to these flames is something of a mystery. Political ineptitude may be a factor—only one Justice serving in the 2004 term, O'Connor, had had significant political experience before becoming a Justice. But probably more important is that these issues tend to divide the lower courts, generating conflicts for the Supreme Court to resolve.

As the number of cases the Court decides diminishes relative to the total number of lower-court cases that raise federal questions, it begins to seem as if the Court is abandoning large swaths of federal law—but of course not federal constitutional law—to the lower courts. To specialists in those fields the Court is a *deus absconditus*.

The more the Court is seen as preoccupied with "hot-button" constitutional cases, the more it looks like a political body exercising discretion comparable in breadth to that of a legislature. Because the federal

4. See the tables entitled "Subject Matter of Dispositions with Full Opinions" in the *Harvard Law Review*'s November issues for 1955 through 2003.

5. These also are statistics compiled by the *Harvard Law Review*.

Constitution is so difficult to amend, the Court exercises more power, on average, when it is deciding constitutional cases than when it is deciding statutory ones. A constitution tends, moreover, to deal with fundamental issues, which arouse greater emotion than most statutory issues, and emotion can deflect judges from dispassionate technical analysis. And they are *political* issues: issues about political governance, political values, political rights, and political power. Constitutional provisions tend also to be both old and vague—old because amendments are infrequent (in part because amending is so difficult) and vague because when amending is difficult, a precisely worded constitutional provision tends to become an embarrassment; it will not bend easily to adjust to changed circumstances, and circumstances change more over a long interval than over a short one.

A constitutional court composed of unelected, life-tenured judges, guided in deciding issues at once emotional and political only by a very old and in critical passages very vague constitution as difficult to amend as the U.S. Constitution is, is bound to be a powerful political organ unless, despite the opportunities presented to the Justices, they manage somehow to behave like other judges. But how can they, when with so little guidance from the Constitution they are asked to resolve issues of great political significance? Political issues by definition cannot be referred to a neutral expert for resolution. A political dispute is a test of strength in which the "minority gives way not because it is convinced that it is wrong, but because it is convinced that it is a minority."[6] Political issues can be resolved only by force or one of its civilized substitutes, such as voting—including voting by judges in cases in which their political preferences are likely to determine how they vote because of lack of guidance from the constitutional text.

The Court is awash in an ocean of discretion. Asked in *Roper v. Simmons*[7] to decide whether the execution of murderers under the age of 18 was constitutional, the Court was at large. The external constraints were nil. The Justices did not have to worry about being reversed by a higher court if they gave the "wrong" answer, let alone being hounded from office or seeing their decision flouted by Congress, the President, or some state official. One can imagine decisions by the Supreme Court

6. James Fitzjames Stephen, *Liberty, Equality, Fraternity* 21 (1993 [1873]).
7. 543 U.S. 551 (2005).

that would evoke constitutional amendments or provoke budgetary or other retaliation by Congress. One can even imagine decisions that the President would refuse to enforce or that would incite a movement to impeach a Justice. There are historical precedents for such a push back. The more judges throw their weight around, the greater the pressure for curbing their independence.[8] And because the Court, though powerful, cannot put its hands on most of the levers of governmental power, Congress or the President, without visibly retaliating, is often able to pull the sting from a constitutional decision.

There was no danger that *Roper* would provoke a reaction from the other branches of government. But consider the *Booker* and *Kelo* decisions, also from the 2004 term.[9] *Booker* enlarged the sentencing discretion of federal judges, and there were rumblings in Congress, which suspected that judges would use the additional discretion to impose more lenient sentences. That suspicion seems thus far largely groundless—sentencing practices and average sentencing length appear largely unchanged since *Booker*[10]—but had they changed, or for that matter before they changed, Congress could have reacted by raising the minimum sentences specified in federal criminal statutes. *Kelo* interpreted the "public use" criterion of eminent domain broadly, stirring up such a storm of controversy that Congress and the states have taken steps to deprive the interpretation of its significance by placing limits on the use of the eminent domain power. So the Supreme Court is not omnipotent, even in constitutional cases. But the contention that the judiciary is the "weakest" branch of government[11] is misleading. It is plenty strong.

8. This is a global phenomenon. See *Judicial Independence in the Age of Democracy: Critical Perspectives from around the World* (Peter H. Russell and David M. O'Brien eds. 2001).

9. United States v. Booker, 543 U.S. 220 (2005); Kelo v. City of New London, 545 U.S. 469 (2005).

10. In the 26 months after *Booker* was decided, 61.6 percent of federal sentences were within the applicable sentencing guidelines range, compared to 67.5 percent in the preceding decade. (Computed from data published at the Web site of the United States Sentencing Commission, www.ussc.gov.) A negligible effect on sentence length is documented (though for only the first year after *Booker* was decided—more recent data are not yet available) in United States Sentencing Commission, *Final Report on the Impact of United States v. Booker on Federal Sentencing*, ch. 4 (Mar. 2006). See also Michael W. McConnell, "The Booker Mess," 83 *Denver University Law Review* 665, 676 (2006). Cf. John F. Pfaff, "The Continued Vitality of Structured Sentencing Following *Blakely*: The Effectiveness of Voluntary Guidelines," 54 *UCLA Law Review* 235 (2006).

11. See, for example, United States v. Hatter, 532 U.S. 557, 567 (2001), quoting *Federalist No. 78* (Hamilton), in *The Federalist Papers* 226, 227 (Roy P. Fairfield ed., 2d ed. 1966).

What is true is that, as I noted in chapter 5, the Court is more constrained by public opinion than the lower federal courts are because of its much greater visibility, which is due to the greater impact of its decisions. A court of appeals can get away with declaring the phrase "under God" in the Pledge of Allegiance unconstitutional[12] because its decision is binding in only one region of the country, and even then only until reversed by the Supreme Court, as the decision in that case was, on a technical ground (lack of standing to sue) that enabled the Court to avoid the wrath of both sides in the heated national debate over the role of religion in public life.[13] A radically unpopular decision by the Supreme Court could provoke swifter and fiercer retaliation than the same decision by a lower court. Imagine if the Supreme Court of the United States rather than the Supreme Judicial Court of Massachusetts had created a constitutional right to gay marriage.

This is a clue to what an extraordinary judicial institution the U.S. Supreme Court is. The usual external constraints on judicial discretion are severely attenuated except for public opinion, which operates more strongly on the Supreme Court than on the ordinary courts. Yet that is one of the most problematic of external constraints on judges. Legislators are supposed to be constrained by public opinion; judges are supposed to ignore it.

Nor did any of the internal constraints narrow the Justices' discretion in the *Roper* case. The Justices did not have to worry that someone or something (their own judicial consciences, perhaps) would harrow them for disregarding controlling texts in reaching the result they did. The Eighth Amendment's prohibition of "cruel and unusual punishments" is a sponge. One might think that if not the text of the Eighth Amendment, then perhaps its history, could disambiguate the meaning of the term. That would have made a quick end to young Simmons. But the Court frequently disregards the history of constitutional provisions on the sensible ground that vague provisions (and even some rather definite ones) should be interpreted with reference to current values rather than eighteenth-century ones. Even Justice Scalia, we recall, does not think that flogging criminals would pass muster under the Eighth Amendment today, as it would have in the eighteenth century.[14]

12. Newdow v. United States Congress, 292 F.3d 597, 612 (9th Cir. 2002).
13. Elk Grove Unified School District v. Newdow, 542 U.S. 1, 17–18 (2004).
14. See Ex parte Wilson, 114 U.S. 417, 427–428 (1885).

A sponge is not constraining; nor, in the Supreme Court, is precedent. The Court in *Roper* brushed aside *Stanford v. Kentucky*,[15] which had held that executing a 16- or 17-year-old (Simmons was 17) does *not* violate the prohibition against cruel and unusual punishments. The Court is reluctant to overrule its previous decisions, but the reluctance is prudential rather than dictated by the law. Unlike a lower court, the Supreme Court always has a choice of whether to follow a precedent. If the Court follows a precedent because it agrees with it, the precedent has no independent force, no "authority," any more than a law review article that the Court happened to agree with would have authority. Yet the number of cases in which precedent dictated the outcome might be small even if the Justices were committed to following precedent unbendingly, because then they would write narrow decisions and interpret their predecessors' decisions narrowly, lest the dead hand of past decisions prevent the law from adapting to changed conditions.

Nor does conformity to precedent make a decision "correct" in a robust sense. The precedent may be wrong, yet the Court may decide to follow it anyway. Suppose the Court issues a decision, A, and years later an indistinguishable case, B, comes up for decision. (Actually this is rather unlikely to happen, because the lower court in which B was filed would have applied A, and there would have been no occasion for the Court to hear B. But ignore this point, though it is a reason for doubting that precedent determines many Supreme Court decisions.) Even if all the current Justices disagree with A, the Court might decide to reaffirm it—perhaps to create the impression that the Court is rule-bound rather than rudderless, or perhaps because people have relied on and adjusted to A. So the Court decides B the same way. If later C comes up for decision and is indistinguishable from A and B, the fact that both A and B would have to be overruled for C to be decided as the Court would prefer to decide it becomes an even stronger reason to decide it the same way as the two previous cases. There is nothing in this lengthening line of precedent to suggest that C is "correct," as distinct from institutionally appropriate.

In *Planned Parenthood of Southeastern Pennsylvania v. Casey*, Justices O'Connor, Kennedy, and Souter, in a joint opinion, let slip the mask, and in a part of the opinion agreed to by a majority of the Justices explicitly

15. 492 U.S. 361 (1989).

grounded the policy of adhering to precedent in concerns for the Court's political effectiveness: "There is a limit to the amount of error that can plausibly be imputed to prior Courts. If that limit should be exceeded, disturbance of prior rulings would be taken as evidence that justifiable reexamination of principle had given way to drives for particular results in the short term. The legitimacy of the Court would fade with the frequency of its vacillation."[16] It is unlikely that the Justices meant that it would be "implausible" to impute vast error to earlier Supreme Court Justices. There is nothing implausible about that; it is possible to disagree on entirely plausible grounds with immense reaches of Court-fashioned constitutional law, including the use of the Fourteenth Amendment to make the Bill of Rights (with minor exceptions) applicable to the states, a move that has spawned thousands of decisions. And think of all the decisions that went down the drain when the Supreme Court overruled *Swift v. Tyson.*[17] Probably the three Justices meant only that whatever the Court may think of particular prior decisions, it must adhere to most of them lest the public tumble to the epistemic shallowness of the body of constitutional law that the Supreme Court has erected upon the defenseless text of the Constitution. It is because so many of the Court's decisions could so easily be questioned that error must not be acknowledged more than very occasionally.

Honoring precedent independently of whether it is sound injects path dependence into law: where you end depends to a great extent on where you began. Today's law may be what it is not because of today's needs but because of accidents of judicial appointment many years ago that resulted in decisions that no one agrees with today but that courts let stand as a matter of prudence. The authors of the joint opinion in *Casey* made clear that they thought the famous case they were reaffirming (actually just the core of it), *Roe v. Wade,* had been decided incorrectly. Undoubtedly a majority of today's Court disagrees with a great number of the decisions rendered by a much more liberal Court in the turbulent 1960s. A newly appointed Supreme Court Justice may pay lip service to most of the Court's earlier decisions even if he dislikes the policies on which they rest. But he will construe those decisions narrowly in order to minimize their impact. And when he finds himself, as he often will, in

16. 505 U.S. 833, 866 (1992).

17. 41 U.S. (16 Pet.) 1 (1842), overruled by Erie R.R. v. Tompkins, 304 U.S. 64, 71–78 (1938).

the open area in which conventional sources of law, such as clearly applicable precedents, give out, he will not feel bound by those policies. So if he can command a majority the law will veer off in a new direction. Eventually the old precedents will be interpreted to death or, finally, overruled explicitly.

This process of gradual extinguishment of unloved precedents, illustrated in the Court's 2006 term by the plurality opinion in *Hein v. Freedom From Religion Foundation, Inc.*,[18] written by the Court's newest member (Alito), is rudely referred to as "boiling the frog." If you want to boil a frog, you put him in warm water and gradually turn up the heat; should you put him in boiling water at the start, he would jump out and you would have to put him back and this time hold him down. Either way he would die, though more slowly the first way, and Justice Alito's warm-water opinion likewise augurs the eventual demise of taxpayer standing to challenge religious establishments.

The decisional process that I am characterizing as political and strategic may sound just like the method of the common law. Judges make up the common law as they go along, yet common law decision making is a lawlike activity. It is suffused with policies that reflect political judgments (for example, in favor of capitalism), but differs from constitutional law in critical respects. It is a decentralized, quasi-competitive system of lawmaking because each of the 50 U.S. states is sovereign in the common law fields. It is subject to legislative override. It deals mainly with subjects on which there is a considerable political consensus (who opposes enforcing contracts or providing a remedy for victims of negligence?), so that deciding a case does not require making a political choice. And common law judges proceed incrementally, giving great weight to precedent, hesitating to lay down broad, flat rules. As a result of these things, the common law is more disciplined and predictable, less personal and political, than constitutional law—to such a degree, indeed, as to make "common law constitutional interpretation"[19] an oxymoron.

Evidence of the powerful influence of politics on constitutional adju-

18. 127 S. Ct. 2553 (2007). The opinion drew a forceful dissent from Justice Scalia, who does not believe in the "boiling the frog" approach to precedents, preferring their outright overruling.

19. The title of a well-known article by David A. Strauss, 63 *University of Chicago Law Review* 877 (1996).

dication in the Supreme Court lies everywhere at hand. Consider the emphasis placed in confirmation hearings on the nominee's ideology to the exclusion of his legal ability. Not a single question directed to John Roberts in his hearing for confirmation as Chief Justice of the United States was designed to test his legal acumen. Nowadays a certain minimum competence is demanded (and Roberts did receive some tokens of respect for his outstanding credentials). But above that level the contenders get little credit for being abler legal analysts than their competitors, and sometimes they receive negative credit. That was the fate of Robert Bork, whose intellectual distinction was held against him as making him more dangerous.[20]

Confirmation battles are not mere posturing by politicians who do not understand that Supreme Court Justices are not like them. Think of the Supreme Court's decision, shortly after Samuel Alito replaced Sandra Day O'Connor, upholding the federal partial-birth abortion statute.[21] The decision in effect overruled *Stenberg v. Carhart*,[22] where a few years earlier the Supreme Court had invalidated an essentially identical state statute. Justice Kennedy, the author of the majority opinion in the new decision, had dissented in *Stenberg,* and it is apparent that what made the difference in the outcomes of the two cases was not the minor differences between the statutes but the replacement of O'Connor (part of the 5–4 majority in *Stenberg*) by the more conservative Alito, which gave Kennedy the fifth vote that he needed. Kennedy's attempt to distinguish *Stenberg* was so unconvincing that it makes one think that when he said in *Casey* that overruling weakens the Court, he meant that only *acknowledged* overruling has that effect.

Or glance back through 50 years of distinguished Forewords to the *Harvard Law Review*'s annual Supreme Court issue and ask yourself whether the positions urged in them could be thought interpretive in a deferential sense—interpretation as discovering as opposed to imposing meaning—rather than legislative. When, for example, Harvard law professor Frank Michelman proposed that the equal protection clause be interpreted to require minimum welfare benefits for poor people,[23] could

20. Lawrence C. Marshall, "Intellectual Feasts and Intellectual Responsibility," 84 *Northwestern University Law Review* 832, 833, 836–837 (1990).

21. Gonzales v. Carhart, 127 S. Ct. 1610 (2007).

22. 530 U.S. 914 (2000).

23. Frank I. Michelman, "The Supreme Court, 1968 Term: Foreword: On Protecting the

he have thought his proposal a discovery of the meaning of equal protection? What he was saying *sotto voce* was that as a liberal he would like to see the Supreme Court do something for poor people and that the Court could do so, without being laughed at *too* hard, by employing the rhetoric of equal protection deployed in his Foreword. If one is not a welfare-state liberal, Michelman's argument—his brief, really—falls flat even if one would bow to a persuasive argument that welfare rights really are found in the equal protection clause. No such argument is available.

In *Roper* the Supreme Court was not interpreting a directive text, hewing to a convincing historical understanding of the Constitution, or employing apolitical principles of *stare decisis* or common law adjudication. It was doing what a legislature asked to allow the execution of 17-year-old murderers would be doing: making a political judgment. That is true of most of the Court's constitutional decisions, even of the most celebrated constitutional decision of modern times, *Brown v. Board of Education*.[24] On legalist grounds, *Brown* could without any sense of strain have been decided in favor of the school board by a literal interpretation of the equal protection clause and a respectful bow to *Plessy v. Ferguson*,[25] which had upheld "separate but equal" a half century before *Brown,* and the reliance that the southern states had placed on *Plessy* in configuring their public school systems.[26] The "rightness" of *Brown* owes nothing to legalist analysis, and its acceptance may be due largely to the civil rights revolution led by Martin Luther King, Jr., that followed it.

The implicit ground of the decision was the Court's disapproving recognition that the segregation of public facilities in the South was intended to keep black Americans in a servile state, separate and unequal, stamped by their compelled separation as racially inferior ("no dogs or negroes allowed"). This system was contrary to American ideals, gratuitously cruel, and an embarrassment to the United States in its conflict with international communism. It was also based on inaccurate beliefs about the capabilities of black people—and to show that a policy is

---

Poor through the Fourteenth Amendment," 83 *Harvard Law Review* 7 (1969). On the political underpinnings of constitutional law scholarship, see Barry Friedman, "The Cycles of Constitutional Theory," *Law and Contemporary Problems,* Summer 2004, pp. 149, 151–157.

24. 347 U.S. 483 (1954).

25. 163 U.S. 537 (1896).

26. Herbert Wechsler famously doubted whether *Brown* had been decided correctly. Wechsler, "Toward Neutral Principles of Constitutional Law," 73 *Harvard Law Review* 1, 31–34 (1959). Learned Hand thought the decision erroneous. Hand, *The Bill of Rights* 54–55 (1958).

based on factual error is an especially powerful, because objective, form of criticism. That is why sophisticated modern religions avoid making claims that could be falsified empirically, such as that tossing a goat into a live volcano will bring rain.

Against the decision in *Brown* it could be argued, first, that if instead of forbidding public school segregation the Court had insisted that states practicing segregation spend as much money per black as per white pupil, the expense of maintaining parallel public school systems might have forced integration more rapidly than the Court's actual decision, which was not fully implemented for decades.[27] Second, to decide *Brown* the way it wanted to, the Court had to overrule a long-established decision, heavily relied on by the segregationist states in fashioning their institutions, educational and otherwise, and to do so in the face of evidence that the framers and ratifiers of the equal protection clause had intended only to protect blacks against the withdrawal of the standard police protections that whites received, so that blacks would not be outlaws in a literal sense.[28] Third, for reasons of *politesse* the Court was unwilling to state forthrightly that segregation was racist and instead had to cite unconvincing social science evidence concerning the psychological effect of segregated schooling. But the second and third criticisms just identify *Brown* as a political decision and the opinion as a political document. It was a politically sound decision and a politically sound opinion, and apparently that is good enough, for no responsible critic of the Court questions the soundness of *Brown* anymore.

Brown has achieved such prestige that a plurality of the Justices, in a recent decision curtailing affirmative action (reverse discrimination) in public schools, intimated (and one of the members of the plurality, Justice Thomas, stated outright) that *Brown* holds that the Constitution is "colorblind"—that is, that it forbids discrimination in favor of blacks or

27. In 1951–1952, the average expenditure per pupil in white public schools in the South was $132.38, compared to $90.20 in black public schools. Truman M. Pierce et al., *White and Negro Schools in the South: An Analysis of Biracial Education* 165 (1955) (tab. 39). See also Robert A. Margo, *Race and Schooling in the South, 1880–1950: An Economic History* 24–26 (1990). Thurgood Marshall "wanted black children to have the right to attend white schools as a point of leverage over the biased spending patterns of the segregationists who ran schools." Juan Williams, "Don't Mourn Brown v. Board of Education," *New York Times*, June 29, 2007, p. A29.

28. David P. Currie, *The Constitution in the Supreme Court: The First Hundred Years, 1789–1888* 348–349 and n. 143 (1985). More on these points in the next chapter.

other minorities as flatly as it forbids discrimination against them.[29] Whatever the merits of the "colorblind" interpretation of equal protection, it is disingenuous (as well as unpragmatic, as I suggested in chapter 9) to ascribe it to *Brown*. The Justices in *Brown* were not thinking about affirmative action, but about the plight of blacks under the apartheid regime then prevailing in the southern (and some border) states. The invocation of *Brown* in the recent decision was fig-leafing.

It is the unusual constitutional case in which everyone agrees to waive legalist objections by observing that, yes, it was decided on political grounds, but they were good grounds and it would be pedantic to demand more. In this regard *Plessy v. Ferguson* differs from another famous overruled decision, *Lochner v. New York*.[30] Although a number of respectable legal thinkers believe that the maximum-hours statute invalidated in *Lochner* was a bad statute rightly invalidated,[31] no one wants to reinstate racial segregation. Typically, as with *Lochner*, there is persisting disagreement over the political desirability of a famous (or notorious) constitutional decision, and this disagreement blocks consensus on whether the decision was correct.

Although *Brown* is a classic legislative decision, there are cases in which Justices vote for results that they would not support were they legislators whose constituents permitted them a free choice. Examples from the 2004 term include *Florida v. Nixon*,[32] in which Justice Ginsburg wrote the Court's opinion reinstating a death sentence that a state supreme court had reversed on federal constitutional grounds, and (less certainly) *Illinois v. Caballes*,[33] in which Justice Stevens wrote the Court's opinion holding that a dog sniff conducted during a lawful traffic stop

29. Parents Involved in Community Schools v. Seattle School District No. 1, 127 S. Ct. 2738 (2007). For penetrating criticism of the opinions, see Stuart Taylor, Jr., "Is There a Middle Ground on Race?" *National Journal,* July 9, 2007, http://nationaljournal.com/taylor.htm (visited July 13, 2007).

30. 198 U.S. 45 (1905).

31. See, for example, Randy E. Barnett, *Restoring the Lost Constitution: The Presumption of Liberty* 211–218, 222–223 (2004); Richard A. Epstein, *Takings: Private Property and the Power of Eminent Domain* 128–129, 279–282 (1985); Bernard H. Siegan, "Protecting Economic Liberties," 6 *Chapman Law Review* 43, 91–96, 100–101 (2003); and references cited in David E. Bernstein, "Lochner Era Revisionism, Revised: *Lochner* and the Origins of Fundamental Rights Constitutionalism," 92 *Georgetown Law Journal* 1, 6 nn. 16, 18 (2003).

32. 543 U.S. 175 (2004).

33. 543 U.S. 405 (2005).

was not a search because it could not reveal anything other than the presence of an unlawful substance and so did not invade a legitimate interest in privacy.

Justices occasionally, and sometimes credibly, issue disclaimers that a particular outcome for which they voted is one they would vote for as a legislator. I believe Justice Scalia when he says that his vote to hold the burning of the American flag as a form of political expression that is constitutionally privileged[34] was contrary to his legislative preferences;[35] and I believe Justice Thomas when he says that he would not vote for a law criminalizing homosexual sodomy even as he dissented from the decision invalidating such laws.[36] But such discrepancies between personal and judicial positions usually concern rather trivial issues, where the judicial position may be supporting a more important, though not necessarily a less personal, agenda of the Justice. No one except a military veteran is likely to get excited about flag burning (and sure enough, the three veterans on the Court when the flag-burning cases were decided, though politically diverse, all dissented, joined by Justice O'Connor). Not only is flag burning rare and inconsequential, but it is likely to be even more rare if it is not punishable—for then the flag burner is taking no risks, and his action, being costless to him, does not signal deep conviction to others and so loses its symbolic and hortatory significance. (Where would Christianity be without its martyrs?) And only someone deeply disturbed by homosexuality could mourn the passing of the sodomy laws, since by the time the Supreme Court declared them unconstitutional they had been repealed or invalidated on state law grounds in most states and had virtually ceased to be enforced in the remaining ones, though people deeply hostile to homosexuality may have valued the laws as symbolic statements. One thing important to Justice Scalia is promoting an approach to the Constitution that would, if adopted, entail the eventual overruling of *Roe v. Wade* and other decisions of which he deeply disapproves. And one thing important to Justice Thomas (as well as to Scalia) is opposing the kind of "living constitution" rhetoric

34. United States v. Eichman, 496 U.S. 310 (1990); Texas v. Johnson, 491 U.S. 397 (1989).

35. See, for example, Frank Sikora, "Justice Scalia: Constitution Allows 'Really Stupid' Things," *Birmingham News*, Apr. 14, 1999, p. 3D; Margaret Talbot, "Supreme Confidence: The Jurisprudence of Justice Antonin Scalia," *New Yorker*, Mar. 28, 2005, pp. 40, 42–43.

36. Lawrence v. Texas, 539 U.S. 558, 605 (2003) (dissenting opinion).

deployed by Justice Kennedy in homosexual rights cases,[37] a rhetoric that invites conforming constitutional law to the personal preferences of "progressive" jurists. In effect, Justices Scalia and Thomas trade a minor preference for a major one.

But this is not a satisfactory explanation for Scalia's vote in the flag-burning cases. Nothing in the text of the Constitution, or in the eighteenth-century understanding of freedom of speech, supports the proposition that prohibiting the burning of the flag infringes free speech. The First Amendment forbids Congress to pass laws abridging "freedom of speech." But the term is not defined and cannot be taken literally because that would make libel, slander, criminal solicitation, betrayal of military secrets, the broadcasting of obscenities in prime-time television, child pornography, fraudulent advertising, publishing stolen trade secrets, infringing copyrights, public employees' speech within the scope of their employment, and falsely shouting "Fire!" in a crowded theater all constitutionally privileged acts—which the Supreme Court has held they are not. Burning a flag is not even "speech" in a literal sense. So without offending a textualist or an originalist the Court could have ruled that, like assassinating one's political opponents or parading naked through the streets in order to promote nudism, burning things is not "speech," though it can be highly expressive.

So maybe Justice Scalia is not really a textualist or an originalist. Or maybe textualism-originalism should be thought a component of a broader concept of legalism that makes a place for the doctrine of precedent. That would be an uneasy alliance, since most of the threads in the fabric of constitutional law are nonoriginalist precedents. Anyway, adherence to precedent cannot explain Scalia's vote in the flag-burning cases. As the dissenting Justices explained, there was no ruling precedent. There *was* a constitutional doctrine, tenuously rooted in the text of the First Amendment, to the effect that any public expressive activity is privileged unless it does significant harm. The doctrine is far from clear, but it would be muddier still were there an exception for flag burning; and Scalia prefers rules to standards, a preference common among legalists, as we know, because it enlarges the area for legalist decision

---

37. See, for example, id. at 579 ("as the Constitution endures, persons in every generation can invoke its principles in their own search for greater freedom").

making. But it is not a preference that can be derived by legalist techniques, all of which favored the dissenters in the flag-burning cases.

Scalia's vote in *Booker*, the case that demoted the federal sentencing guidelines from mandatory to advisory status, may seem to have cut against his legislative preferences more sharply than his vote in the flag-burning cases. Yet neither *Booker* nor the version that Scalia would have preferred, which would not have required even the qualified adherence to the guidelines that Justice Breyer's majority opinion requires, is likely to cause a reduction in the average severity of criminal sentences. (We saw earlier that apparently it has not had such an effect.) The guidelines had narrowed the sentencing variance among judges, but the narrowing did not make the average defendant worse off (unless he was a risk preferrer). The average severity of federal sentences did rise during the regime of the mandatory guidelines.[38] But that was because of choices made by the Sentencing Commission in picking specific guidelines, not because the guidelines required that sentences be based on judicial fact-finding rather than, as in the old days, on judicial whim. Anyway, Congress has the last word on how severely to punish federal crimes, and Scalia does not object to sentencing schemes that allow judges to pick a sentence anywhere between the floor and the ceiling set by Congress. A "rule of law" aficionado like Justice Scalia might be expected to oppose increasing the discretion of sentencing judges, but pockets of discretion, such as sentencing and jury trials, have rarely bothered judges who prefer rules to standards.

It is not an adequate reply to criticism of a controversial decision that a Justice joined to say that he was voting against his "desire." People have multiple desires, often conflicting, and they must weigh them against each other in coming to a decision—the lesson of *Buchanan v. Warley*, discussed in chapter 1. A Justice may desire that burning the American flag be punished but desire more that constitutional standards such as freedom of speech be recast as rules that have few exceptions. Justice Scalia surely disapproves of extravagant awards of punitive damages to tort plaintiffs, but he disapproves more of the concept of substantive due process that his colleagues have used to impose a constitutional

---

38. United States Sentencing Commission, *Fifteen Years of Guidelines Sentencing: An Assessment of How Well the Federal Criminal Justice System Is Achieving the Goals of Sentencing Reform* 42–43 and fig. 2.2 (2004).

limit on those awards.[39] Such doctrinal beliefs are as personal or political as the desire for a particular outcome; they are not the product of submission to the compulsion of the constitutional text or of some other conventional source of legal guidance (though the judge may think they are) because there are no such compulsions in the cases that I have been discussing. The conventional "left" and "right" ideologies are not the only things that matter to Supreme Court Justices. But the other things that matter to them need not be professional legal norms, especially ones incapable of guiding decisions because their application requires a clear constitutional text or a binding precedent—and remember that the Court is never bound by precedent.

Sometimes, moreover, what is involved in voting against one's seeming druthers may be a calculation that the appearance of being "principled" is rhetorically and politically effective. It fools people. So it is worth adhering to principle when the cost to the judge's substantive objectives is slight.

I do not mean to be portraying the Justices as cynics who consciously make the trade-offs that I have been describing. I assume they accept the conventional law-constrained conception of judges and believe they conform to it. They would be uncomfortable otherwise, for they would experience cognitive dissonance. Most jobholders believe their job performance conforms to their employer's reasonable expectations; many are mistaken.

The expanded role of law clerks in the work of the Supreme Court (as in that of the lower courts) has produced an unearned increase in the judicial comfort level. Supreme Court law clerks are more numerous and experienced (because all now have spent at least a year in a lower-court clerkship before coming to the Court) than they used to be.[40] They are also on average somewhat abler because law schools draw a higher average quality of applicants than they used to,[41] probably as a consequence

39. See TXO Production Corp v. Alliance Resources Corp., 509 U.S. 443, 470 (1993) (Scalia, J., concurring); BMW of North America Inc. v. Gore, 517 U.S. 559, 598 (1996) (Scalia, J., dissenting); State Farm Mutual Automobile Ins. Co. v. Campbell, 538 U.S. 408, 429 (2003) (Scalia, J., dissenting).

40. See Todd C. Peppers, *Courtiers of the Marble Palace: The Rise and Influence of the Supreme Court Law Clerk* (2006); Artemus Ward and David L. Weiden, *Sorcerers' Apprentices: 100 Years of Law Clerks at the United States Supreme Court* (2006).

41. William D. Henderson and Andrew P. Morriss, "Student Quality as Measured by LSAT Scores: Migration Patterns in the U.S. News Rankings Era," 81 *Indiana Law Journal* 163 (2006).

of the astronomical salaries of elite lawyers. There is almost no legal outcome that a really skillful legal analyst cannot cover with a professional varnish. So a Supreme Court Justice—however questionable his position in a particular case might seem to be—can, without lifting a pen or touching the computer keyboard, but merely by whistling for his law clerks, assure himself that he can defend whatever position he wants to take with enough professional panache to keep the critics at bay. A law clerk is not going to tell his Justice "It won't write"—the symbol of the self-disciplining effect of authorship. It would be a confession of inadequacy. So "delegation of the opinion-drafting function to law clerks may increase the propensity of Justices to decide cases based solely on their policy preferences."[42] The more that is delegated (because of more and better clerks), the more sway the propensity can be expected to have.

It is true that some constitutional cases can be decided by conventional legalist techniques, just by placing the facts alongside the constitutional text. But they tend to be hypothetical rather than real cases. If Congress passed a law requiring that all books be submitted to a presidential board of censors for approval to be withheld if any of them criticized any federal official, adjudging the statute unconstitutional would not require the Justices to make a political judgment. But cases that clear arise infrequently, and when they do they rarely reach the Supreme Court. And the cases that are unclear in a legalist sense are rarely clear in a political sense. *Brown* was exceptional. Many of the landmark Supreme Court decisions were decided by close votes and would have been decided the other way had the Court been differently but no less ably manned. Even *Brown*, which was unanimous, might have been decided differently had Earl Warren not been Chief Justice.[43]

If constitutional law is saturated by political judgments, a Justice has a choice between accepting the political character of constitutional adjudication wholeheartedly and voting in cases much as legislators vote on bills, or, feeling bashful about being a politician in robes, setting for himself a very high threshold for voting to invalidate on constitutional grounds the action of another branch of government. The first, the "ag-

42. David R. Stras, "The Supreme Court's Gatekeepers: The Role of Law Clerks in the Certiorari Process," 85 *Texas Law Review* 947, 961–962 (2007). See also Stras, "The Incentives Approach to Judicial Retirement," 90 *Minnesota Law Review* 1417, 1422 n. 22 (2006).

43. Michael J. Klarman, *From Jim Crow to Civil Rights: The Supreme Court and the Struggle for Racial Equality* 302 (2004).

gressive judge" approach ("judicial activism"), expands the Court's authority relative to that of the other branches of government. (Judges like to refer to these as the "political branches," as if the federal judiciary itself were not a politically powerful branch of government.) The second, the "modest judge" approach ("judicial self-restraint"), tells the Court to think very hard indeed before undertaking to nullify the actions of the other branches of government.

But we must distinguish between two senses of "judicial activism." In one sense, the sense in which I have just used the term, it means enlarging judicial power at the expense of the power of the other branches of government (both federal and state).[44] In another but misleading sense it refers to the legalist's conceit that his technique for deciding cases minimizes judicial power by transferring much of that power back, as it were, to elected officials (not only legislators but also the members of the state conventions that ratified the Constitution), from whom the judges are thought to have wrested it by loose construction. The two senses may seem the same, both trying to rein in judges. They are not. The legalist implements his approach by literal (textualist) or historical (originalist) interpretation of statutes and the Constitution, and such interpretation, though nominally referrable back to elected officials, often has the effect of curtailing the powers of the nonjudicial branches. Think of what a literal interpretation of the commerce clause, of the First Amendment's free-speech clause, or of the Second Amendment's right to bear arms would do to the government's ability to keep military secrets, punish criminal solicitation, regulate transportation or communications that do not cross state lines or national boundaries, and forbid the sale of heavy weaponry to private persons. The Constitution of 1787 envisioned a much smaller federal government than we now have, and legalist techniques could be used to carve the government back to its eighteenth-century dimensions. Legalists of the "Constitution in Exile" school think that the Constitution as a whole is greatly underenforced, while legalists in the Bush Administration think that Article II (presidential power) is greatly underenforced.

Judicial modesty or self-restraint, understood as the rejection of judicial activism in the sense of judicial aggrandizement at the expense of the other branches of government, is not a legalist idea but a pragmatic

---

44. Richard A. Posner, *The Federal Courts: Challenge and Reform* 318 (1996).

one. The notion of Holmes and Brandeis that the states are laboratories for social experimentation is at once quintessentially pragmatic in exalting experimentation over a priori judgments and a keystone of a policy of judicial modesty, although pragmatism could be thought to counsel activism in cases in which a statute challenged on constitutional grounds limits experimentation, such as the federal ban on partial-birth abortion that the Supreme Court has upheld.

Versions of judicial modesty include Thayer's principle that statutes should be invalidated only if they are contrary to any reasonable understanding of the constitutional text[45] and Holmes's "can't helps"[46] or "puke" test: a statute is unconstitutional only if it makes you want to throw up.[47] Holmes was not speaking literally, of course; he meant only that a conviction of error is not enough—there must be revulsion. But there is a difference between the two approaches. Thayer's is a one-way approach, Holmes's a two-way. Thayer's approach limits—it never expands—judicial review. Holmes's approach allows judges to stretch the constitutional text when necessary to avoid extreme injustice. Holmes's Constitution has no gaps—it is noteworthy how rarely his constitutional opinions quote the constitutional text.

The difference between their approaches illuminates *Griswold v. Connecticut*,[48] which invalidated a Connecticut statute—anachronistic in 1965 (only Massachusetts, another heavily Catholic state, had a similar statute) and well-nigh incomprehensible today—that forbade the use of contraceptives, with no exception even for married couples. A Thayerian would disapprove of the decision because the statute was not unconstitutional beyond a reasonable doubt; indeed, it is difficult to find a provision of the Constitution on which to hang one's hat in a case about contraception. A Holmesian might find the statute so appalling (not only because of its theocratic cast, but also because its only practical effect was, by preventing birth control clinics from operating, to deny poor married couples access to contraceptive devices other than condoms[49])

45. James B. Thayer, "The Origin and Scope of the American Doctrine of Constitutional Law," 7 *Harvard Law Review* 129, 138–152 (1893).
46. *Holmes-Laski Letters: The Correspondence of Mr. Justice Holmes and Harold J. Laski*, vol. 2, p. 1124 (Mark DeWolfe Howe ed. 1953).
47. Id. at 888.
48. 381 U.S. 479 (1965).
49. The use of condoms was permitted on the ground that their purpose was to prevent the spread of venereal diseases—which is, of course, only one of their purposes. For a discussion of the invalidated statute, see Richard A. Posner, *Sex and Reason* 324–328 (1992).

that he would vote to invalidate it despite the difficulty of grounding his vote in the constitutional text. A Holmesian might react similarly to *Harmelin v. Michigan*,[50] in which the Court refused to invalidate a life sentence for possessing a small quantity of cocaine. Actually there was a bigger constitutional handle in that case for invalidating the sentence— the cruel and unusual punishments clause of the Eighth Amendment— than there was for invalidating the statute in *Griswold*.

In the modest role the Justice is still a politician, but he is a timid one. He wants the Supreme Court to play a role a bit like that of the House of Lords after its authority shrank to the delaying of legislation voted by the House of Commons. The Court can keep its thumb in the dike only so long; if public opinion is overwhelming, the Justices must give way, as any politician would have to do.

If the Justices acknowledged to themselves the essentially personal, subjective, political, and, from a legalist standpoint, arbitrary character of most of their constitutional decisions, then—deprived of "the law made me do it" rationalization for their exercise of power—they might be less aggressive upsetters of political applecarts than they are. But that is probably too much to expect, because the "if" condition cannot be satisfied. For judges to acknowledge even just to themselves the political dimension of their role would open a psychologically unsettling gap between their official job description and their actual job. Acknowledging that they were making political choices would also undermine their confidence in the soundness of their decisions, since judges' political choices cannot be justified by reference to their professional background or training. Judges do not like to think that they are expressing an amateurish personal view when they decide a difficult case. Some judges "agonize" over their decisions; most do not; but both sorts feel a psychological compulsion to think they are making the right decision. (Some judges think that just by virtue of their having been made judges, their decisions must be right, or at least as right as any other judge's.) A judge who does not become comfortable with his decision by the time it is handed down might ever after be tormented by doubts that it was correct. No one likes to be tormented, so judges do not look back and worry about how many of their thousands of judicial votes may have been mistaken. As the years pass they become increasingly confident because they have behind them an ever-longer train of decisions that they doubt

---

50. 501 U.S. 957 (1991).

not are sound. Anent self-torment, I admit that Justice Blackmun was not a happy camper.[51] But his decisions were no less predictable, and certainly no less aggressive in their assertion of judicial power, than those of Justices who take a more relaxed attitude toward their judicial duties.

Judicial modesty is not the order of the day in the Supreme Court. I instanced *Roper;* a further example is the already mentioned *Booker.*[52] Legislatures typically specify for each crime a minimum and a maximum sentence—often far apart, thus creating a wide sentencing range—and let the judge pick any sentence within the range to impose on the particular defendant. The mandatory sentencing guidelines curtailed judges' sentencing discretion, but *Booker* restored it, though not completely, because the Court ruled that the judge must still compute the defendant's guidelines sentence and that any departure from it must be reasonable in light of sentencing factors set forth in the Sentencing Reform Act.[53]

The guidelines required that the sentence be based not only on the facts about the defendant's conduct that the jury had found beyond a reasonable doubt but also on facts that the judge found at the sentencing hearing by a mere preponderance of the evidence. The defendant might have been indicted for and convicted of possessing with intent to distribute two grams of cocaine, but if the government at the sentencing hearing persuaded the judge by a preponderance of the evidence that the defendant had actually possessed with intent to distribute 200 grams, he would have to sentence the defendant in accordance with the guideline applicable to the larger quantity.

Yet under the pre-guidelines regime, which no Justice thought unconstitutional, sentencing had been even more lax procedurally. The sentencing judge could impose the statutory maximum sentence without any evidence at all having been presented at the sentencing hearing concerning the actual amount of the illegal drug that the defendant had possessed above the statutory minimum found by the jury.

51. Linda Greenhouse, *Becoming Justice Blackmun: Harry Blackmun's Supreme Court Journey* (2005).

52. See United States v. Booker, 543 U.S. 220, 229–234 (2005) (Justice Stevens's opinion for the Court); id. at 244–247 (Justice Breyer's opinion for the Court). Stevens and Breyer each wrote a majority opinion, Stevens on the unconstitutionality of the guidelines as mandatory sentencing directives, Breyer on their constitutionality as merely advisory.

53. 18 U.S.C. § 3553(a).

Why the mandatory feature of the guidelines should have been thought to violate the Sixth Amendment, a provision designed for the protection of criminal defendants, is a mystery. Gearing sentences to findings made on the basis of evidence gave defendants *more* procedural rights than they had had before the guidelines, when judges could pick any point in the statutory sentencing range when determining a sentence. Because judges' discretion had been greater (hence the greater variance in sentences), defendants' rights had been fewer, since a plea to a judge to exercise his discretion in favor of imposing a lenient sentence is a plea for mercy rather than a claim of right, unless his discretion is tightly cabined, as it was not in the pre-guidelines sentencing regime.

Invalidation of the mandatory feature of the guidelines did not solve the problem of procedural informality in sentencing. The government can still put on a bare-bones case yet count on a heavy sentence if the judge is known to be unsympathetic to the class of offenders to which the defendant belongs. And the judge must still compute the guidelines sentence, which may be high because of evidence first presented at the sentencing hearing. Although he is not bound to impose that sentence, imposing it is the course of least resistance because any deviation must be justified to the appellate court as "reasonable," whereas a guidelines sentence can be presumed by that court to be reasonable.[54]

However the Sixth Amendment issue should have been resolved, the Court's resolution reflected an ingenious compromise, forged by Justice Breyer, under which the guidelines, though demoted to advisory status (in other words, to being genuine "guidelines"), retain considerable bite. The sentencing judge must still, as I noted, calculate the guidelines sentence, though he can give a different sentence. But some departures from guidelines sentences had been authorized by the Sentencing Commission itself,[55] so that all the Court did in the end was to loosen the bindings a little more—and in doing so make more work for the district judges. The Sentencing Reform Act contains a laundry list of factors that the judge is to consider in picking a sentence within the statutory limits.[56] Until *Booker*, the use that a sentencing judge could make of the factors was severely circumscribed by the statute itself in order to ensure

---

54. Rita v. United States, 127 S. Ct. 2456 (2007).

55. See, for example, United States Sentencing Commission, *U.S. Sentencing Guidelines Manual* §§ 3B1.2, 3E1.1, 4A1.3 (2004).

56. 18 U.S.C. § 3553(a).

the guidelines' mandatory character.[57] Since judges must still calculate the guidelines sentence but now must consider the statutory sentencing factors as well, the Court has increased the burden of sentencing—with benefits that are obscure. The mandatory guidelines regime could not be thought inconsistent with a reasonable understanding of the Sixth Amendment; it was not revolting either. So it flunked neither Thayer's test of unconstitutionality nor Holmes's. A modest judge would have voted to reject the constitutional challenge to the guidelines.

For completeness I note that some constitutional issues can be resolved satisfactorily on grounds neither legalist nor political in any contentious sense of those words. Here is an example, albeit a hypothetical one. Article I, section 9, of the Constitution—the "suspension clause"—authorizes Congress to suspend habeas corpus in times of invasion or rebellion. In the eighteenth century, when the Constitution was promulgated, habeas corpus had the limited function of protecting a person against being detained by the government without judicial acquiescence in the detention. Habeas corpus enabled the detainee to require the government to satisfy a judge of its legal right to hold him. So if he was a convicted criminal, all the government had to prove was that he had been convicted by a court that had jurisdiction to try him.[58] But later Congress expanded federal habeas corpus and today it is a means by which convicted criminals, having exhausted their direct appellate remedies, can challenge their conviction or prison sentence on constitutional grounds.

Suppose now that Congress curtailed or even eliminated federal habeas corpus as a postconviction remedy, though there was no rebellion or invasion. Would that be a violation of the suspension clause? An originalist would say no; a "living Constitution" buff would say yes; a textualist (here illustrating a fissure in the textualist-originalist school) would also have to say yes (habeas corpus is habeas corpus). But one does not need a theory to recognize that a judge's ruling that "curtailing an optional statutory enlargement violates the suspension clause would create an irrational ratchet. Habeas corpus could always be enlarged, but once enlarged could not be returned to its previous, less generous scope without a constitutional amendment. Once this was understood, there

57. 18 U.S.C. § 3553(b).
58. See, for example, Henry J. Friendly, "Is Innocence Irrelevant? Collateral Attack on Criminal Convictions," 38 *University of Chicago Law Review* 142, 170–171 (1970).

would be few if any further enlargements."[59] If an expansion of habeas corpus could thus be rescinded only by amending the suspension clause, this would mean that Congress could entrench a statute against repeal, just as if the expansion of habeas corpus had been authorized by a constitutional amendment. The effect would be to enlarge Congress's power beyond the boundaries set for it in Article I and to bypass the procedure specified in Article V for amending the Constitution.

A decision by Congress to eliminate all postconviction remedies could still be challenged. But the proper ground would be due process rather than the suspension clause, which limits a much more ominous form of government action—executive or military detention, bypassing the courts altogether. Rejecting a claim based on the suspension clause, however, though it would have political significance as well as legalist and pragmatic justifications, would not be "political," because liberals and conservatives ought to be able to agree on the result.

Still, the bin containing cases that are at once politically contentious and legalistically indeterminate is chronically overflowing in the Supreme Court. It is no surprise that the search for an alternative to conceiving of the Court as a political organ has been a preoccupation of the Supreme Court Forewords published annually in the *Harvard Law Review* for the past half century. One of the most interesting is Henry Hart's.[60] It focuses on the effect of caseload on the judicial process in the Supreme Court. Hart is usually thought an apostle of the legal process approach. But it would be more accurate to describe him as a Progressive reformer in a sense that associates him with such diverse persons and movements as Max Weber, Woodrow Wilson, Louis Brandeis, and the New Deal, and thus with the exaltation of expertise, in the American setting with the celebration of the administrative agency as the epitome of law made rational, expert, and modern, and even with the legal realist movement. I think Hart in his Foreword was trying to say that if only the Supreme Court would behave in the hyperrational fashion of idealized administrative agencies, its decisions would be legitimate by virtue not of their pedigree (of being sound interpretations of past political settlements, such as the Constitution) but of the expertness of the decision makers. The Court would be a superlegislature because it was super. But

---

59. LaGuerre v. Reno, 164 F.3d 1035, 1038 (7th Cir. 1998).

60. Henry M. Hart, Jr., "The Supreme Court, 1958 Term: Foreword: The Time Chart of the Justices," 73 *Harvard Law Review* 84 (1959).

it would not be political in the usual sense, as legislatures are; its model would be a politically neutral civil service guided by reason rather than public opinion. Justice Jackson's famous dictum[61] would be reversed: the Court would be final because it was infallible. What was holding the Court back, Hart thought, was that it was failing to allocate its time sensibly. The Justices were not taking enough time to discuss the cases thoroughly because they were granting certiorari profligately and therefore hearing too many unimportant cases. Hart's was the Progressive dream of policy emptied of politics by procedure.

A pipe dream, actually. From a distance of half a century, Hart's Foreword seems either naïve to the point of almost total cluelessness or intellectually dishonest in arguing that what was preventing the Justices from fulfilling the Progressive agenda was that they were using their time inefficiently. He seems to have had no sense of how judges, including Supreme Court Justices, actually used (and use) their time. Even when he wrote, it was not true that "writing opinions [was] the most time-consuming of all judicial work, and the least susceptible of effective assistance from a law clerk."[62] Today, as we know, most judicial opinions, including many Supreme Court opinions, are largely ghostwritten by law clerks. Though there were fewer law clerks per judge (or Justice) in the 1950s, when Hart was writing, even then many of the Justices' opinions were written by clerks, as Hart either did not know or pretended not to know. He may not have realized that because writing judicial opinions is for most judges a chore rather than a joy, the availability of law clerks eager to lift that chore from their judges' shoulders allows judges plenty of time to discuss the cases with each other—if they want to.

A giant "if." The naïveté of Hart's "time chart" (his tabulation of the time that Justices devoted to their various judicial tasks, proving to his satisfaction that they lacked the time to deliberate adequately) was noted at the time by the legal realist Thurman Arnold. His rudely accurate assessment of Hart's Foreword—"there is no such process as [the maturing of collective thought], and there never has been; men of positive views are only hardened in those views by [judicial] conferences"[63]—

---

61. Brown v. Allen, 344 U.S. 443, 540 (1953) (concurring opinion) ("We are not final because we are infallible, but we are infallible only because we are final").

62. Hart, note 60 above, at 91.

63. "Professor Hart's Theology," 73 *Harvard Law Review* 1298, 1312 (1960). Arnold continued:

was summarily dismissed by Hart's dean, Erwin Griswold.[64] The rough tone of Arnold's article and the transparency of his political motivations made his diatribe easy to disparage. But his central point was correct.

Griswold wrote that "the volume of the work of the Court is staggering," the Justices being busy "reading long records" and "writing reflective opinions."[65] These things were not true when he wrote and are not true today. Justices do not read the full records of the cases they decide—much, sometimes all, of the record of a case is irrelevant, and most of the relevant parts have been distilled in the opinions of the lower courts. The Justices delegate much of the opinion writing. And the opinions are rarely "reflective"; they are briefs in support of the decision.

Griswold acknowledged that the process of adjudication at the Supreme Court level is "not a merely mechanical one" (he meant not legalistic).[66] But he described it as "a tightly guided process. The scope of individual decision is properly narrow."[67] That is not true either; the Justices exercise vast discretion, thrashing about in a trackless wilderness. Griswold went on to paint the judicial process in heroic colors, very flattering to judges and a mystification to the public:

> It is a process requiring great intellectual power, an open and inquiring and resourceful mind, and often courage, especially intellectual courage, and the power to rise above oneself. Even more than intellectual acumen, it requires intellectual detachment and disinterestedness, rare

---

There is no possibility that I could pool my wisdom with Professor Hart's so that the wisdom of both of us, "successfully pooled," would "transcend the wisdom of" either of us. The reason is that I do not think his wisdom is real wisdom, and I am sure that he has the same opinion of mine. To lock the two of us in a room until I came to agree with the theology of Professor Hart by the process of the "maturing" of our "collective thought" would be to impose a life sentence on both of us without due process of law.

Id. Arnold was correct. He had the advantage over Hart of having been an appellate judge, albeit briefly.

64. Erwin N. Griswold, "The Supreme Court, 1959 Term: Foreword: Of Time and Attitudes: Professor Hart and Judge Arnold," 74 *Harvard Law Review* 81 (1960).

65. Id. at 84.

66. Later, when he was Solicitor General, Griswold was explicit about the existence of an open area in which a judge's "political and philosophical preconceptions and outlooks will inevitably, and rightly, be of great importance." Erwin N. Griswold, *The Judicial Process* 24 (1973).

67. Griswold, note 64 above, at 92.

qualities approached only through constant awareness of their elusiveness, and constant striving to attain them.[68]

These attributes are desirable, but they are not *required*; they are not part of the job description. Few Justices have had "great intellectual power," nor is such power usually conjoined with "an open and inquiring" mind or "the power to rise above oneself." Justices Holmes, Brandeis, and Jackson are uncontroversial examples of great Justices, but would anyone think them intellectually detached and disinterested (Holmes was emotionally detached) or "striving to attain" these qualities?

Like Griswold, Hart would not admit the limitedness of the average Justice, and so the mediocrity (as it seemed to him) of Supreme Court opinions cried out for an explanation. The one he offered was that the Justices were hearing too many cases and so lacked sufficient time to discuss them with each other and thus allow the power of collective thinking to save them from making mistakes. He did not mention the lack of deliberation in English courts (see chapter 5), though in the 1950s, when he was writing, the English judiciary was admired by American legal thinkers despite its disavowal of collective thinking.

Hart's effort to be precise about the amount of time the Justices had in which to deliberate miscarried because of his ignorance (and again, I do not know whether this was actual or feigned) of their working conditions and, more important, of the nature of judicial decision making. He seems to have thought that the typical case the Supreme Court agreed to decide was a complex puzzle that would take even very bright people a long time to unravel. Most cases, certainly most constitutional cases, are not of that character. Indeterminacy, a common feature of cases that get to the top of the judicial pyramid, is not the same thing as complexity. It is the difference between politics and science.

As for those cases that *are* complex, the data that might enable them to be solved as puzzles are usually unobtainable, or at least are not obtained, and so those cases cannot be decided by methods analogous to solving puzzles or designing operating systems either. *Roper v. Simmons,* for example, had an "obtainable but not obtained" dimension—empirical data that the Justices were unable (or perhaps just unwilling) to process, showing that they are not about to become the expert administrators of Hart's vision of adjudication. They ignored a statistical literature

68. Id. at 94.

on the deterrent effect of capital punishment[69] that bolsters the commonsense proposition that there is indeed an incremental such effect. This might have given the Justices pause by making the interests of the murder victims more perspicuous. But the Justices are not comfortable enough with statistical theory and methodology to want to hang their hats on statistical studies that fall short of being conclusive, as the studies of the deterrent effect of capital punishment do.[70] They fear being taken in.

Maybe they are right to be diffident about relying on statistical studies. But if so they should be consistently diffident. The Justices in the *Roper* majority should not have relied on a psychological literature that they mistakenly believed showed that persons under 18 are incapable of mature moral reflection.[71] One does not have to be a social scientist to know that such an inference cannot be correct. Chronological age does not coincide with mental or emotional maturity; age 18 is not an inflection point at which teenagers suddenly acquire an adult capacity for moral behavior. The studies on which the Court relied acknowledge that their findings that 16- or 17-year-olds are less likely to make mature judgments than 18-year-olds are statistical rather than individual[72] and

69. See Hashem Dezhbakhsh and Paul H. Rubin, "From the 'Econometrics of Capital Punishment' to the 'Capital Punsihments' of Econometrics: On the Use and Abuse of Sensitivity Analysis" (Emory University, Sept. 2007), and studies cited there (most finding deterrent effect, some not); Dezhbakhsh et al., "Does Capital Punishment Have a Deterrent Effect? New Evidence from Postmoratorium Panel Data," 5 *American Law and Economics Review* 344, 364–365 (2003); Joanna M. Shepherd, "Murders of Passion, Execution Delays, and the Deterrence of Capital Punishment," 33 *Journal of Legal Studies* 283, 305 (2004); and other studies cited in Paul Rubin, "Statistical Evidence on Capital Punishment and the Deterrence of Homicide: Written Testimony for the Senate Judiciary Committee on the Constitution, Civil Rights, and Property Rights," Feb. 1, 2006, http://judiciary.senate.gov/testimony.cfm?id=1745&wit_id=4991 (visited June 13, 2007).

70. See, for example, John Donohue and Justin J. Wolfers, "A Reply to Rubin on the Death Penalty," *Economists' Voice,* Apr. 2006, http://bpp.wharton.upenn.edu/jwolfers/Press/Death%20Penalty(BEPressReply).pdf (visited May 13, 2007); Craig J. Albert, "Challenging Deterrence: New Insights on Capital Punishment Derived from Panel Data," 60 *University of Pittsburgh Law Review* 321, 363 (1999); Ruth D. Peterson and William C. Bailey, "Is Capital Punishment an Effective Deterrent for Murder? An Examination of Social Science Research," in *America's Experiment with Capital Punishment: Reflections on the Past, Present, and Future of the Ultimate Penal Sanction* 251, 274–277 (James R. Acker et al. eds., 2d ed. 2003).

71. Roper v. Simmons, note 7 above, at 568–575.

72. See Jeffrey Arnett, "Reckless Behavior in Adolescence: A Developmental Perspective," 12 *Developmental Review* 339, 344 (1992) ("It is not being suggested here that all adolescents are reckless, only that adolescents as a group engage in a disproportionate amount of reckless

do not support a categorical exclusion of 16- and 17-year-olds from the ranks of the mature. At most the studies demonstrate a need for careful inquiry into the maturity of a young person charged with capital murder. The Court thought juries incapable of such an inquiry—but if so, they are incapable of ever deciding when a murderer is bad enough to be executed or good enough to be spared.

The principal study cited by the Court acknowledges that "the definitive developmental research has not yet been conducted, [and] until we have better and more conclusive data, it would be prudent to err on the side of caution."[73] Caution might well be thought to argue not, as the authors of the quoted study believe, for outlawing the death penalty for 16- and 17-year-olds but rather for leaving the judgment to the states, though for those Justices who find capital punishment a disturbing practice, caution may mean forbidding it whenever there is the slightest doubt about its propriety. Unless the Justices are naïve about social science (which they may be, however), these studies could not have figured in the decision, as distinct from the advocacy of the decision in the Court's opinion.

The picture of Supreme Court Justices poring over esoteric scholarly articles to come to a decision is an unrealistic one. The expert-administrator model of Supreme Court adjudication misconceives how judges reach decisions. Experienced appellate judges read the briefs in a case, discuss the case with their law clerks, listen to oral argument, perhaps dip into

---

behavior"). Arnett makes no distinction between persons under and over 18; in fact, he defines adolescence "as extending from puberty to the early 20's." Id. at 340. And he does not directly discuss murder or other serious crimes. A study cited not by the Court but by Laurence Steinberg and Elizabeth S. Scott in "Less Guilty by Reason of Adolescence: Developmental Immaturity, Diminished Responsibility, and the Juvenile Death Penalty," 58 *American Psychologist* 1009 (2003), discusses "teens" in passing but, like Arnett, does not classify them by age. See Baruch Fischhoff, "Risk Taking: A Developmental Perspective," in *Risk-Taking Behavior* 133, 142, 148 (J. Frank Yates ed. 1992).

73. Steinberg and Scott, note 72 above, at 1017. See also id. at 1012–1014. The Steinberg-Scott study, coauthored by law professor Elizabeth Scott, is an advocacy article. Its last sentence is: "The United States should join the majority of countries around the world in prohibiting the execution of individuals for crimes committed under the age of 18." Id. at 1017. The only "study" cited by the Court other than the Arnett and Steinberg-Scott articles is not a study at all, but an old, speculative book by Erik H. Erikson, *Identity: Youth and Crisis* (1968). The Court did not cite a study that concludes that adolescents "may be just as competent as adults at a number of aspects of decision making about risky behavior." Lita Furby and Ruth Beyth-Marom, "Risk Taking in Adolescence: A Decision-Making Perspective," 12 *Developmental Review* 1, 36 (1992). For other cautionary notes, see Fischhoff, note 72 above, at 148, 152, 157.

the record here and there, maybe do some secondary reading, *briefly* discuss the case at conference with the other judges, and from the information and insights gleaned from these sources, filtered through preconceptions based on experience, temperament, and other personal factors, make up their minds. It is not a protracted process unless the judge has difficulty making up his mind, which is a psychological trait rather than an index of conscientiousness.

So it is unlikely that the Justices would do a better job if they decided fewer cases and thus had more time to spend on each one. But we need not rest on conjecture. We have the results of a natural experiment. The Justices now do decide fewer cases and thus have more time to spend discussing each one—should they desire to. Although the number of paid petitions for certiorari has doubled since 1958 (the unpaid—*in forma pauperis*—petitions are mostly frivolous and easily disposed of), the number of law clerks has also doubled and an ingenious "pool" system of processing petitions for certiorari has been adopted that enables the Justices to delegate most of the screening function to the clerks. (Instead of each clerk's writing a cert. memo for his Justice, one clerk writes a cert. memo for all eight Justices in the pool.[74]) Most important, the Court has been deciding fewer and fewer cases and is now issuing opinions in only about 70 cases a year, compared to 129 in 1958. In the 2006 term, it decided only 68 cases.

Not that number of decisions is the sole measure of a court's workload. The cases could be getting tougher, and this might be reflected in longer opinions or in more separate opinions. But the decline in the number of decisions by the Supreme Court has not been offset by an increase in separate (that is, dissenting and concurring) opinions. The total number of opinions, not just of decisions, has declined. Nor have these declines been offset by a significant increase in opinion length (since the early 1970s). And so the total word output of the Justices has declined along with the number of opinions.[75]

Why the Supreme Court's caseload and output have declined is a mystery. (The fact that the decline has coincided with an increase in the quality and number of the Justices' law clerks is a disturbing commentary on the effect of bureaucratization on productivity.) The Court's

74. Justice Stevens is the holdout.
75. For statistics and sources, see Richard A. Posner, "The Supreme Court, 2004 Term: Foreword: A Political Court," 119 *Harvard Law Review* 31, 35–39 (2005).

mandatory jurisdiction has, it is true, been curtailed by Congress; the Court used to hear appeals that it would not have heard had they been petitions for certiorari, which is why that jurisdiction was curtailed. Yet that has not been a major factor in the caseload decline,[76] because prior to Congress's action the Court had "taken it upon itself to rewrite the statute and to treat most appeals as the equivalent of petitions for certiorari, subject only to discretionary review."[77] Anyway, the Court might have taken up any slack created by the curtailment of its mandatory jurisdiction by accepting more cases for review, important cases that it had not had time for when it was burdened by the mandatory jurisdiction.

It did not do so. One reason may be that the lower courts—perhaps because of the Court's penchant for laying down rules explicitly designed to guide them, or perhaps because of a growing professionalism in those courts as a result of more numerous and experienced clerks, the rise of computerized research, and more careful screening of candidates for lower-court judgeships—stray less frequently from the Court's directives. And here we may find the silver lining in the increased senatorial scrutiny that candidates for appointment to the federal courts of appeals have been required to undergo ever since it became clear in the early 1980s that President Reagan was using these appointments to try to change the ideological profile of the courts of appeals. The scrutiny is largely political in motivation and character and as a result tends to exclude candidates who are in either tail of the political distribution. So the courts of appeals are more centrist than they used to be, and the more centrist they are, the fewer intercircuit conflicts they produce for the Supreme Court to resolve and the fewer wild departures for the Court to rein in.

The decline in the Court's output provides a test of Hart's workload hypothesis—and does not support it. There is no evidence that the steep decline in the Justices' workload since the 1980s has led to better decisions. The decisions *may* be better, either because of an increase in the average quality of the Justices or the increase in the number and quality of their law clerks—the opinions are on average more polished, more

76. Margaret Meriwether Cordray and Richard Cordray, "The Supreme Court's Plenary Docket," 58 *Washington and Lee Law Review* 737, 751–758 (2001); Arthur D. Hellman, "The Shrunken Docket of the Rehnquist Court," 1996 *Supreme Court Review* 403, 410–412.

77. Erwin N. Griswold, "Rationing Justice—The Supreme Court's Caseload and What the Court Does Not Do," 60 *Cornell Law Review* 335, 346 (1975).

"professional" in appearance, than in days of yore—but not because the Justices have been conferring more. By all reports they have been conferring less because Chief Justice Rehnquist ran a crisper conference than his predecessor, Warren Burger. (Chief Justice Roberts is reported to be less impatient than Rehnquist was.) There are diminishing returns from effort. Probably even in Hart's time the point had been reached at which further judicial effort per case would not have yielded commensurate benefits.

Hart's acolytes might reply that all he meant was that if the Justices deliberated more they would produce better opinions, not that they would deliberate more if they had the time. But that is not the thrust of his Foreword. The thrust is that if only the Justices would stop granting certiorari in trivial cases—such as cases under the Federal Employers' Liability Act in which the only question was whether the plaintiff had enough evidence of the defendant's negligence to get to a jury—they would deliberate more. What was wanting, he seems to have thought, was not the will but the time.

That was wrong. But Hart's more interesting error was to think that dramatic improvements in the quality of judicial decision making would ensue if only the Justices talked out their differences at greater length. Hart was confused not only about the character of constitutional disputes but also about the nature of reasoning. This is apparent in the famous purple passage in which he said that

> the Court is predestined in the long run not only by the thrilling tradition of Anglo-American law but also by the hard facts of its position in the structure of American institutions to be a voice of reason, charged with the creative function of discerning afresh and of articulating and developing impersonal and durable principles of constitutional law.[78]

In everyday usage, the "voice of reason" means a reasonable response to a situation—calm, impartial, prudent, practical—rather than a response driven by a commitment to "principles." Drawing from a more technical vocabulary, we might speak of problem solving—that is, of reasoning from common premises—as "instrumental reason." Hart seems to have thought that "reason" in either of these senses (which he may not have distinguished in his own mind) would bring about convergence on con-

78. Hart, note 60 above, at 99.

stitutional doctrine if only the Justices would take the time to argue out their differences.

Hart's is a seminar model of the appellate process that comes naturally to academics. It is no accident that his claim that the Justices were not spending enough time in discussion echoed similar complaints by Justice Frankfurter and before him by Justice Brandeis.[79] All three were brilliant, articulate intellectuals; two were distinguished professors. It is a source of frustration to brilliant people to be unable to persuade their intellectual inferiors, and a natural reaction is to seek more time to persuade, knowing that they can out-argue their duller colleagues. What they may not realize, being intellectuals and therefore exaggerating the power of reasoned argument, is that such argument is ineffectual when the arguers do not share common premises and—what turns out to be related—that people do not surrender their deep-seated beliefs merely because they cannot match wits with the scoffers. (Robert Bork's intellectual distinction did not disarm his opponents.) In such situations the principal effect of arguing is, as Thurman Arnold noted and the psychological literature on group behavior confirms,[80] to drive the antagonists farther apart—or at least to cause them to dig in their heels.

When the premises for deciding a matter are shared, instrumental reason can generate conclusions that will convince all participants and observers; and collective deliberation may help in enabling conclusions to be derived from common premises. The process is kept honest by empirical verification: the airplane of novel design either flies or does not fly. But in most constitutional disputes, the disputants are not arguing from common premises. One thinks public safety more important than the rights of people accused of crimes; the other thinks the opposite. One views the actions of the police through the lens of a potential victim of a crime, the other through the lens of a person wrongfully accused. One worries about subtle forms of sexual harassment; the other (invariably male) worries about being falsely accused of harassment. One considers affirmative action naked discrimination; the other considers it social justice and a political necessity. One considers the banishment of religion

79. Dennis J. Hutchinson, "Felix Frankfurter and the Business of the Supreme Court, O.T. 1946–O.T. 1961," 1980 *Supreme Court Review* 143 (1980).

80. See, for example, Cass R. Sunstein, "Deliberative Trouble? Why Groups Go to Extremes," 110 *Yale Law Journal* 71 (2000); Daniel J. Isenberg, "Group Polarization: A Critical Review and Meta-Analysis," 50 *Journal of Personality and Social Psychology* 1141 (1986).

from public life a sacrilege and a moral disgrace; another fears that religion will penetrate and subvert government, turning the United States into a theocracy unless the government has no truck whatsoever with religion; a third fears that entangling religion with government, however slightly, hurts religion. One views abortion from the standpoint of the hapless fetus, the other from the standpoint of a woman forbidden to terminate an unwanted pregnancy. One values the states as laboratories for social experimentation; the other regards state government as provincial and local governments as little better than village tyrannies. One holds Thayer's view of judicial review; the other holds Justice Brennan's. The Justices either overlook the social scientific studies that might narrow some of these gaps or, as we saw in *Roper*, use them tendentiously.

The attitude of Supreme Court Justices toward deliberation is illustrated by Chief Justice Rehnquist's decision, when he fell seriously ill in the fall of 2004, to participate until he got better only in the decision of cases in which his would be the deciding vote. This bespeaks a voting model, not a deliberative model, of Supreme Court adjudication. In a deliberative model, the participation of all members of the Court in every case is important not only because the Justices are assumed in that model to be open to persuasion but also because each may be able to contribute to making the opinion in even a unanimous decision the best that it can be. In a voting model, participation is unimportant if one's vote is not going to be decisive.

Rehnquist was behaving in character. He had written illuminatingly about the nature of the deliberative process in the Supreme Court—so different from what Hart had imagined (or perhaps pretended to imagine) it to be:

> When I first went on the Court, I was both surprised and disappointed at how little interplay there was between the various justices during the process of conferring on a case. Each would state his views, and a junior justice could express agreement or disagreement with views expressed by a justice senior to him earlier in the discussion, but the converse did not apply; a junior justice's views were seldom commented upon, because votes had been already cast up the line. Probably most junior justices before me must have felt as I did, that they had some very significant contributions to make, and were disappointed that they hardly ever seemed to influence anyone because people didn't change their votes in response to their, the junior justices', contrary

views. I felt then it would be desirable to have more of a round-table discussion of the matter after each of us had expressed our ideas. Having now sat in conferences for nearly three decades, and having risen from ninth to first in seniority, I realize—with newfound clarity—that my idea as a junior justice, while fine in the abstract, probably would not have contributed much in practice, and at any rate was doomed by the seniority system to which the senior justices naturally adhere.

. . . If there were a real prospect that extended discussion would bring about crucial changes in position on the part of one or more members of the Court, that would be a strong argument for having that sort of discussion even with its attendant consumption of time. But my years on the Court have convinced me that the true purpose of the conference discussion of argued cases is not to persuade one's colleagues through impassioned advocacy to alter their views, but instead, by hearing each justice express his own views, to determine therefrom the view of the majority of the Court. This is not to say that minds are never changed in conference; they certainly are. But it is very much the exception and not the rule, and if one gives some thought to the matter, this should come as no surprise.[81]

What he was describing is perilously close to the traditional English model of judicial decision making without deliberation.

For all the deficiencies of his Foreword, Henry Hart was right that the Justices' institutional "surround" might constrain (rather than, as I have been emphasizing, unconstrain) their judicial performance. Even if the Supreme Court is really just a legislature in most of its constitutional cases, the method of selecting Justices, the terms and conditions of their employment, the resulting qualities and attitudes of the Justices, and the methods they use in legislating differ from the corresponding methods and circumstances of legislators. The differences may be so great that the product, even if legislative in a sense, so differs from the characteristic product of the official legislatures—is so much more disciplined, impersonal, reasoned, nonpartisan—as to be "lawlike" in the same sense that the common law, although also legislative rather than interpretive, is lawlike. Maybe when all the characteristics of the Court as an institution are considered—especially the fact that the Justices try to justify their decisions in reasoned opinions, which, even when they are advocacy products largely drafted by law clerks wet behind the ears, reflect a de-

---

81. William H. Rehnquist, *The Supreme Court* 254–255, 258 (2001).

gree of deliberation and a commitment to minimal coherence that are not demanded of legislative bodies—the correct conclusion is that the Justices' legislative discretion is really rather narrowly channeled. Maybe Hart's mistake was to focus too narrowly on the effect of caseload on judicial behavior.

The findings of the attitudinalists, along with other evidence examined in this book, suggest otherwise, of course. Yet those findings should not be allowed to obscure a major difference between Supreme Court Justices and (other) legislators, a difference stemming from the fact that legislators are elected for short, fixed terms and Justices are appointed for life, as well as from the difference in role expectations between politicians and judges. As a consequence of these differences, Justices are less partisan than elected officials—that is, less emotionally and intellectually tied to a particular political party. Democratic and Republican Justices are invariably less Democratic and Republican than their counterparts in elected officialdom, often to the chagrin of the appointing President. Appointment to a life-tenured position liberates federal judges from partisan commitments.

Nonpartisanship, unlike ideological neutrality, is an attainable ideal; indeed, it is the nearly automatic consequence of the Justices' not having to stand for election or kowtow to politicians, or indeed to anyone else. But "nonpartisan" is not the same as "nonpolitical." A person can be the former without being the latter—can even be the latter without being the former, for there are people whose identification with a political party is unrelated to a political preference, being a matter of family tradition or personal friendships rather than of political conviction. Still, with political parties in a two-party system being coalitions and as a result lacking intellectual coherence, Supreme Court Justices have motive and opportunity to forge for themselves a coherent, party-independent political identity. They are still political, but they are more detached and thoughtful than the "official" politicians. So maybe—this is the implicit view of many constitutional scholars, and of some Justices as well—Justices are better legislators than the members of Congress and state legislatures and would be better still if the institutional setting could be made more conducive to deliberation. (There is an echo of Henry Hart in this suggestion.)

The suggestion is difficult to defend convincingly, however, because of differences between judges and the official legislators that undercut the claim of judges' legislative superiority. Except for Justice Thomas, the current Justices of the Supreme Court grew up in privileged circumstances and do not rub shoulders with hoi polloi. Sheltered, cosseted members of the upper middle class, and, most of them, quite wealthy, the Justices are less representative of the American public than elected officials are. They also lack ready access to much of the information that elected officials obtain routinely in the course of their work. They have much smaller, less specialized staffs, and as lawyers they have professional biases and prejudices that can distort their legislative judgments. Cocooned in their marble palace, attended by sycophantic staff, and treated with extreme deference wherever they go, Supreme Court Justices are at risk of acquiring an exaggerated opinion of their ability and character. In a democratic society of great size and complexity, it is difficult to justify giving a committee of lawyer aristocrats the power not just to find or apply the law and make up enough law to fill in the many gaps in the law that is given to them, but also to create out of whole cloth, or out of their guts, large swatches of law that as a practical matter they alone can alter.

A great weakness of the Court as a legislative body is that it does not have its hands on enough of the levers of power to effectuate grand designs. (This could of course be thought its saving grace—that the Court is mischievous rather than prepotent.) The Court was able to eliminate the stigma of officially segregated schools, but not segregation itself. It could create new procedural rights for criminal defendants—a major project of the Court in the 1960s—but legislatures could and did offset the effect by increasing the severity of criminal sentences. Maybe fewer innocent people were convicted, but those who were served longer sentences;[82] the total misery of the wrongfully convicted was not lessened. The Court altered the structure of state legislatures by requiring that both the lower and the upper houses of every state legislature be apportioned by population, but possibly without effect on the content of state legislation.[83] The Court created a right to abortion, but in states

82. In the 1960s, the average federal criminal sentence was 34.4 months. It rose to 40.4 months in the 1970s and to 59.6 months for the period between 1994 and 2003. Bureau of Justice Statistics, U.S. Department of Justice, *Sourcebook of Criminal Justice Statistics—2003* 424–425 (1996) (tab. 5.23).

83. Stephen Ansolabehere and James M. Snyder, Jr., "Reapportionment and Party Realignment in the American States," 153 *University of Pennsylvania Law Review* 433, 434 (2004); William H. Riker, "Democracy and Representation: A Reconciliation of *Ball v. James* and *Reynolds v.*

where abortion is unpopular a variety of legal and extralegal pressures continue, more than 30 years later, to deny many women access to abortion.[84]

At the opposite extreme from Hart's technocratic conception of the Supreme Court is the idea of the Court as a moral vanguard. Evaluating this idea might not seem to belong in a discussion of *alternatives* to the conception of the Court as a political court; the idea might seem the quintessence of a political approach. I am inclined to agree, but the proponents do not think so. Believers in natural law as a source of or limitation on positive law do not think they are politicizing law. No more did Alexander Bickel, in his influential Foreword published two years after Hart's, in which he cast the Court in the role of a secular Moses that would lead the American people out of their moral wilderness.[85]

Like Hart, Bickel was much taken with "principles." "Principles" in the sense in which both of them, following Herbert Wechsler,[86] used the term echoes the Aristotelian origins of the idea of the rule of law and some of the modern derivatives of the idea, such as the notion of equal protection of the laws and the related notion that legislation should be general and prospective. One way to try to prevent judges from picking and choosing among litigants on inappropriate grounds is to require that legal rules be general in their application rather than pinpointed on specific individuals or groups, just as requiring that legislation be prospective makes it difficult for a legislature to target its enemies. This does not tell us what the *content* of the rules should be. But reading Bickel's Foreword one realizes that he had definite ideas about where the public policy of the United States should be moving and that these ideas were his "principles." They were *political* ideas, and Bickel realized that the Su-

---

Sims," 1 *Supreme Court Economic Review* 39, 41–55 (1982). But see Jeffrey R. Lax and Mathew D. McCubbins, "Courts, Congress, and Public Policy, Part II: The Impact of the Reapportionment Revolution on Congress and State Legislatures," 15 *Journal of Contemporary Legal Issues* 199 (2006).

84. In 2000, 34 percent of women ages 15 to 44 lived in the 87 percent of the nation's counties that have no abortion clinic or other provider, and 86 of the nation's 276 metropolitan areas had no provider. Lawrence B. Finer and Stanley K. Henshaw, "Abortion Incidence and Services in the United States in 2000," 35 *Perspectives on Sexual and Reproductive Health* 6 (2003). See also Guttmacher Institute, "State Policies in Brief: An Overview of Abortion Laws," Sept. 2007, http://guttmacher.org/statecenter/spibs/spib_OAL.pdf (visited Sept. 11, 2007).

85. Alexander M. Bickel, "The Supreme Court, 1960 Term: Foreword: The Passive Virtues," 75 *Harvard Law Review* 40, 77 (1961).

86. Wechsler, note 26 above, at 15–20.

preme Court had to move carefully in imposing them on the nation because other institutions would fight back. For Bickel and his judicial avatar, Guido Calabresi, the Supreme Court is not (quite) political (it is "principled"), but it is in a tense political competition with the elective institutions.[87]

There is an air of condescension in Bickel's Foreword: the Court has an "educational function" that it performs by "engag[ing] in a Socratic dialogue with the other institutions and with society as a whole concerning the necessity for this or that measure, for this or that compromise."[88] It is apparent in this account who is Socrates and who are Socrates' stooges; who is the law professor and who are the law students. As in Hart's Foreword there are many admiring references to Justice Frankfurter, the only professor on the Supreme Court at the time. (Bickel had clerked for Frankfurter.)

The sense of substantive direction, what we might call the teleological mode, is missing from the school of Hart—Hart the Progressive, the technocrat (it is never very clear what substantive principles he embraced). Bickel's project is clothed in references to principles, but the clothing is diaphanous. He wanted to make the United States more civilized by his lights but realized that the Court, because of the limits of its power, could achieve such an aim only if it was politically adroit. That would require it to avoid giving "bad" legislation that it did not yet dare condemn the imprimatur of constitutionality (the Court should exercise its discretionary power to refuse to hear the case), which the ignorant laity would treat as an endorsement, and instead to engage legislatures in a coercive "dialogue."[89] (So here is an echo of Hart's faith in deliberation, but a faint one, because of the one-sidedness of Bickelian dialogue.) Bad state legislation should be invalidated on narrow grounds that give the states the illusion that if they did a better job of articulating the concerns underlying the legislation, or at least expressed their desire for the legislation more forcefully, it might survive.[90] But it would be a Bickelian

87. See, for example, Quill v. Vacco, 80 F.3d 716, 738–743 (2d Cir. 1996) (Calabresi, J., concurring), reversed, 521 U.S. 793 (1997); United States v. Then, 56 F.3d 464, 469 (2d Cir. 1995) (Calabresi, J., concurring); Guido Calabresi, "The Supreme Court, 1990 Term: Foreword: Antidiscrimination and Constitutional Accountability (What the Bork-Brennan Debate Ignores)," 105 *Harvard Law Review* 80, 103–108 (1991).

88. Bickel, note 85 above, at 50. See also id. at 64.

89. Id. at 47–58.

90. Id. at 58–64.

Court's hope that the legislators would have their eyes opened by the Court's tutorial, or that efforts at reenactment would founder on the inertial difficulty of enacting legislation.

Bickel's Foreword discusses at length the Connecticut anti-contraception statute later invalidated in the *Griswold* decision. He was mindful that nothing in the Constitution or in the Court's previous decisions seemed to bear on such a statute; family and sex law had long been thought prerogatives of the states. But he did not want the Court to affirm the constitutionality of—and thus give a boost to—such a bad statute, and so he recommended that the Court invalidate it on the narrow ground that because it was not being enforced it should be deemed abandoned.[91] Such a ruling would allow the state to reenact it. But because it is much more difficult to enact a statute than to leave it unenforced (or weakly enforced, as in the case of the Connecticut statute) on the books, probably it would not be reenacted and so Bickel's goal would be achieved without a confrontation with the state over the power to regulate contraception.

The moral vanguard school of constitutional theory exemplified by Bickel (who actually referred approvingly to "the Court's function of defining the moral goals of government"[92]), although it uses all the tricks of the lawyerly trade to work its will, implicitly conceives of the Supreme Court as a freewheeling legislative body, albeit a more enlightened one than "real" legislatures; conceives of it in fact as a legislature with a bully pulpit from which, not being tongue-tied by partisan commitments, it can preach in clarion tones to the multitude. But being more enlightened it has to bring the elected officials and public opinion along by subtle maneuvers:

> The resources of rhetoric and the techniques of avoidance enable the Court to exert immense influence. It can explain the principle that is in play and praise it; it can guard its integrity. The Court can require

91. "A device to turn the thrust of forces favoring and opposing the present objectives of the statute toward the legislature, where the power of at least initial decision properly belongs in our system, was available to the Court, and it is implicit in the prevailing opinion [Poe v. Ullman, 367 U.S. 497 (1961)]. It is the concept of desuetude." Bickel, note 85 above, at 61. But the Court invalidated the Connecticut statute not on the ground of desuetude, but as an infringement of a constitutional right of privacy (an Aesopian term meaning sexual freedom), Griswold v. Connecticut, 381 U.S. 479, 485–486 (1965). Actually the statute was not wholly ineffectual; it prevented the creation of birth control clinics. Posner, note 49 above, at 205.

92. Bickel, note 85 above, at 79.

the countervailing necessity to be affirmed by a responsible political decision, squarely faced and made with awareness of the principle on which it impinges. The Court can even, possibly, . . . require a second decision.[93]

The Court is a teacher in a class of slow learners consisting of the people and their elected representatives.

We should mark the family resemblance between Bickel's moral vanguardism, despite its cloak of principle, and the active side of Holmes's "can't helps" or "puke" test. Both are delaying games in the sense that if public opinion adamantly favors some policy that the Justices cannot stomach, eventually they will have to give way. The moral vanguard has to stop its march if there is no one following it. But there is an important difference between them. Bickel thought the Justices could educate the masses to fall in line with the Justices' superior insights. Holmes harbored no such hopes, which he would have described as illusions, because he was skeptical of the force of moral reasoning.

Today the leading moral vanguardist on the Supreme Court is Justice Kennedy. But he ignores Bickel's warning against Justices' tipping their hands. Kennedy is a kind of judicial Ronald Dworkin, who also will have no truck with disguises. The slogan of both could be—borrowing from the Army's former recruiting slogan "Be All That You Can Be"—"Make the Constitution All That It Can Be." A newer Army slogan, "An Army of One," could describe Justice Kennedy's Court, given his significance as the sole swing Justice now that O'Connor has retired. In all 24 of the Court's 5–4 decisions in the 2006 term, Kennedy was in the majority.

Justice Kennedy's opinions in *Lawrence v. Texas*[94] (the homosexual sodomy case) and *Roper v. Simmons* make only limited efforts to ground decision in conventional legal materials. They could not do more, operating with nondirective constitutional provisions and in the teeth of adverse precedent. They are appeals to moral principles that a great many Americans either disagree with or think inapplicable to homosexuals and juvenile murderers. The approach is consistent, however, with the judicial philosophy that Justice Kennedy expressed in the interview from which I quoted in chapter 9, when he said that "all of us have an instinctive judgment that we make . . . You make these quick judgments

93. Id. at 77.
94. 539 U.S. 558 (2003).

. . . Judges do the same thing . . . But after you make a judgment, you then . . . have to see if that . . . accords with your own sense of ethics and morality. And . . . [you have to understand] that you have the opportunity to shape the destiny of this country. The framers wanted you to shape the destiny of the country. They didn't want to frame it for you." This is the most powerful judge in America speaking, and, if we may judge from his decisions, meaning what he says—that the framers of the Constitution wanted Anthony Kennedy to shape the destiny of the country in accordance with his own sense of ethics and morality, though it strikes many as quirky.[95]

There is a messianic quality to Kennedy that sorts ill with the conventional conception of a judge. Consider his reliance in both *Lawrence* and *Roper* on decisions of foreign courts. I discuss the pros and cons of such reliance in chapter 12; its imprudence is shown by the surprising antipathy it has aroused[96]—surprising because the citations in judicial opinions rarely receive attention in the lay press. But more interesting is the relation of citing foreign decisions to moral vanguardism. It seems that Kennedy is a natural lawyer—a believer in the existence of universal moral principles (the source of his "own sense of ethics and morality") that inform—and constrain—positive law. If the principles are indeed universal, they might be expected to leave traces in the decisions of foreign courts.

Strip *Roper v. Simmons* of its fig leaves—the psychological literature that it misused, the global consensus to which it pointed, the national consensus that it concocted by treating states that have abolished capital

95. Consider this strange passage from Kennedy's opinion for the Court in the partial-birth abortion case, Gonzales v. Carhart, note 21 above, at 1634: "Respect for human life finds an ultimate expression in the bond of love the mother has for her child." Loving your child and therefore wanting him to live shows no respect for human life in general. Most Nazis loved their children. And what has the point to do with partial-birth abortion? Most women who have an abortion do not think they are killing a child. If that is what they are doing, the implication (which I am sure Justice Kennedy does not accept) is that failure to criminalize abortion is a denial of equal protection of the laws in the original sense of equal protection of the laws: it is the systematic and deliberate withdrawal of police protection from a large class of children. What does it tell us about the commitment to legalism of the four most conservative Justices of the Supreme Court that they should have joined such a wild opinion?

96. See, for example, Dana Milbank, "And the Verdict on Justice Kennedy Is: Guilty," *Washington Post,* Apr. 9, 2005, p. A3; Dennis Byrne, "Trampling All Over State Legislatures," *Chicago Tribune,* Mar. 7, 2005, p. 15; Ed Feulner, "Courting Trouble," *Washington Times,* Mar. 16, 2005, p. A18; Jonathan Gurwitz, "If It Pleases the Court, Law by Consensus," *San Antonio Express-News,* Mar. 13, 2005, p. 3H.

punishment as having decided that juveniles have a special claim not to be executed (the equivalent of saying that these states had decided that octogenarians deserve a special immunity from capital punishment)—and you reveal a nakedly political decision. A decision taking sides on a moral issue that divides the public along approximately party lines and cannot be resolved by expert analysis, let alone by conventional legal reasoning, is a political decision.

A court can as I said be political without being pragmatic, but it can also be political *and* pragmatic. *Zelman v. Simmons-Harris*[97] upheld the constitutionality of funneling public monies to private schools by giving parents vouchers that they can use to pay for their children's tuition. Most private schools are Catholic parochial schools. Although the decision was inescapably political—a taking of sides on an issue that divides the Democratic and Republican parties—it was also pragmatic. There is a great deal of dissatisfaction with American public education. A voucher system would encourage competition in public education, and competition in turn could be expected to improve education—either directly by driving the worst school administrations from the market or indirectly by stimulating new approaches to education, or both. But these benefits could not be realized if voucher systems were declared unconstitutional. Such a declaration would strangle a worthwhile social experiment in its cradle.

Opponents consider vouchers a form of public subsidy to the Catholic Church. Should that turn out to be their effect (as is unlikely, since they stimulate the creation of new secular private schools by providing parents with the wherewithal to bypass public schools in favor of secular as well as religious private schools), there will be time enough to invalidate them. Because Supreme Court Justices are unlikely to develop a taste for social science, social experiments are necessary to generate the data needed for intelligent constitutional rule making.[98] Granted, decisions create reliance and even bring into existence interest groups that will defend the decisions—busing as a remedy for school segregation attracted the enthusiastic support of companies that manufacture or lease school buses. So if vouchers spread like wildfire, the Court might have difficulty putting out the flames.

97. 536 U.S. 639 (2002).
98. Michael C. Dorf, "The Supreme Court, 1997 Term: Foreword: The Limits of Socratic Deliberation," 112 *Harvard Law Review* 4, 60–69 (1998).

Five years after *Zelman* there is no evidence either that school voucher systems are multiplying rapidly or, as the dissenting Justices worried, that they are fomenting religious strife. Yet if someone were to challenge the arguments for the voucher decision—whether on the ground that even indirect financial assistance to parochial schools is an "establishment" of religion according to the best understanding of the Court's previous decisions, or that a voucher system will fatally weaken public education and by doing so undermine a variety of civic values—there would be no killer riposte. Although the impact of voucher systems on public schools, and on educational performance generally, is an empirical issue, there was no way in which the Court could have determined its validity before the systems went into effect.

With *Zelman* compare the decision in the *Seattle School District* case striking down public school affirmative action programs.[99] Activist and unpragmatic, the decision is in conflict with the spirit of *Zelman*. Rather than encouraging experimentation in our troubled education system, it throws a monkey wrench into the efforts of public schools to cope with the vexing issue of race. The plurality opinion in *Seattle School District* pretends most unpragmatically that invalidation of the affirmative action programs was compelled by the sanctified precedent of *Brown v. Board of Education,* thus excusing the Justices from having to consider the practical consequences of their decision. While reading *Brown* broadly, the Justices read the Court's decisions that actually involved affirmative action, as *Brown* of course did not, narrowly. The dissenters—the four liberal Justices—complained loudly. But they behave like the conservative Justices when the shoe is on the other foot. *Zelman* and *Seattle School District* are equally grist for the attitudinal mill. Both involve the issue of judicial intervention in the management of schools. In *Zelman* the conservative Justices, who favor private education and religion and dislike affirmative action, voted against judicial intervention and the liberal Justices voted for it. In *Seattle School District* the liberal Justices, who favor public education and affirmative action and do not wear religion on their sleeves, voted against judicial intervention and the conservative Justices voted for it.

Zelman was a good decision from a pragmatic standpoint because it allowed a social experiment to be conducted, *Seattle School District* a bad

99. Note 29 above.

one because it interrupted a social experiment on legalist grounds without considering the likely consequences of its intervention.[100] In between is *Kelo v. City of New London*, which upheld the condemnation of private property for use in an urban development project as a "public use," and thus within the state's eminent domain power, even though the condemned land was to be transferred to the private developers of the project.[101] The only reason the Court gave for thinking that the project might benefit the public rather than just the private developers and (new) owners was that "the area [of the redevelopment project, a waterfront area in downtown New London, Connecticut] was sufficiently distressed to justify a program of economic rejuvenation."[102] This question-begging justification ("distressed") opened the way to the parade of horribles in Justice O'Connor's dissent, in which we read that "the specter of condemnation hangs over all property."[103] If "economic rejuvenation" is a public use, what is to prevent a city from condemning the homes of lower-middle-class families and giving them free of charge to multimillionaires, provided it can show that the new owners would be likely to pay enough for various local goods and services, and in property and other local taxes, to offset the expense of compensating the owners of the condemned properties at market value?

The majority and dissenting opinions spar over the original meaning of the term "public use" and over the correct interpretation of the previous cases in which the condemnation of property for the purpose of transferring it to a private entity had been challenged (and in this back-and-forth the majority has the better of the argument). They do not ask practical questions: What is the reason for eminent domain? Does the New London development plan comport with that reason? What have been the economic and social consequences of such development projects?

The power of eminent domain seems at first glance a strikingly arbitrary method of taxation. When the power is exercised, the condemnor

---

100. In chapter 9, I gave another example of an unpragmatic Supreme Court decision—*Clinton v. Jones*.

101. 545 U.S. 469 (2005).

102. Id. at 483.

103. Id. at 503. Note the echo—could it be deliberate, the work of a law clerk with a sense of humor?—of the opening sentence of the *Communist Manifesto*: "A spectre is haunting Europe, the spectre of communism." Karl Marx and Friedrich Engels, *The Communist Manifesto* 1 (1998 [1848]).

is required to pay only the market value of the condemned property. Ordinarily an owner's subjective valuation will exceed the property's market value because the property fits his needs or tastes particularly well or because relocation would be costly. Otherwise he probably would have sold it. A private purchaser who wanted the property would therefore have to pay a price sufficiently higher than the market value to compensate the owner for the loss of these idiosyncratic, property-specific values. Awareness of such values explains why courts are more likely to deem inadequate a damages remedy for breach of contract, and thus to order specific performance, when the contract is for the sale of land than when it is for the sale of a fungible type of property. The eminent domain power allows the government to obtain property by paying just its market value and by doing so to extinguish idiosyncratic values; in effect they are taxed away to help pay for the acquisition. If the market value of a condemned property is $100,000 and its total value (including idiosyncratic value) is $125,000, condemnation in effect enables the government to pay for the property with $100,000 out of its own coffers and $25,000 out of the owner's pocket.

The only justification for this form of taxation is the existence of holdout problems, problems best illustrated when the power of eminent domain is employed, whether on behalf of government, in the case of highways, or of private firms, such as railroads, telephone companies, and pipeline companies, that provide point-to-point services. The ability of a railroad, for example, to operate between two points depends on its acquiring an easement from every one of the intervening landowners, and knowing this each landowner will hold out for a very high price. Eminent domain in these situations is an antimonopoly device.[104]

Holdout problems are not limited to right-of-way situations. They can arise whenever someone wants to assemble a large tract of land that is divided into many individually owned parcels. So a pragmatist would want to ask whether that was the situation in New London; if not, it would be a good case for placing a limit on the concept of public use. It is hard to tell from the opinions. The city wanted to redevelop a 90-acre tract adjoining a site on which Pfizer had decided to build a large research facility. The plaintiffs owned 15 lots in parts of the tract that were

104. On the simple economics of eminent domain, see Richard A. Posner, *Economic Analysis of Law* § 3.7, pp. 55–61 (7th ed. 2007); Steven Shavell, *Foundations of Economic Analysis of Law* 123–136 (2004).

either to be developed for office space, in the hope that Pfizer's proximity would attract other businesses, or to be used for parking, for retail stores catering to visitors, for facilities ancillary to a nearby marina, or for some combination of these uses. Conceivably, leaving the plaintiffs' 15 homes in place, scattered throughout these areas and thus giving rise to what New London's brief colorfully termed the "spotted leopard" problem, would make it difficult to develop the areas for their intended uses; imagine a parking lot dotted with houses. If so, the plaintiffs had holdout power that may have justified the use of eminent domain to obtain their property.

The Court mentions the holdout issue only in passing. The opinions do not even indicate the size of either the plaintiffs' lots or the 2 parcels (out of the 7 that constituted the 90-acre tract that was condemned) that contained those lots, although from the briefs one learns that one of the parcels was 2.4 acres in size and the plaintiffs' lots occupied 0.76 acres in it, which was almost one-third of the total area and so might indeed have presented a holdout problem. But as I will note shortly and the Court briefly acknowledged,[105] it is uncertain whether private developers actually need the aid of eminent domain to solve holdout problems.

The majority opinion does not acknowledge that whether a change in land use is a good thing is not the same question as whether eminent domain is a proper method of bringing about the change. If a property would be worth more in a different use and there is no holdout obstacle to transacting with the existing owner, the market will take care of shifting the property to its more valuable use; there is no need for the government to assist.

The minimal attention given to the issue of holdouts (even though it was discussed at length in the briefs and mentioned at the oral argument[106]) supports Justice O'Connor's concern that the decision signifies the abandonment of any limitation on "public use" except that the condemning authority be acting in good faith. But her argument would have been more convincing had she given some examples of actual, as distinct from imagined, abuses of the eminent domain power. She gave none but merely—in typical lawyer fashion—cited a few cases, a brief, and a single study that she made no attempt to evaluate despite its be-

105. 545 U.S. at 489 n. 24.
106. Transcript of Oral Argument, pp. 39–40, www.supremecourtus.gov/oral_arguments/argument_transcripts/04–108.pdf (visited May 2, 2007).

ing an advocacy document of doubtful objectivity.[107] If the inference from this meager documentation is that abuse of the eminent domain power is infrequent—an inference supported by the sparseness of the references to eminent domain in the scholarship on urban redevelopment[108]—then it is hard to work up indignation about municipalities' being allowed to continue exercising the power. Placing limits on that exercise can be reserved for a case in which it is plain that the power was abused.

A point O'Connor might have made but did not is that private developers who want to assemble a large contiguous parcel of land seem generally able to do so by employing "straw man" purchasers.[109] That it is difficult for government to operate with the requisite secrecy is a bad argument for allowing government to use eminent domain on behalf of private developers; it should let the developers fend for themselves.

A political interpretation of the *Kelo* decision is that liberal Justices give the benefit of the doubt to the government when it opposes property rights, while eminent domain is a bête noire of conservatives because it overrides those rights. The four liberal Justices, joined by Justice Kennedy, made up the majority, though Kennedy, while joining Justice Stevens's opinion, wrote a concurring opinion indicating reservations about eminent domain that do not appear in Stevens's opinion. The three most conservative Justices—Rehnquist, Scalia, and Thomas—dissented, joined by O'Connor, whose opinion demonstrates her solicitude for property rights.

An alternative explanation for the result in the case is simply that the

107. 545 U.S. at 503. The study, undertaken on behalf of private developers, is a detailed examination of a large number of recent eminent domain proceedings. Dana Berliner, "Public Power, Private Gain: A Five-Year, State-by-State Report Examining the Abuse of Eminent Domain" (2003), www.castlecoalition.org/pdf/report/ED_report.pdf (visited May 2, 2007). In many of the cases discussed, the court rebuffed the attempt to use eminent domain. In others, though the use of eminent domain appears questionable, the report's presentation is one-sided, and it is difficult to make a judgment about the reasonableness of the use of the power. The report does not discuss holdout problems.

108. Note, for example, the sparse index references to eminent domain in *Revitalizing Urban Neighborhoods* 276 (W. Dennis Keating et al. eds. 1996), and the absence of such references in Charles C. Euchner and Stephen J. McGovern, *Urban Policy Reconsidered: Dialogues on the Problems and Prospects of American Cities* 343 (2003). Even scholars hostile to urban development projects rarely refer to eminent domain. See, for example, James V. DeLong, *Property Matters: How Property Rights Are under Assault—and Why You Should Care* 378 (1997).

109. Daniel B. Kelly, "The 'Public Use' Requirement in Eminent Domain Law: A Rationale Based on Secret Purchases and Private Influence," 92 *Cornell Law Review* 1, 20–24 (2006).

Court's majority was prudently reluctant to become involved in the details of urban redevelopment. A flat rule against a taking in which the land that is taken ends up in the hands of private companies would be unsound and was not urged by the dissenters. An amicus curiae brief on behalf of the American Farm Bureau Federation gave a number of examples of what appear to be foolish, wasteful, and exploitive redevelopment plans. It is unclear how representative the examples are, yet it would not be surprising to discover that most redevelopment plans are unholy collusions between the real estate industry and local politicians. But if so, there is little the Supreme Court can do. The more limitations the Court placed on the private development of condemned land, the more active the government itself would become in development. Had the City of New London built office space, parking lots, and the like on land that it had condemned, a challenge based on the "public use" limitation would have been unlikely to succeed—unless the Court confined "public use" to holdout situations and was prepared to try to determine, case by case, whether a genuine holdout situation existed. But this is a thicket the Court is not minded to enter, as evidenced by *Eldred v. Ashcroft,*[110] which upheld the constitutionality of the Sonny Bono Copyright Term Extension Act against the argument that extending the copyright term from life plus 50 years to life plus 70 years was inconsistent with the purpose of the Constitution's empowering Congress to authorize copyrights only for "limited Times." It *was* inconsistent, but the courts do not have the intellectual tools for determining how long copyright protection should last.

Another complication unremarked by the Court in *Kelo* is that tightening up the public use requirement, and thus curtailing the government's power to use eminent domain, would increase the expense to the government of acquiring property. The higher expense, except insofar as it deterred acquisitions, would beget higher taxes, which might have as arbitrary an incidence as the taxation of idiosyncratic land values through exercise of the eminent domain power. Along with the possibility that constricting the concept of public use would induce the government to develop property itself, the unpredictable tax effects of curtailing the eminent domain power illustrate the difficulty the Supreme Court has in bringing about durable social change when it does not con-

110. 537 U.S. 186 (2003).

trol the full array of public policy instruments. The Court cannot regulate the taxing power or prevent the government from engaging in real estate development.

Paradoxically, the strong adverse public and legislative reactions to the *Kelo* decision[111] are evidence of its pragmatic soundness. When the Court declines to invalidate an unpopular government power, it tosses the issue back into the democratic arena. The opponents of a broad interpretation of "public use" now know that the Court will not give them the victory they seek. They will have to roll up their sleeves and fight the battle in Congress and the state legislatures—where they may well prevail. Property owners and the advocates of property rights are not a helpless, marginalized minority. They have plenty of political muscle, which they are free to use, since there is no constitutional impediment to the government's declining to exercise the full range of powers that the Constitution, as interpreted by the Supreme Court, allows it. The responses of Congress and the states will constitute a series of social experiments from which much will be learned about the proper limits on eminent domain.

So the result in *Kelo* may be pragmatically defensible, but the Court articulated no pragmatic defense. This is typical, and is the obverse of the practice of citing foreign decisions as authority. Pragmatic reasons do not sound very lawlike, whereas citing decisions of a judicial body— any judicial body—sounds quintessentially lawlike in a system, which is the U.S. system, of case law. Moreover, to go beyond the simplest type of pragmatic reasoning—such as let's keep out of this briar patch—would require the Court to develop a taste for empirical inquiry. Like most judges, Supreme Court Justices (abetted by their law clerks, from whom experience has yet to rub off the legalist undercoat applied to them by

111. See, for example, John Ryskamp, *The Eminent Domain Revolt: Changing Perceptions in a New Constitutional Epoch* (2007); Daniel H. Cole, "Why *Kelo* Is Not Good News for Local Planners and Developers," 22 *Georgia State University Law Review* 803 (2006); Abraham Bell and Gideon Parchomovsky, "The Uselessness of Public Use," 106 *Columbia Law Review* 1412, 1413–1426 (2006); Donald E. Sanders and Patricia Pattison, "The Aftermath of *Kelo*," 34 *Real Estate Law Journal* 157 (2005); Timothy Egan, "Ruling Sets Off Tug of War over Private Property," *New York Times*, July 30, 2005, p. A1; Kenneth R. Harney, "Eminent Domain Ruling Has Strong Repercussions," *Washington Post*, July 23, 2005, p. F1; Adam Karlin, "Property Seizure Backlash," *Christian Science Monitor*, July 6, 2005, p. 1. According to the National Conference of State Legislatures' tracking of eminent domain legislation, www.ncsl.org/programs/natres/ EMINDOMAIN.htm (visited Oct. 4, 2007), 32 states have enacted legislation provoked by *Kelo*.

their law school education) are more comfortable with opinions that remain on the semantic surface of issues, arguing over the meaning of malleable terms such as "public use" or "cruel and unusual punishments" rather than over the consequences of adopting one meaning over another. This has the political value, moreover, of disguising the political character of Supreme Court decision making.

Justice Breyer (of whom I shall have more to say in the next chapter) is generally regarded as the most pragmatic member of the current Supreme Court. Yet he dissented in *Zelman,* joined *Clinton v. Jones* (though with an uneasy concurrence, sensing trouble ahead), is an enthusiastic citer of foreign decisions (but at least he is fluent in French), and joined Justice Stevens's majority opinion in *Kelo* without writing separately to explore the interests at stake. But he redeemed himself by his vote and separate opinion in *Van Orden v. Perry,*[112] one of the two Ten Commandments decisions the Court handed down on the last day of its 2004 term. In the other, *McCreary County v. ACLU,*[113] a five-Justice majority including Breyer invalidated the display of the Ten Commandments in a county courthouse. He switched sides in *Van Orden,* creating a five-Justice majority to permit a monument inscribed with the Ten Commandments to remain on display on the grounds of the Texas state capitol. The majority agreed only on the result, because Justice Breyer did not join Chief Justice Rehnquist's opinion. There are passages in that opinion that I imagine struck rather the wrong chord for Breyer, notably the statement that "recognition of the role of God in our Nation's heritage has also been reflected in our decisions."[114] Whether God has actually played a role in the nation's history is a theological question, the answer to which depends first on whether there is a God and, if so, whether He intervenes in the life of nations and has some special fondness for the United States. It is odd for the Supreme Court to offer answers to these questions. But perhaps all that the Chief Justice meant by "God" was invocations of God, and all that he meant by "heritage" was the national culture.

Rehnquist was on solid ground in enumerating some of the countless invocations of the Deity in American public life, including many approving references to the Ten Commandments. He inferred that "the in-

112. 545 U.S. 677 (2005).
113. 545 U.S. 844 (2005).
114. 545 U.S. at 687.

clusion of the Ten Commandments monument" in a varied, one might even say (though with no disrespect intended) motley, assemblage of monuments on the Texas state capitol grounds—dedicated to everything from "Heroes of the Alamo" (of course) to Texas cowboys, Texas school-children, volunteer firemen, and Confederate soldiers[115]—"has a dual significance, partaking of both religion and government."[116]

The implication is that a secular purpose can redeem a religious dis-play even if the secular purpose is not paramount, and Breyer was un-willing to go that far. Instead he looked into the history of the Ten Com-mandments monument and discovered that it had been donated to Texas by the Fraternal Order of Eagles, a primarily secular organiza-tion that "sought to highlight the Commandments' role in shaping civic morality as part of that organization's efforts to combat juvenile delin-quency."[117] From this and other facts, including that it had taken 40 years for anyone to complain about the state's sponsoring a religious dis-play, Breyer concluded that the monument's predominant purpose was to convey a secular message about the historical ideals of Texans.

The reference to the many years without a lawsuit seems at first en-counter off-key—it fairly invites the American Civil Liberties Union to sue the minute it learns of any new display of the Ten Commandments on public property. But as Breyer explained, the dearth of complaints "helps us understand that as a practical matter of *degree* this display is unlikely to prove divisive," whereas "to reach a contrary conclusion . . . might well encourage disputes concerning the removal of longstanding depictions of the Ten Commandments from public buildings across the Nation. And it could thereby create the very kind of religiously based di-visiveness that the Establishment Clause seeks to avoid."[118] In other words, if, as the Justices who dissented in *Van Orden* appear to believe, the Constitution forbids any and all "governmental displays of sacred re-ligious texts,"[119] a decision so holding would trigger an ACLU-led cam-paign to purge the entire public space of the United States of displays of the Ten Commandments, ubiquitous as they are. It is hard to imagine not only a more divisive but also a more doctrinaire and even absurd

115. Id. at 681 n. 1.
116. Id. at 692.
117. Id. at 701.
118. Id. at 704 (emphasis in original).
119. Id. at 735 (Stevens, J., dissenting).

project, faintly echoing as it would the campaigns of Mexico, Republican Spain, and the Soviet Union in the 1930s against the churches of those countries, not to mention the destruction of religious images by the Iconoclasts of eighth-century Byzantium.

What the dissenters in *Van Orden* missed is the dual religio-secular character of the Ten Commandments, which resembles the dual religio-secular character of Christmas and renders the invocation of the Ten Commandments innocuous in most settings—though perhaps not, as the plurality opinion in *Van Orden* suggests, in all. Christmas is a religious holiday for believing Christians, but it is also a national holiday, and a secular holiday for children, for shoppers and retailers, and even for most atheists (they are shoppers, and some of them are even children). So salient is the secular dimension that it requires rather a special effort to remind people of the religious significance of Christmas. The Ten Commandments are similarly multifaceted. They are a set of religious commands for believing Christians and Jews, a set of moral imperatives (thou shalt not kill, thou shalt not bear false witness, etc.) as binding on the nonbeliever as on the believer, a literary rendition of moral duties, a Hollywood spectacular,[120] a milestone of Western intellectual history, and, to the cynical, a set of clichés and anachronisms (such as do not covet thy neighbor's cattle) and pathetic overstatements of duty. Most of the commandments are not explicitly religious, and those that are get the least attention—who but the Taliban has been worrying lately about graven images, or even about taking the Lord's name in vain? The spirit of Justice Souter's dissent in *Van Orden* puts one in mind of bowdlerizers and the (literal) fig-leafers. For he would permit the display of the Ten Commandments on public property only if they were secularized by placing Moses in the company of nonreligious figures such as Plato, Beethoven, or Equity—preferably with the text of the commandments, like the private parts of a fig-leafed statue, invisible.[121]

The obvious criticism to make of Breyer's opinion in *Van Orden* is that it does not enunciate a rule that would enable the lower courts and the

120. Earnings from the Cecil B. DeMille movie *The Ten Commandments* helped to finance the Eagles' project, which DeMille personally encouraged, of placing Ten Commandments monuments throughout the United States. See "Supreme Court Issues Rulings on Ten Commandments Cases," *Ten Commandments News,* June 15, 2005, http://10commandments.biz/biz/newsletter/2005/june/supreme_court_ten_commandments.php (visited May 2, 2007). When it comes to establishment clause issues, the taint of commerce is the saving grace for religion.

121. 545 U.S. at 740–741 and n. 4.

pro– and anti–Ten Commandments forces to determine how far the government can go in the display of the commandments on public property. But that is not a good criticism once the political character of constitutional adjudication is acknowledged. Compromise is the essence of democratic politics and hence a sensible approach to dealing with indeterminate legal questions charged with political passion—this is Bickelian prudence minus Bickelian teleology. To describe the display of the Ten Commandments as an "establishment" of religion is far-fetched from the standpoint of the text or original meaning of the establishment clause of the First Amendment. On its face and in light of its history, the clause is simply a prohibition against Congress's creating an established church, like the Church of England. To get from there to forbidding the State of Texas to display the Ten Commandments on its capitol grounds in company with the Heroes of the Alamo, or even the State of Kentucky to display them in a courthouse, requires a complicated chain of reasoning with too many intellectually weak links to convince doubters. In these circumstances, to give a complete victory to the secular side of the debate (or for that matter to the religious side) could be thought at once arrogant, disrespectful, and needlessly inflammatory. If the Supreme Court is inescapably a political court when it is deciding constitutional cases, we may at least hope that it might be restrained in the exercise of its power, recognizing the subjective character, the insecure foundations, of its constitutional jurisprudence:

> . . . O, it is excellent
> To have a giant's strength, but it is tyrannous
> To use it like a giant.[122]

This is an admonition for Justices of the Supreme Court, and indeed for all judges, to ponder.

122. William Shakespeare, *Measure for Measure,* act 2, sc. 2, ll. 107–109.

11

Comprehensive Constitutional Theories

I noted in preceding chapters the allure of comprehensive theories as a way of dispelling the uncertainty of resolving cases in areas in which the orthodox legal materials of decision run out. The pressure to develop such theories is particularly acute in constitutional law, where the inadequacy of the orthodox materials is most conspicuous. The most recent entry in a crowded field is the theory advanced by Justice Breyer in his book *Active Liberty*.[1] It is a little unfair to use Breyer's book to illustrate the limitations of comprehensive constitutional theories. A Supreme Court Justice writing about constitutional theory is like a dog walking on his hind legs; the wonder is not that it is done well but that it is done at all. The dog's walking is inhibited by anatomical limitations, the Justice's writing by political ones. Supreme Court Justices are powerful political figures; they cannot write with the freedom and candor of obscure people. Still, my subject is judges, and a book by a sitting Supreme Court Justice articulating his judicial philosophy bears importantly upon it.

Beginning in the 1970s, the initiative in constitutional debate passed to the conservatives. They proposed—and, owing largely to accidents of appointment, to a marked extent achieved—a rolling back of liberal doctrines (notably in regard to states' rights, police practices, and executive power) and of the methodology of loose construction that had enabled liberal Justices to offer a plausible justification for those doctrines. The liberals continue to win a share of victories in areas such as homosexual rights and capital punishment, but for the most part their stance

1. Stephen Breyer, *Active Liberty: Interpreting Our Democratic Constitution* (2005).

324

has been defensive:[2] defense of the Warren Court and *Roe v. Wade,* defense of a broad interpretation of the commerce clause and congressional power generally and a narrow interpretation of the Second Amendment and presidential prerogative. Breyer is a liberal, but he wants to do more than defend liberal decisions piecemeal. He wants an overarching approach to set against the textualism and originalism of his judicial foes, but one more modest and democratic, less elitist and academic, less removed from the actualities of the judicial process, than Ronald Dworkin's moral theory of constitutional law. Breyer's book will be widely read. The short book of Scalia's against which his book is directed has been cited in more than a thousand law review articles.[3] What Breyer's book is unlikely to do is to persuade his colleagues or other judges. The victories of conservative judges have been due not to the power of their ideas but to the electoral success of Republicans, the political hue of the judicial appointments to which that success has given rise, and a general rightward drift in American public opinion.

Breyer follows Benjamin Constant in distinguishing between the "liberty of the ancients" and the "liberty of the moderns," and aligns "active liberty" with the former. He fails to note that Constant was writing *against* the "liberty of the ancients," which Rousseau had introduced in France with tragic results, and in favor of the "liberty of the moderns."[4] To Constant, the liberty of the ancients signified the collective exercise of sovereignty, with no concept of individual rights against the state.[5] It is an extreme version of what we now call "direct democracy," illustrated by referenda in California and Switzerland and by the New England town meeting. The "liberty of the moderns," in contrast, is liberty from state oppression. It is what Isaiah Berlin called "negative liberty."[6] It is what citizens of Athens and of revolutionary France lacked. Its instruments include representative democracy (not direct democracy, as in

---

2. "Judicial liberals have been playing defense for close to 40 years." Linda Greenhouse, "On the Wrong Side of 5 to 4, Liberals Talk Tactics," *New York Times,* July 8, 2007, § 4, p. 3.

3. Antonin Scalia, *A Matter of Interpretation: Federal Courts and the Law* (1997). It is a short book, all right, but it is not really *his* short book. His contribution to it is limited to a lead essay, "Common-Law Courts in a Civil-Law System: The Role of United States Federal Courts in Interpreting the Constitution and Laws," id. at 3, and a reply to critics, id. at 129.

4. Benjamin Constant, "The Liberty of the Ancients Compared with That of the Moderns," in *Political Writings* 306 (Biancamaria Fontana trans. 1988). With reference to Rousseau, see id. at 319 320.

5. Id. at 311–312.

6. Isaiah Berlin, "Two Concepts of Liberty", in *Liberty* 175 (Henry Hardy ed. 2002 [1958]).

ancient Athens), separation of powers, federalism, and the type of legally enforceable rights against government that are found in the Bill of Rights.

Breyer understands by "liberty of the ancients" the liberty that Athenian citizens enjoyed for much of the fifth and fourth centuries B.C.[7] because their city was a democracy. Constant, on the contrary, believed Athens to have been the ancient state that "most resembles the modern ones" and Sparta a better example of the liberty of the ancients.[8] Yet Athens exemplified ancient liberty too. The Athenian Assembly, to which all citizens belonged, had plenary power; there were no legislators other than the citizens themselves when attending its sessions. To prevent the emergence of a political class, the few executive officials were chosen mainly by lot, for one-year terms, though some were elected and could be reelected.[9] Similarly, there were no judges except randomly selected subsets of citizens—jurors who voted without deliberating, unguided by jury instructions, since there were no judges to give such instructions. For that matter, there was no legal profession, though orators such as Demosthenes would draft speeches for the litigants to give at trial. There was plenty of litigation, but there were no rights to life, liberty, or property enforceable against the state. The only justice was popular justice.

Breyer wants the Supreme Court to do more to promote the "active liberty of the ancients,"[10] and underscores the point by remarking that "'active liberty' . . . bears some similarities to Isaiah Berlin's concept of 'positive liberty.'"[11] That was Berlin's term for the "liberty of the ancients" as revived by Rousseau and extended, Berlin thought, by modern totalitarians![12] But of course Breyer does not really want to turn the United States into a direct democracy on the model of ancient Athens, or on any other model. He says that "'delegated democracy' need not repre-

7. Josiah Ober, *The Athenian Revolution: Essays on Ancient Greek Democracy and Political Theory* 31 (1996); R. K. Sinclair, *Democracy and Participation in Athens* 68, 80 (1988). Some of the other Greek city-states were also democratic during this period.

8. Constant, note 4 above, at 309–312, 314, 316.

9. Sinclair, note 7 above, at 68–69, 80; John V. A. Fine, *The Ancient Greeks: A Critical History* 390–402 (1983). So even the Athenians flinched from the full implications of direct democracy. Sinclair, note 7 above, at 193–195; Richard A. Posner, *Law, Pragmatism, and Democracy* 154 (2003).

10. Breyer, note 1 above, at 5. He even contrasts "active liberty" with "modern liberty." Id. at 40–41.

11. Id. at 137 n. 6.

12. Berlin, note 6 above.

sent a significant departure from democratic principle,"[13] and by "delegated democracy" he means simply representative democracy. The "liberty of the ancients" is a historical curiosity that Breyer, who is not a classicist or an intellectual historian, should have left to the experts in such matters. It does no work in his book. It is a failed effort to theorize a political program. The program closely resembles that of John Hart Ely, who argued that the major thrust of the Warren Court had been to make American government more democratic,[14] but not democratic in the direct-democracy sense. Breyer, like Ely, wants to show that our judiciary, though an oligarchy, is, even at its most aggressive, a force for democracy. (In the next chapter we shall see this paradox being pushed even harder by the former Israeli supreme court justice Aharon Barak.) The specific issues pressed by Breyer differ from Ely's, but this mainly reflects changes in the policy agenda over the quarter century that separates their two books.

It may seem curious, given the influence on Breyer of Ely's theory, that he should refer to Ely only in passing.[15] It is not that he is trying to steal Ely's thunder; that would be wholly out of character for Breyer. It is I think a reluctance to acknowledge the academic provenance of his theory. The Justices do not want to take their cues from academics—this is an aspect of the alienation of the academy from the judiciary that I discussed in chapter 8. Justice Scalia is the most influential Supreme Court theorist, but his theory is distinctly homegrown. Although like Breyer he is a former academic, his advocacy of the originalist theory of constitutional interpretation does not come with an academic pedigree. There is an increasing preciosity to constitutional theory[16] that is off-putting to judges. And there are grounds for believing that if Justices are politicians in robes, constitutional theorists are politicians in academic gowns (a belief supported by, among other things, the academic briefs in *Rumsfeld*

13. Breyer, note 1 above, at 23.

14. John Hart Ely, *Democracy and Distrust: A Theory of Judicial Review* (1980).

15. Breyer, note 1 above, at 146 n. 14.

16. Well illustrated by Akhil Reed Amar, "*America's Constitution* and the Yale School of Constitutional Interpretation," 115 *Yale Law Journal* 1997 (2006), and Akhil Reed Amar and Jed Rubenfeld, "A Dialogue," 115 *Yale Law Journal* 2015 (2006). The "Yale School of Constitutional Interpretation" that Amar celebrates is completely unmoored from text and precedent; it is the current manifestation of the "bad boy" legal realism that I mentioned in chapter 4. For criticism, see Laurence H. Tribe, "Taking Text and Structure Seriously: Reflections on Free-Form Method in Constitutional Interpretation," 108 *Harvard Law Review* 1221, 1240–1249 (1995).

v. *FAIR*). Liberal judges and lawyers are urged to challenge Scalia on his own turf by redescribing themselves as textualists-originalists and arguing that the original meaning of the constitutional text is that judges are to be nonoriginalist interpreters.[17] This is a rhetorical gambit, politically motivated.

As a Supreme Court Justice, writing in the glare of public scrutiny that such judges receive, Breyer cannot acknowledge that he wants to impose his concept of "active liberty" on the Constitution. Convention requires him to find the concept in the venerable parchment.[18] Manfully he tries. He recognizes that it is an uphill struggle: "The primarily democratic nature of the Constitution's governmental structure has not always seemed obvious."[19] Indeed not—and for the excellent reason that the structure is not "primarily democratic." It is republican, with a democratic component. The Constitution's rejection of monarchy (no king), aristocracy (no titles of nobility), and a national church (no religious oaths of office) was revolutionary. But the governmental structure that it created bore no resemblance to that of ancient Athens and was, and remains, incompletely democratic.

Of the major components of the federal government—the executive branch, consisting of the President, the Vice President, and other high officials; the judiciary; the Senate; and the House of Representatives— only the last was to be elected by the people. And since the Constitution conferred no voting rights but instead allowed the states to fix the eligibility criteria for voters for members of the House (except that the criteria had to be the same as those the state prescribed for voters for members of the lower house of its own legislature), states could limit the franchise by imposing property or other qualifications for voting. The President and Vice President were to be chosen by an Electoral College whose members would in turn be chosen by the states according to rules adopted by each state legislature; there was no requirement of popular election of the Electoral College's members. Other executive branch officials would be appointed by the President or by federal judges. Sena-

17. See, for example, Jack M. Balkin, "Abortion and Original Meaning" (forthcoming in *Constitutional Commentary*).

18. "The belief that a judge's job is to interpret rather than legislate retains considerable resonance. That may be why the justices have never undertaken to advance a rationale for their behavior. To declare openly what they are doing would be to throw gasoline on the smoldering debate about the legitimacy of the Court's activism." Robert H. Bork, "Enforcing a 'Mood,'" *New Criterion*, Feb. 2006, p. 63.

19. Breyer, note 1 above, at 21.

tors would be appointed by state legislatures, whose members were not required by the federal Constitution to be elected. Supreme Court Justices (and other federal judges, if Congress took up the option conferred on it by the Constitution to create federal courts in addition to the Supreme Court) would be appointed by the President, subject to senatorial confirmation, for life. Political parties were not envisaged; the best men (*hoi aristoi*) were expected to rule, rather than the survivors of party competition. There was no trace of direct democracy in the Constitution of 1787, and thus no provision for initiatives, referenda, or recalls. The framers purported to be speaking on behalf of "We the People," as the preamble states, but there is no novelty in adopting a nondemocratic regime by plebiscite; ask Napoleon. Even the ratification of the Constitution was by state conventions rather than by direct popular vote. The Constitution guarantees a republican (that is, a nonmonarchical) form of government to each state, but not a democratic government.

If the framers had "confidence in democracy as the best check upon government's oppressive tendencies,"[20] why is there so little democracy, and none of it direct democracy, in the document they wrote? The Bill of Rights, it is true, added a dollop of direct democracy in its guarantees of the right to a jury trial in criminal and some civil cases (although American juries, unlike ancient Athenian ones, are supervised by professional judges). But the major thrust of the Bill of Rights was to limit legislative and executive power—to place liberty in opposition to democracy—and thus to vindicate the "liberty of the moderns," not the liberty of the ancients that Breyer purports to find in the Constitution.

What we see in the structure of our eighteenth-century Constitution is not an echo of Athens but the adaptation of the institutions of the British eighteenth-century monarchy to a republican ideology. The President corresponds to the king; he exercises the traditional monarchical prerogatives of pardoning, conducting foreign affairs, appointing executive officials and judges, and commanding the armed forces. He is of course not directly elected. The Senate and the Supreme Court correspond to the House of Lords (the House of Lords Appellate Committee is Britain's supreme court[21]), and the House of Representatives corresponds to the House of Commons: elected, but by a restricted franchise.

20. Id. at 23.
21. Or rather was; in 2005 the United Kingdom created a supreme court to replace the House of Lords Appellate Committee. Gary Slapper and David Kelly, *The English Legal System* 133–134 (8th ed. 2006).

Subsequent amendments and changing practices and institutions made the Constitution more democratic, but Breyer insists that the original Constitution, the Constitution of 1787, was animated by the spirit of Pericles. There is irony in an anti-originalist trying to give a historical pedigree to his anti-originalist approach. Breyer's lack of interest in the background and the actual texture of the Constitution is consistent with the loose-constructionist approach that he champions in his book and in his judicial opinions.

Breyer offers a series of illustrations of how the concept of active liberty would, if accepted as the true spirit of the Constitution, shape constitutional law. He begins with free speech. He contrasts political and commercial speech, arguing that the former is entitled to much greater protection because it is central to democracy. But he also defends, against free-speech objections, campaign finance laws that limit political advertising.

The notion of the primacy of political speech is common, but it is misleading and unhelpful. It ignores a principle of rational decision theory that is fully applicable to legal pragmatism: that consequences should be evaluated at the margin. The question should not be whether political speech is more valuable than commercial speech in the sense that prohibiting all political speech would be worse than prohibiting all commercial speech. That is never the issue. The issue always is a comparison of the harm done by a marginal curtailment of one value with the benefit to another value from the curtailment. It is easy to imagine restrictions on political speech that would do less harm than restrictions on commercial speech; compare a prohibition against advocating suicide bombing with a prohibition of all commercial advertising. And where does scientific and artistic expression fit into Breyer's hierarchy of speech categories? He does not say, though it is especially easy to imagine restrictions on freedom of scientific inquiry that would be far more destructive of the nation's power and prosperity than minor restrictions on political expression.

Breyer argues that limiting contributions to political campaigns should not be held to infringe freedom of speech. He recognizes that to forbid a person to spend $1 million to buy a television commercial extolling a candidate curtails expression. But he thinks that limiting the right of the rich to buy campaign advertising is justified by the contribution that such a limitation would make to active liberty. The First Amendment is to be understood "as seeking to facilitate a conversation among ordinary citizens that will encourage their informed participation in the electoral process," and campaign finance laws have a "similar objective. They seek to democratize the influence that money can bring to bear upon the electoral process, thereby building public confidence in that process, broadening the base of a candidate's meaningful financial support, and encouraging greater public participation."[22] The fear is that without limitations on individual campaign contributions, candidates will confine their fund-raising to the handful of fat cats, and the ordinary people will become alienated from the political process because they will assume that policy is shaped by the interests of the rich and that the people's voice is not heard.

No evidence for this implausible speculation is offered. The wealthy are not a monolith; they have conflicting interests and opinions. Also they lack the votes—there are too few wealthy people—to swing elections, and so political advertisements are aimed at average people. And it is odd to think that the fewer political advertisements there are, the greater the amount of political participation there will be. Furthermore, if some candidates court the wealthy, others will be spurred to raise money from the nonwealthy—something the Internet has made easier to do.

I am not suggesting that Breyer is wrong to think that campaign finance laws do not violate the First Amendment. If there is no evidence that they promote democracy, there is likewise no evidence that they curtail free speech enough to undermine democracy or do any other harm to society. And concern about the possibly malign effects of private spending on political campaigns is hardly frivolous, for otherwise voters would be allowed to sell their votes. But it is no help in resolving challenges to campaign finance laws to suggest that the test of their constitutionality should be "proportionality." Breyer wants the law's "*negative* impact upon those primarily wealthier citizens who wish to engage in more electoral communication" to be weighed against "its *positive* impact upon the public's confidence in, and ability to communicate through, the electoral process . . . Does the statute strike a reasonable balance between electoral speech-restricting and speech-enhancing consequences? Or does it instead impose restrictions on speech that are dis-

22. Breyer, note 1 above, at 46–47.

proportionate when measured against their electoral and speech-related benefits, taking into account the kind, the importance, and the extent of those benefits, as well as the need for the restriction in order to secure them?"[23] "The inquiry is complex," writes Breyer.[24] No, it is indeterminate.

The problem is not that he is asking the court to weigh imponderables. For while "weighing imponderables" sounds like an oxymoron ("imponderable" is from the Latin *ponderare,* meaning "to weigh"), it isn't quite. Often a judge can know, even without quantification, that one interest at stake in a case is weightier than another. In a negligence case neither the burden of precautions nor the probability and magnitude of the accident that will occur if the precautions are not taken may be quantified or even quantifiable, yet it may be apparent that there is a grave risk of a serious accident that could easily be averted (negligence), or that the cost of the precautions would be disproportionate to the slight risk of a minor accident (no negligence). That is the "tolerable windows" approach that I advocated in chapter 9. But the key terms in Breyer's test, such as "impact upon the public's confidence in, and ability to communicate through, the electoral process" and the "importance" of a challenged law's "electoral and speech-related benefits," are so nebulous that they cannot be weighed against each other at all. High-level abstractions such as "democracy" and "active liberty" can be arrayed with equal plausibility on either side of constitutional questions. They are makeweights. A decision invalidating a statute on constitutional grounds may seem undemocratic, but even if it is not a democracy-enhancing decision (as reapportionment decisions are widely thought to be) it can be defended as an application of the "higher democracy" embodied in the Constitution. So originalists are democrats along with loose constructionists. Likewise federalists, who want to honor the democratic choices made at the state and local levels, and nationalists who want to honor the democratic choices made at the federal level.

Breyer is one of the nationalists, despite his acknowledgment that a nation as populous as the United States needs a federal system in order to give the citizenry a sense of full participation in political life because

23. Id. at 49 (emphasis in original).
24. Id. at 50.

issues at the state and local levels are often both more important and more intelligible to people than issues involving the national government. Disagreeing with a majority of his colleagues,[25] he argues that the federal government should be allowed to compel state officials to assist in enforcing federal law, as by requiring local sheriffs to check on compliance with federal gun control laws. He thinks that unless the federal government can force state officials to assist in administering federal programs, it will need a larger bureaucracy and so will expand at the expense of state and local government. A more likely consequence of federal commandeering of state officials would be more federal programs because some of their costs would have been shifted from the federal treasury to the states. State officials would be drafted as de facto federal employees. That is the antithesis of federalism.

Continuing in a nationalist vein, Breyer challenges the decisions in which the Supreme Court has limited federal regulation by defining interstate commerce more narrowly than it had done since the 1930s.[26] He argues that federal laws based on an expansive understanding of interstate commerce are democratic because "the public has participated in the legislative process at the national level."[27] But remember that he has acknowledged that political participation is less participatory at the national than at the state level, an acknowledgment inconsistent with criticizing the Court for expanding the scope for political participation at the state level by narrowing the scope for federal regulation.[28] Oddly, considering his commitment to salting law with democracy, he does not remark the fact that, as I noted in chapter 5, state government is more democratic than our national government.

Consistent with his reputation (not wholly earned, as we saw in chapter 10) as a pragmatic judge, Breyer urges his colleagues to "ask about the consequences of decision-making on the active liberty that federalism seeks to further" and to "consider the practical effects on local

25. Printz v. United States, 521 U.S. 898, 935 (1997); New York v. United States, 505 U.S. 144, 149 (1992).

26. United States v. Morrison, 529 U.S. 598 (2000); United States v. Lopez, 514 U.S. 549 (1995).

27. Breyer, note 1 above, at 62,

28. Michael W. McConnell, in a review of Breyer's book, shows that Breyer systematically favors federal over state and local authority and argues that such favoritism is inconsistent with "active liberty." McConnell, "Book Review," 119 *Harvard Law Review* 2387, 2394–2397 (2006).

democratic self-government of decisions interpreting the Constitution's principles of federalism."[29] But when consequences can only be conjectured, the judge is left at large. When would one know that a law had impaired such elusive phenomena as "active liberty" or "local democratic self-government"?

Breyer endorses the approach proposed by Alexander Bickel and more recently by Guido Calabresi for promoting "dialogue" between courts and legislatures (see chapter 10). Here is Breyer's version:

> Through a hard-look requirement, for example, the Court would communicate to Congress the precise constitutional difficulty the Court has with the statute at issue without resorting to permanent invalidation. Congress, in reenacting the statute, would revisit the matter and respond to the Court's concerns. A clear-statement rule would have the Court call upon Congress to provide an unambiguous articulation of the precise contours and reach of a given policy solution. Those doctrines would lead the Court to focus upon the thoroughness of the legislature's consideration of a matter.[30]

This one-sided dialogue would tie Congress and state legislatures in knots. Offered by Breyer as an olive branch to a democratically elected branch of government, it would expand judicial power at the expense of legislatures by invalidating legislation because it failed to meet the criteria of thoroughness, clarity, and precision.

In another part of the book Breyer points out that new technologies have altered the landscape of privacy. He urges courts to forgo offering definitive answers when there is so much uncertainty and such rapid change. Instead the answers should be allowed to "bubble up from below" in a process "best described as a form of participatory democracy."[31] Breyer illustrates with a decision that he joined in which the Court held the First Amendment violated by a federal statute that forbade broadcasting a private cell phone conversation, which an unknown person had intercepted with a scanner and delivered to a radio station.[32] Breyer wrote a concurring opinion that emphasized three points and indicated that he might have voted differently had at least one of them been absent: the radio station had been an innocent recipient of the tape

29. Breyer, note 1 above, at 63.
30. Id. at 64–65.
31. Id. at 70.
32. Bartnicki v. Vopper, 532 U.S. 514 (2001).

of the illegally intercepted conversation; the conversation, which was between two union officials, was a matter of public interest because it contained a threat to damage property; and the conversation was about business rather than about intimate private matters, so the affront to privacy in broadcasting the conversation was less than it might have been.

All this has little to do with "participatory democracy" (the empty slogan of 1960s radicals) or for that matter with new technologies. The decision subordinates the privacy of conversations to the media's interest in disseminating matters that the public may be interested in learning about. The principal effect may be to discourage the use of analog cell phones (which are easier to eavesdrop on than wire telephones, and which are anyway on their way out—an already old new technology) for the discussion of sensitive matters. The irony is that the media know well the value of privacy of communications for themselves—newspapers and other news media are desperate to avoid having to identify their reporters' confidential sources—but do not respect the same privacy interests of the subjects of their stories. Decisions that fail to protect the privacy of communications may result in fewer communications, with a resulting loss to freedom of speech and so, one might have thought, to active liberty.

In a discussion of affirmative action, Breyer declares his agreement with certain "practical considerations"[33] that Justice O'Connor mentioned in the part of her opinion for the Court in *Grutter v. Bollinger*[34] that upheld the affirmative action program of the Michigan Law School. They are that American businesses and the American military consider affirmative action important to their operations and that effective integration of a group into the nation's civic life requires that "the path to leadership be visibly open to talented and qualified individuals of every race and ethnicity."[35] What O'Connor was saying, though one must read between the lines to get it, was that black people in America, because on average they lag so far behind whites, need a helping hand to raise them to a level at which they will feel well integrated into American society, rather than constituting a disaffected underclass.

Pragmatically appealing as that ground for affirmative action may be, it has nothing to do with democracy. Athens thrived on exclusion. Most

33. Breyer, note 1 above, at 81.
34. 539 U.S. 306 (2003).
35. Id. at 332, quoted in Breyer, note 1 above, at 82.

of the population consisted of women, slaves, and aliens, none of whom had the rights of citizens; citizens comprised no more than 20 percent, and perhaps as little as 10 percent, of the adult population.[36] I would not labor the point had not Breyer sounded a Rousseauian note in the series of rhetorical questions by which he seeks to tie O'Connor's analysis to active liberty: "What are these arguments but an appeal to principles of solidarity, to principles of *fraternity*, to principles of *active liberty*?"[37] Solidarity and fraternity, yes; these were ideals of Athenian society as of the French Revolution. But they are not, as Breyer implies, democratic ideals. Nondemocratic societies have frequently achieved high levels of solidarity, sometimes, as in the case of Nazi Germany, with the aid of racist policies.

Breyer's book makes some good arguments against strict construction and in favor of using statutory language and other clues to infer a statute's purpose and then using that purpose to guide interpretation. But he fails to engage the strongest argument against the purposive approach—that it tends to override legislative compromises. (He also overlooks the related possibility of multiple purposes that may be in conflict.[38]) The original or underlying purpose of a statute may be clear enough, but that purpose may have been blunted in drafting in order to obtain majority support. If so, using the pristine purpose to resolve ambiguities might give the supporters of the statute more than they were able to achieve in the legislative process. That would be undemocratic.

Is Breyer's commitment to democracy or just to policies that he happens to favor? There is a revealing slip when he says that "an interpretation of a statute that tends to implement the legislator's will helps to implement the public's will and is therefore consistent with the Constitution's democratic purpose."[39] The slip is in referring to a single legislator rather than to the legislature. Legislation is passed by cobbling together a majority of often fractious legislators representing different

36. For various estimates, see M. I. Finley, *Democracy Ancient and Modern* 51 (1985); A. W. Gomme, *The Population of Athens in the Fifth and Fourth Centuries B.C.* 26 (1933) (tab. 1); Mogens Herman Hansen, *The Athenian Democracy in the Age of Demosthenes: Structure, Principles, and Ideology* 93–94 (1999 [1991]).

37. Breyer, note 1 above, at 82 (emphasis in original).

38. McConnell, note 28 above, at 2405; Cass R. Sunstein, "Justice Breyer's Democratic Pragmatism," 115 *Yale Law Journal* 1719, 1731–1736 (2006).

39. Breyer, note 1 above, at 99.

interests. Compromise is inescapable and can obliterate single-minded purpose. The public is not a singularity either.

This is not to suggest that the purposive approach is wrong. Most of the gaps in statutes are unintentional, and there is no way to fill the gaps sensibly without reflecting on what a statute seems to have been aimed at accomplishing. But that is the counsel of good sense rather than anything to do with democracy (Blackstone was not a democrat, nor was Aristotle, who had made the same point 2,000 years earlier[40]). This is further shown by Breyer's proposal that the best way to implement the purposive approach is to adopt the "fiction" of the "reasonable legislator."[41] The interpreter asks not what the actual legislators thought but what a "reasonable" legislator (again singular) would have thought. It is the judge who decides what is "reasonable," for remember that the "reasonable legislator" is a fiction. To suggest that this approach will "translate the popular will into sound policy"[42] is heroic, even if one passes over the uncertainties buried in the concept of the "popular will." The concept of the "reasonable legislator" is a tool for maximizing the judge's discretion in statutory interpretation, as the judge is bound to regard himself as being "reasonable" and therefore as knowing what a reasonable legislator would do.

What is true and important is that legislators may be content to have the judiciary impose "reasonable" interpretations on their legislative handiwork; otherwise the legislators will have to spend a lot of time amending their and their predecessors' enactments. Textualists do legislatures no favor by insisting that statutes speak clearly; the conditions of the legislative process, and in particular the need to compromise in order to get statutes passed, make it impossible for legislatures to promulgate unambiguous statutes. Judges clean up after legislators, which is fine, and even in a sense democratic.

The concept of the reasonable legislator recurs when Breyer turns to administrative law. *Chevron U.S.A. v. Natural Resources Defense Council,*

---

40. See Aristotle, *Rhetoric*, bk. 1, § 13; W. G., "On Construing Statutes by Equity," 6 *American Law Register* 513 (1858).

41. Breyer, note 1 above, at 97–101. Breyer is borrowing here from Henry M. Hart, Jr., and Albert M. Sacks, *The Legal Process: Basic Problems in the Making and Application of Law* 1378 (William N. Eskridge, Jr., and Philip P. Frickey eds. 1994 [1958]).

42. Breyer, note 1 above, at 101.

Inc.[43] held that when a regulatory statute is ambiguous, the court should defer to the regulatory agency's statutory interpretation, if reasonable, on the theory that in such cases statutory interpretation, though a quintessentially judicial task, has been delegated by Congress to the agency that enforces the statute, subject to only light judicial review. Breyer proposes that to determine in a particular case whether this delegation has occurred the judge should "ask whether, given the statutory aims and circumstances, a hypothetical member [i.e., a reasonable member of Congress] would likely have wanted judicial deference in this situation,"[44] or, contrariwise, would have wanted to decide the question for himself. That is the wrong question. By hypothesis, the statute is ambiguous. Congress did not decide for itself, or if it did, we do not know what its decision was. The question is whether Congress should be taken to have wanted the courts or the regulatory agency to resolve the ambiguity. About all that can be said in answer to that question is that if the issue in the case is a technical one that is within the scope of the agency's expertise but not the judges', the court might as well defer; otherwise not. The idea of "delegation" in *Chevron* is a fiction. It is doubtful that *Chevron,* heavily cited though it is, altered judicial review of administrative action.[45]

Textualists (or textualists-originalists), such as Breyer's frequent sparring partner Scalia, argue, as Breyer notes, that the kind of loose-construction approach that Breyer champions "open[s] the door to subjectivity."[46] It does, and the only good response is that textualism or originalism is just as protean as "active liberty." Breyer's response is different. It is that "a judge who emphasizes consequences, no less than any other, is aware of the legal precedents, rules, standards, practices, and institutional understanding that a decision will affect."[47] But "aware of" does not mean "committed to." Breyer joined *Lawrence v. Texas* (see chapter 10), which

43. 467 U.S. 837 (1984).
44. Breyer, note 1 above, at 106.
45. William N. Eskridge, Jr., and Lauren E. Baer, "The Supreme Court's Deference Continuum: An Empirical Analysis (from *Chevron* to *Hamdan*)" (forthcoming in *Georgetown Law Journal*). The authors find that the government almost always wins cases turning on the interpretation of a statute, especially in areas in which the agencies have relevant expertise and the judges do not.
46. Breyer, note 1 above, at 118. For systematic defenses of textualism, see John F. Manning, "What Divides Textualists from Purposivists?" 106 *Columbia Law Review* 70 (2006); Caleb Nelson, "What Is Textualism?" 91 *Virginia Law Review* 347 (2005).
47. Breyer, note 1 above, at 118–119.

overruled *Bowers v. Hardwick*,[48] and he joined *Roper v. Simmons,* which, as we saw in chapter 10, overruled *Stanford v. Kentucky. Lawrence* and *Roper* are bold "liberal" decisions. Neither exhibits a careful attention to consequences. The sodomy statutes struck down in *Lawrence* had virtually no consequences, since by the time the case was decided they were almost never enforced. They had become little more than a statement, to which few were listening, of social disapproval of homosexuality, and the Court substituted its own, more "enlightened" moral view. And we recall that the psychological studies offered in *Roper* to show that juveniles lack adequate moral maturity to appreciate the significance of murdering were misunderstood by the Court.

In defense of his dissent in *Zelman,* the school voucher case (see chapter 10), Breyer says in his book that he "saw in the administration of huge grant programs for religious education the potential for religious strife."[49] This "seeing" of a "potential" is a conjecture that unless voucher programs were permitted to go into effect would never be either confirmed or falsified. There is a parallel to *Lochner.* When it was decided in 1905, a body of respectable opinion held that laws limiting hours of work were enlightened measures that would improve the welfare of the working class at slight social cost. The question for the Supreme Court was whether to invalidate such measures on the ground that they deprived employers of "liberty of contract," a term not found in the Constitution, in circumstances constituting a denial of "due process of law," a term not obviously related to the content of a law as distinct from its form or from the circumstances of its enactment. Holmes pointed out in his dissent that to invalidate New York's maximum-hours law would require the Court to choose between economic theories, for it could hardly be thought that the framers of the Constitution had made the choice for the Justices. By knocking down the law the Court killed a social experiment.

To foreclose social experiments adopted by elected legislatures is not only unpragmatic, it is undemocratic. Breyer votes more often than his conservative colleagues to uphold federal statutes, but his democratic credentials, as well as his commitment to federalism, are placed in question by his joining decisions such as *Lawrence* and *Roper,* in which the

48. 478 U.S. 186 (1986).
49. Breyer, note 1 above, at 121–122.

Court struck down state legislation, and by his dissent in *Zelman*. He is also an enthusiastic citer of foreign constitutional decisions, and that is a form of elitism, for decisions by foreign courts are not events in American democracy.[50]

Fuzzy contours are a notable feature of Breyer's constitutional doctrines, and he defends fuzziness in his book, arguing that "insistence upon clear rules can exact a high constitutional price."[51] He asks whether "three strikes and you're out" laws, which can result in a criminal's being sentenced to life even though his third crime was a minor one, such as a theft of golf clubs or videotapes, can be adjudged cruel and unusual punishment. The Court thought not.[52] Breyer dissented. He acknowledges in his book that the position he advocated in his dissent "would leave the Court without a clear rule."[53] One is put in mind of his dissent in *Eldred v. Ashcroft* (see chapter 10), where he proposed that a statute extending a copyright term "lacks the constitutionally necessary rational support (1) if the significant benefits that it bestows are private, not public; (2) if it threatens seriously to undermine the expressive values that the Copyright Clause embodies; and (3) if it cannot find justification in any significant Clause-related objective."[54] That is a standard to give standards a bad name. And it is a reminder that if judges are going to be occasional legislators—and Supreme Court Justices frequent legislators—they have to be able to formulate rules and standards that will provide the kind of guidance that explicit legislation provides.

Although Breyer is the Justice most knowledgeable about intellectual property in general and copyright in particular, his dissent in *Eldred* attracted no support from his colleagues; Justice Stevens, the other dissenter, did not join Breyer's dissent. Breyer has confessed his inability to persuade his colleagues to his views about economic regulation,[55] an-

50. See chapter 12. As McConnell, note 28 above, at 2399, remarks: "I presume the 'people' whose active liberty is at issue are the American people. Either the foreign court decisions to which the Supreme Court refers are 'consistent with the [American] people's will' as expressed in our laws, in which case references to foreign decisions are redundant, or those decisions are inconsistent with the people's will, in which case giving them nontrivial weight would seem problematic from Justice Breyer's own point of view." The interior quotation is from Breyer, note 1 above, at 115.

51. Breyer, note 1 above, at 128.

52. Lockyer v. Andrade, 538 U.S. 63 (2003); Ewing v. California, 538 U.S. 11 (2003).

53. Breyer, note 1 above, at 129.

54. Id. at 245.

55. Stephen Breyer, "Economic Reasoning and Judicial Review: AEI-Brookings Joint Center 2003 Distinguished Lecture" 2 (AEI-Brookings Joint Center for Regulatory Studies, 2004).

other field in which, like intellectual property, he has expert knowledge that his colleagues lack. He attributes his inability in part to his colleagues' preference for "bright-line rules" in the law, which he thinks difficult to reconcile with economic reasoning because "economics often concerns gradations, with consequences that flow from a little more or a little less . . . I tend to disfavor absolute legal lines. Life is normally too complex for absolute rules."[56] But complexity is a reason for having rules. It is unpragmatic to ignore the economizing properties of rules.

Breyer has said that judicial "independence is a state of mind. It reflects an indifference to improper pressure and a determination to decide each case according to the law."[57] I do not question the sincerity of his commitment to judicial independence, but I do wonder what the word "law" means to him. Unless one can take seriously his endeavor to derive "active liberty" from the Constitution, which one cannot, and thinks that Breyer can derive all his judicial votes from "active liberty," hence giving them a constitutional pedigree, which is also out of the question, "law" for Breyer, or at least constitutional law, seems more his own creation than a body of thought external to his personal views. I am tempted to describe him as a *bricoleur*—one who uses "the instruments he finds at his disposition around him, . . . which had not been especially conceived with an eye to the operation for which they are to be used and to which one tries by trial and error to adapt them, not hesitating to change them whenever it appears necessary."[58] Breyer's instruments include not only Athenian direct democracy and modern American pragmatism but also Ely's "representation-reinforcing" theory of constitutional adjudication, Henry Hart's "reasonable legislator" theory of statutory interpretation, Ronald Dworkin's claim that constitutional and statutory provisions should be interpreted to make them the best possible statements of political morality,[59] economic analysis, and deference to the conventional legal materials of precedent and statutory text. Such eclecticism leaves a judge with complete freedom to indulge

56. Id. at 6–7.

57. Stephen Breyer, "Judicial Independence: Remarks by Justice Breyer," 95 *Georgetown Law Journal* 903, 904 (2007).

58. Jacques Derrida, *Writing and Difference* 285 (1978). Borrowing from foreign law (see next chapter) has been described as a form of "bricolage." See, for example, David Schneiderman, "Exchanging Constitutions: Constitutional *Bricolage* in Canada," 40 *Osgoode Hall Law Journal* 401 (2002), and references cited there. Justice Breyer is an enthusiastic citer of foreign decisions as authority in American law.

59. Ronald Dworkin, *Freedom's Law: The Moral Reading of the American Constitution* (1996).

his political instincts—liberal, conservative, or moderate—as it can accommodate any result that a judge might want to reach for reasons he might be unwilling to acknowledge publicly, such as a visceral dislike for capital punishment, abortion, affirmative action, or religion in the public sphere.

Breyer is a nondoctrinaire liberal—which means, by the way, that you will not find in his book the constitutional "vision" for which some liberal law professors yearn.[60] Whether you agree with his judicial approach is likely to depend on whether you agree with his politics—as is equally true, however, of his antagonists, and of his and their predecessors on the Supreme Court stretching back to John Marshall.

Judge McConnell states disapprovingly that Breyer wants to "place greater emphasis on 'purposes' and 'likely consequences' than on language, history and tradition."[61] "His emphasis on 'workable outcomes' and 'real-world consequences,' and his claim that his approach would avoid 'seriously harmful consequences,' evidently based on his own balance of costs and benefits, all tend to identify Justice Breyer as a pragmatist."[62] Actually he is an intermittent pragmatist whose pragmatism is heavily leavened with liberal political commitments—a combination that marks him as an heir of the legal realists. In articulating a comprehensive theory, Breyer is wearing a mask, the better to compete with the conservatives on their preferred plane of theory.

But they are wearing masks too, even though originalism and its sibling, textualism, like pragmatism—but unlike active liberty (or the ideology of "state neutrality" that, as I noted in chapter 4, Howard Gillman ascribes to the Justices of the *Lochner* era)—is not *intrinsically* political, although its *motivation* I take to be political, in the sense that the outcomes it is likely to produce will on the whole conform to the political preferences of the theorist and that otherwise he would not have adopted it. Originalism is easily unmasked. Here is an example of how easily. A potentially very great embarrassment for originalists, especially for those who, being or aspiring to become judges, lack the tenured academic's freedom to be outrageous, is that the unflinching embrace of originalism would require overturning many cases that have achieved canonical status. Judge McConnell, a self-described textualist-originalist,

60. See Greenhouse, note 2 above.
61. McConnell, note 28 above, at 2390, quoting Breyer, note 1 above, at 8.
62. McConnell, note 28 above, at 2408, quoting Breyer, note 1 above, at 115–116, 129.

is acutely aware of the problem. He lists as plausible examples of doctrines that violate his principles "protection against sex discrimination under the Equal Protection Clause, application of the Equal Protection Clause to the federal government, expansion of the Commerce Clause to permit federal regulation of intrastate commercial activity, or prohibition of gross malapportionment of state legislative districts."[63] But, he says, these questionable decisions are sanctified by "overwhelming public acceptance . . . This overwhelming public acceptance constitutes a mode of popular ratification, which gives these decisions legitimacy and authority."[64] He quotes James Madison's admission that he changed his mind about the unconstitutionality of creating a national bank because he regarded "the acquiescence of the people at large . . . as a construction put on the Constitution by the nation."

In other words, the Constitution can be amended by popular opinion, a view congenial to a politician, but not, one would have thought, to an originalist. There is no textual support, and as far as I know no relevant historical support either (Madison was writing almost 40 years after the constitutional convention), for such a heresy. What is more, it actually licenses political judging. For it says to the judge: if you think you understand the direction in which public opinion is moving, get out in front of the parade, decide the case without reference to originalist dogma, and if your political instincts are correct your decision will be accepted—including by originalists!

Notice that McConnell does not list the application of the equal protection clause to public school segregation as an example of a ruling that violates originalist tenets. Although recognizing that "in the fractured discipline of constitutional law, there is something very close to a consensus that *Brown* was inconsistent with the original understanding of the Fourteenth Amendment,"[65] McConnell set out to prove the consensus wrong, well aware of the stakes for the political and academic ac-

---

63. McConnell, note 28 above, at 2417.

64. Id.

65. Michael W. McConnell, "Originalism and the Desegregation Decisions," 81 *Virginia Law Review* 947, 952 (1995). See also McConnell, "The Originalist Justification for *Brown*: A Reply to Professor Klarman," 81 *Virginia Law Review* 1937 (1995). Klarman's response to McConnell's article includes a powerful criticism of originalism as a theory of constitutional interpretation. Michael J. Klarman, "*Brown*, Originalism, and Constitutional Theory: A Response to Professor McConnell," 81 *Virginia Law Review* 1881, 1915–1928 (1995).

ceptability of originalism.[66] The only evidence he turned up, however, was that most Republican Congressmen, in debates in the 1870s on civil rights legislation to implement the Fourteenth Amendment (which had been ratified in 1868), said they thought the amendment did entitle white children to go to black schools and black children to go to white schools. But there is nothing more treacherous, in the treacherous arena of legislative history, than postenactment legislative history, whereby the losers in the legislative arena hope to persuade the courts to give them the victory after all. (One has heard of winners' history. This is losers' history.) If postenactment history can be used to disambiguate a statute or a constitutional provision, a court has enormous discretion in interpretation. Judge McConnell is perhaps something new: a postoriginalist.

A consistent originalist would say that if the Fourteenth Amendment required racial integration of the public schools, it would say so. There is nothing in the term "equal protection" that seems to forbid separation, even separation on grounds ordinarily considered invidious, such as sex and race, when for example it takes the form of separate restrooms for men and women or racial segregation in a prison to prevent a race riot; in such settings, "separate but equal" is no oxymoron. To prove that school segregation was tantamount to the arbitrary withdrawal of legal protection from blacks would thus have required evidence, and the plaintiffs in the *Brown* case had not offered much evidence. Everyone *knew* the social meaning of segregation, of course, but that is not the kind of "evidence" with which legalists, including, one would have thought, textualists-originalists, are comfortable. (Nor is it what McConnell relied on.) Writing after McConnell's article was published, a leading student of the history of race law, Michael Klarman, concluded that "the original understanding of the Fourteenth Amendment plainly permitted school segregation . . . To the justices who were most committed to traditional legal sources, such as text, original intent, precedent, and custom, *Brown* should have been an easy case—for *sustaining* school segregation."[67]

What is strangest about McConnell's analysis of *Brown* is his acknowledgment that when the Fourteenth Amendment was passed, "school de-

---

66. Michael W. McConnell, "The Originalist Case for Brown v. Board of Education," 19 *Harvard Journal of Law and Public Policy* 457 (1996).

67. Michael J. Klarman, *From Jim Crow to Civil Rights: The Supreme Court and the Struggle for Racial Equality* 26, 447 (2004) (emphasis in original).

segregation was deeply unpopular among whites in both North and South, and school segregation was very commonly practiced," but that "these were not ordinary times"; instead it was "a time when *a political minority*, armed with the prestige of victory in the Civil War and *with military control over the political apparatus of the rebel states, imposed* constitutional change on the Nation as the price of reunion, *with little regard for popular opinion.*"[68] Originalists defend originalism as protecting democracy by preventing the courts from usurping legislative authority in the name of the Constitution; and recall that McConnell defends nonoriginalist precedents as democratically legitimate when ratified by popular acquiescence. But in his depiction, the Fourteenth Amendment, as interpreted to ban school segregation, is usurpative rather than democratic. He defends the interpretation by reference to the *irrelevance* of democratic preference. What one is seeing here is the theorist fixing his theory around a political imperative—a full-throated acceptance of the correctness of the *Brown* decision.

Originalism is not a theory of judicial self-restraint, in the sense of limiting judicial encroachment on the powers of the other branches of government.[69] And its manipulability makes one doubt even the core originalist claim that originalism reduces judicial discretion. There is a further reason to doubt it. There are two basic legalist tools for achieving a reasonable degree of certainty in a case law system. One is constitutional and statutory texts; the other is precedent. But these are in tension. An originalist has to be suspicious of precedent, because at best it is a judicial gloss of an authoritative text and at worst it is judicial creation *ab nihilo*. Justice Scalia's acceptance of precedent is avowedly pragmatic. In a world governed by originalism, as in a civil law system (in which detailed legal codes make textualism a more feasible strategy than in our system), the role of precedent as a stabilizing force in the law would be diminished. Pragmatists, loose constructionists, and "living Constitution" buffs reject literal interpretation of authoritative texts, subordinating the language of the texts to their purpose. But they tend to have a greater respect for precedent than originalists do, because to them constitutional law is a creature of precedent rather than of text.

68 McConnell, "Reply to Professor Klarman," note 65 above, at 1938–1939 (emphasis added).
69. Keith E. Whittington, "The New Originalism," 2 *Georgetown Journal of Law and Public Policy* 599, 609 (2004).

Exaggerating for emphasis, we can say that one school seeks certainty in text and disparages precedent, and the other seeks certainty in precedent and disparages text. The first is methodologically Protestant (though many of its practitioners are Catholic), and the second is methodologically Catholic (though most of its practitioners are Protestant or Jewish). It is unclear that either school delivers more certainty, predictability, or stability to constitutional law than the other. The Supreme Court is divided at the moment between the two schools 4–4, with Justice Kennedy shuttling unpredictably between them.

So can one take originalism—or any comprehensive theory of constitutional interpretation—seriously? One way to try to answer this question would be to compare the votes of politically aligned judges who espouse different judicial philosophies, such as Breyer (active liberty), Stevens (no discernible judicial philosophy, but leaning toward pragmatism), and Souter (no discernible judicial philosophy, but not very pragmatic); Scalia (originalist) and Rehnquist (no discernible judicial philosophy); Calabresi (Bickelian) and his colleague Jon Newman (again, no discernible judicial philosophy); McConnell (originalist) and any of his colleagues on the Tenth Circuit; Easterbrook (strongly originalist[70]) and Posner (pragmatic). My impression is that politically like-minded judges usually vote the same way despite their different judicial philosophies. Justice Scalia, in a passage I quoted in chapter 1, suggested that judges who have different philosophies tend nevertheless to agree in many cases because judges are "moderate,"[71] and there is surely merit to the suggestion. But a more important factor is that judicial philosophies have little causal efficacy. They do not weaken the force of political preferences. They supply not "actionable" reasons but rationalizations for actions taken on other grounds, though a fuller test of this proposition would require comparing judges who have similar judicial philosophies but different political leanings (such as Justices Scalia and Ginsburg—both legalists), and asking whether their decisions tend to converge or, as I predict, diverge.

70. See, for example, Frank H. Easterbrook, "Foreign Sources and the American Constitution," 30 *Harvard Journal of Law and Public Policy* 223 (2006); Easterbrook, "Abstraction and Authority," 59 *University of Chicago Law Review* 349, 372–378 (1992).

71. Antonin Scalia, "Originalism: The Lesser Evil," 57 *University of Cincinnati Law Review* 849, 862 (1989). See note 60 in chapter 1.

12

Judicial Cosmopolitanism

A debate is raging in judicial and academic circles over whether, or more precisely in what circumstances—for what purpose, to what end—the Supreme Court should cite a decision by an international or other foreign court.[1] The qualifications are vital. *Anything* can be cited as a source of information bearing on an adjudication. Suppose a judge happened to read a decision of the German Constitutional Court concerning the right to an abortion and discovered in it a persuasive argument against abortion (or perhaps facts about the motives for or procedures of abortion) that he had not seen before; and suppose he wanted either to give credit where credit was due or simply to identify a source, because judges, like most other lawyers, are obsessive citers (a reflex designed to conceal the ungrounded character of much legal reasoning). Or the foreign decision might be material in a legal sense, for example because the con-

1. See Austen L. Parrish, "Storm in a Teacup: The U.S. Supreme Court's Use of Foreign Law," 2007 *Illinois Law Review* 637 (2007); Mark C. Rahdert, "Comparative Constitutional Advocacy," 56 *American University Law Review* 553 (2007); John O. McGinnis and Ilya Somin, "Should International Law Be Part of Our Law?" 59 *Stanford Law Review* 1175 (2007); James Allan, "Jeremy Waldron and the Philosopher's Stone" (University of Queensland Faculty of Law, Feb. 2007, forthcoming in *San Diego Law Review*); Mark Tushnet, "When Is Knowing Less Better Than Knowing More? Unpacking the Controversy over Supreme Court Reference to Non-U.S. Law," 90 *Minnesota Law Review* 1275 (2006); James Allan and Grant Huscroft, "Constitutional Rights Coming Home to Roost? Rights Internationalism in American Courts," 43 *San Diego Law Review* 1 (2006); Jeremy Waldron, "Foreign Law and the Modern *Ius Gentium*," 119 *Harvard Law Review* 129 (2005); David S. Law, "Generic Constitutional Law," 89 *Minnesota Law Review* 652 (2005); Roger P. Alford, "In Search of a Theory for Constitutional Comparativism," 52 *UCLA Law Review* 639 (2005); Ken I. Kersch, "The New Legal Transnationalism, the Globalized Judiciary, and the Rule of Law," 4 *Washington University Global Studies Law Review* 345 (2005).

tract on which the U.S. suit was based specified that it would be interpreted in accordance with the law of some foreign country. That would be a case in which foreign law would supply the rule of decision for an American case.

International law, influenced or even created by foreign judicial decisions, can also be a basis for a claim or defense in an American court. Article I, section 8, of the Constitution authorizes Congress to "define and punish . . . Offences against the Law of Nations," and the Alien Tort Claims Act authorizes suits in federal court to enforce tort claims based on violations of international law.[2] Admiralty law is a body of international law enforced in our federal courts. An English decision from the eighteenth century might be cited to establish the original meaning of "cruel and unusual punishments" in the Eighth Amendment; this would be an example of noting a genealogical relation between foreign and U.S. law.

These are examples of unexceptionable citation to foreign decisions. The debate is over the as yet relatively few[3] cases in which a foreign decision is cited for its *precedential* effect by judges (more particularly Supreme Court Justices) searching for a global consensus on an issue of U.S. constitutional law. That search is the latest hopeless effort to ground controversial Supreme Court judgments in something more objective than the Justices' political preferences. Earlier generations sought legal fixity in natural law, deemed universal and therefore suprapolitical. The quest failed because of unbridgeable disagreements on what the principles of natural law are, or at least on what they require in particular cases. A global judicial consensus might seem a reasonable approximation to such a principle.

But this means treating foreign decisions as authority in an American court—that is, as having persuasive force just by virtue of being the decisions of recognized legal tribunals, never mind how compelling the tribunals' reasoning is. So Justice O'Connor acknowledged when she said that "conclusions reached by other countries and by the international community should at times constitute persuasive authority in American courts."[4]

---

2. 28 U.S.C. § 1350.

3. David Zaring, "The Use of Foreign Decisions by Federal Courts: An Empirical Analysis," 3 *Journal of Empirical Legal Studies* 297 (2006).

4. Sandra Day O'Connor, "Proceedings of the Ninety-Sixth Annual Meeting of the American Society of International Law: Keynote Address," 96 *American Society of International Law Proceedings* 348, 350 (2002).

We need to distinguish, however, between a *controlling* authority and an authority that is not controlling. A decision by a higher court in the same judicial system, and, depending on the precise doctrine of precedent embraced by a court, an earlier decision by one's own court, must be followed regardless of whether the current judges think it sound. No one supposes that foreign decisions should have *that* kind of authority. But often a court will cite a decision that lacks authority in the strong sense because it was rendered by a court in a different jurisdiction (it might be the decision of another state supreme court or another federal court of appeals, for example), but to which the court will give some weight by virtue of its having been decided by a sister court assumed to have similar values, traditions, and outlook. Apart from the intrinsic persuasiveness of the decision, just the fact that it *is* a decision by such a court carries some weight. If many sister courts have converged on a particular rule or doctrine, the fact of convergence will push a court confronted with the question for the first time toward the same result unless it has strong contrary feelings.

There are grave objections to citing foreign decisions as authority even in the weak sense of the word. Some objections go to the heart of the question whether American judges should be searching for global consensus—what Justice Kennedy was in quest of in *Lawrence* and *Roper.* But I begin with a more mundane objection. It is the promiscuous opportunities that such a practice of citing opens up. The objection is brought into focus by the common judicial practice of limiting the classes of case that may be cited as precedents. Many courts in the United States do not permit an advocate to cite to them, as precedents, opinions that are not published in the official reports (mainly nowadays the volumes of case reports published by West Publishing Company). Such opinions receive less careful attention from judges than the ones they decide to publish, so allowing them to be cited as precedents would increase the amount of research that lawyers and judges would have to do, but without conducing to better decisions. The Supreme Court economizes on its time by giving little weight to decisions by the federal courts of appeals and the state supreme courts. Such decisions are rarely cited except to indicate what the state of the law was when the Supreme Court intervened. Yet the judicial systems of the United States are relatively uniform and their product readily accessible, while the judicial systems of the rest of the world are immensely varied (the world contains 192 nations besides the United States), and most of their decisions are difficult to access, as a practical matter, by our monolingual judges and law clerks. Were foreign decisions freely citable, any judge wanting a supporting citation would have only to troll deeply enough in the world's corpus juris to find it, though there might well be doubts about just what he had found. Perhaps Justice Scalia would turn from denouncing the citation of foreign decisions by his court to casting his own net wide enough to haul in precedents supporting his views on homosexuality, abortion, capital punishment, and the role of religion in public life.

The citing of foreign decisions in U.S. courts is additionally objectionable as one more form of judicial fig-leafing, of which we have enough already. Few judges are so cosmopolitan in outlook as to want to take their cues from foreigners. In politically fraught cases, such as *Lawrence* and *Roper,* judges take their cues from their personal experiences, values, intuitions, temperament, reading of public opinion, and ideology. None of these influences on adjudication at the highest level has been shaped by the study of foreign judicial decisions. Some foreign nations criminalize sodomy; others do not. Is it to be supposed that the Justices in *Lawrence* weighed the arguments made in other nations about the criminalization of sodomy?

Judges are likely to cite foreign decisions for the same reason they prefer quoting from a previous decision to stating a position anew: they are timid about speaking in their own voices lest they make legal justice seem too personal. They are constantly digging for quotations from and citations to previous cases to create a sense of inevitability about positions that they in fact are adopting on grounds other than deference to precedent. In-depth research for a judicial opinion is usually conducted after, rather than before, the judges have voted, albeit tentatively, on the outcome. Citing foreign decisions is an effort to further mystify the adjudicative process, as well as to disguise the political character of the decisions at the heart of the Supreme Court's constitutional jurisprudence. The more political a court, the harder it tries to appear nonpolitical.

Justice Scalia thus is consistent in crusading against the citing both of foreign decisions and of legislative history. Both are forms of window dressing.[5] But when the window dressing is taken away, what is left?

5. On legislative history, see, for example, R. Shep Melnick, *Between the Lines: Interpreting Welfare Rights* 253 (1994) ("little more than window dressing"). Which brings to mind the following joke. A devout Jew is startled, walking past the office of the local mohel (the person

Scalia thinks it's originalism. Actually it is more window dressing. The citation of foreign decisions, like the citation of legislative history, also has a wasteful, "arms race" character. If one judge starts citing such sources, opposing judges are placed under pressure to go digging in the same sources for offsetting citations. The net contribution to sound judicial decision making may be nil. But the citation of legislative history creates an additional and more serious arms race problem: legislators become motivated to produce tendentious legislative history in an effort to sway judicial interpretation, and their efforts beget responses by legislators who want to nudge judicial interpretation in a different direction.

Furthermore, foreign decisions emerge from a complex social, political, historical, and institutional background of which most of our judges and Justices are ignorant.[6] To know how much weight to give to the decision of the German Constitutional Court in an abortion case, you would want to know how the judges of that court are appointed and how they conceive of their role, and especially how German attitudes toward abortion have been shaped by peculiarities of German history, notably the abortion jurisprudence of the Weimar Republic, thought by some to have set the stage for some of Nazi Germany's legal atrocities, such as involuntary euthanasia.[7] The European rejection of the death penalty, which advocates of abolishing the death penalty in the United States cite as evidence of an emerging international consensus that ought to influence our Supreme Court, is related both to the past overuse of it by European nations (think of the executions for petty larceny in eighteenth-century England, the Reign of Terror in France, and the rampant employment of the death penalty by Nazi Germany and the Soviet Union) and to the less democratic cast of European politics, which makes elite opinion more likely to override public opinion there than in the United States.

To cite foreign law as authority is to suppose fantastically that the

---

who performs circumcisions in accordance with Jewish law), to see pocket watches displayed in the window. He enters and says, "Mohel, why are you displaying watches in your window?" The mohel replies, "What would you like me to display?"

6. As argued in Ruti Teitel, "Comparative Constitutional Law in a Global Age," 117 *Harvard Law Review* 2570 (2004), reviewing Norman Dorsen et al., *Comparative Constitutionalism: Cases and Materials* (2003).

7. Richard E. Levy and Alexander Somek, in their article "Paradoxical Parallels in the American and German Abortion Decisions," 9 *Tulane Journal of International and Comparative Law* 109, 115–116 (2001), discuss the German Constitutional Court's "repeated emphasis," in cases involving abortion, "on the negative example set by Nazi-Germany."

world's judges constitute a single community of wisdom and conscience. That is the position the Justices are gesturing toward when they try to justify their citation of foreign decisions as authority by invoking a "decent respect to the opinions of mankind,"[8] a phrase in the Declaration of Independence that they have taken out of context and by doing so have inverted its meaning.[9] The Supreme Court Justices, or at least those who like to cite foreign courts, are sophisticated cosmopolitans who naturally are influenced by what they know of what other countries do. But are they not arrogant, even usurpative, in trying to impose their cosmopolitan values on Americans in the name of our eighteenth-century Constitution?

A neglected institutional difference between the U.S. Supreme Court and foreign constitutional courts is that it is easier in most other countries to nullify by constitutional amendment the ruling of a constitutional court. It can usually be done by a legislative supermajority.[10] Rarely is there anything that corresponds to the biggest hurdle to nullifying a constitutional ruling of our Supreme Court—the requirement that three-fourths of the states ratify a proposed constitutional amendment

8. See, for example, Knight v. Florida, 528 U.S. 990, 997 (1999) (Breyer, J., dissenting from denial of certiorari).

9. As Eugene Kontorovich explains,

> The Declaration actually says that "a decent respect to the opinions of mankind requires that they should declare the causes which impel them to the separation." In other words, America should give reasons for its actions. The Declaration is a public-relations document designed to explain and justify the colonists' actions. This is the opposite of the spin put on it by internationalist lawyers, who say it shows that we "learn from others." Rather, the Declaration seeks to teach other nations . . . In 1776, there was no basis in international law for throwing off the rule of a sovereign monarch. Doing so contradicted the dominant opinion of nations, which were themselves monarchies. Had the colonists taken the court's approach [in *Roper v. Simmons*], they would have said, "Well, everyone else is doing taxation without representation, there must be something to it."

Kontorovich, "The Opinion of Mankind," *New York Sun*, July 1, 2005, p. 9. See also Kontorovich, "Disrespecting the 'Opinions of Mankind': International Law in Constitutional Interpretation," 8 *Green Bag* (2d ser.) 261 (2005).

10. Of the 47 countries that have a constitutional court for which the requisite data are available, 79 percent allow a two-thirds vote by the legislature to overrule a decision. See Venice Commission, "Decisions of Constitutional Courts and Equivalent Bodies and Their Execution," March 9–10, 2001, www.venice.coe.int/docs/2001/CDL-INF(2001)009-e.asp (visited May 2, 2007), as supplemented by other Web sites, such as the University of Richmond's Constitution Finder, http://confinder.richmond.edu (visited May 2, 2007), that contain foreign constitutional texts.

after a two-thirds vote in both houses of Congress in favor of it. The easier it is to overrule a constitutional decision by amending the constitution, the less cautious, the less respectful of public opinion and strong disagreement a constitutional court can afford to be. Just as dogs bark more ferociously when they are behind a fence, judges indulge their personal views more blatantly when they know they do not have the last word. Think of the uncomfortable position in which Justices Black and Douglas would have found themselves had their dissenting position that obscenity is fully protected by the First Amendment commanded the assent of a majority of the Justices. Our Justices are fooled if they think that all the audaciously progressive opinions expressed by foreign constitutional judges would be the same if those judges had the power our Justices have.

The decisive objection to citing foreign decisions as authority is the undemocratic character of the practice. Even decisions rendered by judges in democratic countries, or by judges from those countries who sit in international courts, are outside the U.S. democratic orbit. This point is obscured because we think of our courts as "undemocratic" institutions. That is imprecise. Not only are most state judges elected, but federal judges are appointed and confirmed by elected officials, the President and the members of the Senate. So even our federal judges have a certain democratic legitimacy. The judges of foreign countries, however democratic those countries may be, have no democratic legitimacy in the United States. The votes of foreign electorates are not events in our democracy.

I am not suggesting that our judges should be provincial and ignore what people in other nations think and do. Just as our states are laboratories for social experiments from which other states and the federal government can learn, foreign nations are laboratories from whose legal experiments we can learn. The problem is not learning from abroad; it is treating foreign judicial decisions as authority in U.S. cases, as if the world were a single legal community.

The yen to cite foreign decisions is part of a movement—call it "judicial cosmopolitanism"—that treats the entire world as if it were one judicial jurisdiction. The problems with such an approach go far beyond citation practices and are well illustrated by two books—one by a Canadian law professor, David Beatty, and one by an Israeli judge, Aharon Barak—that I shall discuss. But in criticizing judicial cosmopolitanism I shall be taking no position on the validity of the *philosophical* concept of cosmopolitanism, with which the judicial concept is easily confused. The philosophical concept has a long and distinguished lineage that runs from Diogenes the Cynic to Martha Nussbaum, through the Stoics, Cicero, Grotius, Kant, and many other notables. Epitomized by Diogenes' term "citizen of the world," it teaches that our duties to other human beings do not stop at the border; that our common humanity transcends, or at least rightly competes with, loyalties to family, friends, co-ethnics, co-nationals, and others with whom we have "local" ties, psychologically and politically important though these ties are.[11] Nowadays it is most often advanced as an argument in favor of generous foreign assistance by rich nations.[12] It has nothing to do with whether American judges should be taking their cues from judges in other nations, even if our common humanity is believed to underwrite a universal natural law that should guide courts, as some cosmopolitan philosophers, Kant for example, have believed.[13] Whatever the source or content of natural law, to think it a proper recourse for the Supreme Court or evidenced by foreign judicial decisions is a leap not justified by anything in philosophical cosmopolitanism. Kant's concern with "cosmopolitan right—one's willingness to do what is required by the general principle of sharing this limited world with others"[14]—is as remote from the current issue of judicial cosmopolitanism as international charity is.

David Beatty entitles his defense of judicial cosmopolitanism *The Ultimate Rule of Law,*[15] and the adjective primes us to expect an augmented concept of the rule of law. Traditionally, as we know, the term has meant two distinct though related things: that legal cases are to be decided according to their legal merits rather than according to the personal merits of the litigants (this is the law's impersonality and the judge's duty of dis-

11. On philosophical cosmopolitanism, see, for example, *The Political Philosophy of Cosmopolitanism* (Gillian Brock and Harry Brighouse eds. 2005); Martha C. Nussbaum, "Duties of Justice, Duties of Material Aid: Cicero's Problematic Legacy," 8 *Journal of Political Philosophy* 176 (2000).

12. See, for example, Gillian Brock, "Egalitarianism, Ideals, and Cosmopolitan Justice," 36 *Philosophical Forum* 1 (2005).

13. David Held, "Principles of Cosmopolitan Order," in *The Political Philosophy of Cosmopolitanism,* note 11 above, at 25–27. See generally *Perpetual Peace: Essays on Kant's Cosmopolitan Ideal* (James Bohman and Matthias Lutz-Bachmann eds. 1997).

14. Jeremy Waldron, "What Is Cosmopolitan?" 8 *Journal of Political Philosophy* 227, 242 (2000).

15. David M. Beatty, *The Ultimate Rule of Law* (2004).

interestedness); and that even the highest officials in society are subject to the law rather than being above (immune from) it. A corollary of the second sense is that unless the law is reasonably clear, so that it can guide judges in applying it and provide a basis for monitoring judicial conformity to the law, judges will perforce be deciding cases on something other than legalist grounds. They will be the nation's rulers rather than the law's servants. The threat that unclear laws pose to the rule of law is especially acute in the case of constitutional adjudication when the highest judges are exercising final authority without guidance from the constitutional text or other sources external to their own will on how to exercise it.

Beatty is aware of the problem and offers the following surprising solution: Judges dealing with constitutional issues are not to attend to the constitutional text, to precedents ("in constitutional cases, precedents are at best superfluous"[16]), or to analogies. They are not to think of their task as interpretive at all. They are to attend exclusively to the facts of the case. Beatty argues that although constitutions differ greatly from one another "none of this rich variation in constitutional texts . . . has had any effect on the way judges think about laws that intentionally provide more training and employment opportunities for men than women. All the details and adornments that are so important to those who negotiate and draft constitutions and international human rights treaties have absolutely no bearing on how these cases are resolved."[17] That does not trouble Beatty because "when judges are prepared to look at all the facts of a case honestly and impartially, they have no difficulty seeing and doing what is right"[18]—and he means legally right.

Beatty considers his approach a form of pragmatism, though his preferred term is "proportionality": "Proportionality makes pragmatism the best it can possibly be."[19] This is not an idiosyncratic renaming; "proportionality" is a standard commonly used by courts outside the United States,[20] and we recall that it has been appropriated by Justice Breyer,

16. Id. at 90.

17. Id. at 81.

18. Id. at 112. Or as he puts it elsewhere, "Everyone's interests are better served when the courts base their decisions on a close and careful evaluation of the facts than when they spend most of their energy trying to divine answers from the words of the text." Id. at 57.

19. Id. at 187.

20. See, for example, Vicki C. Jackson, "Ambivalent Resistance and Comparative Constitutionalism: Opening Up the Conversation on 'Proportionality,' Rights and Federalism," 1 *Uni-*

our most cosmopolitan Supreme Court Justice. To pass constitutional muster, Beatty argues, a law must represent a proportional, rather than an excessive, response to some perceived social need. Proportionality so understood is indistinguishable from the quintessential pragmatic technique of balancing competing interests.

Beatty claims that fact-based adjudication will yield an *objective* resolution of constitutional issues in the sense of a resolution unaffected by ideology or emotion. "When judges remain completely detached from the substantive values that are at stake in a case, and take seriously all the evidence that shows what a law really means for those it affects most, the cases show that the right answer is usually pretty clear."[21] He therefore disparages efforts to create constitutional theories that generate substantive results, confident that judges guided by facts will converge more or less automatically on outcomes of which he approves. About "originalism" he comments pungently that "directing judges to resolve the flashpoints of social conflict in their communities against the understandings of people who lived as long as two hundred years ago, leaves them, it turns out, free to come down on whatever side of a case their consciences tell them is right."[22] He points out that adopting Dworkin's moral theory of constitutional interpretation would make "the people lose control of the moral development of their communities to a professional elite."[23] With the aid of such examples Beatty argues convincingly that constitutional adjudication cannot be made objective, impersonal, and apolitical by a demonstration that there is one correct constitutional theory.

So judges should take their cue not from theorists—all of whom are easily refuted—but from their own practices, which mainly involve, Beatty insists, finding facts. He instances the common law: "The great genius of this ancient legal tradition is its pursuit of theory and overarching principles from the bottom up."[24] It is "the method of induction."[25] He contends that this is not only how courts *should* approach

---

versity of Pennsylvania Journal of Constitutional Law 583 (1999); Gregory C. Alexander, *The Global Debate over Constitutional Property: Lessons for American Takings Jurisprudence* 189–294 (2006).

21. Beatty, note 15 above, at 98.
22. Id. at 9.
23. Id. at 33 (footnote omitted).
24. Id. at 34.
25. Id.

constitutional adjudication but how they *do* approach it. For evidence he takes the reader on a tour of the world's constitutional courts, arguing that despite differences in the wording of constitutional texts, in legal culture, in doctrine and precedent, and so forth, the courts come up with remarkably uniform results, though the U.S. Supreme Court is a frequent outlier. About all that the cases have in common is similar facts, so it must be, he concludes, the facts that are driving the outcome.

Beatty is thus the heir of those legal realists who thought that facts were all that drove judicial decisions. He is mindful, however, of the "is-ought" problem that such an approach gives rise to. How can a study of facts alone, however searching and scrupulous, generate a conclusion that the position of one of the parties to a case is right and the position of the other is wrong, without a normative framework? He never answers this question directly. But he seems to think that proportionality just happens to be the legal norm on which the global judicial community has converged. The world is a pretty big place, though, and Beatty cites decisions from only 15 of its 193 nations (plus decisions of 2 European tribunals and 1 United Nations tribunal). And 11 of the 15 are former British possessions. This is not a representative sample of world judicial opinion.

Yet he may be right that the highest judges in most countries are paying relatively little attention to what their countries' constitutions actually say. The United States is such a country. But people who recognize this judicial insouciance usually conclude that the judges are stepping out of line and forgetting that they have less democratic legitimacy than the legislative and executive branches of government. Beatty, however, revels in the fact (if it is a fact) that "people all over the world have chosen to put courts at the centre of their systems of government."[26] He likes this because while interpretivism may in practice be quite unconstrained,[27] as he argues convincingly, fact-based adjudication is not because for him there is always a fact of the matter that once found resolves the case. It is a fact that the state should provide financial support for religious schools, a fact that the state must recognize homosexual marriage, and so on. Since all that judges are doing is finding facts, their

26. Id. at 35.

27. He calls it "profoundly undemocratic" because it "imposes virtually no constraints—no disciplining rules—on the discretion of judges." Id. at 56. That is the pot calling the kettle black.

activity is apolitical. They are not competing with the elected officials whose acts they invalidate in the name—but it is only in the name—of the constitution.

The facts speak to Beatty more clearly than they will to many of his readers because what he considers facts others would describe as opinions. For example, he commends the German Constitutional Court for having ruled that Bavaria "does no wrong if it allows voluntary prayers to be spoken in its schools but it does if it affixes crucifixes to classroom walls" because "for non-Christian students, the sectarian nature of the cross and the fact that they could never escape its glare made its force much more powerful than voluntary prayers."[28] Without more detail concerning the court's analysis, which Beatty does not supply, this sounds like an arbitrary judgment precariously perched on the odd choice of the word "glare" to describe the appearance of a crucifix.

He applauds the Japanese Supreme Court for having permitted a local government to make a financial contribution to a Shinto groundbreaking ceremony for a public gymnasium.[29] He remarks that "most people, including those on the city council who voted for the expenditure, regarded it primarily as a secular ritual dedicated to the safe construction of the gymnasium that lacked a religious meaning of any significance."[30] In other words, the court was denying the religious significance of the ceremony, just as an American court would be inclined to deny the religious significance of the intonation of "God save the United States and this honorable court" that opens its sessions. Still, it would be remarkable in the American context to authorize public expenditures for elaborate religious ceremonies. The Shinto case transports the American reader to a disorientingly different political culture. The groundbreaking ceremony was sponsored by the city's mayor, presided over by four Shinto priests, involved a Shinto altar and other sacred Shinto objects and purification rituals involving the spectators, and lasted 40 minutes.

Shinto had been the Japanese state religion until the United States occupied Japan at the end of World War II and had been intolerant of other religions. Despite this history and the emphatically religious character of

28. Id. at 46–47.

29. Kakunaga v. Sekiguchi (1977), translated and reprinted in Lawrence W. Beer and Hiroshi Itoh, *The Constitutional Case Law of Japan, 1970 through 1990* 478–491 (1996).

30. Beatty, note 15 above, at 68. By "secular ritual" I assume he means the equivalent of pledging allegiance to the flag or singing "The Star-Spangled Banner."

the groundbreaking ceremony, the Japanese Supreme Court ruled that because "the average Japanese has little interest in and consciousness of religion" (with many of them indeed believing in both Shinto and Buddhism, as a result of which "their religious consciousness is somewhat jumbled"), and because Shinto is not a proselytizing religion, "it is unlikely that a Shinto groundbreaking, even when performed by a Shinto priest, would raise the religious consciousness of those attending or of people in general or lead in any way to the encouragement or promotion of Shinto."[31] It is apparent that the decision depends on particulars of Japanese culture rather than on general principles that an American or Canadian court might draw on.

Beatty's faith in the objectivity of fact-based adjudication stems from a belief that "factual claims can be tested for how accurately they conform to an independent empirical world, as it actually exists."[32] But this is rarely done, or doable, in the adjudicative context. One will have sensed already a rather casual attitude on Beatty's part, as on that of the courts whose decisions he discusses, toward empirical testing. He is not above criticizing judges for "inflating the importance of facts"[33] and "decreeing what facts mattered the most"[34]—as if it were possible to conduct fact-based adjudication without making judgments of relevancy. Beatty himself does this when he states in defense of a U.S. Supreme Court decision striking down state residency requirements for entitlement to welfare benefits that "need, not length of residence, is the proper criterion for distribution."[35] He overlooks the fact that a likely consequence of outlawing state residency requirements is to induce states that provide generous welfare benefits to reduce them, lest the state become a magnet for poor people in other states.

He is willing to resolve constitutional issues by shifting the burden of proof to the side whose position he disfavors, as when he notes with approval that "laws that regulate how people do their work are more likely to be found wanting where it cannot be shown that they advance the well-being of the community in some significant way,"[36] or when he says

31. Beer and Itoh, note 29 above, at 483.
32. Beatty, note 15 above, at 73.
33. Id. at 107.
34. Id. at 108.
35. Id. at 142.
36. Id. at 131.

that "no evidence is ever provided that would support the claim that if gays and lesbians had the same rights and freedoms as heterosexual couples, . . . the moral character of the community and especially its young would be threatened in any way."[37] He does not explain why the burden of presenting convincing evidence should rest on the defenders of the challenged marriage laws rather than on the attackers.

In discussing a case that invalidated the exclusion of homosexuals from the military, Beatty approvingly remarks that the court "noted the lack of 'concrete' and 'actual or significant' evidence that allowing gay men to enlist in the armed forces would prejudice its morale, fighting power, or operational effectiveness in any way."[38] He does not require that there be "concrete" and "actual or significant" evidence that homosexuals are harmed by the exclusion. Nor is he bothered by a lack of concreteness when he says that "laws that establish a broadcasting system [must] guarantee that the full spectrum of opinion in the community will be heard."[39] What is "the full spectrum" of opinion, and who is to decide? Must every lunatic have access to a broadcast studio? Beatty contends that government has a constitutional duty to subsidize religious schools but "may make funding conditional on religious schools agreeing to teach the same curriculum that is used in state-run schools."[40] If the curriculum is identical, in what sense are they religious schools? He also says that "proportional funding remains scrupulously neutral as between the competing pedagogical philosophies of secular majorities and religious minorities."[41] But a religious school cannot implement its pedagogical philosophy if it must teach the curriculum specified for public schools.

He argues that "there is no legal basis to permit traditional marriage laws [banning homosexual marriage] remaining in force for even one more day," since the "evidence" in favor of permitting homosexual marriage is as "one-sided" as the evidence for permitting homosexual sodomy.[42] The only "evidence" he gives is that "it is no longer possible to

37. Id. at 110. Incidentally, despite much talk of "rights" throughout the book, Beatty claims that the concept of "proportionality" "makes the concept of rights almost irrelevant." Id. at 160.

38. Id. at 113.

39. Id. at 145 (footnote omitted).

40. Id. at 179.

41. Id. at 180.

42. Id. at 114–115.

argue that allowing [homosexuals] to swear a legal oath of marriage will have a tangible effect on anyone else's welfare or well-being."[43] What about intangible effects? Remember that Beatty insists that judges should decide constitutional cases without regard to substantive values. John Stuart Mill's philosophy of tolerance for acts that, though they may offend, inflict no tangible harm on third parties is substantive and controversial.

Beatty's assessments of specific case outcomes are generated not by testable (let alone tested) factual claims but by such ideological assertions as that in law "liberty and equality . . . mean exactly the same thing. Regardless of whether a law is attacked under the banner of equality or liberty, its legitimacy and its life depend on whether it can pass a rigorous evaluation of its ends, its means, and its effects against the principle of proportionality that connects all three."[44] (Notice the burden shifting implicit in the word "rigorous.") Indeed, he claims that "liberty, equality, and fraternity all mean the same thing."[45] Within a page of stating that "ethical and prudential arguments [in constitutional cases] make no sense," he equates "proportionality" to a "universal principle of distributive justice that is controlling in all constitutional democracies and determinative of all human rights."[46] Elsewhere he suggests that "proportionality" means "entitlements to fair shares of whatever is being legislated."[47] Yet he also concedes that "what is just, what is in proper proportion, in any case is particular to each community."[48] And hence it is proper to restrict abortion more in Ireland than in Japan.[49] But then why is it not proper to limit homosexual marriage in Alabama though not in Massachusetts?

Pragmatic judges will agree with Beatty that consequences should be front and center in the adjudicative process, but not that the *only* consequences worth considering are the consequences for the people immediately affected by a judicial decision. Institutional consequences should also be considered, and they include the damage to the democratic process, and to the law's stability, that would be inflicted by a wholehearted

43. Id. at 114.
44. Id. at 116.
45. Id. at 158.
46. Id. at 116–117.
47. Id. at 133. See also id. at 144–158.
48. Id. at 167.
49. Id. at 168.

embrace of Beatty's program of fact-based, law-free constitutional adjudication. There would be a breathtaking expansion of judicial power at the expense of the power of drafters and ratifiers of constitutions, legislators, other officials, and the public at large. And because judges would be constrained only by their commitment to impartial factual inquiry, and not by any text (constitutional, legislative, or judicial), because the practical limits of adjudication prevent a deep judicial engagement with the facts bearing on constitutional controversies, and because those facts will differ unpredictably from case to case, lawyers and lower-court judges would be utterly at sea in trying to figure out how future disputes should be resolved.

Still, Beatty's criticisms of constitutional theorists are spot-on. And he vindicates his faith in the power, or at least the potential power, of judicial engagement with facts in a number of his discussions of specific cases. Thus he points out that the maximum-hours law invalidated in *Lochner v. New York*[50] had been intended to put small nonunion bakers out of business.[51] And he notes that despite the holding in *Employment Division v. Smith*[52] that the free exercise of religion does not embrace the use of peyote in American Indians' religious ceremonies, a number of states had made an exception to their drug laws to permit such use, without the sky falling.[53]

But the greatest interest of Beatty's book lies elsewhere—lies in its unintended cautionary function. The book is a warning against dissolving legal pragmatism into "only the facts, ma'am" adjudication. Legal pragmatism is disciplined by a structure of norms and doctrines, commonly expressed in standards such as negligence, good faith, and freedom of speech, that tells judges what consequences they can consider and how (in what relation to each other, for example). Take away the framework and what judges do does not merit the word "law." In the arresting glimpse that it gives of an emerging global community of aggressively interventionist constitutional judges, Beatty's book warns us against hopping too quickly on the world-law bandwagon.

One of the most prominent of the aggressively interventionist foreign judges is Aharon Barak, a long-serving justice (eventually chief justice)

50. 198 U.S. 45 (1905).
51. Beatty, note 15 above, at 135–136.
52. 494 U.S. 872 (1990).
53. Beatty, note 15 above, at 52.

of the Supreme Court of Israel, recently retired. He is a world-famous judge who dominated his court as completely as John Marshall dominated our Supreme Court. Were there a Nobel Prize for law, Barak would probably have been an early recipient. Yet his book on judging[54] is Exhibit A for why American judges should be wary about citing foreign judicial decisions or, more broadly, about taking their cues from foreign judges on the theory that the judges of the highest courts of all civilized countries constitute a loose-knit community something like that constituted by the supreme court justices of all the states in the United States. Although Barak is familiar with the American legal system and supposes himself to be in some sort of sync with liberal American judges, he actually inhabits a completely and, to an American, weirdly different juristic universe.

Robert Bork has said that Barak "establishes a world record for judicial hubris."[55] Barak is John Marshall without a constitution to expound. Israel does not have a constitution in the usual sense. The Knesset (the Israeli parliament) has passed several "basic laws," one of which—Basic Law: Human Dignity and Freedom—provides that "the life, body or dignity of any person shall not be violated" and that "every person is entitled to protection of his life, body and dignity."[56] But while the Knesset can call some of its laws "basic" if it wants to, there is grave doubt that it is authorized to promulgate constitutional as well as ordinary statutory provisions.[57] This may be why Barak's book contains barely any references to the "constitutional" text.

Yet without a secure constitutional basis, Barak created a degree of judicial power undreamt of by our most aggressive Supreme Court Justices. He puts Marshall, who did less with much more, in the shade. (He borrowed from Marshall the trick of first announcing a novel rule in a case in which he concludes that the rule does not apply, so that people get accustomed to the rule before it begins to bite them.) Among the rules of Israeli law that Barak's judicial opinions have been instrumental in creating are that any citizen can ask a court to block illegal action by a government official even if he is not personally affected by it (that is,

54. Aharon Barak, *The Judge in a Democracy* (2006).
55. Robert H. Bork, "Barak's Rule," *Azure*, Winter 2007, pp. 125, 131.
56. Barak, note 54 above, at 85 n. 154.
57. Joshua Segev, "Who Needs a Constitution? In Defense of the Non-Decision Constitution-Making Tactic in Israel," 70 *Albany Law Review* 409 (2007).

even if he lacks "standing to sue" in the U.S. sense); that any government action that is "unreasonable" is illegal ("put simply, the executive must act reasonably, for an unreasonable act is an unlawful act"[58]); that a court can forbid the government to appoint an official who has committed a crime, even though he has been pardoned, or is otherwise ethically challenged, and can order the dismissal of a cabinet minister because he faces criminal proceedings; that in the name of "human dignity" a court can order the government to alleviate homelessness and poverty;[59] and that a court can countermand military orders, decide "whether to prevent the release of a terrorist within the framework of a political 'package deal,'"[60] and direct the government to move the security wall that keeps suicide bombers from entering Israel from the West Bank.[61] These are powers that a nation *could* grant its judges. For example, many European nations and even some U.S. states authorize "abstract" constitutional review—that is, judicial determination of a statute's constitutionality without waiting for a suit by someone actually harmed by the statute. But only in Israel (as far as I know) do judges confer the power of abstract review on themselves, without benefit of a constitutional or legislative provision. One is reminded of Napoleon's taking the imperial crown out of the Pope's hands and crowning himself.

Barak bases his conception of judicial authority on abstract principles that in his hands are merely plays on words. The leading abstraction (reminiscent of Breyer's *Active Liberty*) is "democracy." Political democracy in the modern sense means a system of government in which the key officials stand for election at relatively short intervals and thus are accountable to the citizenry. A judiciary that is free to override the decisions of those officials curtails democracy. For Barak, however, democracy has a "substantive" component, namely a set of rights ("human rights" not limited to political rights, such as the right to criticize public officials, that support democracy), enforced by the judiciary, that clips the wings of elected officials.[62] This is not a justification for a hyperactive judiciary, but merely a redefinition of it. Notice the parallel to Justice Breyer's conflation of liberty and democracy in his notions of "ac-

58. Barak, note 54 above, at 248.
59. Id. at 85–88.
60. Id. at 180.
61. Id. at 284.
62. Id. at 25–26. "Human rights are the core of substantive democracy." Id. at xi.

tive liberty," "the liberty of the ancients," and our "democratic Constitution."

Another portmanteau word that Barak abuses is "interpretation." To him it is a practice remote from a search for the meaning intended by the authors of legislation. He says that the task of a legislature in passing statutes is to "bridge the gap between law and society" and the task of the judge in interpreting a statute is to "ensure that the law in fact bridges the gap between law and society."[63] This is very odd—isn't the statute the law, rather than the intermediary between the law and society? What he seems to mean, as further suggested by his statement that "whoever enforces one statute enforces the whole legal system,"[64] is that a statute should be interpreted to harmonize with the spirit or values of the legal system considered as a whole. But in practice that means with the judge's ideal system, as no real legal system has a unitary spirit or common set of values. Alternatively, the judge should consider the statute's "objective purpose . . . to realize the fundamental values of democracy,"[65] with "objective" having nothing to do with legislative intent. So a regulation that authorizes military censorship of publications that the censor "deems likely to harm state security, public security, or the public peace" was interpreted by Barak's court to mean "would create a near certainty of grave harm to state security, public security, or public peace."[66] The court treated the statute as a first draft that the judges were free to rewrite.

Barak invokes the "separation of powers" as further support for his conception of the judicial role. What he means by the term is that the executive and legislative branches are to have no control over the judicial branch. What *we* mean by separation of powers, so far as judicial authority is concerned, is that something called the judicial power of the United States has been consigned to the judicial branch. That does not mean that the *branch* is independent of the other branches. If each of the powers (executive, legislative, and judicial) were administered by a branch that was wholly independent and thus could ignore the others, the result would be chaos. The branches have to be mutually dependent in order to force cooperation. So "separation of powers" implies "checks

63. Id. at 17.
64. Id.
65. Id. at 138.
66. Id. at 6.

and balances," and the judicial branch has to be checked by the other branches and not just do the checking. The President nominates and the Senate confirms (or rejects) federal judges, and the Congress fixes their salaries and the courts' budgets, regulates the Supreme Court's appellate jurisdiction, decides whether to create other federal courts, and can remove judges by impeachment. The judicial power of the United States can be exercised only in suits brought by persons who have standing to sue in the sense of having a tangible grievance that can be remedied by the court. And because the judicial power is not the only federal power—there are executive and legislative powers of constitutional dignity as well—the judiciary cannot tell the President whom to appoint to his cabinet.

Armed with such abstractions as "democracy," "interpretation," "separation of powers," "objectivity," "reasonableness" (it is the concept of "reasonableness" that Barak would have used to adjudicate the "package deal" for the release of the terrorist), and (of course) "justice" ("I try to be guided by my North Star, which is justice. I try to make law and justice converge, so that the Justice will do justice"[67]), the judiciary is a law unto itself.

Barak's jurisprudence may seem to hold no interest for Americans other than as an illustration of the world's diversity. In reality it bears importantly on the issue of whether American judges should cite foreign cases as authority. Some of our judges, as we know, think that just the fact that a foreign court has decided a case in a certain way entitles the decision to some, though perhaps not a great deal of, weight in deciding a factually similar American case. But what we learn from Barak's book is that some foreign legal systems, even the legal system of a democratic nation that is a close ally of the United States, are so alien to our own system that their decisions ought to be given no weight by our courts. American judges distinguish between how they might vote on a statute if they were legislators and whether the statute is unconstitutional; they might think it a bad statute yet uphold its constitutionality. But in a Barakian court it would be impossible to tell whether a judgment of unconstitutionality was anything more than the judges' opinion that it was a dumb statute, something they would have voted against had they been

67. Id. at 107.

members of the legislature that enacted it. Such an opinion would have no significance for issues of constitutionality in our system.

When Bork attributed "judicial hubris" to Barak he was using as his benchmark the American system. Many Israelis think Barak hubristic,[68] but whether he is or is not in the Israeli setting is irrelevant to Bork's judgment. All Bork means is that a judge who thinks like Barak is playing outside the boundaries within which American judges operate. There are plenty of hubristic American decisions, but their authors make some effort to tether them to orthodox legal materials, such as the constitutional text. The tether is often long and frayed—when for example a judge decides that criminalizing abortion or refusing to grant a marriage license to a homosexual couple is a deprivation of liberty without due process of law, or upholds an antiabortion law on the ground that a mother's love for her child epitomizes respect for human life. So there is a sense in which Barak merely carries to its logical extreme a tendency already manifest in the decisions of supreme courts in the United States. It is a matter of degree. But at some point a difference in degree can rightly be called a difference in kind.

Barak's book is not introspective. He purports to derive his judicial approach from the abstractions I mentioned, but they cannot be the real source of the approach. For they are empty verbiage, as when Barak says that "other branches [of government] seek to attain efficiency; the courts seek to attain legality."[69] Or when, in defending a ruling made during the 1991 Gulf War requiring the Israeli army to distribute more gas masks to residents of the West Bank, he says that "we [the court] did not intervene in military considerations, for which the expertise and responsibility lie with the executive. Rather, we intervened in considerations of equality, for which the expertise and responsibility rest with the judiciary."[70] Elsewhere in the book he defends judicial balancing of competing interests, and it is obvious that in the gas mask case the court had to balance against considerations of equality whatever military reasons

---

68. See, for example, Caroline B. Glick, "Israel's Judicial Tyranny," *Jerusalem Post,* Nov. 18, 2005, p. 24; Jonathan Rosenblum, "Drunk with Arrogance," *Hamodia,* Jan. 18, 2002, www .jewishmediaresources.com/article/326 (visited May 2, 2007). For a defense of Barak's activism, see Barak Medina, "Four Myths of Judicial Review· A Response to Richard Posner's Criticism of Aharon Barak's Judicial Activism," 49 *Harvard International Law Journal Online* 1 (2007), www.harvardilj.org/online/116 (visited Oct. 6, 2007).

69. Barak, note 54 above, at 216.

70. Id. at 289.

the army gave for distributing fewer gas masks on the West Bank than in Israel proper, such as that Iraq was more likely to aim its missiles at Jews than at Arabs. A few pages after discussing the gas masks Barak says inconsistently that when deciding whether to invalidate a security measure "the court asks if a reasonable person responsible for security would be prudent to adopt the security measures that were adopted."[71]

All this is not to say that Barak was a bad judge or is a bad constitutional theorist. For although like most legal theorists he purports to be discussing the law at large rather than his own local law, also like most theorists it is really the latter that is his subject. Legal thinking does not cross national boundaries easily[72]—that is the main point of this chapter. Barak is by all accounts brilliant, as well as austere and high-minded— Israel's Cato. Israel is an immature democracy, poorly governed; its political class is mediocre and corrupt; it floats precariously in a lethally hostile Muslim sea—and it really could use a constitution. Barak stepped into a political and legal vacuum and with considerable ingenuity generated a series of, in Laurence Tribe's words on the dust jacket of Barak's book, "surprisingly agreeable outcomes." Barak was a legal buccaneer— and maybe that was what Israel needed, and perhaps still needs.[73] Of course, there is no acknowledgment of this in the book. Barak writes not only without self-doubt but also without a sense that his jurisprudence may reflect local, even quite personal, conditions and experiences. He survived the Holocaust as a child in Lithuania. This can help us understand his approval of an Israeli law that would be thought unacceptably illiberal in the United States: that no candidate of an antidemocratic party can be permitted to stand for election to the Knesset—for the Nazi Party came to power in Germany democratically. Like our judges, Aharon Barak is a prisoner of his experiences.

71. Id. at 305.

72. A point I have made in discussing the jurisprudence of Ronald Dworkin, H. L. A. Hart, and Jürgen Habermas, in my book *The Problematics of Moral and Legal Theory*, ch. 2 (1999).

73. See, besides Medina, note 68 above, Eli M. Salzberger, "Judicial Appointments and Promotions in Israel: Constitution, Law, and Politics," in *Appointing Judges in an Age of Judicial Power: Critical Perspectives from around the World* 241 (Kate Malleson and Peter H. Russell eds. 2006). It would be an impertinence for me to opine on how Israel should structure its judiciary.

Conclusion

The essential datum with which I began my effort in this book to develop a positive theory of judicial decision making was that there is a pronounced political element in the decisions of American judges, including federal trial and intermediate appellate judges and U.S. Supreme Court Justices. The evidence is overwhelming, though judges themselves tend to brush it aside. They brush it aside because they *know* they are not Democratic or Republican hacks. In so doing they fail to understand that the scholarship that shows that judging is "political" need not be understood to be using the word to denote crass, partisan political commitment. A judge may be a staunch conservative, but he does not ask himself: "How would George W. Bush, who appointed me, vote in this case?" Judges are reluctant to confess even that they are not complete political eunuchs engaged solely in applying rules they did not create to facts they find, like baseball umpires. Many of them believe in all honesty that their decisions are not influenced in the slightest by their political leanings. This widespread honest belief may be the strongest counter to the evidence of political judging. But it is turned by Bayes's theorem, which shows how preconceptions influence decisions. Preconceptions often are unconscious. Much thinking, including that of busy judges who must make decisions under uncertainty, is telescoped thinking—emotional, intuitive, or commonsensical—that does not proceed step-by-step from explicit premises and so offers wide play for unconscious preconceptions. Bayes acquits judges of the charge of hypocrisy.

So judging is political. It is also "personal" in the sense that judges' personal attributes—including background characteristics, such as race

369

and sex; personality traits, such as authoritarianism; and professional and life experiences, such as having been a prosecutor or having grown up in turbulent times—influence judging. Personal attributes do this indirectly as well as directly, by contributing to the formation of a judge's ideology and thus of the political inclinations that affect judicial decisions. But judging is not just personal and political. It is also impersonal and nonpolitical in the sense that many, indeed most, judicial decisions really are the product of a neutral application of rules not made up for the occasion to facts fairly found. Such decisions exemplify what is commonly called "legal formalism," though the word I prefer is "legalism." But they tend to be the decisions in routine cases.

What is it about the judicial labor market that determines the balance, which varies among judges and courts, among the personal, the political, and the legalist factors in judging? That is the central question that this book has addressed. Coming up with an answer has required examining the motivations and constraints that play on judges in different judicial systems, including private judicial systems (such as commercial arbitration), elected judiciaries, and the career judiciaries found in civil law systems such as those of Continental Europe. I discussed these other systems only briefly, however, mainly to test my conclusions regarding the determinants of the behavior of U.S. federal judges, my primary focus.

Judges are employees, and employers use a variety of carrots and sticks to cause their employees to be faithful agents. But because of the immense social and political value of an independent federal judiciary, the employer (the United States—specifically, the President and the Senate) has been given few of the usual carrots and sticks with which to motivate its judicial employees. The biggest carrot the government has is, paradoxically, the promise of independence itself, for that makes a judgeship attractive; and the biggest stick it has is conflict-of-interest rules (such as the rule forbidding a judge to sit in a case in which he has a financial stake, however small), which fairly *compel* judges to be independent by enforcing upon them an almost monastic isolation from possible temptations to surrender independence for other personal advantages. The contrast in these respects with other types of judicial system is profound and has the effects on judicial behavior that one would expect.

There are two more external influences on federal judges besides those that promote judicial independence—a promotion carrot and a reversal-by-a-higher-court stick. These are weak influences, but even if there were no external influences on the behavior of federal judges at all, judicial decision making would not be random. It would be shaped by a host of *internal* constraints on judicial behavior—things that move judges when they do not anticipate an external reward or punishment whichever way they decide. For most judges the biggest internal constraints on their judging are, first, the desire for self-respect and for respect from other judges and legal professionals generally, which a judge earns by being a good judge, and, second (and closely related), the intrinsic satisfactions of judging, which usually are greater for a good judge than for a bad one. This creates an "Aha!" moment for legalists, who argue that a good judge is a judge who follows rules rather than making them—making rules is the job of legislators—and so good judges must be legalists after all and forswear the personal and the political. But legalists can no more than other judges avoid harboring preconceptions that may inflect their interpretation of rules and their resolution of factual disputes, and also influence the outcome of their application of rules to facts to yield a decision. Legalists are closeted pragmatists.

Legalism fails at a deeper level to refute the hypothesis that personal and political leanings influence judicial decisions. Many of the cases that arise in our dauntingly complex, uncertainty-riven legal system—featuring an antique constitution, an overlay of federal on state law, weak political parties, cumbersome and undisciplined legislatures, and executive-legislative tugs-of-war (so unlike the situation in parliamentary regimes)—cannot be decided by the straightforward application of a preexisting rule. The initial statement of a rule, whether in legislation, the Constitution, or a precedent-creating judicial decision, is usually just a first cut at regulating the activities that fall within the statement's ordinary meaning. The subsequent refinement of the rule by judges, whether through interpretation of a legislative enactment or the distinguishing of precedents, is aimed at fitting the rule to a particular situation, and that is not an operation based on logic or on the straightforward application of a rule to facts anticipated in the drafting of the rule.

Legalists invent canons of construction (principles of interpretation) and distinctions between dictum and holding; embrace statutory and constitutional literalism but carve narrow exceptions for literal readings that produce absurd results; exalt rules over standards; wash their hands of messy factual issues by adopting principles of deferential appellate review; and in these and other ways expand the reach of legalism beyond its syllogistic core. Some commend "legal reasoning by analogy" as a legal technique, mistakenly thinking that it can save case law from contamination by policy and politics. But all the expansions require legislative judgments and thus the exercise of discretion, which turns out, in the currently most influential incarnations of legalism, to be guided by a political judgment: that there are too many legally enforceable rights. Today's exaltation of legalism is to a significant extent a reaction by politically conservative legal thinkers, including a number of prominent judges, to the expansion of rights and liability—particularly the rights of tort (including civil rights) plaintiffs, breach-of-contract defendants, prisoners, consumers, workers, and criminal defendants—by the judicial activists of the Warren Court in the 1960s and their successors who, continuing into the 1970s, issued further activist decisions, notably *Roe v. Wade,* and by their counterparts in the state courts. The claim that the courts shifted the balance too far in favor of rights—also that they are continuing to do so in cases involving capital punishment and homosexual rights—is a perfectly reasonable claim, but it is political. Because conservatives have discovered that it is rhetorically more effective to call activist liberal decisions "lawless" than to call them "too liberal," the legalists have become the face of legal reform, and the unsophisticated commend them for bringing stability to the law by renouncing political judging. There is a better, a pragmatic, argument for judicial self-restraint based simply on reluctance to interfere with social experiments, for without the knowledge that such experiments yield, the prospects for durable social reform are stunted.

Even if judges *wanted* to forswear any legislative, any political, role and be merely the "oracles" of the law, transmitting directives rather than directing, they could not do so in the conditions in which they find themselves. A combination of structural and cultural factors imposes a legislative role on our judges that they cannot escape. So the question becomes, what prevents the descent of the judiciary into an abyss of unchanneled discretionary justice that would render law so uncertain and unpredictable that it would no longer be law but instead would be the exercise of raw political power by politicians called judges? A bad answer is that to avoid the abyss judges must commit themselves to a comprehensive theory—such as economics, originalism (insofar as it is distinct from legalism), moral theory, or Justice Breyer's "active liberty"—to guide their decisions. None of the theories commands a consensus in the judiciary because all are based on—and, being putty in the hands of clever judges, are shaped around—controversial ideologies. None commands a consensus in the legal academy either. This weakens the effect of academic criticism of judicial behavior (potentially an effective constraint on an activity, such as judging, so carefully sheltered from the more powerful incentives and constraints that keep ordinary employees, and other agents, in line), although the greater weakening of the efficacy of academic criticism has come from the alienation of the academy from the bench that I described in chapter 8.

The principal force tending to stabilize judicial decision making is the existence of a limited, a field-specific, ideological consensus in such fields of law as contracts and commercial law, much of torts, much of property law, much of bankruptcy law, most of antitrust law, and pockets of intellectual property law. Judges who agree on the premises for decision can reason their way to outcomes that reflect and augment a coherent body of doctrine. In some cases they reason syllogistically. In others they engage in policy analysis uncontaminated by ideology—more precisely, uncontaminated by *contested* ideology, because when an ideology is uncontested it is not even perceived to be an ideology but rather is treated as common sense. American law has achieved the necessary minimum of coherence, stability, and "objectivity" (in the sense in which an objective proposition is one that commands the assent of persons of otherwise antagonistic views) in those fields in which legal pragmatism—practical, policy-oriented reasoning—can conduce to reasonably predictable because ideologically uncontroversial results and in which legalist techniques can dispose satisfactorily of masses of routine cases.

The consensus that enables judges to decide cases by logical or instrumental reasoning may be founded on a social consensus, for example the current consensus of American elites, and much of the general public as well, in favor of free markets. Or it could be based just on the happenstance of judges' having uniform views, maybe because they are drawn from a narrow social or professional stratum, the members of which think alike on relevant issues.[1] Our judges are somewhat diverse in so-

---

1. That turns out to have been the secret of the "legal process" school of the 1950s, resolute in "eschewing substantive values," but foundering "in the face of the emerging social conflicts that defined the 1960s." William M. Wiecek, *The Birth of the Modern Constitution: The United*

cial origins. But the preconfirmation screening process and the confirmation gauntlet that nominees must run (and the corresponding filters for state judges) combine to toss out of the applicant pool judges who swim outside the mainstream. So behind the consensus that I have identified as the principal force stabilizing our unruly American law is a selection process that guarantees a certain level of consensus.

Not that 100 percent predictability is possible in any field of law in a legal system that relies as heavily as ours does on case law. When law is perfectly predictable, cases are not brought—all legal disputes are settled—and so precedents are not kept up to date, and as a result when society changes and the old precedents no longer fit, the law becomes unpredictable, which generates litigation and so incites the production of new precedents. The decisions of a diverse judicial corps, moreover, are bound to be less predictable than those of a uniform one. But the former is epistemically more robust. Its decisions are smarter because the judges collectively have greater knowledge and insight than if they were intellectual peas in a pod. There is a tension between good law and certain law that critics of the legal system who decry legal uncertainty overlook.

The stabilizing force of consensus is weaker in the Supreme Court than in the lower courts, especially in constitutional cases. Legalism is out of the question because of case selection (the easy cases are likely to be decided satisfactorily in the lower federal courts); because the Constitution is vaguer than most statutes and is in some respects embarrassingly obsolete; because the Court decides such a small percentage of cases and thus has only limited control over the lower federal courts (which tend therefore to go their own way, generating conflicts that the Court may take many years to get around to resolving); because the Justices are not bound by the Court's precedents or subject to review by a higher court; and because constitutional cases are, in consequence of the Constitution's focus on fundamental political rights and structures, forever presenting contentious political issues for the Court to resolve.

States Supreme Court, 1941–1953 460–461 (2006). As Brannon P. Denning, reviewing Wiecek's excellent book, pointedly remarks of Justice Frankfurter, the guru of the legal process movement, "Frankfurter's prescription for judicial restraint . . . was personal , almost idiosyncratic in its reliance on the judge to know when to act and when to stay his hand." 99 *Law Library Journal* 621, 624 (2007).

That contentiousness rules out not only legalism but also in many cases instrumental reasoning (reasoning from agreed-upon premises) as well. The result is that the Supreme Court is not merely not a legalist court; it is a political court. We saw this in the spring of 2007 when the Court veered abruptly to the right in a series of 5–4 decisions as a result of the replacement of a moderately conservative Justice by an extremely conservative one. Pragmatism remains in play. But it seems that the consequences that the Justices are interested in are mainly political consequences, though they are reluctant to acknowledge this, perhaps even to themselves.

Justices do not deliberate collectively a great deal; they vote. Constitutional law is a function not of conventional legal analysis or disinterested policy analysis but of ideology, reflecting the political balance that determines who is appointed to the Supreme Court and the play of public opinion on the executive and legislative branches, and through them on the appointment process. The incessant efforts to stabilize constitutional decision making through comprehensive theory are an embarrassing failure. The latest example is the quest for global judicial consensus on matters such as capital punishment, a quest certain to founder on the diversity of the world's legal systems and American ignorance of foreign cultures, including foreign legal cultures. The quest replaces time with space—the pretense that judges just enforce past political settlements with the pretense that when judges strike off in a new direction they do so just to bring American constitutional law into conformity with the best legal thinking in the world as a whole.

What reins in the Justices is none of these things; it is an awareness, conscious or unconscious, that they cannot go "too far" without inviting reprisals by the other branches of government spurred on by an indignant public. So they pull their punches, giving just enough obeisance to precedent to be able to present themselves as "real" judges, rather than as the more than occasional legislators that they really are.

The problem of political judging in the form in which it presents itself in constitutional adjudication in the Supreme Court is not unique to constitutional law or to the Supreme Court. Until a quarter of a century ago the problem was acute in antitrust law, and for all one knows it may become so again. Despite its antiquity the Sherman Act of 1890 remains the principal charter of federal antitrust law. But the Act is so vague that federal antitrust law is really a creation of the courts, primarily the Supreme Court.[2] Until the 1950s the economics of antitrust were poorly understood even in law schools and economics departments, and in addition it was widely believed that distributive justice and even political liberty were important values that antitrust law should be understood to serve. Technical ignorance and ideological disagreement were rife and infected judicial doctrine. Eventually, advances in economic analysis, coupled with more conservative appointments to the Supreme Court and other federal courts and with changes in public opinion about the free market that were accelerated by the demise of the Soviet Union and most other communist societies, created a consensus that antitrust law should be concerned only with economic efficiency and also brought about a considerable degree of agreement on what antitrust principles would best promote efficiency. It took almost a century, then, for antitrust law to achieve the condition of what Thomas Kuhn called "normal science." The Supreme Court has not achieved a comparable consensus in most areas of constitutional law, though it has in some (mainly having to do with economic regulation—the *Lochner* era is well behind us—and with some aspects of criminal procedure in noncapital cases), which in consequence have largely dropped from sight.

The progress in antitrust law owes nothing to legalism. Judges and Justices did not learn to read the Sherman Act more carefully. Instead they learned more about how the economy operates. When law is conceived of as an autonomous discipline, improvement is impossible. The evolution of antitrust law is a triumph of pragmatism. But pragmatism is not a panacea for what troubles American law, or an antidote to political judging. It tells judges to have regard for the consequences of their doctrines and decisions, but it cannot tell them how to weight those consequences. The weighting is the result of a complicated interaction—mysterious, personal to every judge—of modes of reasoning (analysis, intuition, emotion, common sense, judgment), political and ideological inclinations, personality traits, other personal characteristics, personal and professional experiences, and the constraints implicit in the rules of the judicial "game." Logic plays only a limited role in adjudication, espe-

2. See, besides references in the introduction, Daniel A. Farber and Brett H. McDonnell, "'Is There a Text in This Class'? The Conflict between Textualism and Antitrust," 14 *Journal of Contemporary Legal Issues* 619 (2005).

cially at the appellate level and that mainly in routine cases, relative to psychology—an understudied influence on judicial behavior.

American law is very costly, like American medicine. But just as in the case of medicine one is hard-pressed to figure out what to do to lower those costs without lowering quality by more than the cost savings would justify. Even so obvious a reform as raising judicial salaries steeply in order to attract a better quality of judge could, as we saw, backfire. The academic efforts to develop performance measures for judges merit encouragement, and I have suggested marrying the quantitative methods that are used to develop such measures to critical studies of judges. But we are a long way from having comprehensive objective measures of judicial performance. Maybe, however, a keener recognition that legalism is not the path to reform would induce greater awareness that the path lies through pragmatism, not legalism, and with that awareness might come constructive efforts to improve pragmatic judging.

For that recognition to take hold, however, will require a change in the way in which law is taught in law schools. Realism about judges is sorely lacking there. Law is taught as if judges were second-class professors, professors manqué—legal analysts lacking the specialized knowledge of the law professor. The motivations and constraints operating on judges, and the judicial mentality that results, are ignored, as if judges were computers rather than limited human intellects navigating seas of uncertainty. As a result students are not taught how to present a case to a judge in a way that will strike a responsive chord. The curious judicial passivity that results from judges' being accustomed simply to decide whatever is brought to them to decide, rather than to initiate anything, has made most judges shy about telling lawyers how they should be presenting cases to maximum effect, thus helping themselves by helping the judges. The nation needs a better bridge between bench and bar, and its construction must be largely the work of the law schools.

Acknowledgments

I have incorporated material from the following articles of mine, though with much revision and amplification: "The Role of the Judge in the Twenty-first Century," 86 *Boston University Law Review* 1049 (2006) (chapters 3 and 4); "Judicial Behavior and Performance: An Economic Approach," 32 *Florida State University Law Review* 1259 (2005) (chapter 5); "Reasoning by Analogy," 91 *Cornell Law Review* 761 (2005) (chapter 7); "A Note on *Rumsfeld v. FAIR* and the Legal Academy," 2006 *Supreme Court Review* 47 (2007) (chapter 8); "The Supreme Court, 2004 Term: Foreword: A Political Court," 119 *Harvard Law Review* 31 (2005) (chapter 10); "Justice Breyer Throws Down the Gauntlet," 115 *Yale Law Journal* 1699 (2006) (chapter 11); "No Thanks, We Already Have Our Own Laws," *Legal Affairs*, July/Aug. 2004, p. 40 (chapter 12); "Constitutional Law from a Pragmatic Perspective," 55 *University of Toronto Law Journal* 300 (2005) (chapter 12); "Enlightened Despot," *New Republic*, Apr. 23, 2007, p. 53 (chapter 12).

I thank Heather Afra, Max Barker, Alicia Beyer, Justin Donoho, Justin Ellis, Jonathan Fackler, Nevin Gewertz, Brandon Hale, Allison Handy, Zachary Holmstead, Matthew Johnson, Tara Kadioglu, Meghan Maloney, Shine Tu, and Michael Welsh for their excellent research assistance and their careful cite-checking, and Michael Aronson, my editor at Harvard University Press, for his encouragement and suggestions. Scott Baker, Michael Boudin, Lee Epstein, William Eskridge, Ward Farnsworth, Barry Friedman, Mitu Gulati, Brian Leiter, Jonathan Lewinsohn, Barak Medina, Shelley Murphey, Frederick Schauer, Andrei Shleifer, and Cass Sunstein have my gratitude for making many helpful comments on portions of the manuscript. Dennis Hutchinson's careful critical reading of the entire manuscript deserves a special acknowledgment. I also owe a large debt to Judge Boudin for discussions that altered my analysis in significant ways and to Professor Shleifer for challenging my judge-centered attempts at unraveling the puzzle of judicial behavior.

Index